APPELLATE COURTS AND LAWYERS

Contributions in Legal Studies
Series Editor: Paul L. Murphy

Stability, Security, and Continuity: Mr. Justice Burton and Decision-Making in the Supreme Court, 1945–1958
Mary Frances Berry

Philosophical Law: Authority, Equality, Adjudication, Privacy
Richard Bronaugh, editor

Law, Soldiers, and Combat
Peter Karsten

THOMAS B. MARVELL

APPELLATE COURTS AND LAWYERS

INFORMATION GATHERING IN THE ADVERSARY SYSTEM

CONTRIBUTIONS IN LEGAL STUDIES, NUMBER 4

GREENWOOD PRESS
WESTPORT, CONNECTICUT • LONDON, ENGLAND

Library of Congress Cataloging in Publication Data

Marvell, Thomas B   1939-
    Appellate courts and lawyers.

    (Contributions in legal studies ; no. 4 ISSN 0147-
1074)
    Includes bibliographical references and notes.
    1. Appellate courts--United States.   2. Adversary
system (Law)—United States.   3. Judicial process—
United States.   I. Title.   II. Series.
KF8750.M37   347'.73'24   77-94743
ISBN 0-313-20312-1

Library of Congress Catalog Card Number: 77-94743
ISBN: 0-313-20312-1
ISSN: 0147-1074

First published in 1978

Greenwood Press, Inc.
51 Riverside Avenue, Westport, Connecticut 06880

Printed in the United States of America

10 9 8 7 6 5 4 3 2 1

To Alice and Mary

Contents

Part I

Introduction

CHAPTER 1

Foreword

Appellate judges, like all of us, cannot make decisions without information. The quality of their decisions depends largely on the amount, accuracy, and relevancy of the information obtained. What kinds of information do judges use? Where and how do they get the information, and why do they obtain it there? How do they evaluate factual information? How do information-gathering problems affect the types of decisions made? These questions require a far-ranging study of the courts.[1]

Appellate courts are interesting organizations in this regard because they rely on the adversary system—on presentations by opposing counsel—for the bulk of their information (though much also comes from other sources, mainly law clerks' research and judges' background knowledge). Information from the adversary system, moreover, ordinarily comes only from lawyers representing opposing positions in a single dispute, but the courts use that information for two different and sometimes conflicting functions: resolving that dispute between the parties and, by making precedent, controlling future relations between people not before the court. This quite often leads judges to disagree about what information they should use and how they should obtain it.

This book emphasizes the practical, nuts-and-bolts features of deciding appeals more than, but not to the exclusion of, the logic of decisions and the judges' philosophies. The latter two are the predominant topics in appellate court studies by lawyers and political scientists, very likely because scholars are rarely faced with the same information about appeals that judges are. They rarely have the mass of factual information describing a dispute or the background practical experience that judges use to decide issues. The temptation is strong to focus on the more familiar areas of logic and philosophy. This book attempts to view appellate work from the judges' standpoint, to view problems judges deem important as they define them. It is an empirical study; most of the data comes from the judges themselves and from the records of cases on appeal.

The focus is on the middle range of appeals. Little of the discussion is about appeals containing issues of no importance to the development of the law, and only one or two chapters pertain to those rare cases containing issues of major public policy significance. Rather, the book is written with an eye to the ordinary case in which an appellate court makes a moderate adjustment to existing law.

Information gathering, again, is the central topic. The term "information" means any assertion, except a purely normative one, about facts, ideas, rules, or relationships. It does not imply that the assertions are correct or relevant; that must be determined by the judges. A great mass of information goes into deciding appeals. This book, especially in the later chapters, concentrates on the less abstract kinds of information, which are more amenable to empirical research. They are: (1) the issues upon which a case may be decided, (2) legal authority, such as statutes and prior opinions, (3) the facts of a case—that is, facts about what happened in the dispute and background factual assumptions needed to determine and evaluate them, (4) practical considerations and facts of life used in developing the law, called "social facts" here, and (5) empirical data, for example, statistical studies, used to determine social facts. These encompass the major portion of information used in deciding appeals; however, there are other important types only touched upon here, such as the possible ways an issue can be framed and the various lines of reasoning that might be extracted from a legal authority.

Information gathering is a complex subject and is interlaced with most of what goes on at the courts. It requires a comprehensive, but often detailed, view of the appeals deciding process. Most of what is said in this book falls under four broad topics.

The first is a description of how attorneys and others present information to judges. This is mainly a discussion of appellate procedure and of the law clerks' duties. Both are largely information-processing activities.

The second is an analysis of the information sources, contrasting the adversary system with other sources. How much of each type of information comes from counsel, from amicus briefs, from outside experts, from law clerks and staff attorneys, and from the judges' background knowledge? To what extent do counsel smother their presentations with time-wasting extraneous materials? And how successful are the judges' attempts to suspend the adversary system, for example, by requiring counsel to present facts and legal authority against their positions?

The third looks into why judges rely on the adversary system for some types of information more than for others. In general, they rely on counsel more for issues and facts of the case than for legal authority and social facts. The second half of the book explains the many interlocking factors behind these differences; the most important factors are those having to do with how judges use the various types of information and with the problems of finding and evaluating the information.

The fourth topic is how the problems of finding and evaluating information affect the kinds of decisions made. The problems are different for each type of information. There are many appellate decision-making rules that operate to, and are often designed to, alleviate them. For example, the judges tend to decide issues narrowly because information about the social consequences of broader rules may be lacking.

These topics cannot be adequately studied without substantial background knowledge of the general subject area. Hence a number of background topics are discussed in addition to the four main topics. For example, this first chapter later discusses judicial secrecy and the inaccessibility of the judges' thinking processes; these are two important restraints on what can be said about appellate decision making. Because appellate attorneys and law clerks are major actors in the information-gathering area, their general activities and their influence upon decisions are given considerable attention. Among the other essential background subjects are the case load problems of appellate courts, the distinction between the courts' lawmaking and dispute-deciding functions, the stages at which judges make up their minds, and the extent to which written opinions reflect the judges' actual conscious reasons for their decisions.

The four main topics, along with the various background subjects, are highly interrelated, too much so to be presented serially, chapter by chapter. Rather, the book is divided into separate parts along simpler lines. The first three chapters are introductory. The rest of this chapter discusses various points about the empirical research of appellate courts. The second chapter is a short preliminary description of appellate courts and their work. The third chapter is an introductory discussion of the adversary system and includes topics such as the judges' opinions about the adversary system and about the major mistakes made in the briefs and oral arguments. Part II consists of four chapters that describe the progress of an appeal: the appellate lawyers' work, their means of presenting information to the courts, the work of law clerks and other court employees who gather information for the judges, and then the judges' processes of reaching decisions and writing opinions. Part III discusses the five types of information listed earlier—the importance of each type, how it is used, where it comes from, the special problems of obtaining and evaluating facts, and how much extraneous material is presented by counsel. Part IV summarizes and elaborates on the main topics outlined earlier, looking especially at how appellate courts deal with the problems of finding and evaluating information.

APPROACH AND RESEARCH METHODS

Only a rough outline of the methodology will be given here; Appendix A contains a more thorough discussion, and the notes explain the research relevant to specific topics.

The overall strategy is to learn as much as possible about a broad area of activity at appellate courts, rather than to focus on a narrow topic and a few variables. The latter strategy leads one to extract artificially a few aspects out of their milieu, such that one has little idea what they mean. Likewise, theories and theoretical frameworks are de-emphasized here. Although this is a quantitative study, it shuns both numerical figures and attempts to find exact relationships between variables; these present an aura of exactness that is hardly ever justified by social scientists' ability to gather data. Lastly, information is gathered from many different types of sources, rather than the typical reliance on one or two sources, because cross-checks are helpful and because any one source has its own limitations.

The book concentrates on state supreme courts and federal circuit courts, giving less attention to the U.S. Supreme Court and the state intermediate appellate courts. The core of the research is a study of the supreme court of a northern industrial state, called the "focal court" because I promised its justices not to name it. I interviewed nearly all its present and recently retired justices and many law clerks, staff members, and attorneys who argued before the court; and I studied the opinions, briefs, and oral arguments in 112 cases argued during a one-year period ending June 1972. Five other courts were researched somewhat less thoroughly—the First and Sixth Circuit Courts of Appeals, the Rhode Island and Ohio Supreme Courts, and the Massachusetts Supreme Judicial Court. I interviewed the great majority of judges on these courts and some law clerks and staff members, and I studied their cases, though less systematically than those in the focal court. In all I interviewed forty-six judges, thirty-three law clerks, seventeen staff members, and thirty-six appellate lawyers. The interviews were conducted over four years, from late 1971 through 1975. They were generally tape-recorded. Ten judges refused to be interviewed. For some reason only five of thirteen judges in Ohio (on the Ohio Supreme Court or on the Sixth Circuit with offices in Ohio) agreed to be interviewed; elsewhere all but two judges were interviewed, and a number were interviewed several times.

A major question in research of this sort is the generalization of the findings beyond the organizations and time period studied. Considerable use is made, especially in Part III, of one year's appeals in the focal court. The handling of these cases may well differ from that at other courts and from the focal court's operations at other times, for example, because of different types of appeals, different court organization, or different judges. The findings from the year's appeals, however, is supplemented by interviews and a much more limited study of cases at the five other courts. Still, the six courts may not be typical, especially because they are all in the northeast quarter of the country. For this problem, I have relied on the enormous body of law and political science literature about appellate courts; the literature contains enough information about most topics to indicate how typical the six courts are. Much of this literature consists of published speeches given by judges, of which there are hundreds, mainly descriptions of the inner workings of their courts or advice to lawyers about how to present appeals. Other valuable sources of information are judges' hearing testimony and judicial conference discussions.

The method of presenting the data must be given a quick mention. Differences between the six courts or between groups of courts elsewhere are not mentioned unless the data clearly indicate a difference. Instead of littering the text with percentage figures and giving a false impression of exactness, I have defined certain words to mean specific percentage ranges. These are listd in Appendix A. For example, "nearly all," "generally," and "most" refer to 85-95 percent, 70-85 percent, and 55-70 percent, respectively. I rarely had time to ask each judge about all the points discussed here. Unless at least nearly all spoke to a point, I have indicated, mainly in the notes, how much information was obtained. Lastly, quotations from the interviews are used for two purposes: to give one of many similar statements as an example, or to emphasize a point with what I consider an astute or colorful statement. Examples are clearly labeled as such; all other quotations fall in the second category. Virtually all the quotations were taken from tape-recorded interviews.

This book is written both for those with and without extensive knowledge of appellate courts. Preliminary discussion needed for the latter group, however, is kept as short as possible, and much is confined to Chapter 2. Most detailed discussions of interest to only appellate court scholars are in the notes.

TWO LIMITS ON THE STUDY OF APPELLATE COURTS

In any area of research, data gathering problems prevent some lines of inquiry. One should establish these boundaries at the outset. For the study of appellate courts (and most any other organization) two obstacles stand out: (1) the secrecy surrounding many decision-making activities, and (2) the inaccessible nature of a decision maker's thinking process. The information-gathering approach was chosen for this study largely because it is less hindered by these obstacles than other broad approaches to the empirical study of appellate courts.

JUDICIAL SECRECY. Appellate court decision making is actually quite open when compared with that at the top levels of many organizations. The oral arguments, briefs, records, and written opinions are virtually always available to the public. Still the core of the decision-making process remains hidden in apparently every American appellate court.[2] All internal communication about the cases (draft opinions, talk, and memorandums) is confidential. Until the decision is announced, no outsider is supposed to know which judge is writing on a case or how a case will be decided. Judges take special pains to keep their conferences closed; not even the law clerks are allowed in except at a few rare courts. And the numerous articles and books by judges and law clerks about decision-making procedures speak in generalities, rarely mentioning specific behind-the-scenes events.

The main reason that judges and law clerks give for this secrecy is to ensure open discussion when making decisions[3]—a typical justification for secrecy in organizations. One judge said bluntly:

I think we ought to be able to say to each other absolutely any damn thing that's on our minds and it should go no further than our conference table.
Q — This is to keep the conversation free?
A — Free, and so that we would have *no* hesitation and no *fear* of being misquoted for one thing, and quoted when we don't want to be quoted for another.

The feeling here is that secrecy enhances decision-making efficiency in a collegial group. It enhances the free expression of one's reasoning and the blunt criticism of others'. It allows a judge to state tentative views and later to change his mind without seeming inconsistent to the outside world, thus fostering the prized judicial trait of "keeping an open mind" until all arguments have been heard.

Although the free flow of discussion is by far the major rationale for secrecy, there are others. Nearly half the judges said they were concerned that an outsider could gain financially should he get advance knowledge of a decision: a civil litigant could settle his case upon discovering that he was about to lose, or someone might be able to make money on the stock market when a decision has a large impact on a company. The latter actually happened in 1919 when a U.S. Supreme Court clerk leaked information to friends.[4] Two reasons less frequently mentioned are that attorneys and others might try to influence or otherwise bother a judge who is known to be writing on a case, and that continual rumors about what is happening in pending appeals might damage the prestige or integrity of the court. Another likely reason sometimes given, though not by judges, is to prevent criticism of the judges' decision-making methods.[5] Their jobs certainly would be less pleasant if their deliberations were constantly in public view.

On the whole, judges and law clerks are firmly committed to this secrecy.[6] Comments like "It would be *monstrous* if the judicial process was open to the public," are typical of the judges' feelings in the interviews. Office procedures at the courts emphasize the preservation of secrecy, even to the extent of having, in at least one court studied, a paper shredder to make sure discarded draft opinions and memorandums are not plucked from the trash. Another court periodically debugs the judges' quarters. A difficult problem is law clerks' discussion of cases in places where they can be over-heard, such as in restaurants or in courthouse halls. The clerks continually gossip about the cases, and they must always be aware that "walls have ears," as one judge said. In fact, the clerks seldom violate the secrecy rules, though a few complained that the emphasis on secrecy was overdone. The leaks that cause the most trouble and concern are those picked up by news-papers.[7] I learned of a half-dozen incidents similar to this one recounted by a clerk:

There was a flap last year when apparently there was—somehow the information got out that a particular judge was writing a particular opinion, and they never really did trace down the source of the thing, so they figured it was courthouse gossip, you know.
Q — they really tried to—
A — oh, yeah, the chief judge was just furious, and he told the judges to tell their law clerks and personnel, you know, "If anyone ever lets out something like that, they'll be immediately fired."

In this atmosphere the current enthusiasm for openness in government, as evidenced by the freedom of information and sunshine laws, will have little effect on appellate courts. This is true even though a few scholars have recently called for less secrecy,[8] and even though deliberations at some foreign appellate courts, notably in England and Switzerland, are open to public view.[9]

It is, therefore, unlikely that a researcher will ever be given free access to the inner workings of appellate courts. This rules out any extensive firsthand knowledge about what people actually do there. Accurate and complete secondhand information is nearly as hard to come by, especially because judges are reluctant to discuss individual appeals and to criticize their col-leagues. A full and contemporary description of the judges' bargaining, influences, and other interactions will have to await a judge who is willing to defy convention and write frankly about his experiences in these matters.

INACCESSIBILITY OF THE JUDGES' THINKING PROCESSES. The second main obstacle when studying appellate courts is the problem of getting a com-prehensive view of the judges' thinking processes. This is partly due to judicial secrecy; more important, the judges themselves cannot describe, and probably do not know, much of what goes on in their minds when making decisions. This is a key point about appellate judges and, I suspect, about all decision makers. Justice Cardozo began his great *The Nature of the Judicial Process* with:

The work of deciding cases goes on every day in hundreds of courts throughout the land. Any judge, one might suppose, would find it easy to describe the process which he had followed a thousand times and more. Nothing could be farther from the truth. Let some intelligent layman ask him to explain: he will not go very far before taking refuge in the excuse that the language of craftsmen is unintelligible to those untutored in the craft.[10]

Cardozo then analyzes the principles behind his decision making, a task rarely attempted by judges since. But his skillful prose often is not concrete enough to help one understand how he decides.

There is no, and probably never can be any, definite proof that judges cannot describe how they decide; rather, this assumption comes from the paucity of their attempts, the inability of myself and others to elicit descriptions of it in interviews, and a few statements by judges explicitly acknowledging this point. I will concentrate on the latter here. The most poignant published statement is by Justice Schaefer of the Illinois Supreme Court; after quoting Cardozo to the effect that judges do not candidly talk about the subconscious elements in their decision making, he said:

Perhaps there has been a lack of candor. I do not think so. Rather it seems to me that we lack the ability to describe what happens. I have tried to analyze my own reactions to particular cases. When I have tried in retrospect, I have doubted somewhat the result, for the tendency is strong to reconstruct along the lines of an assumed ideal process. William James said, "When the conclusion is there we have already forgotten most of the steps preceding its attainment." And, when I have tried to carry on simultaneously the process of decision and of self-analysis, the process of decision has not been natural. I suspect that what is lacking is not candor but techniques and tools which are sensitive enough to explore the mind of man and report accurately its conscious and subconscious operations.[11]

Next, here are two lengthy passages from my interviews given by experienced and highly respected judges. Besides the matter at hand—their acknowledged inability to describe how they decide—these two passages give about as much insight into how decisions are made as can be found anywhere (though judges seem to differ greatly in their decision methods). The first is by a federal judge:

Q — How much of the discussion among the justices is about this general knowledge about facts of life as opposed to the strict authorities?
A — Well, I think they're always talking about it whether they realize it or not. I think when a judge speaks about the *justice* of a case, it's a shorthand way of weighing the values involved here on one side against those opposing it. I think the balance is struck in this sense. But in doing so he's talking about ethics. He's talking about religion. He's talking about economics. He's talking about history. He's talking about all of these things, whether he does it expressly. It's implicit.
Q — They do talk about justice a lot in the conference room?
A — Oh, I think so. Certainly they do. Maybe there isn't a dichotomy. You don't sit down and say "Well, first we'll decide where's the justice of the matter and next we'll

see whether—whether the precedents will let us come *out* that way." I've never been in a conference where anything that *formal* was done. But I've had the impression many times that this is what a colleague *might* be doing. And then he might approach it from the other way. He might say, "Well, now let's see, where do the precedents take us here? And now I have to ask myself, 'Wouldn't my sense of justice be outraged if I followed them?'" So he might approach it from that viewpoint, but *probably* not consciously from either direction, but it's lurking there.

Q — You yourself do that?

A — I suppose so. I don't *formalize* it. If you did, you'd never get anything done. It's like an *athlete*. You see a professional athlete who is—and a judge is a professional in his field—an outfielder, say, in baseball. At the crack of the bat he runs to some part of the outfield, and when he gets there and puts up his glove, and there's the *ball*. And someone not a student of the game might wonder why in the world he's running in that direction, and what does he know. And if he ever thought about it, he's saying, "Now, this is probably an outside pitch, but it's a pull hitter, and there's a wind blowing in right field" and so forth. But if he—"and he's a long ball hitter. He's a line drive man," or whatever. But if he tried to sort all these things out, he'd *never* get out there in time to get the ball. And it's sort of a shorthand *cognition* of all of the factors that go into *accomplishing* this. Well, arriving at a judgment is, I think, a somewhat similar, but much more complex, process.

The last statement is by a state judge; I asked what most of the disagreements between the justices were about and he answered:

A — I think it's differences in philosophy.

Q — The philosophy, rather than the practical applications—aspects of—

A — And the practical applications, yeah, that's part of it. Has this guy got a white or a black hat on him? Does this group of litigants have a white or black hat? What are the objectives, what are you trying to accomplish? These are not all stated, but these are in the back of everyone's mind. The unstated things.

Q —You mean they look at the equities between the two parties in the case?

A — The parties and the litigants and how they feel. Yeah. A lot of it's—just—you know, people say that judges are viscerally oriented. And it's true. . . . Sometimes its a group of litigants. Sometimes it's a *particular* litigant, as to how you look at the case, and the legal equities and the personal equities, and how you feel the law is— you know, what you think of the law. It's awfully hard to pin down, but somehow or another out of all this, you develop an attitude of how you think the case should be resolved.

Besides saying that they cannot easily describe their decision process, these three judges illustrated a number of other points that emphasize this inability. Notice the use of (1) "subconscious," (2) "justice," "equities," and having "a white hat or black hat," and (3) "viscerally oriented."

First, in the interviews a number of judges volunteered that part of the decision making is or may be "subconscious" or "subliminal." Cardozo explained at great length that "subconscious forces" are a major element,[12] and I am sure the reader would admit the same with respect to his own decisions. It would be very difficult to determine how much of a judge's decision making is in the subconscious realm or what actually goes on there.

Secondly, when explaining decisions, the great majority of the judges interviewed used the word "justice" or, less often, "equity," "fairness," and looking at who has "the white or black hat." Likewise, judges who write about the decision process are equally fond of such words; "justice" appears on one page in six of Cardozo's *The Nature of the Judicial Process.* This is typical of judges' writings. So "justice" and the like are very popular words among judges when describing at least some facets of their jobs.[13] But they are such broad and nebulous words, with so many different meanings, that they thoroughly hide what goes through the judges' minds. Judges rarely define these terms, but from the context it seems that they use them to refer to any one or a combination of: (1) considerations other than legal authority that go into forming a rule, (2) considerations other than legal authority that go into arriving at a result between the litigants, and (3) following the existing authority. Even if one could straighten out the broad sense in which one of these terms is used, he would still be far from understanding what leads a judge to believe that a particular decision is just, fair, or whatever. Also, of course, the innumerable philosophical and jurisprudential writings attempting to define these concepts give further testimony to their illusiveness.

Thirdly, equally vague is the use of "visceral reaction" and similar terms like "intuition" and "feeling" to describe how decisions are reached. A number of judges used these terms in the interviews, though at times referring only to their initial vote on a case.[14] One judge described his approach to an issue as "sort of instinctive as far as I was concerned. I felt something was wrong—almost like a seventh sense." And another said about his view of lower court rulings in some cases, "It just leaves a bad taste in your mouth." Both then said they had to fit their feelings into existing legal authority before arriving at a final decision.

The law clerks are just as likely as the judges to use such broad, unhelpful terms when describing appellate decision making. Favorite expressions are deciding by "gut reaction" and according to "who got screwed." Recourse to this kind of language sugests that they are able only in a very general way to learn how judges decide cases. In fact, when asked if they could predict, upon first reading the briefs, how the judges would vote in a case, most said they had great difficulty in doing so (but several said that they could predict their own judges quite well after a year or so based on past positions in similar issues). An Alabama law clerk has written a typical statement along this line: "To some limited extent, a clerk could learn how individual judges tend to approach cases," for example, their views on stare decisis, but "predicting the way a justice will vote is an inherently difficult task."[15] And one of the clerks interviewed summed up this matter saying:

The reasons [for decisions] still remain hazy and foggy. And any particular mix of precedent versus policy versus civilized humanism and so on is—you know, you don't know what the brownies are going to come out like, but you know that the ingredients are all in there stirring and bubbling around.

Students of appellate courts have had trouble looking into the judges' minds. Several political scientists have taken the bull by the horns and straightaway asked judges how they go about reaching a decision, but the answers have been decidedly unhelpful.[16] Numerous other political scientists have tried to circumvent the problems just outlined by looking only at the judges' votes and, through various statistical manipulations, trying to discover underlying philosophies behind the votes; but votes alone are a meager foundation for this kind of guesswork. The most successful description of appellate decision making by a nonjudge is Karl Llewellyn's *The Common Law Tradition, Deciding Appeals.* He said that judges have little idea of how they reach their decisions, stressing "the inarticulateness of the vast body of appellate judges about how they do their work and why—their inarticulateness even to themselves."[17] Then, based on an enormous knowledge of judicial opinions and on conversations with his judge friends, he proceeded to tell the judges how they make decisions, but in terms, such as "situation sense," so imprecise that they add little to the judges' "justice."[18]

IMPLICATIONS OF THESE LIMITS. These two obstacles have been emphasized because a social science study must begin with an understanding of where useful data can be found. And one must be candid about the problems behind the methods used and the conclusions reached. Although trite, it is necessary to keep in mind that human action and thought are so complicated that one has trouble writing about them above the commonsense level without wandering into unfounded speculation. No social science study can be far from drowning in this uncertainty; that fact should be acknowledged. Social science loses credibility whenever the uncertainty is hidden behind pretentious theory or showy statistical techniques.

The two obstacles plague any appellate court study, unless simply a critique of reasoning found in published opinions, and one must never lose sight of them. However, the information-gathering topic is, in astronomers' terminology, a "window" through which one can get substantial glimpses of appellate decision making in spite of the obstacles. Much of the information gathering is done in public through briefs, records, and oral arguments. The bulk of the rest—for example, independent research—can be studied through straightforward questions in interviews, questions of the type that judges and law clerks are not reluctant to answer. This skirts, by and large, the secretive internal deliberations—the bargaining, persuasion, and other interactions. It also skirts, though less successfully, the murky area of how various pieces of information are combined to produce decisions in conjunction with the judges' philosophies, particular interests, and perhaps moods on particular days.

In general, the obstacles are a greater hindrance as the study progresses along the four major topics that were outlined at the beginning of the chapter. The first topic, describing how information is presented to the judges, runs into very few problems of this sort. The second, the judges' reliance on the adversary system, runs into problems mainly because it requires some knowledge about what information the judges use and about the relative importance of that information. Judges may be unaware of using some information and thus would not mention it in the interviews, oral arguments, written opinions, and law review articles—which are where I looked for evidence of what information is used. Judges also may not mention important information they do consciously use; thus Chapter 7 contains a lengthy discussion of how well written opinions reflect the reasons for the judges' decisions. This subject, as will be seen, involves both obstacles. The last two topics—why the adversary system is relied on for some types of information more than for others and how the problems of finding and evaluating information affect the kinds of decisions made—involve causation and the judges' motives, thus necessarily running into the second obstacle. The two topics, however, follow directly from the earlier topics, and they are sufficiently interesting and important to justify tackling the substantial problems involved.

CHAPTER 2

Structure and Operation of Appellate Courts

This chapter is a short background description of appellate courts, intended for those not fully familiar with them. It concentrates on state supreme courts and the U.S. circuit courts, emphasizing the six courts researched for this study. Special attention is given to points that become important later, especially the judges' work load problems and the distinction between law-making and dispute-deciding functions. Chapters 5 through 8 will describe appellate court operations in much more detail.

TYPES AND STRUCTURE OF APPELLATE COURTS

Appellate courts can be classified according to three major distinctions. The first is between state and federal courts. Very briefly, federal courts can decide only a limited range of cases, mainly those involving federal law or involving the U.S. government as a party. State courts decide litigation involving someone or something within the state, using either federal or state law.

The second distinction is between courts of last resort and intermediate appellate courts. The latter take appeals from trial courts and administrative agencies, and their decisions can be reviewed by a court of last resort. In the federal system the major intermediate courts are the eleven U.S. Circuit Courts of Appeals (often called simply "circuit courts"). Cases decided there can be decided again by the court of last resort for the federal system, the U.S. Supreme Court. This happens, however, for less than 2 percent of the circuit court decisions. In the state court systems the highest court is almost always called the "supreme court" of the state. They are considered courts of last resort even though the U.S. Supreme Court can review (though it rarely does) any decision involving federal law, and the lower federal courts quite often review their decisions in criminal appeals containing federal constitutional questions. Almost thirty states have intermediate appellate courts, which are usually called "courts of appeals." All but the

Rhode Island court of the four state courts studied here sit above an intermediate court. Some states have one central intermediate court, often a very large court. Other states have several small intermediate courts based in different cities around the state. As a general rule, judges on courts of last resort are formally called "justices," and those on intermediate and trial courts "judges."

Thirdly, appellate courts have greatly varying degrees of discretionary jurisdiction. This is a court's authority to select from the cases submitted those that it wishes to decide and to leave the lower court decision standing in the rest. Courts of last resort that sit above intermediate courts typically have a large degree of discretionary jurisdiction. A few, including the focal court and, as a practical matter, the U.S. Supreme Court, have discretion in virtually every case. Others, such as the Ohio and Massachusetts courts, must take several, and sometimes large, categories of appeals, especially constitutional questions and murder convictions; but their jurisdiction is largely discretionary. Intermediate courts and almost all supreme courts in states without intermediate courts have little discretionary jurisdiction. Still, to varying degrees they can refuse to decide some cases. Examples are when the lower court decision is attacked after the deadline for appeal, when the parties seem not to have a stake in the outcome of the controversy, and when the case is outside the court's jurisdiction. Also they may have discretionary jurisdiction over certain classes of cases, especially civil appeals involving small sums and appeals from preliminary rulings in the trial court.

The number of judges varies from three in some intermediate court divisions to over twenty in the largest statewide intermediate courts. State supreme courts typically have five or seven justices—odd numbers to lessen the chance of tie votes. Many courts sit in panels, allowing less than the full court to decide cases. U.S. circuit courts and nearly all state intermediate courts sit in three-judge panels, and a number of state supreme courts (only the Massachusetts court in this study) use panels of three, four, or five members. The circuit courts and supreme courts can also sit en banc—that is, with all the members sitting.

Appellate courts are small organizations, employing some 20 to 150 people. Each judge has his chambers, called his "office," with a secretary and from one to five personal law clerks. The clerks are young lawyers, nearly always hired for only a year or two, who help with legal research and a variety of other tasks. Occasionally the offices are in the judges' home-towns some distance from the court itself. Circuit judges are generally scattered all over the several states of their circuits. Most focal court and Ohio Supreme Court justices have offices far from their court. But in most states supreme courts all the offices are at the court's seat.

The rest of the court employees are organized into various divisions at the court's seat, such as the clerk's office, the reporter's office, and the administrative office. These posts will be described later as they become relevant to the discussion.

DECIDING APPEALS

In courts having wide discretionary jurisdiction a major part of a judge's job is deciding which cases the court will hear. The litigant who lost below must apply for leave to appeal, or certiorari as it is called in some courts, and must file a brief supporting the application. (This application is sometimes called a "petition," and the briefs should be distinguished from those submitted if the case is accepted and heard.) Then, ordinarily, his opponent contests the application with his own brief. At the focal court these briefs tend to be very similar to those submitted later if leave is granted. Courts differ greatly in how they process these applications and often change their procedures in response to the increasingly large numbers of applications. Until fairly recently the Ohio justices held oral argument on the applications; now the justices simply read the briefs, which are required to be very short, and then vote. Under the focal court's old procedure each application was given to a justice, and he then circulated a memorandum to the other judges describing and recommending action on the application. Now, however, each application goes to one of four staff attorneys who writes a memorandum of about three to six pages long. His suggestion as to whether the court should take the case becomes final in a few days unless a justice disagrees, in which case the court votes on it. The Massachusetts Supreme Judicial Court (SJC) was given wide discretionary jurisdiction in 1972, and the court established a complex procedure. In brief, a panel of three judges studies, with the help of staff attorneys, all appeals sent to either the SJC or the intermediate court, keeps some cases for the SJC, and sends most to the intermediate court. The latter's decisions can be, but rarely are, reviewed by the SJC.

One of the most obscure aspects of appellate courts is the criteria used to determine when leave will be granted.[2] Guidelines in state constitutions, statutes, and court rules are written in broad terms. The Ohio Supreme Court, for example, is directed to accept cases "of public or great general interest." Probably the most important factor in state courts is whether the justices think, upon first glance, that something is wrong with the lower court's work. Other major criteria are whether the issue is considered significant and whether the issue has been decided different ways by the intermediate courts. In some states, also, lower courts can send cases they consider important directly to the supreme court. At any rate, the courts with discretionary jurisdiction only decide some 1 to 10 percent of the appeals decided below; and the criteria for taking cases, however vague, mean that these appeals tend to contain close issues—issues which are likely to produce disagreement among the justices.

The actual appeals-deciding procedures are much the same from court to court. In most courts, and in all but the Massachusetts court here, the judges read the attorneys' briefs before oral arguments. Then they listen to and question each attorney for fifteen to thirty minutes of arguments. Afterward, the judges confer and register tentative votes. One judge is assigned to write the opinion. The assignment is made before oral arguments on some courts and afterward on others, and it is made by drawing lots or some other random method on some courts and by the presiding judge on others. The assigned judge and his law clerk often do library research and study the trial record, which includes a transcript of the testimony. They write a draft opinion and circulate it to the other judges. The others may comment on the draft, correcting mistakes and suggesting changes, either in informal conversation, in memorandums, or in a later "opinion conference." They also may write concurring opinions, reaching the same result for different reasons, or dissenting opinions, reaching different results. The final vote on the case is essentially the judges' indications as to which opinions they will go along with, and the original opinion writer may end up in the minority.

The major departures from this procedure are shortened routes for cases considered clear-cut. U.S. circuit courts, especially, often do not hold oral arguments and do not issue opinions, relying heavily on staff attorneys to weed out the insubstantial appeals and to do the research outside the briefs. Even some courts with discretionary jurisdiction, including the focal court and the U.S. Supreme Court, decide a large number of cases in a summary fashion when they believe the lower courts are clearly right or clearly wrong.

ADMINISTRATION

The job of an appellate judge involves much more than deciding appeals. Some of this is related to the cases; for example, judges rule on hundreds of applications for bail, requests for delays in submitting briefs and records, and requests to stay lower court decisions pending appeal. More tangential are overseeing bar admissions and attorney discipline. However, the biggest part of noncase work is the administration of the court system.

In the past two decades the administrative activities have grown by leaps and bounds. On the focal court, at least, some of the justices now consider these duties as important as deciding appeals. The administrative side encompasses two overlapping functions: supervision of the lower courts and procedural rule making. Supervision consists of, among other things, compiling statistics about the courts in the jurisdiction, preparing the courts' budget, and trying to cut down backlogs in trial courts. The chief justice is in charge of the supervisory work, helped by an administrator and often a large staff. The second type of administration is rule making. Courts of last resort generally have power to regulate procedure in the lower courts, and a number can override legislation in so doing.

TIME AND WORK LOAD

Information gathering, the focus of this book, is closely connected with time and work load problems; the amount of information that can be gathered greatly depends on the time available to receive or search for it. Almost all the judges I interviewed volunteered some comment about being short of time. The most vehement comments were made at courts without discretionary jurisdiction. Three poignant examples are:

We really are just hung up by the thumbs by the case load.

It is a lot of work. My feeling is if you knock for two nights in a row, you're in trouble. you know. . . . [And later, as a reason for mandatory retirement age] cause this is a wearing job. This is *murder*. You get intellectually pooped. You get *dry*. I'm getting rapidly to the point where I cannot write, "I see the horse" and make sense after a while, you know.

Judicial time is one of the most critical items in our society. . . . I would travel (and have traveled) miles to listen to anyone who might tell me how to save five minutes a day.[3]

The present situation in the U.S. circuit courts is especially severe. The yearly case load has been doubling every seven or eight years, a rate of growth several times greater than the increase in judges. Each circuit judge sits on about 300 to 400 cases a year and writes some 60 or 70 opinions (over twice as many cases and opinions as at the focal court). A 1973 seminar for circuit judges was entitled "Time, Our Most Precious Commodity," and the case load problems have lead to numerous studies and commission reports. State supreme courts with discretionary jurisdiction can, of course, control their case load; but the justices have additional duties, especially administration, that take up much of their time.

The increased interest in administration has reduced time available for deciding cases. The chief judge spends more time on administration than the other judges, and that position has become a grueling honor. Courts of last resort have greater administrative duties, but even the circuit court chief judges spend perhaps a third of their time there.[4] On many courts, however, the extra load is somewhat mitigated by giving the chief judge an extra law clerk and other staff help or by lessening his case load. On the focal court, where the chief justice spends an enormous percentage of his time on administration, he is assigned half as many cases as the other judges. Administrative work by associate judges is partly voluntary and varies greatly from court to court and judge to judge. On the circuit courts they spend very little time on these activities. On the focal court they spend a quarter to a half of their time there, somewhat more than at the other three state courts.

With few exceptions, appellate judges work much longer than the regular 40-hour week; some work over 60 hours. In one study, the Third Circuit judges kept track of their working hours for a year and logged an average of 2,300 hours—or 47 hours a week assuming three weeks of vacation. The study concluded that the judges work about 50 percent longer hours than other professional people engaged in comparable work.[5] Judges actually do not work that much in their offices, often arriving at midmorning and going home early; much of the work is done at home—much in the evenings and on weekends—where many have their own small law libraries. The law clerks, though often critical of judges, almost never accused them of lacking industry. They work especially hard during the court sessions when they read briefs late in the evenings to prepare for oral arguments.

The courts can meet the work load problems in a variety of ways. The most obvious is limiting the number of cases to be decided. The courts can get some relief by throwing cases out under strict interpretations of procedural or jurisdictional rules. They can also discourage appeals by increasing the costs or by lessening the chance that the lower court will be overruled (e.g., by more readily accepting the trial courts' findings of facts). But these have only a limited effect and tend to be unpopular. A new tack, used on the Second Circuit and several other courts, is to bring the attorneys together and try to persuade them to settle the case and drop the appeal.

Courts of last resort can be relieved of case load pressures by increasing their discretionary jurisdiction and by creating or expanding intermediate courts. This helps only up to a point, however; as the case load continues to rise, more time is needed to decide which cases to accept. Much of the work here is delegated to staff members, but the focal court justices, at least, spend nearly as much time on this process as on the actual deciding of cases.

The U.S. circuit courts have very little discretionary jurisdiction because of the general belief that each litigant should have the right to at least one appeal. The major ways to lessen case loads are to split the more overloaded circuit courts into two courts and to lessen the courts' jurisdiction by leaving some types of cases—for example, suits between people from different states or tax cases—to the state courts or to specialized federal tribunals.

The standard way to relieve intermediate courts has been adding more judges. But judges often resist expansions. The internal operation of a large court is complicated, coordination is difficult, and more judges might mean less prestige for any one judge. There are, however, several ways of increasing judicial manpower without increasing the number of regular judges. For example, a whole host of people can sit on the circuit courts: senior circuit judges, judges from other circuits, district court judges, and even active and retired Supreme Court Justices. All but the last are used extensively. The busier circuit courts have over seventy judges sitting during a year. Senior judges are semiretired, hear somewhere around half the normal case load, and sit in addition to the judges authorized on the court. Outside judges or retired judges are also used in half the state supreme courts, including the Ohio Supreme Court among the four courts studied here.

A typical response to overload is the delegation of work. First, the judges can delegate decision making to their colleagues. They can sit in panels so that only part of the court need hear an appeal. Intermediate courts have already gone about as far as they can along this route; panels of fewer than three are very rare and are greatly disliked. Also the court can leave the decision largely in the hands of the judge assigned to write the opinion. This used to be a common result of high case loads, but it is now frowned upon, and all judges who hear a case are expected at least to read the briefs.

The most extreme delegation to nonjudges is the commissioner system used in a few state supreme courts, a system that has been losing favor recently. The commissioners do everything the judges do, including opinion writing and sitting in conferences, except that they do not vote on the cases. Most of the help judges now recieve is from law clerks and staff attorneys, whose main job is gathering information for the judges, as Chapter 6 will discuss. The number of law clerks has more than doubled during this decade. Staff attorneys, who differ from law clerks in that they are not attached to specific judges, have proliferated at an even greater rate.

The ultimate response to an excessive case load is to spend less time on some cases, especially those considered routine. One method in wide use is writing very short opinions or no opinions at all. Another is to do away with oral arguments and even, at a few courts, full briefs. The circuit courts especially have used these shortcuts, often using staff attorneys to select (with review by the judges) the cases to be given abbreviated treatment.

DISPUTE DECIDING AND LAWMAKING

A very important and often discussed distinction is that between the dispute-deciding and lawmaking aspects of deciding appeals. The distinction goes under many names—a common one is error correcting versus institutional or policy functions—always referring to the difference between deciding which litigant wins the case and deciding precedent for future cases. Although appeals are presented to courts as a contest between parties to a suit, often the decision is later applied to other disputes involving other people. That is the doctrine of stare decisis; courts build laws by applying past rulings to present appeals. Moreover, lawyers and citizens may rely on these past rulings to guide their affairs.

This distinction is an important background assumption in this book. It is one explanation for why judges obtain different types of information from different sources. The distinction, however, is sometimes hazy, since it involves the judges' thought processes. Hence, like many distinctions in the law, it is only an approximation.

Dispute deciding is simply determining which litigant wins the case. As a general rule, it has much less impact than lawmaking because it only affects the parties. Lawmaking decisions produce rules that are often applied to many existing and future disputes, and in criminal procedure cases, especially, decisions may in effect decide thousands of cases lower in the court system. On the other hand, some dispute-deciding rulings have an enormous impact, such as that which forced President Nixon to hand over the Watergate tapes; and some affect many people, such as class actions, labor injunctions, or school desegregation suits. The dispute-deciding aspects of a decision cannot be changed except in an appeal or other timely review involving essentially the same parties. The lawmaking part of a decision can be changed in later cases involving totally different parties—that is, precedent can be overruled.

Virtually all decisions require the dispute-deciding function. As will be discussed in the next chapter, courts are reluctant to decide an appeal if the decision would not directly affect a litigant—for example, if one side lacks standing or if the case is moot. Courts without discretionary jurisdiction tend to emphasize dispute deciding more than courts with discretionary jurisdiction. As a practical matter, however, this difference is not great because much law is created by the former, and the latter sometimes summarily reverse lower court decisions they dislike.

Whether a case involves lawmaking aspects in addition to dispute-deciding aspects depends on the judges' perceptions of the issues. If they label the issues as only involving, as it is often put, "the application of the facts of the case to settled and well-defined rules of law," then they are deciding the dispute only. If they see the law as incomplete or wish to change the law, then they are making law. Many judges in the past refused to admit they were making law when they did so, but that position is rare now.

Lawmaking is absent in a range of issues that falls between: (1) when the judges believe the facts fall unquestionably within a specific rule, and (2) when they decide the case by applying the facts to a broad, loose rule, and they do not wish to confine their future discretion by refining the rule. Cases falling in the latter end are more common; attorneys do not often appeal in the face of a specific and clearly applicable rule. The major class of issues falling solidly in the second category (and the major class of solely dispute-deciding issues) are those termed "fact issues." As will be discussed in Chapter 11, courts are reluctant to overturn findings of fact made below by the trial court or administrative agency; they study the evidence to see whether the findings are "supported by substantial evidence" or fall under some other vague criteria, and they do not evolve specific rules. Another common type of fact issue is determining whether a mistake made by a trial judge is a "reversible error"—roughly, whether the mistake might have affected the jury's decision.

Labeling an issue as containing lawmaking content or not often affects the form of opinion produced. Lawmaking opinions are addressed to a wide audience. They must be carefully drafted to explain the ruling to lawyers, judges, and others who will use them as precedent. On the other hand, if the judges feel that no lawmaking is involved, hardly anyone but the litigants and the judges working on the case care about the opinion. Thus appellate courts are to an ever-increasing degree leaving these opinions unpublished or even not writing opinions and sending the parties short memorandums instead. At courts that do not publish these opinions, the number of published opinions is the best indication of the number of lawmaking cases decided.[6] At the Massachusetts and Ohio courts 80 to 90 percent are published. At the focal court about 60 percent are; its remaining decisions are summary decisions. The circuit courts publish opinions in about a third to a half of their cases.

There is considerable tension and interaction between the two functions —that is, between reaching what the judges consider a just result in the particular situation and producing a ruling that the judges would like to be applied to similar situations in the future. On one side is the old saw that "hard cases make bad law": The particular equities of a case may, in the judges' opinion, run counter to the present rules and the wisest rule for litigation of this type in general. On the other hand, the particular facts and equities of a case are often used as evidence of what the sound rule for situations of this sort should be; the information used in dispute deciding is also useful in lawmaking.

Appellate courts make law in a system designed primarily for dispute deciding. In the great bulk of cases the issues are presented by two opposing litigants interested in winning their cases, but the court must make law affecting many others not represented before the court. Whether or not this is fair, it is how stare decisis works.[7] It leads, however, to tension in information-gathering matters, because information may be considered sufficient for dispute-deciding decisions but not for the more far-reaching lawmaking decisions.

CHAPTER 3

An Introduction to the Adversary System

The adversary system is no more and no less than a means of gathering and evaluating information. People seeking a favorable decision bring information to the decision maker, and the information is evaluated through one adversary attacking another's presentation. As a general rule, the adversaries are outside the decision maker's organization and are not subject to his control, although, as in any human arrangement, there are many restraints on how the adversaries should act. The investigatory method is the opposite of the adversary system; the decision maker and his agents find and evaluate the information themselves. For example, when buying new machinery, a manufacturing company relies on the adversary system if it depends on outside salesmen to suggest that new machinery is needed, what types of machines are available, and how well they work. Each salesman touts his own machines and attacks the others', and the buying company relies solely on these representations. On the other hand, the company uses the investigatory system to the extent that its employees research the need for new machinery and check out the possible machines.

As a practical matter, no one relies totally on the adversary system, if only because past experiences and accumulated knowledge must enter into a decision. But some organizations rely more than others on this source of information. Appellate courts' reliance is equaled by that of few other types of organization. Trial courts rely on it more, but I can think of no others. Legislatures and administrative agencies gather much information through hearings and from lobbyists, but they often have large staffs of investigators. Appellate courts, nevertheless, do use much information obtained from outside the adversary system, mainly legal authority and social facts. The extent and reasons for this departure are major topics later in the book.

Although it would be difficult to prove, there seems to be a general movement in this country toward the adversary system. For example, the juvenile justice system and the civil commitment process (e.g., commitment of the mentally ill) have become less paternalistic in that due process notions are now emphasized and adversary lawyers often used. Outside of the legal system, there is a much discussed proposal for a "science court" to evaluate the benefits and dangers of technologies. Scientists would present their varying views before a panel of experts; they would cross-examine others and attack their view; and then the panel would come to a decision on the basis of this information.

Probably the main benefit of—and rationale for—the adversary system is that self-interest motivates the parties to present the best arguments in their favor.[1] Ideally, the parties will give all the necessary information. Judge Hamley of the Ninth Circuit has written:

The appellate court lawyer [must] be a pleader for and upholder of his client's interest. He must be a partisan for the cause he espouses. Consistent with a high standard of ethical and fair conduct, his every choice of plan or action must be dictated by its supposed tendency to bring acceptance of his view. It is expected that the attorneys for both sides will follow this course in preparing their briefs and presenting oral argument. If they do so, the court of review, in whom the judging process is lodged, will be able to reach the right and just decision. This, at least, is the theory of our adversary system, as applied to appellate review.[2]

As will be seen later, however, this theory is often far from realized. Attorneys may be lax in preparing their appeals; they may not know what information the judges want; or both sides may wish that certain information not be presented.

Another rationale for the adversary system in courts is that litigants believe it to be a fair system. If one has his day in court, is given a chance to answer points used against him, and believes that the judges seriously consider his arguments, then a loss may be more palatable and the judicial system more tenable. Whether that happens in real life is not a topic here, though Chapter 4 gives some evidence of such an effect on the attorneys.

Appellate judges are fond of the adversary system. I asked most of those interviewed what they thought of it and how well it worked in presenting information to the court. Nearly all said it was a good system.[3] Two of the more elaborate comments were:

Q — What do you think of the way the adversary system works in getting information to you? Is it generally pretty good?
A — Oh, I think so. It's probably better than leaving it up to the court to do it. In the first place the court wouldn't have the same *motivation*. The adversary system is sort of consistent with the whole idea of capitalism too: that self-interest compels people more than anything else.

You could devise a system, I suppose, of a kind of a beneficient court that was supposed to look into all the important facts, and decide the case like a caseworker or social service caseworker or something like that. The danger is that the judges are lazy like everyone else, and the investigators may be lazy, and perhaps they would end up not developing the facts as well as a person motivated by his own self interest.

Judges often call a strict allegiance to the adversary system an "umpire" approach, and they often call departures from it the "search for justice" or "search for truth" approach. In the umpire approach, the judge passively absorbs information given by opposing contestants and, without attempting to gather further information, decides the issues according to who has presented the better arguments. This approach is not popular among appellate judges. None subscribed to it in the interviews (although a couple claimed they knew of judges who did). One judge gave this explanation of why he did independent research beyond the briefs:

I have a responsibility for something more than just deciding which litigant made the best showing. I know there are differences of opinion among judges about this. Some judges say they're just umpires, and they decide who scored the most runs. But I think that a much better or more *accurate* view—the more socially *acceptable* view—is that we have a responsibility for reaching a *correct* and *just* result.

Probably all appellate judges do independent research and use arguments not given by the attorneys. Also, there is a general feeling that one should alleviate an imbalance of counsel: I asked half of the judges if they felt obliged to do extra research when an attorney did a much poorer job than his opponent, and the great majority said they did; most felt rather strongly that they should.

The distinction between dispute deciding and lawmaking is very important here. On the dispute-deciding side the judges must ask: Should the court make a possibly wrong ruling for one side on the basis of incomplete information? Should a litigant suffer because his attorney does a poor job? And should the court make sure all information used has been openly presented by one side so that the other can contest it? On the lawmaking side the question is different: Is it fair or wise for the court to rely on counsel in the present case when the ruling may affect other disputes involving people not before the court? Much of this book is concerned with how the judges answer these questions. Roughly, they answer the first series yes and the final question no; much depends, however, on the type of information involved.

The legal adversary system exists in its purest form (though increasingly less pure) in the trial court fact-finding process. Nearly all facts about the dispute are presented by counsel. Here a decision affects only that one case; if counsel does a poor job, ordinarily only he and his client suffer. In fact, most discussion in the legal literature about the umpire versus searching-for-truth roles is about the fact-finding process in trial courts.[4] Moreover, the term "adversary system" is often associated mainly with this aspect of the legal system. Even though asked in the interviews about the adversary system in their court, a number of judges answered at least partly in terms of presenting evidence at the trial level.

When it comes to lawmaking, reliance on the adversary system would be risky. The stakes tend to be higher than when deciding disputes, because precedent is created and more people are affected. Also, the attorneys' incentive is to present information designed to help win his case; so he may try to hide information or may not see the relevance of information needed for lawmaking. One of the several judges who mentioned this problem in the interviews said about appellate advocacy:

I'm well aware of the circumstance that *nobody* is trying exactly to tell us just how we ought to do our job in the sense of how to make the law come out properly. They're trying to win the case. In fact, they're trying to trick us into applying the law to the advantage of their client. I use the word "trick" with quotes around it. And really, that you have to watch everybody in an adversary, or any other situation possibly, to make sure that they're not trying to pull the wool over our eyes. . . . So an adversary situation forces people to be militantly on their own behalves, and they're not necessarily going to spend an awful lot of time worrying about *our* problems, and try to make *order* out of the case in the context of the continuing flow of decisions.

On the other hand, there need not be such a mismatch between the adversary system and lawmaking. Some attorneys—though probably not many below the U.S. Supreme Court level—are more interested in the precedent created than in the narrow outcome of the dispute. More important, any attorney who is sufficiently knowledgeable ordinarily would argue toward the judges' lawmaking function, because the judges take that into account when deciding who wins the immediate litigation. In fact, as will be seen later, that in general is what the attorneys try to do.

Lawmaking by appellate courts in a dispute-deciding framework presents several other problems: (1) Lawmaking on a subject must await a case presenting the subject and, ordinarily, the raising of the specific issue by counsel. (2) In the ordinary case only two sides present information to the court (although each side is often represented by a team or a succession of counsel). There is less chance of receiving full information than in congressional or administrative hearings, where many adversaries appear. Lawmaking problems need not be bipolar. There can be solutions that neither side desires and that the court must evaluate on its own. (3) The dispute-deciding adversary system focuses on only one specific fact situation, the situation involved in the dispute; hence courts tend to receive a very narrow view of the facts of life, making difficult comprehensive lawmaking in any one appeal.

Appellate courts have, to some extent, adjusted the adversary system to meet these problems through two devices: taking amicus briefs and deciding

two or more cases with similar issues at the same time. These two will be discussed in Chapter 5, where it is concluded that, in practice, they add little
beyond what the two adversaries alone present.

Lawmaking in the dispute-deciding framework, on the other hand, does
present some countervailing benefits. It can, as was said, provide the motivation for adversaries to present information to the court. If nothing else,
it is a cheaper way of getting information than through hired assistants.

Also, although the facts tend to be focused on a narrow slice of life,
information about this slice of life ordinarily is well developed because it
has been presented in a dispute-deciding context at the lower tribunal.
Appellate judges, then, have considerable information with which to determine a fair and wise rule for the issue before them. Lastly, the dispute-
deciding framework often provides appellate courts with feedback information about the effects of their lawmaking; new disputes in the area may
be appealed later.

The rest of this chapter will elaborate these general considerations about
the drawbacks of the adversary system and about what is done to counter
them. The major topics are the generally low quality of appellate advocacy,
at least in the eyes of the judges; what, precisely, the judges find wrong with
the briefs and arguments; the apparently substantial impact of imbalance of
counsel on the outcome of appeals; and the problems of preserving adverseness in litigation and, thus, the attorneys' incentive to present their case
well. These discussions are intended as both a foundation and a road map
for the later chapters on specific aspects of appellate procedure, details of
decision-making methods, and various types of information used by the
judges.

QUALITY OF THE ATTORNEYS' WORK

The advocate is a partner of the court in the important enterprise of dispensing justice.
I am concerned about the future of this partnership in light of what many perceive to
be a decline in the quality of advocacy. . . . In our adversary system, the quality of
justice dispensed by the courts is ultimately dependent on the quality of advocacy
provided by the bar. If lawyers fail as advocates for want of skill or dedication, then
judges surely will fail as well, and the coin of justice will be debased beyond recognition.[5]

This statement by Judge Kaufman of the Second Circuit is typical; appellate judges often say that the quality of their work depends greatly on the
quality of counsel's work. They view good briefs and arguments as a help
and poor ones a bother. Obviously, competent advocacy is necessary for the
adversary system to work well; when it is not present, Justice Traynor has
said, "An element of chance then enters the solution, for even the most
painstaking court may fail to uncover what the adversaries failed to reveal."[6]

Anyone familiar with the writings and speeches of appellate judges knows that they often complain about the lawyers. Based on these sources plus statements in interviews, it appears that most are not at all pleased with the general run of briefs and arguments.[7] Judge Lumbard, also from the Second Circuit, claims that only one in five is passable, and one in ten good.[8] But that is an extreme view. Judges are ordinarily more charitable than that, though their opinions differ considerably—except on one point, that the quality varies greatly. The majority view among those I interviewed was that most lawyers' work is adequate; yet only several seemed satisfied with it on the whole. They were reluctant to give, as Judge Lumbard did, exact figures, but one had graded each oral argument and found that "one third of them were very good, one third very bad, and one third competent." The remaining judges, a substantial minority, either said that most of the briefs and arguments are inadequate or, without giving any proportions, spoke very strongly about the poor advocacy. One experienced circuit judge, when asked about the quality of advocacy, said it is "usually poor" and added:

I was much disappointed to discover that some of my friends that sit on the Supreme Court—by which I mean in Washington—exhibited the same disappointment. In due course I'll come to my theory on why—*one* of my reasons why I think that is so. . . . Obviously partly it's so because all lawyers are not as good as they should be. But I think the situation has become exacerbated by the very large incomes that lawyers make. I don't say they shouldn't, but it means that they charge on an hourly basis more than they can possibly put into the ordinary run-of-the-mill case; and a brief that is as good as it should be, even though it's not an important case, runs up too many book charges.

Several others said that the caliber of advocacy has deteriorated, usually adding that it no longer pays top lawyers to do appellate work. In fact, for some time people have been complaining that appellate lawyers were better in the past.[9] Another explanation for poor advocacy was given mainly in Rhode Island; the justices thought less of the attorneys than those on the other five courts, blaming the poor work on the absence of an appellate bar.

The great majority of law clerks complained about the attorneys' work, usually more vehemently than any of the judges. They called the arguments and briefs "terrible, worthless, meaningless," "abhorrent," "exceedingly poor," and "lousy." Actually, of the clerks who gave proportions, half said the majority were adequate; yet their shock upon encountering the briefs and arguments was greater than the judges'.

What types of attorneys do a better job? Half the judges and lawyers commented on this. Several mentioned that lawyers with appellate experience are more often competent and that general practitioners are less often so, although some judges are fond of pointing out exceptions to the latter statement. In criminal cases it was said, especially at the focal court, that public defenders tend to do better than assigned counsel or, less often, prosecutors.

Worst of all are the pro se defendants—those representing themselves. Their petitions are often "prepared in confusing layman legalese,"[10] and one circuit judge has written that reading them is "the most irritating and most disagreeable task which I have been called upon to perform as a judge."[11] On the civil side, several clerks and judges said the attorneys are better in cases involving large sums of money: the litigants hire better attorneys because there is more money at stake. Also the government lawyers before the federal courts are considered good, especially those representing the Internal Revenue Service and the National Labor Relations Board.[12]

It is interesting that attorneys, in their writings and in the interviews here, have almost as low an opinion of the courts' products as the judges and law clerks have of theirs (the attorneys' complaints, however, are sometimes based on ideological differences as well as views about the quality of opinions). Perhaps one should expect this mutual lack of respect. The two groups are highly dependent on one another's work and must deal with it constantly; yet at the same time they are independent in any organizational sense and cannot order each other to act as they would wish.

WHAT IS DONE ABOUT POOR ADVOCACY. The judges do very little to upgrade the quality of advocacy. They could to a great many things. They could publicly upbraid attorneys for poor work or praise them for good work. They could ask for new briefs or for further briefing on specific topics. On some courts they could regulate which attorneys practice before them. Courts with discretionary jurisdiction could consider the caliber of the attorneys' work when deciding what case to take. Judges could help attorneys by telling them early in the progress of an appeal what issues to concentrate on. They could foster further schooling in the art of appellate advocacy. And they could make speeches and write articles or pamphlets telling the bar how to proceed. These have all been done, but traditionally, except for the last, done rarely. Many judges are reluctant to do anything that would reflect badly on an attorney, ruling out many of these possibilities. One said in the interviews:

There are occasions when we would very much like to have better briefs, and it's very hard to *solve* that problem because it almost comes close to implying malpractice if we in effect strike the brief and send it back to the parties and ask them to try again.

In the last couple of years, however, two committees, consisting largely of judges, have been formed to evaluate ways to improve advocacy. One is considering standards for attorneys who appear before federal courts, and the other is fostering programs that train lawyers to present better briefs and oral arguments.[13]

Two other, rather indirect means of controlling the quality of advocacy will receive considerable attention both in this chapter and later in the book. The two are directly opposite, though not necessarily contradictory. First, judges attempt to make the adversary system less than totally adversary in nature. Notice that Judge Hamley, quoted earlier, said that the adversary system is based on the attorneys' attempts to present their side forcefully "consistent with a high standard of ethnical and fair conduct." Here the judges ask counsel to present information favorable to opponents—by, for example, presenting a balanced statement of facts in the briefs and bringing up important adverse precedent—partly in the hopes that one side will help fill in the gaps left by his opponent. This, as might be expected, meets with only limited success. Second, judges use various mechanisms, such as standing and mootness rules, that help ensure adverseness among the parties and, thus, the incentive upon which the adversary system is based. But these rules do not often come into play.

Although appellate judges do little to improve advocacy, they do routinely attempt to mitigate the problems of inadequate information from the briefs and oral arguments. These attempts will be discussed at length in later chapters. By and large they are used in the lawmaking side only. The most important, of course, is independent research by judges, law clerks, and staff attorneys. Two others were mentioned earlier, receiving amicus briefs and hearing jointly several cases presenting similar issues. Along the same line, a few judges get informal advice from experts outside the court. And, very important, judges like to restrict the scope of their decisions—for example, through judicial restraint or by ruling only on the specific points needed to decide the case—and thus lessen the chance of, and extent of, damage caused by faulty decisions based on incomplete information.

ATTORNEYS' SHORTCOMINGS

Just what would the judges like from counsel, and where do they believe counsel fall short? The best approach to this question is through judges' writings about appellate advocacy, in which they tell appellate lawyers how to do their work and complain about the mistakes made. Over eighty judges have written on this topic in the past several decades.[14]

Of course, the length and thoroughness of the writings vary greatly. Many of them are quite short; thus only rarely is any specific comment made by more than half the judges. Only (and all) comments made by at least fifteen judges are mentioned here. Every judge would agree with most of the major comments, but I assume that the relative frequency of comments reflects, at least roughly, the relative concern judges attach to them.

The judges' comments about appellate advocacy fall into four broad categories:

First, the least interesting, and probably least important, is their wish to have information presented in a pleasant, convenient, and easily understood form. For the most part this involves relatively insubstantial things that annoy the judges and waste their time. They are, in order of decreasing frequency:

• There should be a short summary of the case—the issues and the lower court ruling—at the beginning of the briefs and oral arguments, so that the judges can understand the relevance of the discussions that follow.

• Attorneys should follow the court rules as to the form and filing times of the briefs.

• The statement of facts in the briefs should contain references to the record supporting every assertion of fact.

• An attorney should not make unseemly attacks on his opponent or the trial judge.

• The clarity of one's writing style is important.

• Issues should be stated clearly.

• Citations of cases should be correct.

• The briefs should be readable and written in a good literary style.

• When asked a question in oral arguments, an attorney should not postpone the answer till later when he had planned to cover the topic (because he might not get around to it and because the judge is interested in the topic right then).

• If more than one counsel represents the same side of an appeal, only one should give the oral argument, and he should be prepared to answer questions on any part of the case.

• The statement of facts in the brief should be in chronological order and not in the order the facts developed at trial (so that the judges can more easily grasp them).

• Charts and exhibits should be used in oral arguments whenever they might help the judges understand complicated factual situations.

The second broad category is direct or indirect requests for more information from attorneys. By far the most frequent of these, found in almost half the judges' writings, is that the attorneys know the facts of the case—that they study the record thoroughly before writing the briefs or giving oral arguments. The reason, apparently, is that judges want counsel to present all the important facts and to be able to answer questions about what the record contains. Several judges specifically request that the statement of facts in the briefs or arguments thoroughly present the relevant facts.

Legal argument is emphasized less. Only about a quarter of the judges mention that the attorneys should research the law thoroughly, and even fewer mention that the legal argument be thorough.[15] Less often still are requests that attorneys argue the justice or equity of their clients' positions in addition to the strictly legal arguments. this does not mean that the judges care little about the quality of counsel's legal research and legal argument.

Surely all care about it. Rather, it suggests that they are less bothered about the quality of advocacy here than in the statement of facts. Judges may believe attorneys do a better job in presenting the legal argument. More likely, as many judges commented, they believe that the factual presentations are more important than the legal arguments.

This second category also includes some suggestions not related to specific types of information. A common and broad warning is that attorneys should prepare thoroughly for oral arguments. Also, several judges mention each of the following: An attorney should refute his opponent's arguments and should directly face the weak points in his case; he should not evade the judges' questions in oral arguments; and he should plan his oral argument time carefully to make sure he covers all his major points before time is up.

The judges give the most emphasis to the third broad category, that counsel be succinct. Here the judges are calling for less information; they ask counsel to delete information not relevant to the decision and to limit the repetition of relevant information. The most frequent comment by far, made by 70 percent of the judges, is that attorneys limit the number of issues discussed in the briefs or arguments. This topic is a major part of Chapter 8; for the moment it is enough to say that an issue is a bundle of facts and laws upon which the appellant wishes to reverse the lower tribunal, and limiting the number of issues presented is equivalent to limiting the number of decisions the judges are asked to make and, thus, the amount of information they must consider.

There are many other requests to limit information. About half the judges say the briefs and oral arguments in general should be "brief," "concise," or "succinct." An equal number say the same thing in reference to the statement of facts in the briefs or arguments. A substantial minority say that counsel should limit precedents cited to those that are the most relevant. A number also say that counsel should end his oral argument and sit down when he has covered all he had planned to cover, rather than repeat points already made.

Two further comments are aimed both at shortening attorneys' presentations and at making the judges' jobs more pleasant. Half complained about attorneys who read in oral arguments from prepared statements, from precedents, and especially from their briefs. Judges find listening to this tedious and feel it wastes time, since they can read the material themselves. Likewise, several asked counsel not to place long quotes in the briefs, preferring more compact descriptions of the material, which in any case they will read in the original if important.

This emphasis on conciseness is significant. The effectiveness of the adversary system depends not only on the parties' ability to present the relevant information but also on their ability to stick to what is relevant and to present it in a compact form. Briefs and arguments are of little help if the judges

must extract the information they want out of a mass of extraneous stuff.
Justice Tate of Louisiana wrote:

Probably the outstanding fault of most briefs, however, is not that they include too
little information, but that they include too much. The lawyer will enable the judge
to understand his client's position much better and more efficiently if the lawyer will
take the time to weed out the irrelevant and the unnecessary, and to concentrate on
the essential and serious issues, rather than to leave this labor to the judge. If the
lawyer does not do so, the judge may simply peruse the brief and, realizing that it will
not give him much help, go on about his research and review without much further
reference to the brief.[16]

Judges not only want counsel to weed out the irrelevant material but also to
bring to the fore the *most* relevant material. For example, a common complaint is that some lawyers follow legal propositions with long chains of
citations; judges much prefer that counsel mention only the two or three
cases he believes most strongly support his position. They tend to view oral
argument, with the fifteen or thirty minutes allowed a party, as a way of
forcing lawyers to select the most important information—to narrow and
confine the issues, to concentrate on the key facts, and to mention very few
authorities. Several judges used the identical phrase, that counsel "should
go for the jugular" in his oral arguments. Especially courts with excessive
case loads would like counsel to cut the information down to the bones.
"Counsel's whole effort in both brief and argument," said an overworked
New Jersey intermediate court judge, "must be toward getting his message
across with the least unnecessary expenditure of effort by the judges."[17]
And Justice Harlan said when on the Second Circuit:

Most cases have one or only a few master issues. In planning his oral argument the
wise lawyer will ferret out and limit himself to the issues which are really controlling,
and will leave the less important or subordinate issues to the court's own study of the
briefs. Otherwise, one is apt to get tanglefoot, and the court is left pretty much
where it began.[18]

Justice Harlan listed four characteristics of a good oral argument. This
passage deals with "selectivity." Two others are "resiliency," which is basically not evading judges' questions, a point mentioned earlier, and "candor,"
which will be discussed presently. The remaining characteristic is "simplic-
ity"; this again is winnowing the information and means leaving only an
easily understood line of reasoning. Quite a few other judges also asked
counsel to simplify. One warned that "a thing that does not lend itself to
quick and ready explanation is usually a thing that is not capable of being
effectively or honestly explained at all."[19]

Thus a major part of appellate decision making is sifting, refining, and simplifying the often massive amounts of information involved in a case into manageable portions that can be conveniently grasped by a busy judge. And the advocates are expected to play a large role in this process, a greater role, the judges believe, than they now play.

The fourth and last category is judges' suggestions that counsel be candid: Counsel should not knowingly present inaccurate information, and they should supply important information favoring their opponents. The main comment, given by most judges, is that the statement of facts should be objective or, at least, should include all the important unfavorable facts. (Also, though somewhat tangential to this area, several judges warned against giving facts that are not in the record—facts that they are not supposed to consider.) There were also general statements that counsel should always try to be candid throughout the briefs and arguments and, occasionally, statements that the legal authorities should not be misrepresented and that the adverse authorities should be faced directly. (Almost none, however, said specifically that an attorney must tell the court about adverse authorities missed by his opponent, a topic that will be discussed in Chapter 9.) The emphasis on candor is forcefully stated by Judge Prettyman of the D.C. Circuit Court:

But to be an aggressive, competent, forceful, fighting advocate is not to be a slick, cute, tricky one. I have read advice that questions be slanted so as to produce a satisfactory answer, that facts be stated so as to lead a busy court to reach an answer favorable to that party, that irrelevant factors be introduced and emphasized with the object of leading the judges into misapprehension of the real dispute; in sum that, short of actual misstatements, tactics be designed for the sole purpose of winning the lawsuit.[20]

He went on to say that these tactics violate professional ethics and that they are stupid because the opponent or the court will uncover them. Justice Tate, who was quoted earlier, said that counsel may emphasize favorable facts:

However, it is also important that in so doing counsel does not distort or ignore other facts which do not favor his position. He may seek to evade their forcefulness by the context or in the emphasis by which he shows them, or he may explain them, but if he ignores them, and the court subsequently finds them to be of relevant force in the determination of the appeal, counsel risks the loss of the court's confidence in his own fair presentation of the issues, and an assumption by the court that counsel cannot satisfactorily accommodate his case to these unfavorable facts.[21]

Justice Tate here points out an interesting aspect of appellate decision making. Counsel's mistakes and, especially, lack of candor color the rest of his arguments in the eyes of many judges. If they are suspicious of an attorney, they more thoroughly check his information. Half the judges said this. Several wrote in terms similar to Justice Tate's that their opinions about the objectivity of an attorney's statement of facts influence their trust in the whole brief or oral argument. Others spoke to the same effect with reference to candor in presenting authorities, candor in describing issues, or simply candor in general. Also, quite a few judges said that if an attorney presents many insubstantial issues in an appeal, they presume that all the issues are insubstantial. They presume that the attorney cannot or does not want to distinguish the good from the poor issues, and this colors their outlook towards his whole argument.

Judges say occasionally that this suspicion attaches not only to the briefs in the one appeal, but also to the attorney's appellate work in general. Those attorneys, they say, having reputations for lacking candor lose effectiveness because the judges pay less attention to, and cannot accept at face value, their arguments. For example, Justice Denecke of the Oregon Supreme Court coauthored this passage:

If you cite cases for what they don't stand for, or assert that the record contains evidence that isn't there, you are not only violating your professional obligation to the court, but doing your present and future clients a disservice. You can be sure your sins will find you out in the particular case; and, what is perhaps worse, you will build up a reserve of distrust which could take years to eradicate. With some lawyers, a statement regarding either the record or the authority is accepted at face value; with others, every word is taken with a grain of salt, and then checked and double-checked. Honesty is emphatically the best policy.[22]

In this same area, judges say on occasion that an attorney is more effective if he seems sincere in his arguments. "Nothing is quite so effective," said Judge Fahy of the D.C. Circuit, "as the conveyance by the advocate to the court of his deep conviction of the correctness of his position."[23] Here too judges pick up clues as to whether counsel's arguments are, in general, to be believed. Lack of faith in his own arguments suggests they have little merit.

Thus the judges try to blunt the adverseness of the adversary system, and there are any number of reasons why they might wish to do so. An advocate may not supply all favorable information and may not uncover faulty statements by his opponent; so judges ask that opponents help him out. An attorney's statement against his own interests is considerably less suspect than one supporting his interests; so a candid advocate supplies the court with much information that it need not bother to verify. Judges may feel the same way, furthermore, even about self-serving information supplied by counsel with a reputation for candor. Whatever benefit judges derive from counsel's candor, however, counsel may not believe it benefits them. Later chapters will discuss the extent to which counsel actually try to be candid. For the moment, it is interesting that the main incentive (along with vague and seldom enforced ethical proscriptions) that the judges offer attorneys for being candid amounts to lessening adverseness by turning the adversary system back on itself. Counsel are told that they are more effective advocates, and better serve their self-interest, when they act with less than complete adverseness.

THE EFFECT OF IMBALANCE OF COUNSEL

The conflict between candor and full adverseness is, of course, greatest when one side presents better briefs and arguments than the other. Unless the better attorney admits the weaknesses in his case, the court receives lopsided information, which can only be mitigated through information obtained at the court. Judges, we have seen, do not view themselves as umpires simply deciding which attorney gives the best arguments, and they routinely do extra research to bolster the weakly presented side of the case.

Be that as it may, does the caliber of an attorney's work have much impact on the outcome of his appeal? This is an important question for one studying the adversary system. But it is a difficult one, dealing as it does with the baffling subject of causation in human affairs. There can be no real answer in any specific case because no one knows how the case would have been decided if an attorney had presented better or worse arguments. One can only explore the possible effects over many appeals.

The question really consists of two parts. First, how often is there actually an imbalance? One cannot say that equally good briefs and arguments tipped the scales, except to speculate about what would have happened had the quality been different. And the second question is: When there is an imbalance, does the better-prepared side tend to win? This two-part question is studied in three ways by using: (1) judges' and law clerks' feelings on the matter, (2) the relation between winning and certain characteristics of the attorneys, such as Martindale-Hubbell ratings and the length of bar membership, and (3) the relation between outcomes and my own evaluation of the briefs and arguments.

1. I asked most of the judges interviewed how often one attorney does a much better job than his opponent and whether the quality of counsel's work affects the outcome of the case. On the whole they found these questions hard to answer and rarely gave definite proportions. As to the frequency of imbalance, all that can be said is that the judges rarely stated or implied that there is a substantial imbalance in the majority of appeals, and several said it is quite uncommon.

As to the effect of counsel's presentation, most answered that a good argument or brief does or probably does help one's cause. On the other hand, a number of judges, especially in Ohio, said that there is no or extremely little impact, mainly because the judges know the law or do their own research. Typical comments expressing these contrasting views are:

Q — How often does the quality of the briefs and arguments affect the outcome of the case? Can you tell?

A — I don't know how you can tell . . . because it's like the doctor who says "maybe you didn't get well, but you'd have been sicker if I hadn't given you the medicine." But obviously a fellow who makes good arguments is better off than a fellow who doesn't because maybe you won't be bright enough or have enough time to see the point if he hadn't made it.

With all modesty, most of us have been around a long time, and I think you'd have to consider us experts on these things [routine criminal cases], simply on the basis of the time we've been working on it. And it doesn't make an awful lot of difference whether the defense counsel picks up a point or not. One of the members of the panel *will*, and will inject it either at the time of the oral argument, or in a subsequent—if there's stuff that ought to be in it—

Q — Overall, does the caliber of the counsel make much difference as to who wins the case?

A — It makes an amazingly small amount of difference. I say that without hesitation. I've often marvelled at that.

Many judges, also, have written about this topic; the vast majority say that counsel does affect the outcome, especially when the issues are close. Thirty percent of the judges writing on appellate advocacy expressed this opinion. That is a very impressive figure in view of the shortness of many articles; only a few points were made more often. Only three said or implied that the quality of advocacy makes little or no difference, but, then, a judge urging better advocacy is not likely to add that better advocacy will not produce any results. Still, judges' writings elsewhere, not about appellate advocacy, equally stress that the quality of advocacy does affect decisions.[24]

But these are only the judges' impressions and are far from the last word. As the first judge quoted previously implied, they cannot know when an attorney has failed to provide the relevant information unless the court has that information. They cannot really know the impact of counsel. A circuit judge said:

I think that as a judge you like to think that you're deciding a case on its own merits; so you would hope that the case wouldn't depend, at least primarily, on the quality of the attorney. But that's a pretty subjective judgment, because a good attorney— like any real artist—the artistry doesn't show. So that he may be conning you, and if he's really doing a *good* job, you don't think you're being conned. You just think you're being awfully smart in discerning where the truth lies.

In fact, quite a number of judges said that they really did not know whether the quality of an advocate's presentation affected the outcome, though they usually hazarded a guess anyway.

Because of this uncertainty, there can be different interpretations of the same situation—some judges saying that the attorneys' presentations make a great deal of difference, and some saying they make little or no difference. For example, a judge on the same court as the second of the three judges quoted previously said the attorneys' arguments make "an enormous difference" in the judges' final decisions. So a judge's opinion about the effect of counsel reflects not only his observation and experience but also his wishes and, in Judge Medina's words, "perhaps . . . an exaggerated notion of his relative importance in the general scheme of things."[25]

2. Is an attorney more likely to win if he has had more legal experience than his opponent, or is from a better law school, or ranks higher on other criteria that one might associate with his competence? Listed next are five such comparisons based on the attorneys who argued in the focal court over a one-year period:[26] (a) Martindale-Hubbell ratings, which are based on recommendations by fellow lawyers, differed between opposing counsel in not quite half the cases. Those with the lower ratings did as well as those with the higher ratings.[27] (b) Attorneys who had been members of the bar for a shorter time—had less legal experience—actually won a bit more often. (c) As for appellate experience, only about 20 percent of the cases pitted an attorney who did mostly appellate work against one who did not—mainly prosecutors against appointed defense attorneys—and the former did decidedly worse. Also, among the attorneys I interviewed, in most cases opposing counsel had had about the same amount of appellate experience; in the other cases there was no tendency for the more experienced to win. (d) When private attorneys represented both sides of a case, the one from the larger firm lost as often as he won. (e) In one area, however, there was some difference. I classified the attorneys' law schools into two groups—top national schools and all others. Three-fifths of the cases were argued by attorneys who went to schools in the same group, but when there was a difference, the attorney from the better school won almost twice as often as he lost.[28]

Overall these comparisons suggest that there was little imbalance in most cases, and when it existed, it did not affect the outcome. A political science study, using a small nationwide sample of cases, found that characteristics similar to these were weakly related, if at all, to who won appeals.[29] The category of better law schools, however, was somewhat broader than that used in the present research.

One should not make too much of these studies because the characteristics are rather remote indicators of the actual caliber of work done before the courts. The attorney's law school is the remotest of all, at least in terms of time. On the other hand, I did feel when reading the briefs that the work of attorneys from the top schools was a bit better.

3. I studied the briefs and arguments in 109 appeals decided by the focal court and recorded my opinion of the lawyers' work. In nearly 40 percent of the cases opposing counsel seemed to do about the same caliber of work. In the other cases, the attorney who in my opinion did a better job won almost three-fourths of the time. Moreover, the better almost always won the few cases in which the difference between presentations seemed very large.[30]

All three ways of looking to the effect of counsel suggest that the opposing attorneys do work of roughly equal quality in a sizable number of cases. There are varying degrees of imbalance in the remaining cases, though not often a great imbalance. On the whole, too, there is a strong possibility that the adversary system operates substantially in favor of lawyers who do a better job—if, that is, one trusts the judges' impressions or my own impressions.

Incidently, there was very little relation in the appeals studied between the amount of information presented by an attorney and his chances of success. Neither shorter nor longer briefs tended to win more often. Attorneys presenting more legal authority than opponents won more often by a very slight amount, as did attorneys presenting more facts of the case. On the other hand, there was a moderate relationship between attention given to social facts and winning.[31] These findings that attorneys presenting the most information do not have a significant edge is in accord with the judges' emphasis on conciseness in their writings about appellate advocacy.

That attorneys presenting better briefs and arguments tend to win more often, it should be added, does not necessarily mean that the law develops along the lines suggested by better advocates. First, much of an attorney's success is due to his ability to spot issues. Hence any relation between the apparent quality of an attorney's briefs and arguments (i.e., the quality of law, fact, and policy arguments) and winning may exist because good attorneys are good at finding issues as well as at arguing the issues. As will be seen in Chapter 8, the major effect of finding issues is on the dispute-deciding, rather than lawmaking, aspects of appellate work. Second, the judges and their staff tend to do more independent research in major lawmaking cases. Finally, there is probably much less imbalance in the major cases. My impression was that these cases ordinarily received at least one good presentation on each side, in part because a good amicus brief can compensate for poor briefing by a litigant.

ADVERSENESS OF LITIGATION

The adversary system, based as it is on motivations of self-interest, would be ineffective if counsel were indifferent about winning. The next chapter will describe the motivations of appellate counsel; by and large they are interested in winning, although they often have no tangible motivations. Here I will discuss the techniques courts use to restrict their decision making to cases involving real adversaries. Standing and mootness rules require that a litigant have an actual stake in the outcome of the dispute; and the refusal to give advisory opinions, except at a small minority of state supreme courts, means there must be actual litigants involved in a dispute. How well do these techniques ensure that opposing parties are motivated to win appeals —that is, ensure adverseness—and are they in fact intended to ensure adverseness? The discussion here, based on interviews with judges and on the legal literature, is aimed at these questions, rather than the technical details of the often complicated and uncertain doctrines.

STANDING AND FRIENDLY SUITS. Under the standing to sue doctrine a court refuses to decide the merits of a case when it determines that the person advancing the issue has no real stake in its determination. That is, the litigants must have a chance to gain or lose something by the resolution of the dispute in the immediate case, as opposed to by the law produced. In the state courts even a slight stake will ordinarily do.[32] In the federal courts more is required, but determining what is a sufficient stake is a murky, complicated, and shifting subject. The innumerable court decisions and law review articles discussing this hornet's nest have settled very little.[33]

The federal standing doctrine is often explained, at least by the courts, in terms of preserving adverseness. The Supreme Court has traditionally given this explanation, for example, in these passages from cases decided in the early 1960s:

[There must be a] personal stake in the outcome of the controversy [such as to] assure that concrete adverseness which sharpens the presentation of issues upon which the court so largely depends for illumination of difficult constitutional questions.[34]

Within the framework of our adversary system, the adjudicatory process is most securely founded when it is exercised under the impact of a lively conflict between antagonistic demands, actively pressed, which make resolution of the controverted issue a practical necessity.[35]

On the other hand, scholars have been very skeptical of language such as this. They have suggested several other reasons for the federal standing requirements. Examples are limiting the case load, providing courts with some discretion to dodge controversial issues, and disguising substantive rulings for defendants by basing decisions on jurisdictional grounds.[36]

In fact, standing and counsel's motivation are often weakly related. Standing may be denied a person with a large stake in the lawmaking aspect of the case but with no stake in the specific dispute before the court. These litigants often seem, from the face of the court opinions at least, to be motivated strongly to present thorough arguments. On the other side, standing is allowed when the damages alleged are much too small to justify a well-prepared law suit. Some damages are so small that busy state justices sometimes say they would like to pay plaintiff out of their own pockets rather than spend time on the appeal, but of course they cannot.

Yet the Supreme Court has continued to cite the need for adverseness as the major basis for standing.[37] The reason, however, is not so much that the quality of advocacy will be worse when a party has no immediate stake in the outcome; rather, as is suggested by the language quoted previously, the Court is more interested in the development of the factual record: A party without an immediate stake may not present the court with a specific and well-developed fact situation upon which law can be made. The Court wants, and the parties with an immediate stake are more likely to provide, "a complete perspective upon the adverse consequences flowing from the specific set of facts undergirding the grievance," and this is "an integral part of the judicial process, for a court must rely on the parties' treatment of the facts and claim before it to develop its rules of law."[38]

I asked half the judges interviewed for their reasons behind the standing rules. The most common answer was concern with adverseness—but concern with the motivations of counsel to present their case thoroughly more often than concern that the facts might not be fully developed. "I don't think a party *can* present a case with as much strength," said one justice, "if he is not *really* going to live and die with the decision." But less than half the justices gave this reason; the remaining gave a mishmash of answers, reflecting the uncertainty in the area. Several said a prime reason is to keep the case loads down. Other reasons were that the courts should not encourage people to get involved in others' business, that the court may wish not to decide the substantive issues presented, that courts should not foreclose an issue for future litigants unless it must, and that that is just traditionally the way things are done at the courts. The federal judges get many more standing issues than state justices, and several of the latter said they could not give a reason for the doctrine because they had seldom met it.

Two other situations present a clearer lack of adverseness than standing problems; in one the courts tend to decide the issues, in the other they tend not to. The first exists when one side—especially a prosecutor or other government counsel—admits error and tells the court that an issue should be decided against him. This is the ultimate extent of the "candor" inroads on adverseness, and the adversary system is largely annulled. It does not happen often, but when it does appellate courts routinely decide the issues; they may even make law in such a context.[39]

The second situation clearly lacking adverseness is a friendly suit: One side pretends to, but actually does not, desire a ruling in his favor. The same person may gain control over both sides after the litigation is under way, or the suit may be contrived by the plaintiff and defendant for the purpose of establishing a ruling favoring one side. For example, an action may be brought against a government official attacking the legality of a prospective bond issue, although both parties only wish to affirm its legality. In general, courts profess to be wary of friendly suits because adverseness is lacking,[40] but it is impossible to say how often courts decide cases of this sort, especially because they may not know the parties' actual motivations.[41] The focal court, at least, has knowingly decided friendly suits. A justice told me that one was decided because the court "felt it was important and everybody had been waiting around for a decision, expecting to get one, and the court felt that the public interest required that the matter be resolved." He then said the judges thought they could decide the case by themselves without the help of a truly adversary proceeding.[42]

MOOTNESS. An appeal is moot when neither side would gain in the immediate dispute no matter how the court ruled.[43] The typical moot case began with a real controversy that was negated by some later event. For example, the Supreme Court ruled the *DeFunis*[44] case moot because the defendant's law school, whose admissions policies the plaintiff was contesting, had been forced to enroll the plaintiff and said it would allow him to graduate even if the Court were to rule in favor of the school.

The general rule is that moot cases are thrown out, but there are two major exceptions: (1) The case may be decided if the issue is one that is bound to become moot before decision in the appellate court, for example, issues about elections or pregnancies. Here the parties have no stake in the immediate ruling, but without a ruling the issue would remain unsettled, and the court's lawmaking function would be unfulfilled. (2) Many state supreme courts openly decide moot cases whenever they wish to do so. The justification for ignoring mootness ordinarily is that the case contains an important issue that should be addressed quickly. As a practical matter these two exceptions, along with the considerable vagueness in the definition of mootness, often give a court discretion either to embark on or to dodge lawmaking in a case.[45]

There is a tenuous connection between the mootness rules and the desire to preserve adverseness so that parties will be motivated to prepare the appeal well. (Because mootness ordinarily develops after the trial stage, mootness rules have little to do with ensuring an adequate fact record.) The mootness rules can help keep out cases obviously lacking adverseness, provided, that is, the court learns of the mootness. This proviso may be important. Since the record (and thus all the facts an appellate court is likely to have about the case) dates from the time of trial, appellate courts have trouble discovering mootness unless the litigants mention it. The litigants might not do so.[46] When interviewing attorneys I discovered that two cases decided by the focal court within a year became moot soon after briefs were filed, and the court was not told. In one case, the attorneys did not bother to argue because of the mootness. In the other, one gave an ill-prepared argument, which his opponent attributed to the mootness. However, it is as difficult to discover how often courts unknowingly decide moot appeals as it is for friendly suits.

Litigation with obvious adverseness is often thrown out as moot. "In some instances," one circuit judge said, "we have had cases which have been argued vigorously but turned out to be moot. Take the instance of a law suit over a strike that's now ended; that could very well be a moot question." Mootness, like standing, is determined by a party's interest in the outcome of the specific dispute. But some attorneys are concerned mainly with the precedent to be created, and mootness need not diminish their effort. Also, cases can be mooted even after the lawyers have submitted their briefs and made oral arguments; here lack of adverseness is not a factor at all.

Thus the wish to preserve the parties' motivations to present their cases fully seems only a secondary basis for the mootness rules.[47] I asked a number of judges about the reasons behind the mootness rule. Most gave judicial economy as a reason: They do not want to take the time deciding cases they did not have to decide. Another common reason was simply that it is not the courts' function to make decisions when there really is no contest. Only several judges said a reason is that the parties might not be motivated to present their cases thoroughly; actually, an equal number mentioned that they often throw out hotly contested cases as moot. One judge gave as reasons both adverseness and time problems:

That's the same area as advisory opinions, and all of those things. God knows the practical answer in this day and age is that we've got too damn much legitimately before us to be looking for additional things. But I think there are a lot of more fundamental reasons behind it, and we get back to the assistance of counsel among other things. And query, would you get as good assistance from counsel if they just appeal, asking you for an advisory opinion, as you do in a legitimately contested adversary proceeding?

Only one other reason for not deciding moot cases was given. A couple of judges said it was a way to put off ruling on issues, especially controversial ones.

ADVISORY OPINIONS. Although the term "advisory opinion" is often used to describe a decision in a moot or friendly suit, the more technical definition, and the one used here, is the justices' opinion on questions submitted to them by the governor or the legislature.[48] The great majority of appellate courts, including all federal courts, refuse to give advisory opinions. But in eleven states, mostly on the eastern seaboard, the supreme court justices do give them, generally because the state constitution provides for it. Even here, however, only a tiny percentage of the courts' business is advisory opinions; they average only three or four such opinions a year.

There are no litigants, and thus no formal adversaries, in an advisory opinion. The governor or the legislature simply submits the problem and awaits the justices' advice. Still, the adversary system is not totally absent. Most of the eleven courts allow briefs from people who would be affected by the law announced in the opinion, and the courts sometimes request amicus briefs. Ordinarily, though, advisory opinions are given without briefs arguing both sides of the issues.

Judges, on the whole, greatly dislike giving advisory opinions. Eight state courts, for example, abandoned the practice after some experience with it. This dislike has several reasons, all of which, however, can be partially answered: (1) There are no litigants to supply information. But, as was just said, the courts sometimes do get briefs. (2) All those affected by the opinion are not before the court. But judges routinely make law that affects disputes not before the court. (3) Decisions are difficult without concrete facts and without any assurance that all situations affected by the opinion can be foreseen. But these objections do not apply to some clear-cut statutory or constitutional issues, and the opinion requests are sometimes in the form of specific fact situations anyway. (4) There are various philosophical problems concerning the separation of powers between the judicial, legislative, and executive branches. But most of these problems disappear if the state constitution authorizes advisory opinions. (5) The duty adds to the court's work load. But requests are not very frequent, and they may forestall future litigation on the issues.

Mainly because of the first three problems, justices claim that advisory opinions are not really precedent and need not be followed in later cases. Those who have studied advisory opinions, however, claim that the justices and litigants treat them like other opinions; they are virtually never overruled and are often used to support later holdings.

The benefit of advisory opinions is, obviously, that they answer legal problems quickly, lessening uncertainty in the law. A Massachusetts justice said about the justices' authority to give advisory opinions:

I think it's great. . . . They work well. Now, we don't answer questions about freedom of speech very much, unless they're awful easy. But on the question of whether you can hold a town meeting outside the geographical boundaries of the town you save everybody an awful lot of pain and suffering if you can give them the answer. It isn't hard to find the answer to that. You can find the answer, and you send it back to the legislature, and they go ahead and authorize the meeting to be held in the local regional high school, which is the only building in the whole area which is big enough to hold the town meeting.

Massachusetts justices, however, seem to like this function more than others. The typical view in the Rhode Island court is:

And nothing points up the *value* of the adversary system quite so much as *advisory opinions.*
Q — You don't like those?
A — No. We don't like them because the court does not have the time to go into the in depth study that you get in the adversary system, you know. And you're apt to overlook a very important factor and come up with an advisory opinion that you later regret.

Another Rhode Island justice said they "try to avoid them if they can." Even in Massachusetts a justice said, "We have various ways of not answering them when we don't know the answer." In fact, the justices on all eleven courts where advisory opinions are given sometimes refuse requests, in all about 12 percent of the requests. The standards as to when the requests will be refused are not at all clear, but the tendency is to refuse them when they run afoul of the second, third, and fifth objections enumerated previously —when the issue directly affects an existing private dispute that the justices believe should be decided in normal litigation, when the decision requires factual information that the justices cannot get, and when the issue is a tough one and would take much time and effort to decide correctly.

ADVERSENESS—SUMMARY. On the whole, judges prefer to decide cases presented in an adversary context because they will be better informed. And the rules discussed in this section help keep out appeals lacking adverseness. But the relationship between the rules and the preservation of adverseness is rather weak. The justifications for the standing rules, the mootness rules, and the dislike of advisory opinions include the desire for adverseness. But other reasons, mainly time and work load problems, often overshadow this desire. The rules, also, do not bar all appeals lacking adverseness, though it would be hard to guess how often appeals of this kind are actually decided.

The topics in this section pertain directly only to the judges' lawmaking function. By definition, the immediate ruling in a moot case does not affect either party; there are no parties involved in an advisory opinion; and when standing is a problem, the party with a stake in the immediate dispute can, and presumably will, present his side of the case. The courts' worry about the lack of adverseness, then, is that they will not receive enough information for lawmaking. It is often argued that any party willing to press an appeal in spite of mootness or lack of standing must be motivated by a desire to make law and, thus, would be motivated to present the information the court needs. Otherwise, he would not go to the expense and effort of appealing.[49] That is, there really is adverseness in the lawmaking context, and the lack of it in the dispute-deciding context is an unimportant technicality.

But a lawyer's motivation to change the law is not likely to include a motivation to explicate the details of a specific dispute. Judges often use the facts of the case as an aid to lawmaking; this is a major rational for the standing restrictions and the dislike of advisory opinions. Moreover, it is likely that lawyers, especially underemployed and inexperienced lawyers, pursue these cases for the thrill and experience of appearing before a high court, for the advertising value of publicity, or for other reasons not related to a desire to establish a precedent and not necessarily providing a motive to present the case carefully.

Lawyers in normal appeals often incompletely inform the courts; yet the cases are decided and law is made. And judges sometimes—although they are wary of doing so—make broad rulings, write dicta, and decide issues not raised, thus deciding more than what was presented them in the adversary context. Then why worry about the lack of adverseness in an occasional moot case, advisory request, or absence of standing?[50] One judge said in an interview:

There's always been a big debate as to whether the courts are really right in refusing to give advisory opinions. There are some who say we are constantly expressing ourselves, and you can make the argument that we're constantly writing on things that aren't fully briefed. That we generally decide things with inadequate information, without all the contending parties or all the people of interest in front of us. You know, you have inadequate lawyers. . . . The adversary system doesn't supply all the answers, therefore why insist on it in every case? You can make an argument for advisory opinions.

But the argument that courts already make decisions without effective presentation by adversaries only pertains to only one rationale for the mootness, standing, and advisory opinion restrictions. The courts use these restrictions for other purposes as well, both the practical purpose of reducing case loads and the various lawmaking purposes, such as dodging controversial issues and increasing concrete fact description.

The rules in all these areas are quite vague and uncertain, leaving courts considerable discretion as to when they will embark on lawmaking. The judges are unwilling (and are probably unable) to codify rules based on the complicated set of elements that go into deciding whether or not to make law in an appeal. A problem with this, which upsets some, is that litigants may have trouble forecasting, and planning around, the applications of these restrictions. Also many believe that the actual reasons for invoking them often are not admitted in the opinions, an unseemly lack of candor if these critics are correct.

All this leaves open the question of why appellate judges do not use the quality of counsel or the actual quality of briefs and arguments in the appeal as one element when deciding standing and mootness issues and when deciding whether to give an advisory opinion. As far as I know this is not done, openly at least, except when a class action is involved. One criteria when judging whether a class action will be entertained is the ability and experience of counsel representing the class.[51] The courts' concern here, however, is with dispute deciding rather than lawmaking: The judgment in a class action is binding on the members; they are stuck with the work of an attorney whom they ordinarily did not select. The reasons similar considerations are not used in standing and mootness questions and advisory opinions probably are, first, the reluctance to downgrade attorneys publicly (which was discussed earlier in this chapter), and, second, the aura of expediency involved that may be unseemly in light of the important substantive issues often found in these cases.

Part II

The Progress of an Appeal

CHAPTER 4

Appellate Lawyers
and Appellate Work

This is the first of four chapters that in roughly chronological order follow the progress of an appeal from the attorneys' work to the final decision, focusing on the information-gathering aspects of the process. The lawyers, of course, are major actors here. They are the courts' main source of information. They are virtually the sole source inside the adversary system; except in prisoners' complaints laymen virtually never represent themselves in appellate courts. The lawyers manage the first stages of an appeal, through the filing of the briefs, and the courts ordinarily play a passive role until oral arguments.

This description of appellate lawyers and their work comes mainly from two sources, the briefs and arguments in 112 focal court appeals submitted over a year's time and lengthy interviews with three dozen attorneys. The attorneys argued almost a quarter of the cases and typically were those on both sides of a case. A little over 35 percent of the appeals were criminal cases, and the same portion of the lawyers interviewed argued criminal cases. The lawyers were generally interviewed between oral arguments and the court decision; then after the decision they were interviewed a second time, over the telephone. The interviews were very informal and often rambling; I simply asked the lawyers to describe their practices and their appeals, adding specific questions later in areas they had not touched.

This chapter will focus on only a few aspects of the broad topic of appellate lawyering. The purpose is to give a background description of what appellate work is and to explore some reasons why appellate advocacy is not as good as judges would like. The chapter contains three parts: (1) the type of work involved in handling appeals and specialization among lawyers, (2) the degree of adverseness, especially the impact winning or losing has on attorneys, and (3) the attorneys' knowledge of the court. The focal court, it should be emphasized, is a state supreme court with discretionary jurisdiction and, therefore, the issues it decides tend to be more important and more difficult than issues decided by courts with little discretionary jurisdiction (and less important and less difficult than issues before the U.S. Supreme Court). This difference affects appellate work in several important respects, as will be seen.

At the outset one must distinguish between government lawyers and private practitioners. The former are salaried employees in various government agencies—the attorney's general office, the city attorneys' offices, the prosecutors' offices, the bar grievance commission, and the public defender's office. Except for public defenders they represent only the government. Private practitioners represent all types of clients, and they are paid by fee or retainer. Most appellate lawyers are private practitioners. They comprised three-fifths of the lawyers arguing at the focal court and a similar proportion of those interviewed. (Virtually all lawyers at the court fell within one of these two categories though, of course, there are other types of lawyers.)

APPELLATE LAWYERS, APPELLATE WORK, AND SPECIALIZATION

The lawyers who appeared before the focal court differed considerably from the overall population of lawyers in the state and in the nation.[1] Roughly twice the proportion were government lawyers, and only one-third as many worked in corporations. Law firm lawyers before the focal court outnumbered sole practitioners by more than three to one, while the two categories are about the same size among lawyers in general. The law firm lawyers were more likely to be partners; only a third the normal proportion were associates. More focal court lawyers came from large and medium-sized cities; they were half as likely as other lawyers to be small town attorneys. Fewer than normal were older lawyers, and more were middle-aged. Finally, over 40 percent had graduated from top national law schools, about twice the proportion among lawyers nationally. All these comparisons indicate, as much as background characteristics can, that the focal court lawyers are somewhat better than the general run of lawyers. They are, however, far from being a homogeneous group.

The rest of this section will describe the type of work these lawyers do. First, it is necessary to emphasize the complexity of the appellate process. The progress of a case from the original trial court or administrative agency decision through the various appellate stages takes a long time and involves many court decisions. The various possible stages are: a motion for rehearing at the trial level, an appeal to the highest-level trial court, an appeal to the intermediate appellate court, an application for leave to appeal at the state supreme court, and finally the supreme court hearing. Cases vary widely in the routes taken. Any of the steps might be eliminated and some often are. Some cases are sent back down again to repeat earlier levels. In most cases at the focal court, and many other supreme courts as well, the briefs are filed well over two years after the original decision at the lowest level.

An appeal really begins at the first stage, because the factual background and the issues raised must, with few exceptions, be first brought up at the trial or agency hearing. At succeeding levels, then, the attorneys hammer away at and elaborate upon points already made at trial. In fact, the briefs submitted to the focal court are often only slight modifications of those submitted at previous stages.[2] Nevertheless, an attorney may spend a good deal of time restudying the case at each level, even if he has handled the previous level, because he has forgotten much and because there might be new legal developments.

The vast majority of appeals, judging from the attorney interviews, arise from fortuitous events rather than from attempts to place particular issues before the court. Appealable issues blossom during the early proceedings of a case that is otherwise part of the regular course of the attorney's business. (In criminal cases, however, it is now expected that some issue or another will always be found for an appeal.) On the other hand, a few cases, ordinarily very important ones, are designed from the beginning as appellate cases. The trial is seen as only preliminary preparation for the appeal. With these few exceptions, an attorney who appeals a trial court ruling against him is bound to be entering a line of work, appellate work, that he does not regularly meet in his practice.

Attorneys, however, very often, are replaced between the various stages.[3] Only 45 percent of the attorneys arguing before the focal court had carried their case all the way through, and a few cases had been handled by three or more different attorneys at different times. Half the brief writers were not involved with the case at the trial level. Most of this switching occurred in criminal cases, which generally had a new counsel at the appellate stage. Still, even in civil cases over a third of the brief writers had not been at the trial. Apparently, the change of attorneys normally took place upon the first appeal, to the intermediate appellate court; but a new attorney occasionally took over later in the focal court, even at the oral argument stage in a few cases.

I had hoped to find out from the attorneys how much time was spent on the appeals. This proved difficult because work at one level in the progress of a case incorporated work done in earlier levels, often by a different attorney. Also, more than one attorney often worked on a case at the same level. Many scattered time increments would have to be found and added; this often cannot be done by interviewing only one attorney in a case. Still, a substantial minority of the attorneys gave figures for their time spent on all appellate briefs in the case. They claimed a great deal of time, varying from 50 to 350 hours; half claimed at least 200 hours.[4]

The prevalence of new counsel on appeal indicates that the cases are often turned over to appellate specialists after the trial. Lawyers and judges have long debated whether appeals should be handled by the trial lawyer or by an appellate specialist. They give several arguments for their various positions.[5]

The trial lawyer has a head start on understanding the record and the issues involved, but the appellate lawyer can take a fresh look at the problems and is more likely to be open-minded about just where one's strong points lie. The odds are great that the trial lawyer is a specialist in the area of law involved in the case; he is more likely than an appellate specialist to understand the practical implications behind the issues, and he can better integrate the issues into the broad area of law involved. (Except for government lawyers in often litigated areas like criminal, tax, or labor law, lawyers are rarely both appellate specialists and subject matter specialists.) On the other hand, the appellate specialist should know more about what kinds of information the judges want and about how to write briefs and present oral arguments.

Whatever the resolution of this debate may be, a lawyer specializing one way or the other would be expected to give the court more help than one with little experience in either appellate work or the area of the law. By and large, the lawyers appearing before the focal court did specialize in one of these ways, and most of those in criminal cases specialized both ways. But there were greatly varying degrees of specialization.

All the lawyers interviewed specialized to some degree in the types of law they dealt with, as probably almost every lawyer in the country does. Most restricted the great bulk of their work to a narrow area of the law—usually criminal or negligence law, but also labor, bond, real estate, divorce, and other areas. Their appeals were nearly always in their specialty. The other lawyers specialized a good deal less. A number considered themselves general practitioners, but that does not indicate a total lack of specialization and, in fact, their work fell largely within three or four areas. A few of the lawyers specialized only in the sense that they handled miscellaneous civil problems either for the city or state (in the case of government attorneys) or for continuing corporate clients (in the case of private practitioners). The appeals handled by these lawyers were generally within their broad areas of specialization. In all, only four of the thirty-six attorneys were handling issues clearly outside their line of work.

The amount of appellate specialization was considerably less than subject matter specialization. On the one hand, as was just discussed, a new attorney often takes over after the trial (though this is partly because appeals take so long that the original attorney may have died, retired, changed jobs, or lost interest in the case, as happened in several cases handled by attorneys interviewed). On the other hand, appellate specialization seems nearly absent when one looks at figures showing that the vast bulk of attorneys who appear before an appellate court in any one year appear only once. The focal court is typical in this respect. Only one-sixth of the attorneys argued more than once during the year studied (and only one-sixteenth more than twice). This and similar figures for other courts[6] somewhat understate the degree of specialization because there are at least two, and usually three or more, appellate courts that an attorney might practice before in his locale.

Probably half the arguments in the focal court were made by attorneys who specialized in appellate work to some extent. First, an eighth of the attorneys (making more than a fourth of the arguments) fully specialized in appellate work, in that their main job was appellate work. All were government lawyers, the vast majority criminal lawyers in the public defender appellate office or the appellate sections of large prosecutors' offices. This is probably typical of courts with large industrial jurisdictions.[7] Secondly, several attorneys interviewed were appellate specialists in that, although their main job was not appellate work, they tended to be assigned the cases in their firm or agency that reached the appellate level; but this may mean only one or two appeals a year. (It was more common, however, for each person in the firm or agency to handle his own case all the way through.) Except for the public defenders almost none of the lawyers took cases from outside his firm or agency for the appeal. This is probably a rare practice, though two criminal lawyers said that, had their clients been able to afford it, they would have given their appeals to other firms.

One reason for appellate specialization, such as it is, is that appellate work differs from much of what lawyers do. Appellate counsel must read the trial record, determine the issues, research the law, write briefs, and present oral arguments. All these are found elsewhere in legal work, but generally to a much lesser degree. Issue finding and selection are always central to a lawyer's job. Legal research, of course, is common, though it plays a small role in many types of practice. Trial work may include checking the record, brief writing, and even oral arguments, but presenting and developing the facts are far more important there. Briefing and arguing appeals, in sum, are considered a specialized area of the law in the same vein as tax law, criminal law, or trial practice. Good evidence of this is the hundreds of books and articles devoted solely to the subject, just as there are in other areas of legal work.

Appellate specialization, thus, may exist because it is thought those familiar with that type of work do a better job. But another point is important: Some lawyers like appellate work and tend to gravitate there, whereas others dislike it and shy away. I asked the attorneys what they found satisfying or dissatisfying about handling appeals. Several said they disliked it, generally because they disliked legal research and what a couple called the "academic" sort of work. And most of them, as well as a few who enjoyed appeals, said it took too much time. One lawyer said bluntly:

I found this piece of appellate work satisfying because I prevailed. I find appellate work in general dissatisfying because it is time-consuming, laborious, tedious, and office work, and I prefer to be out.
Q — Out at court?
A — Yep.

Those who did not object to appellate work usually said they liked the "intellectual challenge" or the study of legal problems on settled facts. They commonly called the work "cleaner" or "more refined" than trial work because the facts are set in the record.

Appellate work is fun. It's just very *clean*. You know, you're just dealing with the law, and what you can deduce from the facts that are pretty much established from the record. And it's really a challenge to create arguments that are going to be persuasive without overdoing it. It's an intellectual challenge.

What I do as an appellate attorney, deciding what the issues are, and the strategy of where you go, and you know, what you do, I think, is probably the most creative and intellectually complex level a lawyer can function at. I mean, a *trial* is also, but in a very different way, and I'd like to try a few trials sometimes. But most legal jobs are very *dull*. I like it for that reason.

Also the attorneys occasionally said they liked appellate work because they enjoyed oral arguments, because it presents a chance to help create new law in areas they feel strongly about, or because they enjoyed the competitive atmosphere or the thrill of winning. Except for this last point, all of the reasons why appellate work is satisfying or dissatisfying distinguish it from what most of the legal profession does.

In spite of being an academic, library type of work, brief writing often involves two or more attorneys working together, and the briefs probably benefit from the differing views. Only some 30 percent of the focal court briefs had more than one lawyer listed as authors, but other lawyers often contributed without being acknowledged. In fact, the great majority of the brief writers I interviewed received help in some form or another. Usually two or more lawyers worked together on the briefs, at times even lawyers from different firms or offices. Several others drafted the briefs alone and had them checked by colleagues; although, surprisingly, less than half the government attorneys said their supervisors checked their work.

ADVERSENESS AND THE LAWYERS' INCENTIVES

The adversary system, as we have seen, is based largely on the assumption that the adversaries are motivated to present the court with the arguments supporting their positions in order to increase their chances of winning. However, it is not the lawyers whom the court rules for or against, but the litigants. What, if anything, supplies the adverseness, and what motivates the lawyers to present fully their side of the issue? This is an awfully complex question even for the ordinarily complex area of human motivation. One can never be sure he has considered all possibilities. A benefit of the informal interviewing method used here is that major elements are not likely to escape notice (if recognized by the attorneys themselves), but it does require a rather inexact description of the motives. In the following discussion the possible motives are placed in three broad categories: (1) the lawyers' tendency to agree with their side of the appeal, (2) their stake in winning or presenting good briefs and arguments, and (3) their attitudes toward losing. In general, when all these are considered, adverseness is obviously there, but often to a surprisingly small degree.

AGREEING WITH THEIR APPEALS. One would expect lawyers to apply themselves more thoroughly to their cases if they agree with the positions they present. Also, as was brought out in the preceding chapter, quite a few of the judges writing on appellate advocacy said that an attorney is more effective when he appears to believe his arguments sincerely. One of the better texts on appellate advocacy says that one must have an ''inner conviction of the soundness and correctness of his case'' to be an outstanding appellate lawyer.[8] (On the other hand, a few lawyers and judges have said that too strong a feeling for the rightness of one's position can so thoroughly destroy objectivity that one's case is damaged by concentrating on emotional arguments.)

All the lawyers interviewed agreed with their side of the case, most vehemently so. A few did have reservations about parts of their argument. One thought the court should throw out his appeal for lack of jurisdiction, but believed (and the court ruled) that he was correct on the merits; one said his position was ''legally correct,'' though his ''visceral reaction'' was for the other side; and two said they thought the lower court had gone too far in their favor and should be partly reversed. (For example, a lawyer for a criminal defendant said the case should be remanded for retrial, even though the intermediate court ordered acquittal.) But even these four attorneys believed they should prevail when the legal system ran its course. The lawyers also talked about many appeals other than the ones before the focal court at the time, and they virtually always agreed with their sides of these cases as well.

Opposing counsel can believe in opposing positions because each appeal offers many aspects from which one can draw support and because several types of argument can be applied to any aspect. The attorneys interviewed talked at length about their appeals. Opposing counsel generally concentrated on different parts of their case; each stressed the parts in which favorable arguments could be found easily, giving little or no attention to his opponent's strong areas. When they did talk about the same parts of a case, they tended to talk at different levels of abstraction (e.g., factual details or points of legal philosophy), such that their arguments did not conflict with their opponent's.

The arguments given in the interviews were often not those given the court. All said the legal authority supported their position, and quite naturally these arguments were similar to those in the briefs. But their views on public policy and, especially, their views of the equities of the particular case often were not.

The lawyers viewed their clients in a much more favorable light than they viewed the opposing parties, especially because of considerations that were outside of the legal merits of the case and, thus, seldom presented to the court.[9] They generally attacked the motives, methods of operation, or general character of the other side, while praising or sympathizing with their own clients. About half the criticism of opposing parties concerned their motives for bringing the suit—for example, they are out to get one's client, are trying to delay a project, want publicity or political gain, or are looking for a windfall after knowingly disregarding a legal defect in property they had purchased. Several lawyers attacked the character of the other party, mostly prosecutors calling defendants rather ugly names. Occasionally, when the opponent was an organization, an attorney would attack its general mode of operation, especially criminal defense attorneys criticizing prosecutors' tactics in general. The small minority who talked about the other side without criticism consisted of a few attorneys in civil cases who said they could not impute motives to their opponents and about half the prosecutors who said they had no feelings about the defendant—it was impersonal because they never met the defendant or his victim.

On the other hand, the lawyers praised their own clients or sympathized with their plight, and this may, especially if the client is an individual, provide considerable impetus to win. The criminal defense lawyers were the most striking in this regard.[10] To a prosecutor one defendant was a "vicious son of a bitch," whereas defense counsel said about him, "He's an arch criminal. What's an arch criminal like? You know, he's a fairly nice guy . . . a fairly nice fellow." Another defense counsel said:

I don't feel bad that a black person who couldn't possibly get a decent job, who couldn't possibly earn a decent living—I feel bad that somebody got murdered, yea, but I think it's *separable*—what happened to the victim and what you do with the defendant because of it. I think those are mutually exclusive. . . . I feel that [the defendant] was probably justified. He was robbing a store, you know. If he had a job, he wouldn't have had to rob a store. If he had been a businessman, he could have embezzled, you know, and you don't have to shoot people while you're embezzling, you know. No, I don't feel bad, even if he got out on the street.

There was not nearly as much animosity felt for opposing counsel as for the opposing parties. Although the lawyers criticized the caliber of their opponents' work as often as they praised it, they rarely showed a strong dislike for them and only occasionally criticized them for improper acts, for instance, misstating a fact or making an incomplete appendix. Generally, they described relations with opposing counsel as good or friendly, though only several were personal friends. Nearly half had not met their opponents before, and the rest had dealt with them more or less frequently in their work. But no matter how well they knew their opponents, the general rule seemed to be, as a few expressed it, a lawyer should not let his feelings about the case spread to the opposing counsel.[11]

Although the attorneys agreed with their side of the appeals, lawyers do not, as a rule, restrict their practice to representing litigants they agree with. When I asked the attorneys if they ever disagreed with their side of law suits, roughly a third said they never did. The rest said they sometimes disagreed, though for most it was unusual. Lawyers in the second category, which included nearly all the private practitioners, commonly added that they disliked handling such cases, and several said that they probably did not do as good a job. The rationale for arguing positions they disagreed with, as volunteered by half of these attorneys, is that a lawyer has a duty to represent people that come to him regardless of his feelings; everyone is entitled to counsel.[12]

Most of those who always agreed with their side were government attorneys who said they would admit error if they did not agree.[13] On the other hand, half the government attorneys said they had presented positions they disagreed with when ordered to do so, or, in the case of several prosecutors, had brought defendants to trial when they were uncertain of their guilt and thought it best to leave certain factual determinations (e.g., the defendant's motives) to the jury.

On the whole, then, there is a strong tendency for an attorney to agree with his side of a case especially in appellate work. The tendency is much stronger than the law of averages would suggest. It exists partly because some lawyers refuse cases they disagree with. Also, attorneys tend to become more sympathetic with their side after immersing themselves in the case; their ideologies tend to match the positions of the kind of clients they have; and they tend to appeal only when they agree with their side of the case. These three points will be discussed in order.

1. Several attorneys mentioned that they often convinced themselves as they were handling a case that their side was correct. Several more, when talking about their focal court appeals, said they only came to agree with their positions after they had studied the issues for some time. Thus there is some tendency to adapt one's beliefs to the stance taken.[14]

2. The lawyers tend to have outlooks that harmonize with their jobs. Sometimes they select jobs because of their outlooks (e.g., young lawyers who believe the criminal justice system is unfair tend to join the public defenders) and sometimes their job influenced their outlooks (e.g., self-termed liberal attorneys may begin to disagree with the expansion of criminal defendants' procedural rights after joining prosecutors' offices). Attorneys tend to represent one type of client within their speciality—for example, plaintiffs or insurance companies in negligence cases. And their views fit

their types of work. Most of the attorneys representing criminal defendants mentioned that they think prisons are a poor place to send anyone but extremely violent criminals. It was mentioned earlier that four lawyers did not completely agree with their appeals in the focal court. Three of them were among the very few lawyers representing clients who differed greatly from their usual clients—that is, a labor lawyer who usually represents employers but represented employees in this case, a defense negligence lawyer representing a plaintiff, and an assigned defense counsel who disliked criminal work.

3. Attorneys do not often appeal, at least in civil cases, if they believe their position has no merit. Many factors go into whether to recommend appeal to a client. By far the most common, mentioned by nearly all the attorneys who spoke to this subject, is their opinion of the correctness of the lower court ruling or the chances of winning on appeal.[15] That is, they are more likely to appeal if they believe their position has merit, not a very surprising conclusion. On the other hand, several said that they had filed appeals they thought pointless because clients had insisted and had ignored their advice. But these were considered rare because of the cost of appealing. A few, also, said they had initiated appeals as bargaining tools when trying to settle a case after the trial court ruling.

ATTORNEYS' STAKES IN APPEALS. Attorneys, thus, believe their sides should prevail. Presumedly they would like to win for that reason. But is the adverseness of litigation, from the attorneys' standpoint, fueled by anything more substantial? Except for the mere dislike of losing, which will be discussed later, do the attorneys have anything specific to gain or lose by the outcome of the appeals? Often, the answer is that they have little or nothing at stake—no extra fees, no new business, no promotions, and no prestige.[16]

Government attorneys obviously receive no greater fee for winning, because they are salaried, and none of them thought his salary or position threatened or advanced by the outcome. Private attorneys in criminal cases also do not get a higher fee for winning. That accounts for about half the lawyers. In civil cases, some private practitioners (or their firms) were on a contingent basis or under some kind of a bonus arrangement, by which they would gain more—sometimes immensely more—if they won. However, most were simply paid by the hour and would receive the same fee no matter what. Thus for only a small minority was there a financial benefit directly contingent on the outcome. In addition, a good number of private practitioners, including all those in criminal cases, complained that they were getting very little money for their effort. There may be, on the other hand, an indirect financial benefit in that winning would attract more clients. A few said they would like to win for this reason, but that was decidedly a minority position.

Perhaps one would think the lawyers' professional prestige—their reputation among other lawyers—would be enhanced by a victory or by writing good briefs. But by and large the lawyers did not see it that way. I asked most if they thought winning would help their prestige. The majority said it would not make any difference, and half of the rest said any effect would be very slight. I also asked if, when preparing briefs, they tried to impress anybody besides the court—other lawyers or anybody else. The great majority said they did not; a few added that no one but the court and their opponents read the briefs anyway. On the other hand, three private practitioners wished to impress the opposing counsel or lawyers in general. Two government attorneys wished to impress their bosses, but government attorneys generally said they were not interested in doing that.

The infrequency of these incentives is quite startling. Admittedly, one should be wary of peoples' accounts of their motives. The incentives may be much more frequent, and the attorneys may refuse to admit them to others or, more likely, to themselves. On the other hand, there is nothing noticeably degrading about these incentives, and thus little reason not to admit them.

Although the incentives discussed here are those one would consider the most likely in the adversary system, many others are possible. Several attorneys volunteered that their motive was personal satisfaction from doing a good job. A number were motivated by particular characteristics of the case: strong sympathy with the client, the satisfaction of defeating the particular opposing counsel because he was a close friend or an enemy, being annoyed that a court or opposing counsel considered their case frivolous and wishing to prove it was not, and a strong interest in establishing a particular legal principle. But each of these was unusual, the latter surprisingly so.[17] In all, a good number of the attorneys evidenced nothing that they stood to gain by winning, except the fact that they agreed with their side, as was just discussed, and the general desire not to lose, the next topic.

LOSING. Not surprisingly, the lawyers said that they like to win. But they were not often greatly upset by losing. When I asked what it felt like to lose, a few made comments like, "Terrible. It's awful. Go out and get smashed," or "I can't stand to lose." However, the vast majority were much calmer, for example:

Q — Would it upset you much if you lost?
A — Oh, I've practiced too long. I'd be *disappointed* cause I don't like—just as an *advocate,* we don't like to lose any case, but, no, I wouldn't go around and pull my hair out and scream and holler, or anything. I would accept it. Here was a law suit and this is where it disagreed with us. It wouldn't be the first time, and it's not going to be the *last* time either.

A couple of government attorneys said they hardly cared at all whether they won or lost: "As far as *I'm* concerned, as long as I do a competent professional job, I'm not going to really feel all that bad about [losing].''

After the focal court announced its decision, each attorney was asked what he thought of the opinion in his case. All those who lost disagreed with it, as might be expected. Only several, however, seemed upset or angry. Even those who claimed victory usually criticized the court's treatment of their appeals. They disliked some aspect of the ruling, or they disliked the opinion's reasoning. In other words, whether an attorney won or lost, he tended to be annoyed if the court departed from the arguments he had presented.

When talking about what it felt like to lose, the lawyers usually mentioned that it felt worse to lose certain types of cases, especially cases they strongly felt they should have won. Two attorneys said:

Q — How bad does it feel when you lose?
A — Well, I've become less *emotive*. Like, I've been doing this [public defender appellate work] for a year and a half. I've gotten accustomed to arbitrariness. I mean, it's very hard to shake me in any way now. It used to be very disturbing. I mean, especially when you get an inane opinion. It's now—*now* it's disturbing to me when I think the issues are just so clearly—so strong—the guy got so screwed. That's been bothersome.

Judges, I get hot at. You know, some judges if they give me a bad deal—I feel bad when I lose a case like that. I feel the guy messed up.

Several others said they felt worse if the court's opinion was poor or they felt better after analyzing the opinion and realizing it was correct. Several more said a loss is more disturbing when one is personally involved with the client or when the client has a lot at stake in the case.

In general, though, the attorneys took losses in stride. They can do so because they find ways to blunt the effect of a loss. "All good lawyers," one said, "have some mechanism to get over the feeling of losing." A fair number of these mechanisms were evident in the interviews. At times the attorneys mentioned them when explaining why losses are easily borne. At other times they mentioned what seemed to be mechanisms to blunt losses, but were not stated as such. Only a few lawyers did not mention any mechanism; most of these said they hardly ever lost cases (because, for example, they settled their doubtful cases). The following paragraphs list six mechanisms.

1. A quarter of the attorneys said that losing was not very painful because they realized that one cannot win all the time; the losses have to be balanced against the victories. "You can't dwell on either a loss or a win. No career is ever made on one or two cases," and "I'm hardened to a point now where I accept our system. I like it fine when it works in my favor; so I have to accept it when it *doesn't* work in my favor. It's not—we can't always be right.''

2. The lawyers occasionally said that losing bothered them little if the court had acted correctly—if they felt justice was done or the court's opinion made strong arguments for the decision. This is the reverse of the situation just described in which the losing attorney thought he should have won. Normally, what the attorneys had in mind here is that a loss is less devastating when they felt that the court has dealt fairly with them. The clearest statement of this was:

It's *hard* to lose a case. If—if you lose a case and you're given a well-reasoned opinion, that's one thing. But if you lose a case and you don't get a well-reasoned opinion, it's very difficult to take. . . . As long as you're treated fairly and the court—a loss is easier to take when the court has considered all your arguments and is able to tell you in a reasonable, rational way, supported by authorities, that you're wrong. But unfortunately the courts are too busy, and sometimes they don't do that, and it's pretty hard to bear.

As will be discussed in Chapter 8, the attorneys were annoyed when the court based a ruling against them on issues that were not raised, something they considered very unfair. Thus the court itself can often relieve the pain of losing if the opinions persuade the attorneys that the court has met the arguments in an adequate fashion. (Incidentally, the lawyers were very concerned about whether the court was interested in their cases and whether it would consider the issues carefully. These were not subjects I asked about in the interviews, but the great majority commented on one or the other. Several lawyers said they liked questions in oral arguments because questions show that the justices were interested. Several more said that the justices' chatting among themselves or leaving their seats showed that they were not interested in the case.)

3. In some respects, however, an attorney's belief that a court treated him unfairly acts to soften a loss. The attorneys frequently talked about cases in which a court was predisposed to rule against them because of what they believed to be illegitimate considerations. Although only several of these attorneys specifically said this belief made the loss easier to take, it probably often had that effect because the considerations were always factors outside an attorney's control. Thus the loss reflected little on him. Typically, the attorneys made these comments when explaining why the court would or did rule against them. The lawyers seldom explained victories in this manner; the reasons they gave for why the court ruled or would rule for them were nearly always valid arguments of the sort they urged on the court.

The most frequent type of predisposition the attorneys mentioned was that the court was "political." This word has many meanings, the most common being that the elected judges consider the voters' reactions when deciding cases, that they decide cases for the benefit of their political party, and that they decide on the basis of broad philosophical or social policy grounds that, according to the attorneys, should not be considered. The last was also mentioned occasionally without being labeled political but equally seen as improper. (On the other hand, of course, many judges and lawyers believe philosophy and policy to be proper factors in deciding cases.) In addition, a few lawyers claimed that the court would rule against them because it sympathized with the little guy, for instance, plaintiffs in tort cases and defendants in criminal cases. And a few more said that the court was mainly interested in upholding or rebuking a particular lower court judge.

4. In the eyes of the lawyers, whether a case is won or lost is often elusive and often a matter of degree. "*Many times* a layman may not realize it," one lawyer said, "but what looks to him like a *loss* is really a *victory*." The "affirmed" or "reversed" at the end of an appellate court opinion may not define who won. And there may be latitude within which opposing counsel can interpret the outcome. Hence it is not always the case that one thinks he won and the other that he lost. Thus when the focal court ruled against an attorney and I asked what it felt like to lose the case, occasionally the answer was that he had not lost, even though his opponent considered himself the winner. Only once did opposing attorneys both claim definite victory: The appellee said he won because the court had ruled for him on a procedural ground, and the appellant claimed the procedural ruling was unimportant, and the court's dicta discussing the merits supported him. In several cases the court ruled for one side, which claimed victory, but the other side said it had not lost because the case was remanded to the trial court where his side might well prevail. In criminal cases there may be some ambiguity about who won when the case is reversed on some of the counts under which the defendant had been convicted. In two cases, defense counsel considered this a partial victory, and the prosecutor a complete victory.

5. Several lawyers, while admitting that they lost, felt that the loss was mitigated in some way. For example, the defendant was out on parole anyway; the loss meant little because the court dodged the major issue; or the court's decision was less strongly against him than the lower court's ruling. Also, a few said they felt better about losing because the vote was close.

6. Two lawyers said that losing did not bother them at all because the court decides on the basis of what the law is and not on the basis of the attorneys' arguments. Thus the loss had nothing to do with their handling of the appeal. This feeling, however, is the exception. Most of the lawyers discussed whether they felt an appellate court's decision could be affected by how good a job counsel did, and the great majority said it could—though frequently adding that they could not say how great the effect was, or that the attorneys' ability was a factor in only limited types of cases, for example, cases where the law is not clear.

Perhaps it is only natural that an attorney try to lessen the impact of a loss and to make life more pleasant in the face of the high probability that losses will occur. The six mechanisms given here are a formidable list of ways to do this, and nearly all the attorneys mentioned at least one of them. Also, except for the last, all opinions were volunteered; thus they are surely more common than this discussion suggests.

CONCLUSION. There seems to be rather little of the adverseness—the strong contrary motives of contestants presenting information—upon which the adversary system is based. The attorneys do agree with their sides of the appeals; they like to win; and they see a connection between winning and presenting good briefs and arguments. This provides some adverseness. But apparently there is not much else; although one must keep in mind the difficulty of uncovering motives in complex situations. The general desire to win is largely not backed by any particular impetus to win, such as monetary gain, more business, or greater prestige. Likewise, few attorneys professed to be upset greatly by losses, and attorneys have many means of mitigating losses; therefore, losing is but a limited threat that might prompt adverseness. Internal satisfaction for one's self or professional pride may provide for some an incentive to prepare well, but these are not things that apply to the adversary system above and beyond the investigatory system. All this, then, matches the limited concern that judges give adverseness in standing and mootness questions, as well as their attempts to set aside adverseness by requesting candor in the briefs and arguments.

ATTORNEYS' KNOWLEDGE OF THE COURT

In order to present the most telling arguments—and the information most valuable to the judges—counsel should understand the interests and tendencies of the judges, as Karl Llewellyn, among others, stresses.[18] This applies not only to presenting information that will influence the judges, but also to leaving out information the judges will give little weight. The judges writing on appellate advocacy, as was seen in the preceding chapter, constantly complain about getting too much irrelevant information.

By and large the attorneys I interviewed knew little about the court they appeared before. Nearly all, on the threshold, could identify each of the focal court justices. Beyond that there are many facets to this topic, some of which will be discussed shortly: whether the attorneys follow the decisions of the court, how much they know about the individual justices, how well they can predict the outcome of their appeals, whether they knew why the court granted leave, whether they geared arguments to specific justices, and what they knew about the decision-making procedures at the court.

FOLLOWING THE COURT AND KNOWLEDGE ABOUT THE JUSTICES. Most attorneys said they read the advance sheets—the recent opinions—of the focal court, but commonly only the cases falling within their specialties. The others usually tried to read the advance sheets, but were too busy to keep up or just skimmed them. Only a couple said they did not read the advance sheets at all. To this extent, then, the attorneys followed the court fairly well and had the opportunity, at least, to understand what was on the justices' minds.

The attorneys were usually able to talk in a general way at least about the justices' views—able, for example, to give an opinion about which justices were liberal or conservative. Several described in detail the positions of the justices in the area of law they specialized in. On the other hand, a good number said they knew little about the court and the justices' views.

The lawyers frequently said they personally knew one or more of the justices. A substantial minority said they knew most of the court, and a number even considered some justices close friends. The lawyers knew them from political life, as social friends, as former law clerks, or from practicing with them when they were lawyers or under them when they were trial judges. However, except for three former law clerks, there was very little evidence that the attorneys had learned much about the justices' positions as a result of these relationships.

PREDICTING THE OUTCOME OF CASES. A strong indication of how little the attorneys in general knew about the court is their inability to predict the outcome of cases. I asked if they thought the court would rule for them (or, in the case of several interviewed after the cases had been decided, what they had thought the court would do). Nearly one-third said they had no idea, and most of those who did predict did so hesitantly. The predictions were not very accurate; almost 40 percent were wrong, not much better than chance. What is more, they usually said they had little idea how individual justices would vote; though, when they did predict the votes of specific judges, they were wrong on only one-fourth of the guesses. In trying to predict the outcomes and justices' votes, they frequently used indicators requiring no advance knowledge of the justices' thinking. Most relied heavily on the questions in oral argument; they studied the questions to see whether any justices hinted how they might vote. But the questions, as several lawyers said, are uncertain indicators. Also, they occasionaly based their predictions at least partly on what they thought the law to be in the abstract without relation to these particular justices. They seldom mentioned the court's position on similar issues or the views of particular justices known before the arguments.

Attorneys in civil cases were much less adept at prediction than attorneys in criminal cases. Only about 60 percent of the former would make a prediction, and half the ones they made were wrong. This is no better than blind guesswork. Counsel in criminal cases, on the other hand, predicted the correct outcome three-fourths of the time. The reasons, apparently, are that criminal cases were handled mainly by appellate specialists (who almost always predicted correctly) and that the judges' positions in criminal issues were rather clear because of the large criminal case load.

Attorneys appearing before courts without discretionary jurisdiction may do much better at predicting, it should be added, because they handle more one-sided appeals. The criteria for granting leave to appeal, as was discussed in Chapter 2, are uncertain, but on the whole the focal court and others with discretionary jurisdiction concentrate on fairly close issues of law.

KNOWING WHAT ABOUT THE CASE INTERESTS THE JUSTICES. Because of the court's discretionary jurisdiction, any case taken must contain something special that interests the justices. It is important that counsel know what this is, so that he can present arguments on that point. This is no mystery in the bulk of the appeals that contain only one or two clearly important issues. But a good number of lawyers said they had little idea why the court took their cases. This problem was not limited to attorneys who know little about the court; three of the better-informed attorneys wished the focal court would expand its seldom used practice of announcing, when granting leave, what issues it wants emphasized.[19]

Another indication of how well the attorneys know the court is whether they gear arguments to specific judges in the briefs and oral arguments. Less than half said they ever did this, and few did it often.[20] Only a small minority did it in the cases I interviewed them about, and these arguments were generally aimed at the same judge, an outspoken judge who had been on the court for many years. Again, lawyers in criminal cases did this more often; some went to great lengths to tailor their arguments to persuade particular justices. A common reason for not using this tactic was the lawyers' ignorance of the justices' interests, but most gave other reasons: They could not tell who would be assigned the opinion, or the tactic may be damaging because arguments geared to one justice might dissuade others.

KNOWLEDGE OF THE COURT'S DECISION-MAKING PROCEDURES. The attorneys generally knew very little about how the court processes appeals. All that was commonly known was that one judge circulates an opinion and then discusses it with the others in conference. What information they had typically came from talking to former law clerks or listening to speeches by judges. The best informed either were law clerks or had friends who were clerks. The most important knowledge about appellate court internal procedures is that about the judges' preparation for oral arguments, because this information affects the style of an attorney's presentation. For example, less time is spent describing the facts and issues when the judges are known to be prepared. In practice, the focal court justices read the briefs rather thoroughly before the arguments. A substantial minority of the lawyers did not know this and were sometimes surprised by the court's questions. It might possibly help counsel to know which justice has been assigned the case so that he can concentrate on persuading him. But the lawyers commonly did not even know that cases are assigned before oral arguments, and those that did know generally said it was very difficult to tell which justice had the case, for the court keeps the assignments confidential until the decision is announced.[21]

CONCLUDING REMARKS

Appellate lawyers are a greatly varying group, and generalizations do not apply well to them, as to most other aspects of appellate justice. They come from greatly varying types of practice; some specialize much more than others in appellate work and in the subject areas of their appeals; some have much more incentive to win than others; and some know much more about the court and the judges than others. On the whole, though, they seem to have surprisingly little to gain by winning their appeals, and there is surprisingly little actual adverseness underlying the adversary procedures. Moreover their knowledge of the court and of the judges' interests seems less than what one might expect.

It is difficult to pin down the factors that lead to good or poor appellate advocacy. Many interconnecting factors would have to be unraveled. There are few direct relationships between attorney characteristics and the quality of appellate advocacy. An elaborate Federal Judicial Center study of appellate advocacy in the U.S. circuit courts compared several such characteristics with the judges' views of the quality of the lawyers' presentations. The relationships were all very small (and statistically insignificant).[22] Some of the characteristics studied are: (1) the size of the lawyer's office, (2) the lawyer's age, (3) the year of the lawyer's graduation from law school, (4) the extent of the lawyer's appellate experience, (5) the quality of the lawyer's law school, (6) whether the lawyer had taken a course on appellate advocacy in law school, and (7) the lawyer's moot court experience. Again, none of these indicated how well the lawyer would perform in his briefs and oral arguments.

My own, less comprehensive, study of the focal court briefs and arguments came to a somewhat different conclusion.[23] Law firm lawyers seemed to do considerably better work than sole practitioners (and the bigger the lawyer's firm, the better the work tended to be).[24] Lawyers only a few years out of law school seemed quite a bit better than the more experienced lawyers. Lawyers from better law schools and appellate specialists seemed slightly better than average. But it would be foolish to imply causation from these relationships. For example, perhaps only the most skilled recent law graduates obtain jobs that take them before the focal court.

The quality of appellate advocacy seems to depend on a complicated mix of considerations such as those described in this chapter. Sometimes relationships seem fairly direct and clear. Among the attorneys interviewed, the small minority who disliked appellate work wrote markedly poor briefs. The same is true of the few who believed there is no connection between the quality of their work and the outcome of appeals. But this type of thing is unusual. Overall, the prevailing uncertainty prevents one from labeling certain features of attorneys' backgrounds, work, or attitudes as producing good or poor briefs and oral arguments. Hence attempts by courts to improve advocacy by regulating the bar are almost surely doomed to failure.

CHAPTER 5

How Lawyers
Present Information

Appellate lawyers have very few means of presenting information to the courts, namely, through briefs, records, and oral arguments.[1] There are some rather unimportant exceptions: In a few cases judges ask for supplementary briefs or memorandums, or the attorneys submit them on their own; and in many cases petitions for rehearing are filed after the decisions. These exceptions, which provide a very minor portion of the information courts receive from counsel, take place after oral arguments. Where judges read the briefs before arguments, the close of arguments marks a rather strict line between when information comes from counsel and when information comes from research inside the court.

The attorneys' means of presenting information are, with rare exceptions, quite formal and highly restricted by court rules, which are designed to make sure the information is in a convenient form and to make sure each adversary has a chance to answer information presented by his opponent.

In describing the attorneys' information channels, this chapter will focus on the process in decisions on the merits (as opposed to decisions about granting leave or certiorari) in appeals of medium importance. Little attention will be given to the clear-cut appeals common in intermediate courts and to the cases of great consequence that form a very small portion of the business of courts below the U.S. Supreme Court level. Very little, therefore, will be said about the policentric appeals, which involve numerous counsel advancing several divergent lines of argument, common among appeals having extremely wide social implications.

BRIEFS AND RECORDS

At the six courts studied, and probably at every other appellate court as well, all written communication between counsel and the court about the substance of appeals passes through the office of the court clerk (who should not be confused with the judges' personal law clerks). The clerk's staff numbers from two or three in a small court to over thirty in some large intermediate courts. This often seems the busiest part of an appellate court; lawyers continually send in various papers and ask about the court's procedures.

When a case is appealed, the clerk's office receives the record made at the lower tribunal that originally heard the case. The record contains the facts of the case—that is, in general, all the papers filed in the lower tribunal and a transcript of the testimony, which is often very long. Then the appellant sends his brief, followed a month or two later by the appellee's. Sometimes the appellant or both litigants add reply briefs—shorter briefs that answer points made by the opponent. And amici curiae, people who are not parties to the suit, sometimes send in still more briefs. Thus there may be a dozen or more briefs in important cases involving many parties, but that is rare and most appeals involve just the two main briefs.

An appendix consisting of the parts of the record the appellant considers relevant to the case ordinarily accompanies the briefs at the bulk of appellate courts; and the appellee can submit an appendix also if he does not like the appellant's version. Each attorney must give copies of his brief and appendix to the opponent and must give some ten to thirty copies to the clerk's office, which then distributes them to the judges and, after the case is decided, to various law libraries.

Courts have very definite rules regulating the size and format of briefs. For example, Rule 32 of the Federal Rules of Appellate Procedure states that printed briefs "shall be bound in volumes having pages not exceeding 6-1/8 by 9-1/4 inches and type matter 4-1/6 by 7-1/6 inches." Some courts require that briefs be printed as in a book; others allow photocopying and other duplicating methods as long as the copies are easy to read. The length of briefs is often regulated; in the federal courts printed briefs cannot be longer than fifty pages without the court's permission. Briefs longer than fifty pages are probably unusual in any court, but some are well over a hundred. (Most briefs at the focal court were twenty pages or less, and one brief in five was less than a dozen pages. The length varied greatly, even within appeals. In more than a fourth of the cases one side's brief was over twice the length of the other's—but the length of briefs was not at all related to the outcome of cases.)

All this illustrates the extreme emphasis on paper work. Papers are the judges' main source of information and must be handled frequently. Thus the courts require abundant copies, and the form is standardized for easy handling. Also, these rules are needed because all of the circuit courts and the great majority of state supreme courts give copies of the briefs and, if any, the appendixes to law libraries,[2] where shelving may be a problem.

As to the organization of the briefs, probably all courts require a statement of questions, a statement of facts, and an argument section. The statement of questions is a list of the issues the attorney is presenting. The statement of facts is a summary of the facts already in the record and appendix, generally one to ten pages long. The bulk of the brief consists of arguments why the court should decide each issue in one's favor, including the legal authority, various types of legal reasoning, and practical arguments. The appellee's brief sometimes differs from the appellant's in that it may accept the latter's statement of facts or statement of questions, but not the arguments.

READING THE BRIEFS AND PREPARING FOR ORAL ARGUMENTS

Earlier in this century often only one judge, the opinion writer, read the briefs; and the judges who did read the briefs did so after the oral arguments. Now judges seldom decide without reading the briefs, and they usually prepare for arguments. All the judges read the briefs before hearing arguments in the circuit courts and in roughly half the state supreme courts, including all but the Massachusetts court among the six studied here. (It is interesting that three highly respected courts have lagged behind the trend toward preparing for oral arguments. Besides the Massachusetts court, the New York Court of Appeals does not do so, and the Second Circuit only recently began to prepare, after some time as the only circuit court that did not.) Even at courts where all judges do not prepare, some ordinarily do prepare. The others may or may not read the briefs later, but there are probably few courts left besides the Massachusetts court where some judges often decide without reading the briefs.

Judges give various reasons for reading the briefs either before or after arguments. Judges who read the briefs beforehand, it is said, get more help out of the arguments because they know enough about the case to ask the key questions and to ask about areas not adequately covered in the briefs. The arguments are more compact because the attorneys need not spend much time explaining the background of the case. And the judges' conference after the arguments is more productive because they know the case well. The main reasons given for not reading briefs beforehand are that the large case loads do not give them enough time, that their time reading the briefs is better spent reading them alongside the draft opinion, and that judges should go into the arguments without any knowledge about the case so that they will listen to the attorneys with an open mind.[3]

Preparing for arguments is often difficult because some ten to twenty cases are heard in a week, and several courts sit for three or more weeks at a time. Other work, especially preparing opinions, often keeps the judges from studying the briefs until a few days before arguments, resulting in long evenings of reading. A few judges mentioned that they prepare more in the autumn before they are hit by the crunch of opinion writing.

The amount of preparation on the six courts studied varies greatly, both between courts and within courts. At the First and Sixth Circuits, which are typical of circuit courts, the judges ordinarily read each brief thoroughly and read, or at least skim, the appendixes. Some judges or clerks may even look at the actual record in the clerk's office. A great many circuit judges have their clerks write "bench memos" of two pages or so, outlining the facts, the issues, and each party's contentions. Judges use these, especially in the more difficult cases, as advance summaries before reading the briefs or as quick refreshers just before arguments. A 1971-72 study of the Third Circuit showed that almost one-third of the total time spent on cases was spent preparing for arguments,[4] and that appears to be roughly the figure for the First and Sixth Circuits. (The circuit judges now often meet cases during the early stages of appeals other than to prepare for oral argument, mainly to screen out insubstantial appeals for abbreviated treatment. In general, a three-judge panel studies a case soon after it arrives at the court, ordinarily with the help of a memorandum from a staff attorney. The panel then eliminates or shortens oral arguments in many cases or, on some circuits, summarily decides appeals deemed to contain issues with clear outcomes.)

Preparation for arguments varies more among state court justices than among federal judges. The focal court justices read the briefs and appendixes, and they often have learned a good deal about the case when granting leave to appeal. The judge assigned the case or his clerk writes a memorandum similar to the bench memos on circuit courts, and this is circulated to the other judges. Likewise, the Ohio justices become familiar with the case upon granting leave and then read the briefs more or less thoroughly before oral arguments. Rhode Island justices read the briefs before arguments, though some only have time to skim them when the case load is particularly heavy. Some Massachusetts justices do not regularly read the briefs before the arguments, relying on a summary of the case, similar to the bench memos, prepared by staff attorneys and on a quick glance at the briefs. In recent years, however, the trend has been toward more preparation, and now at least two justices read the briefs before arguments.

The focal court and Rhode Island justices confer quickly immediately before arguments to pinpoint the parts of the cases they think important, sometimes even deciding what questions to ask counsel. Only a small minority of appellate courts, however, meet before the arguments. A few of them, notably in New Jersey and California, discuss the cases at length a few days before arguments.

ORAL ARGUMENTS

The next stage in the processing of an appeal is the oral arguments, assuming that the attorneys have not waived them, which seldom happens at the great majority of courts, and assuming that the court has not eliminated them through screening procedures. Eleven state supreme courts and seven circuit courts hear cases in more than one city; the Fifth Circuit, sitting in eight southern cities, is an extreme example. But all of the six courts studied, except the First Circuit, which sits a week each year in Puerto Rico, sit in only one city.

The courtrooms differ from trial courts in that, of course, the dais has seats for more judges and there is no jury box or witness chair. They are large rooms with high ceilings, sometimes very imposing. Chairs or benches at the back of the room seat several dozen spectators, and closer to the dais are tables and chairs for lawyers, law clerks, and court officers.

Appellate courts rarely hear arguments in August, and often not in June, July, or September. Sometimes arguments are held every week, but normally courts sit for a while—from a couple of days to three weeks—and then recess for a month or two. Most of the courts in this study hear arguments one week every month, sitting four or five hours on most or all days of that week. On the other hand, the Sixth Circuit hears cases for three weeks every two months, and the Ohio court hears cases two or three mornings every week. In any event, judges spend, on the whole, only a small portion of their working time listening to arguments, much less than reading the briefs and writing opinions.

Even so, because of the increasing case loads, the trend is toward shorter arguments. The U.S. Supreme Court used to allow virtually unlimited arguments, sometimes lasting for days, but now each lawyer has half an hour in ordinary cases. In the late 1950s the U.S. circuit courts allowed forty-five minutes or an hour to a side; today the ordinary argument is fifteen or twenty minutes, with thirty minutes in more difficult cases. The four state courts here allow a half-hour, as do most others. In practice these time limits often do not determine the length of the argument; lawyers often stop much sooner, and nearly all courts sometimes let them argue past the time limit, especially if the judges question heavily.

The amount of questioning varies greatly from court to court and from judge to judge. At the focal court almost half the average argument was taken up with questions and the attorneys' answers, though occasionally there was no questioning at all. A couple of justices spoke much more often than the others, asking four times as many questions as the least active justice. Most courts question less than this; but the focal court is typical of the courts studied here, except that questioning is rather light in Massachusetts, probably because there is less preparation.

THE IMPORTANCE OF ORAL ARGUMENTS. As a general rule, briefs are a more important source of information to the judges than the arguments. More information can be crammed into the written pages than in a half-hour talk, and the briefs are available later when thinking and writing about the case. Some courts tape-record the arguments, making them available later. Only the focal court and the Massachusetts courts of the six studied do this (though seven other circuit courts and many other state courts do), and the focal court judges, at least, infrequently used the tapes later,[5] which suggests that the information presented in the arguments is used little in opinion writing.

The great majority of judges who commented on the relative importance of the briefs and arguments said that the briefs are on the whole more important.[6] Also, at the focal court the attorneys' arguments gave extremely little information not already in the briefs or records. As is discussed in Part III, no new issues were advanced at the argument stage; few of the authorities cited in the briefs were also mentioned there, and only about 1 percent of the authorities were first brought out there; the vast bulk of the facts of the case are in the record, though when attorneys do give facts outside the record, they generally do so in the arguments; and, lastly, the arguments often do contain social fact arguments not in the briefs, but those the court used in its opinions were taken almost exclusively from the briefs.

This does not mean the judges think that the arguments are unimportant. A great many appellate judges, both those interviewed and those who have elsewhere expressed an opinion on the question,[7] strongly believe that the arguments are a major help. A few others, including the Ohio judges interviewed, believe them to be of but limited importance, and a very few judges have written that they are a waste of time. Some judges say, and probably all would agree, that the arguments help little when their quality is poor or when the outcome of the appeal is clear from the beginning. (The law clerks interviewed thought much less of the value of oral arguments than their judges.[8] They usually did not attend the arguments, unless their judges required attendance—a requirement often resented by the clerks.)

The role of oral arguments has long been a favorite topic of judges' discussions, recently more so in the circuit courts because the high case loads have forced the judges to search for areas in which time can be saved, and eliminating arguments is one of these (not only for the time spent listening to arguments but also for the time spent traveling to the court, which is often hundreds of miles from a judge's office). A decade ago the circuit courts heard almost all appeals, but most have now cut back a good bit and several decide a substantial number of cases "on the briefs"— that is, without arguments. At least two, the Fourth and Fifth Circuits, decide more than half their cases on the briefs. Arguments tend to be abandoned when the issues are simple and well covered in the briefs, when precedent clearly dictates the result, and when only fact issues or questions about admissibility of evidence are presented.[9]

On the other hand, the great majority of state supreme courts hold oral arguments in nearly all cases, and only five decide most cases on the briefs.[10]

The trend in supreme courts has been to hold arguments more often. Intermediate courts, though, are beginning to cut back somewhat.

One reason arguments are important is that just afterward judges on most courts hold a conference and give their tentative views. Presumedly, the views are strongly influenced by arguments fresh on their minds, and judges do not often change their minds later. (This latter fact suggests, as is discussed in Chapter 14, that the information from the adversary system, the briefs and arguments, is more important than that received by independent research, the great bulk of which is done after the postargument conference.)

PURPOSES OF ORAL ARGUMENTS AND OF THE JUDGES' QUESTIONS. The arguments, according to appellate judges, serve different functions than the briefs.[11] Two functions are mentioned much more than others: (1) The most common is that the arguments focus on the more important parts of the attorneys' positions. As mentioned earlier when discussing the judges' writings on appellate advocacy, a major facet of judicial decision making and the adversary system is the judges' wish to narrow the information received down to the most relevant, and the arguments are one means of doing this because the attorneys, allowed only a half-hour or so, can give only selected portions of what they have put in the briefs. The argument "is more meaningful than other offerings," a circuit judge has said, "because the lawyer is finally required to reduce his case to its lowest terms and to submit his best thinking."[12] (2) Almost as many judges, especially in more recent statements, say that a major purpose of the arguments is the chance to ask questions (though at some courts the judges still do very little questioning).[13]

Since questioning is one of the main purposes of oral arguments, what do the judges try to accomplish in the questions? This subject is important not only for the light it sheds on the function of oral argument, but also in later chapters the judges' questions are usd to indicate what types of information they consider when making decisions. It may seem obvious, but it should nevertheless be established, that topics in questions are relevant to the judges' thinking about how the case should be decided. (However, questions often do not indicate the judges' exact thoughts, for judges often express very tentative thoughts or play devil's advocate.)

Based again on the interviews and on judges' writings,[14] judges virtually always say that the prime purpose of questioning is to get help in deciding the case, though they rarely explain in detail just how this is so. Several said specifically that the questions are asked to get "information" from the attorneys, and most other purposes mentioned by more than a few judges amount to the same thing: to find out what the attorneys' positions are, to shed light on specific problems, to learn the facts of the case, and especially to "clarify" the attorneys' arguments. Several also said that they asked questions to make sure counsel addresses the crucial points in the case; this illustrates how the oral arguments can be used as an occasion to narrow the attorneys' presentation down to the most important information, and the same notion probably underlies much of the judges attempts to "clarify" the arguments. One judge interviewed explained it this way:

Q — When you ask questions, what is the purpose of the questions?
A — Just generally to pinpoint what it is they *really* are claiming. *Often* briefs are diffuse, and you get the shotgun approach—you know, everything they can think of. Well, certainly *everything* they bring up was not wrong with that given trial, you know. And it's—once and a while, somebody—I don't make a practice of this—but somebody will say, "Now if you had to choose *one* important point, what is that one important point that you would like to make?" And you would be surprised how it does *then* make the advocate who has been thinking in general terms that *everything* is wrong with the case come down to one thing.

On the other hand, half the judges added that they or their colleagues some-times ask questions for purposes other than to get help from the attorneys, but these questions are said to be uncommon and usually improper. The major improper purposes are belittling attorneys, pointing out where attor-neys are wrong, and showing one's knowledge to impress others. A typical statement was given by a circuit judge:

Q — What do you try to accomplish when you question attorneys in arguments?
A — I think very often—we do *a lot of questioning*. Sometimes, speaking only for myself, I ask questions to try to indicate to the attorney where he's wrong, and I think that's a wasted question. I don't think I should ask that question. I think I should ask questions only to gain information for myself, and not to point out to the attor-ney where he's missing something.
Q — Do you do that because you agree with his side of the case and you want to—
A — I don't know why I do it. Maybe I just do it to show my knowledge. *I don't* think I should do it. I don't think it *adds* anything. I'm not convincing anybody. I'm not going to make him change his mind.

On the other hand, some questions not aimed directly at getting help are ordinarily considered proper: showing the attorneys that the court is familiar with the briefs (so they do not rehash what is already there) and trying to inform, persuade, or otherwise communicate with the other judges. Even in most of these exceptions, however, the questions indicate what kinds of topics the judges are interested in.

THE ATTORNEYS AND ORAL ARGUMENTS. Oral arguments present some special problems for the attorneys, mainly because the two major functions of arguments sometimes conflict. To begin with, attorneys, like the judges, nearly always consider the arguments important. This is the case among the attorneys I interviewed and among the 1,600 attorneys who answered questionnaires in a recent study of attorneys appearing before three U.S. circuit courts.[15] Again, like judges, the attorneys believe the importance of arguments lies mainly in the chance to stress major points and to answer questions from the bench. This also showed up in both my interviews and the circuit court study.[16] (There are other reasons given less often by the attorneys: about half in the circuit court study agreed that litigants feel they have not had their day in court if not allowed oral arguments, and a good number of attorneys interviewed believed the arguments are a chance to present various nonlegal arguments—for example, equity and public policy arguments—that they feel should not be in the briefs.[17] These two are mentioned less often by judges.)

The two main tasks—emphasizing important points and answering questions—do not always mesh, because the questioning interrupts the attorneys' attempts to present their views. Appellate judges often have experience with, and worry about, attorneys who are annoyed by questions; in the judges' writings on appellate advocacy discussed in Chapter 3, over half who wrote about oral arguments told the attorneys that they should welcome questions even if they interrupt a planned presentation because questions show what the court is interested in. Nearly all the attorneys interviewed, however, said they liked questions or considered them a major purpose of the arguments. A number elaborated by saying that they wanted questions so that, as the judges also say, they can see what interests or worries the court and, thus, more effectively argue their case. The same feeling is evident in the circuit court study, where some 60 percent said they agreed with the statement, "Oral argument allows counsel to gauge the feelings of judges and to couch his arguments accordingly."[18] One attorney experienced in appellate work told me:

I was disappointed in the argument because I tried to *bait* the court and draw them out and *get* them to ask questions, and they *didn't* do it.
Q — You were disappointed in the—
A — Yes, I *like* to be challenged by the court, and the reason for it is this: The only way you can find out what may be bothering the judges is if you can provoke them into asking some questions, and then you get a chance to answer what may be bothering them, because you argue the case—and I've seen cases where the judge got all confused or wound up in some extremely inconsequential point, but he regarded it as *significant* point. Now if they didn't ask you about it, you'd never know that that's the one.

The attorneys normally prepare beforehand an argument they wish to present, using an outline only since a court rule forbids, and judges detest, reading. But the judges' questions may disrupt the planned presentation:

Q — What was it like arguing before the court?

A — You know, they start asking you questions. You kind of get all your argument lined up in, you know, a little speech and you're going to hit all the points and all this. And they start asking you questions. Completely throws you off balance. And then when one starts and another one starts and a third one starts, you just might as well give up.

This attitude, however, was unusual; the attorneys almost always expected the judges to interrupt their presentations. More often the attorneys complained that they were prevented from giving the arguments they had planned to give because the questions took up too much of the half-hour allowed each side. There is no problem here when the questioning is light or when the attorney believes the overriding purpose of the arguments is to answer questions. But several attorneys said they liked questions; yet they complained that questions cut into their allotted time so much that they had to abandon some of the points they had wished to emphasize. One said he felt "cheated out of time." Occasionally, they tried to work their argument around the questions; they used the questions as starting points for making points they had prepared. My own impressions, from listening to the arguments, is that this often resulted in answers that only weakly responded to the questions.

Thus counsel's planned presentation and preconceived view of the case may be a hindrance. As another indication of this, a substantial minority of the attorneys interviewed complained that questions were irrelevant or trivial, and several more said some judges showed little knowledge of the case. It is difficult to judge the accuracy of their assessment, but it is likely—and in a few cases it became obvious when the decision came out—that the judges saw the case in a different light than the attorneys, who were unable to adjust. One attorney explained it this way:

You know so much more about *your* case than they do; you have weighed the insignificant and the significant and come up with what you think is *important.* And I would think that there's quite—quite frequently you feel that had they given the consideration that you had, that they wouldn't be asking these questions, and not take up time.

In contrast, a few attorneys said it was not up to them to determine relevancy, for example: "How good [the questions] were depends. That's like beauty. It lies in the eyes of the asker. I may say, 'What the hell, that's a silly question to ask.' It ain't so silly to them."

One last point about the oral arguments: The attorneys generally said they felt at ease standing before the court, at times because they personally knew some of the judges. On the other hand, several who were arguing for the first time said they were scared or nervous. It is likely that their arguments suffered from this though I saw little evidence of it.

AMICUS CURIAE

Amici curiae are not a major source of information for appellate judges; yet they are the most important source outside the court other than the litigants' attorneys. Amici curiae are organizations or, rarely, individuals not a party to the appeal but likely to be affected by the precedent created. They are, then, interested in the lawmaking aspects of deciding appeals, and not the case-deciding aspects. Many types of organizations become amici curiae; common examples are trade organizations, civil rights organizations, trade unions, attorneys general offices, and bar organizations. Though "amicus curiae" means "friend of the court" and though they are not litigants, as a practical matter they are within the adversary system; they argue for a specific outcome of the appeal, they are represented by counsel, and present their information in briefs and, much less often, oral arguments. For the most part the briefs are submitted on their own motion, though courts sometimes request them, especially from bar associations and attorneys general offices. Ordinarily, an amicus must obtain the permission of the court or of the party who's side he supports before he can file a brief.

The amicus briefs are not a very important source of information because they are not submitted often and because they often add little to what is already in the parties' briefs. A 1957 study found that they were submitted in few cases at the vast majority of appellate courts,[19] though they are probably more common now, and they are surely much more common in important appeals. These briefs vary greatly in length and thoroughness; often they are merely statements that the amicus supports a certain result in the case, but others are very detailed presentations, even more detailed than the parties' briefs. Yet it is probably a rare appeal in which an amicus brief adds much beyond the regular briefs. In the 112 focal court appeals studied here, 35 amicus briefs were submitted (only 2 amicus gave oral argument) in 15 cases, mainly the most important cases. This is a good deal more than most courts get, including the 5 others studied here, but it is far overshadowed by the U.S. Supreme Court.

A good number of these amicus briefs at the focal court, though, were only a few pages long and did little more than announce the position of the amicus curiae. The amicus rivaled the parties' briefs in thoroughness in only a dozen cases; in two they were so much better than the briefs of the parties they supported that they were virtually the whole argument for their sides of the appeals. At any rate, the amount of new information in these amicus briefs is quite limited. Of course they did not help present the facts of the case, since they were aimed at the broader aspects of the appeal. And incredibly less than 1 percent of the legal authorities cited in the opinions were mentioned in the amicus briefs and not in the parties' briefs (and less than 5 percent of the authorities cited in the cases in which amicus briefs were submitted). Social facts used in the opinions were equally unlikely to be found only in the amicus briefs, though they were a fairly important source of empirical data.[20] Likewise, a study of all amicus briefs given the Illinois Supreme Court from 1938 to 1958 concluded that they rarely contributed anything beyond the parties' briefs in the way of law, but did contain much economic, social, and political data.[21]

Judges, on the other hand, generally welcome amicus briefs and find them helpful on the whole.[22] A Massachusetts justice said they only came about once a month, but:

Often they're very helpful. Sometimes they're the best brief in the group. They are *extremely* helpful in areas where you have a specialization involved where you need the help of somebody who really knows the field when the parties do not. We had a case recently involving the rights in land where neither party was quite as strong as it ought to be, and the conveyancers' association came in and gave us the story as they saw it, and that kind of thing is *extremely* helpful. . . . On the other hand some of the amicus briefs would be kind of pathetic.

The judges said that the briefs by and large came in only the more important cases and in the advisory opinions, fortunately the two places where they are most needed, and that their benefit was largely due to the specialized knowledge of the organizations. On the other hand, several judges said that, with few exceptions, the amicus briefs were a wasted effort. One of these judges said about amicus briefs in two recent and important cases:

They just said "We are the organization of so and so, and we support these parties." It's just implied political pressure. . . . They're poorly written. You might as well say "All those for the plaintiffs stand up, and then all those for the defendants stand up." It's almost an insult to the court.

In fact, Philip Kurland recently recommended that the U.S. Supreme Court abandon the practice of accepting amicus briefs because they are usually just such briefs and add nothing.[23] The Supreme Court a few decades ago greatly restricted the filing of amicus briefs because it received large numbers of worthless briefs.[24] However, it should not take a judge more than a couple of minutes to detect and discard useless amicus briefs, a small amount of time to spend in the hope of finding help.

ISSUES BRIEFED BY MORE THAN TWO LITIGANTS

Even aside from amicus briefs, appellate courts often receive information from more than only two opposing parties. This happens in four types of situations. First, a third party, an intervenor, may be given permission to join the case at the trial stage; he can present his views there and is bound by the judgment. As a practical matter, because of the public nature of the cases, the four intervenors appearing before the focal court were normally the same thing as amici, except that they first appeared at the trial stage and were allowed a few minutes oral agument. They tended to side with one or the other of the original litigants; and though they presented substantial briefs, they added virtually no authorities cited in the opinions and not brought out by the original parties.

The second situation occurs when more than one of the original parties on one side of the appeal file separate briefs. Although most appeals have several parties on one or both sides, they seldom file separate briefs; that happened in only three cases during the year's study of the focal court. In the third situation, similar to the second, the appellate court joins two or more appeals, and they are argued together and decided in one opinion, though the parties still file separate briefs. This happened five times in the cases studied. These two situations seemed to have given the court some help, because at times one of the briefs was notably more thorough than the other on the same side (as was shown, for example, by citing at least twice as many authorities used by the court than the other), and perhaps only the weaker brief would have been filed had there been only one brief to a side.

In the fourth situation, two cases having a similar issue are before the court at roughly the same time, such that the briefs in the two cases can be used in any one of the two opinions.[25] This happened 13 times, involving 19 of the 112 cases studied, though it involved only one of several issues— occasionally a minor issue—in the various cases. The court on occasion processed several of these cases together, holding arguments on the same day and assigning the opinions to the same judge. But generally the cases were handled separately, and I can only guess that the judges and clerks made use of the separate briefs when writing the opinions. At any rate, these overlaps seem to give the court only limited help. Less than a tenth of legal authorities cited in the opinions were in the collateral briefs and not in the briefs of the parties to the particular case.

All in all, including amicus briefs as well as these four situations, the court received more than only the two opposing briefs in over a third of its appeals. Thus it and probably other appellate courts as well are far from limited to outside information presented by just two adversaries, the typical model of litigation. This is especially true in the more important appeals; the great majority of those that might be considered important, admittedly an imprecise category, had three or more briefs (excluding reply briefs). One case, probably the most important of the year's appeals, had briefs from 10 sources, generally very good briefs—from 5 parties, 2 intervenors, and 3 amici—totaling over 300 pages. Still, it must be emphasized that seldom do these additional briefs add much information beyond that found in the two main briefs.

OTHER INFORMATION FROM COUNSEL
BEFORE THE DECISION

The means described so far of submitting information to appellate courts end after oral arguments. When the judges read the briefs before the arguments, the close of the arguments marks a rather abrupt change from information received from the adversary system to information received by investigation (e.g., legal research at the court). Even so, there are exceptions. This section will discuss the more unusual ways counsel submit information to judges, ways that ordinarily take place after arguments. The most normal of these is judges' requests for memorandums or supplemental briefs on points not adequately covered in the regular briefs or oral arguments. Judges request these in only a very small percentage of the appeals;[26] at the focal court the practice was usually used only to obtain additions to the appendix. Rarer still is reargument—calling for a second oral argument before the case is decided.[27] Beyond these, there are several more informal means of submitting information, which will be discussed presently.

A very important facet of the adversary system in appellate courts is that each adversary must be given a chance to answer his opponent's arguments. Thus the belief that information given by one side must be available to the other underlies all communication between judges and lawyers.[28] Whenever an attorney sends a brief or memorandum to the court, he must send a copy to his opponent. Ex parte communication with counsel about the substance of a case is forbidden, except when one side has turned down a chance to appear—for example, courts will hear oral argument if only one attorney shows up. (Judges, however, do talk to one attorney alone about scheduling an appeal, such as trying to persuade him to file his brief quickly.) Judges often know many of the lawyers who appear before them and often meet them at parties, bar functions, or chance encounters in the street or courthouse. But they try to (and as far as I know always do) shun talk about the merits of pending appeals. Some judges have even restricted their social activities to lessen contacts with lawyers or litigants. Another problem is the rare case in which an attorney or a litigant contacts a judge or, more likely, the court clerk or a law clerk to find out how his case is coming along. In these situations the answer given is that nobody at the court can talk about it.[29]

Within these restrictions there is a small amount of informal communication between counsel and judges. At a very few courts, including the focal court, the judges, or perhaps just one or a few of them, have asked the attorneys to come in or have called them on multiparty telephone lines to confer about specific points that the judges believed the briefs and oral arguments left unresolved. At least three other appellate courts have called in attorneys, and sometimes technical experts, for lengthy conferences after the oral arguments, especially in highly technical and complicated cases. But even the courts that use these unusual procedures use them very rarely.[30]

Also, in a few cases, lawyers send in letters after oral arguments on their own initiative, pointing out a relevant opinion just issued by another court or attempting to answer some point that came up in the arguments. Some judges are annoyed if the lawyer does this without first obtaining the court's permission to file a supplementary brief, especially if the letter does more than just cite a recent case. Other judges, however, are glad to get the information whether it goes through approved channels or not. As one focal court clerk said, lawyers should just mail a letter to the judges, "and say, 'I know it's outside the rules, but just in case the court should consider it . . .' and they'll read it. They want all the help they can get." A judge said that when he was an appellate lawyer, he had someone write down the judges' questions and then sent the court a letter supplying additional answers, without asking for the court's permission. In any event, the lawyer must send a copy to the other side and inform the court that he has done so. If he does not, at best the court will send a copy itself; more likely the judges will become annoyed and refuse to look at the letter.[31]

REHEARINGS

The lawyers' last chance to send the court information is in the rehearing process. After the decision is announced, the loser can petition the court for another review of the case; that is, he can argue that the decision was wrong and should be changed. All those courts responding to a 1957 survey of appellate courts allowed motions for rehearing, and the majority received them in at least 15 percent of their cases.[32] The motions, however, are very rarely successful. "The normal petition for rehearing has about the same chance of success as the proverbial snowball on the far side of the River Styx."[33] A typical attitude toward rehearing is this statement by Judge Goodrich of the Third Circuit:

Most petitions for rehearing are nothing but a rehashing of the argument on appeal. It is quite clear that if the court has worked through a case thoughtfully and rejected a certain line of argument it is not going to change its mind by hearing the argument made again. But every once and a while a case appears where the court has mistaken the facts or misconstrued the point of the case. In that sort of situation it may grant petition for reargument. For judges, while they exasperate lawyers a great deal, really want to do the right thing. But let it be repeated, these instances of mistake based on fact or misconception of the case are few.[34]

The rehearing procedure, thus, is a minor source of information for the judges' decision-making process, though it is a final check against missing important arguments. Rehearing motions probably get more attention on the few courts where the judges do not read the briefs or discuss the cases among themselves.[35]

CONCLUSIONS

Information received by appellate courts from the adversary system is tightly restricted to only a few formal channels; very little information arrives outside the briefs, records, and oral arguments. To my mind, this rigidity is unfortunate and, as Judge Leventhal said in this connection, "appellate judges can and should become less custom-bound,"[36] especially in cases presenting important and complex issues.

In general there should be much more information flow back and forth between judges and counsel so that counsel can address the precise concerns of the judges. At present, virtually the only interaction of this sort is during oral arguments; here counsel may not have the information requested at their fingertips. Justice Jackson wrote:

I used to say that, as Solicitor General, I made three arguments of every case. First came the one I had planned—as I thought, logical, coherent, complete. Second was the one actually presented—interrupted, incoherent, disjointed, disappointing. The third was the utterly devastating argument that I thought of after going to bed that night.[37]

Courts lose that third argument and much valuable information because counsel is not given the time to answer adequately many of the questions.

Flexibility can be added to appellate procedures several ways. These are discussed at length in Appendix B and will be mentioned only quickly here. Courts can ask for more supplemental briefs. This procedure would be very valuable if judges prepare thoroughly before oral arguments, since the need for supplemental briefs will become obvious when counsel is unable to answer questions at the arguments. If the judges prepare far enough in advance, they can ask counsel several days before the arguments to concentrate on several specific points in need of clarification. This would give counsel time to prepare.

Several more suggestions must be limited to cases where judicial secrecy can be relaxed somewhat (giving attention, of course, to the rationales for the secrecy given in Chapter 1). First, the memorandums sent to the judges by staff attorneys should be sent to counsel also, again indicating to them what arguments need to be made (and mitigating the suspicion that the staff has too much influence). Secondly, the court should send draft opinions to the attorneys, pinpointing exactly what is on the judges' minds.[38] This would also cut down the time-wasting and often useless rehearing procedures, since petitions for rehearing could be prohibited if the final opinion does not

differ substantially from the tentative draft. Lastly, a judge should be allowed to telephone or meet with both counsel to discuss specific points that
bother him, though requests for supplemental written information would
do just as well except in highly technical areas where a common background
understanding must be established through a great deal of communication
back and forth.

The present rigidity of the adversary system in appellate courts, it should
be noted, results mainly from the courts' dispute-deciding function. When
courts engage in pure lawmaking, unmixed with dispute deciding—that is,
when they issue rules of court procedure in the administrative side of their
functions—their means of information gathering are quite flexible. Special
committees are often set up to study specific problems and to draft proposed
rules; interested persons (in effect, adversaries) are permitted to comment
on the proposals; and then the court issues, modifies, or rejects the proposed
rules. This, of course, is very similar to administrative agency rule making.
It is by no means a model procedure (e.g., courts do not always provide the
public with an opportunity to comment, and when they do the comments
are ordinarily meager), but it does suggest that appellate judges freely depart from the traditional model of receiving information when given the
opportunity.[39] There is never any need to violate the basic tenet of the
adversary system that an adversary have a chance to rebut another's arguments, for all comments can be made public (as is the trend in administrative
agency rule making).

CHAPTER 6

Sources of Information Outside the Adversary System

Appellate judges supplement the information given by counsel with independent research, done mainly by law clerks and staff attorneys, and in rare cases with advice given informally by outside experts. This chapter describes these sources of information, emphasizing the law clerks. Of course, much information used by the judges but not supplied by the adversary system comes from their accumulated knowledge gained from past experience, but this chapter is concerned with the other people the judges use in their quest for information.

THE LAW CLERKS[1]

Law clerks were first used a century ago by a few Massachusetts and U.S. Supreme Court justices, and other judges have since slowly adopted the practice. Now nearly all appellate judges have at least one law clerk,[2] and those on federal appellate courts and several state supreme courts have two or more.

The clerks are almost always young lawyers, hired right out of law school or within a year after graduation. They rarely stay for more than two years; in fact, they usually just serve from the summer after law school graduation to the following summer. The caliber of clerks varies greatly from court to court; by and large the federal courts attract better students, often from the top of the class in major law schools.

At virtually all courts a law clerk is the personal employee of his judge, who alone hires and supervises him. Staff attorneys, on the other hand, are hired and supervised by the chief judge or the whole court, though they may have many of the same duties as law clerks. The procedures used in hiring law clerks vary greatly from court to court and judge to judge. Prospective clerks may simply respond to notices sent by judges to law school placement offices, or they may be recommended by law school professors, by judges' friends, or by law student sons of fellow judges. The present clerk often helps his judge evaluate the applicants, and several courts now have formal screening procedures to limit the number of candidates sent to each judge. Even with this help, however, judges often spend a good deal of time each fall making the final selection. Probably all go to the trouble of interviewing the most promising applicants.

THE CLERKS' DUTIES. The clerks' duties[3] vary enormously, since each judge controls his clerk and has his own ideas about how a clerk can best help him. Judges, moreover, often use clerks differently from case to case. Nevertheless, a major duty is always research—checking the legal authorities and facts in the briefs and searching for information missed by counsel. "In general," a U.S. Supreme Court clerk has said, "it is the job of the clerk to be the eyes and legs for his judge, finding and bringing in useful material."[4] The clerks are, in fact, the judges' most important means of finding information not given in the briefs and arguments.

Clerks present the fruits of their research in draft opinions and legal memorandums. Judges hold widely divergent views about the delegation of opinion drafting. The trend has been toward clerk drafts, and this is now commonly accepted practice.[5] But there is still criticism of it, most vocally by Judge Edwards of the Sixth Circuit:

I may be a lonely minority with a voice crying out in the wilderness on this score, but I won't have my law clerks write draft opinions. I won't have them write for decision prior to oral argument. And I won't adopt anything that they write in a legal memorandum afterwards as *part* of my opinion. I don't *want* to encourage myself to be lazy, and I know enough of the seeds of laziness to be able to recognize them in myself; so I'm going to adhere to that until I am *forced by this overload to use them for opinion writing*. And *when I do*, I'm going to put *their name on the opinion*, and say that it was written by my law clerk and say that I reviewed it and accepted it and so did my colleagues.[6]

Almost a third of the judges in the present study, largely Rhode Island justices, never allow their clerks to draft opinions, and a few more do so only rarely and only near the end of the clerk's stay. Most judges make substantial use of clerks' drafts; several judges receive them in nearly all cases, but a more common practice is to split the drafting more or less evenly between the judge and his clerk or clerks. Reasons for the different practices, as given by two judges on the same state court, are:

I *cannot* understand a system by which a judge permits a law clerk to write an opinion. It requires so much side information, being a part of the judge, really, of what was left out, *why* things were handled, and various side aspects, that I would rather have a memorandum on the full problem, what the clerk thinks, with a lot of stream of consciousness observation, some of which can be disposed of quickly because I know the procedure.

It's very helpful if you get capable law clerks. A judge should spend his time reading the record and cases and debating with his associates, and then making up his opinion on the cases. The law clerk does the drudgery of drafting. He will write the drafts and I will revise them; sometimes there are six or seven revisions.

The clerks tend to draft opinions less often in their first few months of work, and less often in cases the judges feel contain clear-cut issues. These six courts are typical of appellate courts in the country with respect to opinion drafting by clerks.[7]

Judges' instructions to their clerks when they draft opinions vary from no instructions whatever to, as one clerk said, "almost a dictation of what the opinion should be." Sometimes a judge tells a clerk little more than the desired outcome (and a few times not even that); at other times they discuss the case at length, and the clerk may even write preliminary memorandums. Most judges vary their procedures from case to case between these two extremes.

The judges then review the drafts and make changes. Here again practices are far from uniform. The following are extreme comments by clerks about how much their judges change their drafts:

It depends from opinion to opinion. Not a great deal. I don't know if that's good or bad. That worries me. I think that he probably should. But not a great deal. Mainly to make it clear, to point out a point if he thinks I've left out something.

Well, when I first started they were changed quite a lot. I mean just about total rewrite. But I've gotten to the point now where a word is changed occasionally, sentences are turned around or restructured, but it's basically, you know—but not very drastic changes. Style changes more than anything else.

We would submit draft opinions. They were solely an exercise.
Q — He would chop them up?
A — He would chop them up. He would do worse than chop them up. He would start over. He would throw them away. He wrote his own opinions from start to finish. I think he once liked one of my sentences and that found its way into an opinion. But never more than that.

The practices of the remaining judges who used clerks' drafts fall somewhere in between, though just where is hard to say. The clerks usually said that the amount of editing varied greatly from case to case—between a few minor changes and changes so extensive that they leave little of the clerk's draft. They were no more specific than this; thus estimates of just how much the clerks' drafts are changed is very difficult. A typical comment is:

Q — How much of what you wrote ended up in the final opinions?
A — It's hard to say. Some opinions, most of it, and some opinions very little of it.

Usually I knew which way he wanted to go and *why* before I started the opinion. It was not a thing that I did that he agreed with. We had discussed it earlier—discussed it as we went along; so although I may have written it, actually it was sort of a combined effort.

As this passage suggests, drafts touched the least strongly tend to be in cases where the clerk and judge discuss the case thoroughly before and during the drafting process. Also, a number of clerks said that the changes were fewer after they had been a clerk for some time, once they had learned what their judges wanted in the opinions and become attuned to their writing styles.

Those clerks who do not draft opinions present the results of their research in memorandums; and even clerks in "first draft offices" often write memos, such as the preargument bench memos that were described in the preceding chapter. Judges who draft all their opinions usually ask their clerks for long, detailed memorandums covering all of each case assigned them. These are used by the judge as a source of information when writing opinions, condensing the material in the memos to one-fifth or so of their length. On the other hand, a number of judges who write their own drafts use their clerks to research and submit memorandums on specific points only, rather than covering all the issues completely.

The distinction between memorandums and draft opinions is sometimes hazy. The clerks' memorandums usually suggest how the issues should be decided, and judges' opinions often include sentences or even paragraphs taken from the memorandums. Likewise, clerks' draft opinions are sometimes much longer than they expect the final opinion to be, containing collateral points that the judge might want to know but that need not be in a published opinion.

Clerks help their judges in many ways other than doing research and writing memorandums or draft opinions. They serve as a sounding board for their judges' thoughts and, in general, as someone to discuss the issues with. They often check the facts and citations in their judges' draft opinions and criticize the reasoning used. They may study tentative opinions circulated by other judges on the court; but about half the judges reserve this task for themselves alone, unless they want some research done, which tends to leave the clerks with little knowledge of what is happening in other offices. At courts with discretionary jurisdiction, the clerks often review the applications for leave to appeal and give their judges advice. Several of the clerks interviewed took an active part in the court's administrative side, but most did virtually nothing here.

Clerks do other work, often quite menial, not directly related to deciding cases. Many judges use them as chauffeurs so that they can work while in the car. Also to save judges' time, clerks write speeches or even fetch coffee, collect mail, or run other trivial errands. They may be charged with the upkeep of the library in the judge's office, a tedious task: "My major diddly work is librarian stuff. It's just—I mean I don't think you've ever lived until you've put in pocket parts in the volumes of C.J.S." On the average, federal judges drive their clerks much harder than state justices. Some state court clerks are left with a good deal of free time, which they are likely use in practicing on the side, studying for bar exams, or involving themselves in other outside interests.

CLERK-JUDGE RELATIONSHIPS. On these six courts, and probably on nearly all other courts, the judges and their clerks are normally very close, both in the sense that they have a great deal of contact and the sense that their personal relations are open and friendly. The judges generally spend much time talking to their clerks about the cases and often about other matters as well. Occasionally, the judges and their clerks have a rather distant personal relationship. But typically they are on friendly terms, sometimes extremely friendly. Some typical comments by clerks are:

As you know, my relationship with him was not one of the warmest, and we crossed paths as infrequently as I could make it. . . . I took my work and went and did it and stayed out of his way as much as I could.

He tries to be good friends with all his clerks. Sometimes he is and sometimes he isn't. We were particularly close, I think.

We enjoy the *rapport* that I think is—as far as I am concerned is out of sight. I mean I can pop in that door any time I want to. We don't necessarily have to be talking about [cases]. We can, you know, talk about many and varied *things*, and just a very, very comfortable atmosphere.

The clerks' opinions of their judges varied from strong disgust to almost hero worship, with the majority quite close to the latter end. In the interviews they generally praised their judges profusely,[8] whereas, in contrast, a great many criticized other judges on the court, usually passing out more criticism than praise. Thus, it seems, as one clerk said, that "it's just built in the job to become very pro your judge."

In this rather congenial atmosphere, the flow of information from the clerks to their judges is normally very free. Judges want their clerks to speak their minds about the cases and to argue their positions forcefully,[9] for example:

The primary job of my law clerk is to tear what I have written apart. Tell me how bad it is legally, grammatically. . . .

Q — You like them to be absolutely frank with you?

A — Oh, *yeah*. The better the opinion is, the better *I look*; so they're really helping me, from a vain point of view.

Q — Do you like the clerks to argue with you—to debate with you?

A — Heavens yes. They don't do any *deciding*, but the last thing in the *world* I want is a yes-man. I've always said I can make enough mistakes myself. I don't need any help on that. But I think it's a necessary function of the law clerks.

I encourage free-for-all intellectual combat, no holds barred by the Marquis of Queensbury Rules. As I remind my clerks at various stages of our collective efforts, the First Amendment prevails in my office, preserving to myself only the right to invoke cloture.[10]

In fact, one of the clerks' main duties, according to most judges, is to contest the judges' tentative conclusions they disagree with. They explain this to the clerks when hired, but a few judges complained that some clerks remained too meek or deferential. Several judges added, however, and all would probably agree, that once they have definitely decided how to vote, the clerks should quit trying to persuade them.

Likewise, the clerks feel that they can say anything about the cases to their judges, at least according to those I interviewed, except that several are wary of bothering their judges too much or of attacking their underlying philosophies. Typical, though more elaborate, comments are:

Q — Did you feel that you could say anything to him about the cases?
A — Absolutely anything.
Q — Did you argue with him a lot?
A — Yeah, we did. There was a lot of discussion. He was always willing to talk, and you know, if you felt something, you know, you could tell him. If you thought it was a crummy decision, you told him it was a crummy decision.

Sometimes I guess, I do hole back something. I mean I guess I'm moody also. Sometimes I'm very bold and I'll tell him anything I think of. "This word is ridiculous," or "this expression" or you know, "This whole paragraph doesn't fit." Other times, I'm not as bold, but sometimes, and if there's something that he's really excited about, and I'm, you know, fifty-fifty or really fifty-two-forty-eight against, and he's very excited about it, I guess I'm not really going to say anything.

As a result, many clerks often argue with their judges. But the amount of arguing depends largely on the amount of disagreement. Some clerks seldom argue with their judges, even though they feel free to do so, because they seldom find anything to argue about and do not, as some clerks do, play devil's advocate.

In fact, the clerks generally said they hardly ever disagree with their judges about the outcome of cases, although differences over the details of reasoning are more common. Rarely are there any great differences in philosophy between a clerk and his judge. The clerks' descriptions of themselves vary from radical left to conservative Republican, though most are liberal to some degree. Most considered themselves more liberal than their judges,[11] especially in criminal cases (only one thought himself more conservative than his judge, and a good number said they were about the same), but they generally added that the differences are not very great. A few clerks said that their clerkships had moderated their views—they had become more practical—such that they came to agree more with their judges.

Apparently little of this similarity is the result of selective hiring by judges in order to get clerks with views similar to theirs. Half the judges interviewed talked about this; most said they did not consider the clerks' philosophical views at all when hiring them, and the rest said that this might be a minor consideration or that they did not want clerks with strongly held extreme views—one judge said "I don't want a wild-eyed conservative or a wild-eyed liberal around here." On the other hand, it seems more likely that the clerks gravitate toward judges they agree with, though they were not asked about this.

THE LAW CLERKS' INFLUENCE. The influence of law clerks on appellate decision making is a difficult subject. First, I know of no sensible and usable definition of words like "influence" and "power," and secondly it is nearly impossible to determine whether influence has been exerted in any particular case. However, a broad outline will be attempted, since it is an important topic within the framework of this book.

To begin with, the judges always have the final say. As far as I know, they never delegate the actual deciding of appeals to their clerks or to anyone else, except their fellow judges, for example, in panel decisions.[12] The clerks' influence, therefore, is limited to persuading their judges, which they generally feel free to attempt, as was just seen.

When asked if they had changed their judges' minds about the outcomes of cases, almost two-thirds of the clerks said they had, but in only 1 or 2 or "a few" cases out of the 100 to 400 their judges sat on each year. Several said they never changed their judges' minds, and several more said they could not tell if they had. Clerks have, on very rare occasions, persuaded a whole court to reverse its tentative position. Also a good number of judges commented on whether clerks had changed their minds, and all but a few said it had happened, though they normally added that it was not often. One reason given for these low figures is that judges are very unlikely to change their basic viewpoints overnight in preference for those of the young and inexperienced clerks. Furthermore, and probably more important, the clerks seldom disagree with their judges' decisions, especially after they have discussed the case together. In fact, several clerks explained their slight influence by saying that they could not very well change their judges' minds if they did not disagree.

The discussion so far is overly simple and probably understates the clerks' influence. In the first place, as mentioned by a number of clerks and judges who discussed this topic, whether a clerk changes his judge's mind depends a lot on the extent to which the judge has decided to vote one way or the other. Judges often talk with their clerks and receive memorandums or draft opinions while they are still undecided, and if the judge finally agrees with his clerk, it may or may not imply influence by the clerk. One does not know how the judge would vote if the clerk were not there. For example:

Q — Did you ever change [your judge's] mind about the outcome of a case?

A — Have I ever changed his mind? That's interesting. I think I've changed an immediate reaction, but only by research. I think that once he's given all the materials—you know, giving him a good research job, and makes the decision, no, I don't think I ever persuaded him to change his mind then.

Q — How often have you changed his mind about the outcome of a case?

A — Oh, I'd say about—let's see—a percentage of all the time I've disagreed with him, I'd say, oh, 5 percent.

Q — That's about three cases?

A — Oh, let's see. I mean, there are times when I will influence his decision. If I believe very strongly in a position, I try very strongly to get him to take that position, but there are times when both of us just sort of try to play devil's advocate with each other, and try to think up all the arguments each of us can. You know, and then we sort of come to a consensus of what we think, you know, is the best side. But there are times when we just flat out disagree. You know, just he wants to go one way, and I want to go the other, and I try but I very rarely—once he's made up his mind, that's it. I got to get him before he's 100 percent.

A plain statement by a clerk that he changed his judge's mind in a certain number of cases really means very little. The clerk may have changed an early tentative view that the judge would have changed later in any case even without the clerk's persuasion, or on the other hand his judge might have decided differently in many other cases but for the discussions he had with his clerk during his early consideration of the issues.

A second point, important from the point of view of this study, is that since the clerks are the judges' prime tools of investigation, their research efforts may often affect decisions. This point was well stated by one of the clerks interviewed:

Some of the things I didn't expect was the tremendous amount of power that the clerk has. But again, putting it in perspective of the time element and the allocation of resources, it's understandable now looking back that the judge just doesn't have the time and resources. That's why he had you.

Q — But not all clerks were in the same position you were, were they? [He wrote draft opinions and had a very good relationship with his judge.]

A — If the judge says, "Find out if there's any case law on this," and you go out and look and don't find any—I mean, it's your word. There may be a whole book on it. But if you don't find it, it might as well not exist. That's power. And if it does exist, and you tell the judge it doesn't exist, that's power, because the judge is going to operate on that. No matter what level of rapport you have with the judge, he is not going to go out and research it. He doesn't have time. That's why they hire clerks. Somebody else may find it and *embarrass* him. And we have seven men. That's the whole point of having seven men. But if nobody finds it, it might as well not exist as far as the case is concerned. And if the appellate practice is shitty, you aren't finding the other guys finding it. Then, you know, it just doesn't exist. And so you go on your merry way. I was *tremendously* aware of that.

Thus the thoroughness of a clerk's research may affect the outcome of an appeal. A number of clerks, in fact, did say that the way they changed their judges' minds was through the fruits of their research. But one cannot tell how important this is because there is no way to determine what information the clerk missed or what information the judge would have found without the clerk or whether, even if these were known, the judge's decision would have been different in the different circumstances.

The notion of clerks' influence through information gathering is, perhaps, incomplete without adding a requirement that the clerks use their position to affect decisions they agree with—that is, that they selectively present information supporting the result they wish. Though the clerks were rarely asked about this, I never heard of an incident in which a clerk withheld information from his judge because it would suggest a result he disagreed with. Several clerks did volunteer that they would never mislead their judges. On the other hand, a few clerks mentioned that they sometimes did extra research in specific areas when trying to persuade their judges; that is, they searched for information where the extra information would most likely lead to the result they wished. But, again, the extent of the clerk's influence here is uncertain.

Another possible influence, mentioned rarely in the interviews but often in the literature about law clerks, is the questioning of old ideas and the introduction of new ideas, especially the latest thoughts of law school professors. Judge Skelly Wright argued against substituting professional legal assistants for the short-term law clerks, saying that the professionals would

get farther and farther away from the law and from the fresh air of the law schools that are brought into the judges' chambers each year. I suggest that the thing that keeps the judiciary alive and buoyant and moving forward instead of backwards, as we were inclined to do in the past, are these bright young men who come and stay with us for a limited period of time.[13]

This may be by far the most important influence of law clerks—a subtle modifying of the judges' overall outlooks, rather than directly affecting decisions in specific cases. But, even more than in the earlier discussion, conjecture here must be nearly baseless because one cannot go into the depths of the judges' thinking processes.

Besides the actual outcome of cases, there are other areas where clerks have some influence. They often affect the wording and details of reasoning in the judges' opinions—first, by commenting on their judges' drafts and, second, by writing the drafts themselves. In the second case, though, it should be remembered that the judges either give their clerks detailed instructions about what should be in the opinion or they greatly edit the clerks' drafts. Also, on courts with discretionary jurisdiction a great deal is often delegated to the clerks or to staff attorneys when deciding which cases to hear. Because the judges often do not have time to read the briefs supporting and opposing leave to appeal (i.e., certiorari), they must rely on the information in clerks' or staff attorneys' memorandums to learn about the cases, and clerks often feel they have more influence here then in the actual deciding of cases.[14]

The clerks' influence, in conclusion, seems to consist of presenting judges with ideas and information they would not otherwise have time to discover; as such, it results in more informed decisions, not decisions against the judges' wills, as long as the clerks are capable.

One further point of interest is that clerks often find their positions as underlings somewhat frustrating. When asked about the major drawbacks of clerking, by far the most common complaint was that their judges have the final say. (The only other complaint mentioned by more than a few was an itching to practice law. The major benefits, they said, are learning how appellate courts operate and working under a judge they particularly like.) Half the clerks said that they were frustrated at not being able to vote on the cases or to have the opinions worded as they would wish, even though they may greatly respect their judges. One clerk said:

[When he] let me on my own for two or three days and I have . . . formed a thinking approach to the problem—how to look at it, and analysis. And then I talk to him, and I'm really into my analysis, and his analysis is just different, and you know, just—that's been difficult for me. I guess I think the whole business of being creative or something—my unique approach doesn't fit with his. It just sort of puts a damper in the whole thing with me.

[Then an hour later:] You know, everybody's ego's into something. I mean take if I write a draft, and I spend a lot of time over it, and my ego has gone into it, and I like to think of it as mine. I mean, I'm positive, and then he comes through and, you know, he's the judge, and he must think of it as his, and you know it does bother me.

A few clerks even refuse to write draft opinions when they disagree strongly with their judges, but the prevailing view among clerks is that one should swallow one's pride and write the way the judge wishes even though, as several said, this is an onerous task.

INFORMATION FROM OTHER SOURCES IN THE COURT

Besides the attorneys and the law clerks, judges on the whole receive the most help from their colleagues. As will be seen in Chapter 9, independent research is largely limited to the office of the judge assigned to write the court's opinion. For the other judges, then, a major source of information is the draft opinion, insofar as it presents the fruits of this research. The assigned judge gets some, but not much, information—as opposed to expressions of opinion and requests to alter the draft opinion—from his colleagues. I asked most of the judges how often, when writing an opinion, other judges tell them of authorities they were not aware of, and the answers varied greatly—from "never" to "very, very frequently." Excluding several who said they could not guess how often, most said it happened "not very often" or used similar language. Judges seem to welcome this help, especially in finding recent decisions, though a few seemed to think it implies "you weren't doing your work competently," as one said. On the other hand, as will be discussed in Chapter 12, the assigned judge's colleagues are often an important source of advice about policy and practical implications, especially colleagues with experience in the area of law under consideration.

Judges hardly ever receive help directly from their colleagues' clerks. On a few rare occasions judges temporarily assign their clerks to others in need of help, and sometimes judges chat and argue informally with other judges' clerks, but the clerks generally said they talk regularly about the cases with at most one or two other judges, and several said they virtually never talked with other judges. Any information a judge gets from another's clerk is more likely to arrive secondhand through his own clerk or through the opinions. The clerks often gossip about the court's business, more so if their offices are in the same town, and they may give each other advice about the opinions they are working on, perhaps even bringing up new and relevant authorities. But even this is not an important source of information. In fact, a good number of clerks said they rarely went outside their offices or library for help.

Lastly, judges and their clerks may get advice from other lawyers that are sprinkled throughout the organization of any court. By far the most important of these are the staff attorneys. They are a rather new addition, brought in to help process the increasing case loads, and their number is increasing at a rapid rate. An important job given these attorneys at some courts, especially courts without discretionary jurisdiction, is writing memorandums about the cases, often including research beyond the briefs.[15] In this sense, then, staff attorneys function very much like law clerks (the main difference is that they are not attached to specific judges), and many of the same questions about the clerks' influence apply to them also. Staff attorneys on some state supreme courts, including the focal court, do some independent research when preparing memorandums on the applications for leave to appeal (though the focal court opinions contain virtually no legal authority mentioned by the staff attorneys but not by counsel), and judges or clerks may ask their advice when studying the memorandums. Also, but not often, the administrative office or the court clerk may give advice, especially on procedural questions. Lastly, at most of the courts studied here, and at many other courts,[16] lawyers or secretaries, ordinarily in the reporter's office, check the opinions before publication. Their basic job is to check the citations of authority and to make sure the facts are in the record, but they may also mention some authority that they think should be considered.

INFORMATION OBTAINED INFORMALLY FROM OUTSIDE EXPERTS

Virtually all information judges get directly from people outside the court comes through the adversary system—from the parties and amici curiae. The one exception is the uncommon and controversial practice of asking experts for advice about cases being decided. By this I mean direct contact with experts, and not information from law reviews, texts, or amicus briefs. Also, this is advice on a specific issue the judge is working on, not general discussion of legal problems with professors and friends, especially in judicial seminars, even though this may touch on something the judge is deciding at the time. And it is advice during the deciding of a case, not talk with professors about opinions recently handed down, as some judges do once in a while.

Most of the judges interviewed never get advice from outside experts, and the great majority of the rest very rarely do it. Only a few, mainly focal court justices, get expert advice on more than one or two cases a year, and none much more than that. So this does not rival the attorneys' briefs and the clerks' and staff attorneys' library research as a source of information. Whether a judge will ever go to outside experts depends mainly on the feeling within the court about the propriety of the practice. Only one judge of all those interviewed on the Ohio court and the two circuit courts had gone to experts for advice. At least the majority on the focal, Rhode Island, and Massachusetts courts had, though one or two on each thought the practice wrong.

Generally, the clerks venture out for advice if and only if their judges do. Some judges send their clerks to professors rather than go themselves, and the clerks are not likely to get advice without being directed to do so. However, a few clerks said they felt free to contact professors on their own, and a few more chatted with their attorney friends about the legal issues before the court, sometimes picking up information that way.

This type of advice is ordinarily obtained over the telephone or in informal meetings; written communication about the cases outside regular channels is uncommon. I learned of only three instances in which judges or clerks wrote to professors or friends for advice, though they more often wrote to government agencies for statistics relevant to issues before them.

A wide variety of people are contacted on a wide variety of problems. Law professors are contacted the most, as one would expect, but the clerks and judges also went to attorneys, trial judges, government officials, physicians, and social and physical science professors. More often than not, these are people the judge or clerk already knows well, especially as relatives, personal friends, or former associates. Outside advice is sought on a broad range of problems, but three in particular stand out. Much, if not most, of the information sought at the focal and Rhode Island courts is information about social facts, such as the practical consequences of a proposed ruling. This will be discussed further in Chapter 13. These two courts also ask for advice about the interpretation of the states' rules of court procedure. Law professors helped both courts draft these rules, and the justices have quite often asked them about the meanings of particular provisions. The Massachusetts justices tend to seek advice on technical points of law, often trust law, asking law professors whether they know of any authorities on the subject.

Confidentiality of decision making, which was discussed in Chapter 1, impedes this source of information. Theoretically, outsiders are not supposed to know anything about the court's deliberations. But by asking for advice a judge would imply that he is writing on the case, and he may disclose how he is leaning. For this reason, questions are generally posed in the abstract without giving the name or specific facts of the case. Sometimes, to hide the judge's identity, questions are sent through the court clerk and under the clerk's name.[17] And judges may refrain from going outside on well-publicized cases where the expert would be able to connect an abstract issue to a specific case. On the other hand, a few clerks and judges said they discuss details of cases with professors they trust and do not care if the cases are identified; two judges even showed them draft opinions.

Why is this source of information so rarely used—why did most of the judges interviewed refuse to use it at all, and why did the others use it so seldom? Among the judges who never asked outsiders for advice, the most frequent reason given was that it would be unfair to the parties because they would not have a chance to answer what the expert said. "It's no different," one judge said, "than talking to one lawyer about the case and not having the other one present." Almost half the judges who do not get outside advice gave this as a reason. Also, a number said they have no need for outside advice; they can get the information they want from the briefs and from independent research. Several judges said it was their job, not outside experts', to decide cases and do the research work.[18] (This should not suggest that judges let outside experts determine their votes. I found no evidence that outside experts are used for anything more than a source of information, which the judges evaluate on their own.)

Even among those who had no ethical objections to obtaining outside expert advice, the practice was on the whole rare. The main reasons given by these judges were that help of this sort is not needed often and that the experts are not of much help (though most justices, especially in Massachusetts, found them very helpful when used). Two more restraints were mentioned by a few judges: They must always worry about "what axes do these people have to grind?" as one judge expressed it, and they may not know an expert on the particular problem well enough to ask for advice.

Refusing to get outside advice on the grounds that it would be unfair to the parties is an instance of the adversary system actually restricting the information available to the courts. A major rational for the adversary system, as has been noted in Chapter 3, is as a means of gathering information. But another rational is to make the litigants believe they have been treated fairly, partly through giving them a chance to answer arguments presented against them. This is the root of much of the difference between judges on this subject. Of course, judges often use information gained through independent research without giving the parties a chance to answer; thus some say that if they can look up a law review article by a professor they should be able to talk to him. The counter argument is that the attorneys have the chance, at least, of finding and answering material in the law library, but one really cannot expect counsel to answer everything on point in the law books.

Even the rare use of outside experts on the six courts is probably atypically frequent. The best evidence of this is the reaction to the following provision in Canon 3A (4) of the American Bar Association's proposed Code of Judicial Conduct:

A judge should . . . except as authorized by law, neither initiate nor consider *ex parte* or other communications concerning a pending or impending proceeding. A judge, however, may obtain the advice of a disinterested expert on the law applicable to a proceeding before him if he gives notice to the parties of the person consulted and the substance of the advice and affords the parties reasonable opportunity to respond.

The last sentence was inserted because the code's authors learned that some judges do obtain informal advice from law professors and thought this advice might be valuable at times.[19] The notice requirement obviously reflects the belief that the adversary process requires that counsel be given an opportunity to answer information against his position. But as a practical matter the cumbersome restrictions probably prevent all but the least complex outside help if given orally, as it ordinarily is.[20] Therefore, it is reasonable to assume that the justices who accepted the ABA version of Canon 3A (4) have in the past and believe they should in the future make no or extremely little use of outside advice. Since 1972, when the ABA adopted the Code of Judicial Conduct as a model for the various jurisdictions in the country, the federal court system and the vast majority of the states have adopted all or part of it. The federal courts and most states accepted the ABA version of 3A(4). Three states amended it to prohibit flatly outside advice other than through amicus briefs. Only twelve loosened the restrictions to allow advice without notifying the parties.[21] There is also evidence in the legal literature that justices get outside advice at two other state supreme courts.[22] Thus, in all, judges on probably no more than a fourth of the circuit and state supreme courts combined go to experts for advice, whereas they do so in half the courts studied here.

CHAPTER 7

Reaching Decisions and Writing Opinions

The last three chapters described the attorneys' work, how they present information, the early stages in the process of an appeal, and the activities of the clerks and others who help supply information. This chapter will continue to the last step in the processing of an appeal, the judges' decision-making activities.[1] Some of this goes beyond the main focus of the book —the adversary system and information gathering—but it rounds out the discussion of the appellate process and it is needed in later chapters as background knowledge, particularly knowledge about specialization among the judges and about the relation between written opinions and judges' reasons for decisions.

Much was made, in the first chapter, about how difficult it is to study and say anything definite about what judges think and do when deciding appeals. Judicial secrecy greatly limits access to the interactions of people at the courts, and the judges' mental processes are well hidden. This chapter, then, like all writings on the subject, must be imprecise and must hedge in order not to mislead.

PATH OF AN APPEAL THROUGH THE COURT AND FORMING A JUDGMENT

Judges study and evaluate the ordinary appeal at several different points. How early in this process firm decisions are made differs greatly from case to case and from judge to judge. Nevertheless, one can sketch the successive stages at which decisions become less and less tentative.

At one extreme a judge may have decided an issue even before it was presented in the appeal. The major example, of course, is when he has already decided the issue in an earlier case and has no intention of changing his mind. A more interesting, but much less common, situation is when he has studied, but not decided, the issue and awaits an appeal to serve as a vehicle to express his views.[2] For example, the issue may have been considered at length in an earlier case, but the case was eventually decided on other grounds. This type of predisposition, though, need not dictate the judge's vote; the issue presented might turn out to be a bit different from the issue studied earlier, or the ruling might be based on some other issue in the case.

Tentative judgments are often made at a very early stage in the appeals process. At courts with discretionary jurisdiction the justices study the applications for leave to appeal (or certiorari) to see whether the lower court should be reviewed. Here, as we have seen, a major consideration is often the correctness of the lower court ruling; that is, the judges often make a tentative judgment about the merits well before the case is actually heard. At many courts without discretionary jurisdiction the judges make a similar preliminary study and judgment to determine how much, if any, oral argument will be allowed; one criteria here is whether the decision seems so clear that argument will not help. Some of these courts even summarily decide clear-cut cases upon first looking at the briefs, without argument or conference. Lastly, in a small number of cases, though often very important ones, the judges are asked to stay the lower court judgment, and the judges' impressions about the correctness of the lower court ruling are a major factor in these decisions.

Before oral argument, if it is held, the judges usually read the briefs and, of course, form impressions about the merits. These impressions are aired in a preargument conference at several courts. Normally, though, this is not done, largely because judges fear it might cause them to be less open-minded to counsel's contentions. Next the oral argument can create, strengthen, or change a tentative opinion. Here again judges differ considerably; some say the arguments often change their minds, and others say they virtually never do.

The great majority of appellate courts hold a conference after oral arguments—immediately after them, except that a few courts, such as the First Circuit, meet at the end of a week's arguments or during the next week. The judges take a straw vote and explain their reasons with varying degrees of thoroughness, and this process may lead a judge to modify his position. The judges now have just about everything counsel has to give them; hence unless counsel is totally inadequate or the case is extremely complex, the judges have enough information to form a fairly solid judgment. The vote, though, as is routinely stressed, is not binding and judges are free to change their minds later. But they seldom do, probably in no more than 10 or 15 percent of the cases. This fact is emphasized in Chapter 14, since it indicates the relative importance of information received from counsel and that found by independent research.

One judge is assigned to write the majority opinion, a process that will be described presently, and he circulates a draft to his colleagues. He is the judge most likely to initiate any change in position after the postargument vote because he does more work by far on the case. His clerk's research, his further thinking, or even the opinion-writing process may change his mind. Judges like to point out that an important function of written opinions is that sometimes (but apparently not often) an opinion "just does not write," forcing its author to rethink his conclusions. The other judges are unlikely to have touched the case since the postargument conference unless they had decided there to dissent. Then after they study the draft, they may make suggestions to the writer, or circulate separate opinions if they dislike the draft enough. The assigned judge, once he has circulated an opinion, is very unlikely to change his views drastically; although according to what several judges and clerks said, most judges on rare occasions have been persuaded to rewrite an opinion the other way or to drop it and "sign" a colleague's opposing opinion. Justices in the great majority of state supreme courts, including the four studied here, then discuss the opinions and vote in an "opinion conference," as it is often called. If a judge wishes to study the case further, or if the opinion needs major changes, it is brought again to a later opinion conference. Opinions at a number of courts routinely go through two or more conference discussions. The circuit courts and several state courts do not hold opinion conferences; instead the judges vote and suggest changes through informal meetings, letters, and phone calls.

This is a rough outline of the decision-making procedures (much of it was discussed more thoroughly in Chapter 5, and the interactions involved in producing opinions will be expanded upon later in this chapter), but it suffices to show that judges ordinarily have several opportunities to study and rethink the issues. Changes can occur all along, though in probably most cases a judge's first impression only becomes firmer and firmer in the later stages. Judges often pride themselves on the ability to "keep an open mind," and one reason for judicial secrecy is to prevent irretractable publically held positions. In addition, one of the many definitions of objectivity, a highly prized quality, is the ability to keep an open mind until one has listened to all the arguments and considered the case fully. Information from counsel, from independent research, and from the other judges should not fall on deaf ears before the case is decided.[3] According to comments by a number of clerks and judges, this ideal is fairly close to what actually happens. A few judges though complained that one or two of their colleagues are intransigent once they have circulated a draft opinion, and the clerks, especially, said that a few judges refuse to consider opposing arguments when they feel very strongly about an issue. As will be discussed in Chapter 9, judges may decide how they would like to rule on an issue and then search for authority as support. Nevertheless, if the authority is contrary, with rare exceptions, the judge will change his mind or, infrequently, change the law. Therefore, what is often called "result-oriented" decision making does not mean that judges close their minds to further information.[4]

ASSIGNMENT OF CASES AND SPECIALIZATION

American judges are generalists. All but a few appellate courts have very broad jurisdictions,[5] and judges must decide a wide range of issues. Moreover, judges frown on specialization within the courts,[6] mainly because specialization may hinder the ideal that each judge should form an independent judgment in each case; thus cases ordinarily are not assigned on the basis of the judges' interests or specialized knowledge.

Two methods are used to assign cases: (1) Roughly three-fourths of the state supreme courts use an automatic method; the judges draw cases by lot or, more often, receive them by rotation. The assignments are generally made when the briefs come in, though several courts wait till the postargument conference. (2) Virtually all the remaining state supreme courts and all the U.S. circuit courts leave the assigning to the judgment of the chief judge or the presiding judge of a panel, and this is done after the arguments. There is considerable debate about which system is better.[7] Those advocating rotation say it evens the case load over time, limits feelings that one has been unfairly given the duller and more time-consuming cases, and relieves the already overworked chief judge from the chore of balancing assignments. Those advocating assignment by the chief judge say that it offers more flexibility; without it the slower judges develop backlogs and the few extremely time-consuming cases put an extra load on one or two judges (though, in practice, cases can be and often are reassigned when such problems occur). Also, it is said, better opinions result if the judges' competence and interests are one basis for assignments. Both systems are accused of fostering one-man decisions—that is, less than full understanding of the case by nonassigned judges. Because rotation assignments are normally made before arguments, the assigned judge may be the only judge to prepare before the arguments or even afterward. Assignment by the chief judge based on specialization may leave judges with little knowledge of some types of issues. But in practice the nonassigned judges' understanding of a case depends mainly on the judges' feelings about the amount of work they should do, rather than on the assignment system. In all, the preferred system depends on the judges' attitudes toward specialized assignments and on the chief judge's willingness and ability to assign cases fairly, a task that Judge Medina of the Second Circuit called the hardest and most delicate part of his job.[8]

To be more specific about the relation between assignment systems and specialization, first, assignment strictly by rotation or lot obviously limits specialization because judges must write on whatever issues they get by chance. But the random assignments are not always adhered to. If the assigned judge is in the minority, another judge virtually always writes the majority opinion, often a judge who is particularly interested in the area. Justices on the Rhode Island and focal courts, and probably most others using the rotation system, sometimes swap cases and take cases from overloaded colleagues. The swapping ordinarily occurs because two cases involving similar issues are before the court at the same time or because the judges especially like or dislike certain issues. But this happens in only a few cases. For example, during one year at the focal court, a fifth of the majority opinions were written by judges who did not receive the case by rotation, but in half of these cases the assigned judge was in the minority and filed a dissenting or concurring opinion. In Ohio the justices rarely if ever tamper with the random assignments largely because the judges draw cases by lot after discussing them in the postargument conference, and only the judges in the majority draw. In all, there is little selective handling of cases and, thus, specialization under the rotation or lot systems.[9]

Assignment by the chief or presiding judge, of course, permits more specialization, and practices vary somewhat from court to court. At the Massachusetts court there is very little tendency for cases to go to judges expert in the area, but there is considerable specialization in that traditionally the chief justice retains the bulk of the most important cases for himself. At the First and Sixth Circuits, and apparently at the other circuit courts as well, the assignments are made quite informally; a case often goes to a judge who requests it or otherwise shows the most interest in it. This naturally leads to a tendency for certain types of cases to go to certain judges. But there is a strong feeling that cases in one area of the law should not all be given the same judge and that each judge should write once in a while in each area. These three courts seem to be typical of other courts where opinions are assigned by the chief or presiding judge.[10] By far the major criteria always, it should be kept in mind, is to spread the work load evenly.

Specialization is also limited at the circuit courts by the system of arranging the three-judge panels. At the Sixth Circuit and probably most others, cases are given to panels without regard to the types of issues they contain. Thus the judges must at least sit on a random assortment of appeals.[11]

In spite of this limited specialization on appellate courts, judges do have different amounts of expertise in different areas of the law—gained from experience while on the court because of cases handled or, especially, experience before joining the court. The varying careers of judges produce, in a limited way, courts of specialists; each judge has more in-depth knowledge about the areas of life in which he has worked. This, as will be seen later, provides the courts with sources of information about the practical aspects of these areas.

THE OPINION

The rest of this chapter describes the production of written opinions by appellate courts, the last stage in the decision process, at least when opinions are actually written. (Some courts, especially those without discretionary jurisdiction, decide a large portion of their cases without opinions or with very short memorandums that explain little.) The emphasis will be on the very difficult question: how well does an opinion reflect the judges' reasons for deciding the case? This task is necessary because the next six chapters use opinions as one indication of what information judges use when deciding. Thus the opinion-writing process must be studied in some detail. No definite answers, however, can be given due to the two obstacles to the study of appellate decision making discussed in the first chapter.

An opinion, first of all, obviously does not reflect the reasoning process through which its author arrived at the decision, for the judicial opinion-writing style does not attempt that, and, anyway, the author may not know much about what that process was. Certainly, as is often said, an opinion does not indicate "the doubts with which the judge has wrestled in the process of reaching his decision."[12] Whether the opinion reflects the final reasons —the final results of his deliberations—depends on whether he is conscious of the reasons and whether the conscious reasons are those in the opinion. Unconscious reasons must remain hidden; there is no way to study them. Therefore, whatever is said about opinions reflecting the reasons behind the decisions must be qualified by admitting that there may well be unconscious, unstated reasons.

JUDGES' AND CLERKS' VIEWS ABOUT WHETHER OR NOT REASONS ARE IN OPINIONS. The judges and clerks almost always said that the reasons for decisions are, on the whole, placed in the opinions.[13] Some were more forceful than others about this, but most said unreservedly that the reasons are in the opinions, for example:

Q — Do your opinions accurately reflect the reasons for your decisions?
A — I like to think so.
Q — Are there underlying reasons behind the opinions that you do not put in?
A — No, I would say not. I would say that the opinion is supposed to be an honest representation of what the thinking of the judge on the court is. It's never occurred to me that it wouldn't be.

Few other judges or clerks, however, used "honest" or similar terms in this context. There is no strict rule that opinions must reflect judges' reasons; it is just the preferred writing style. About a third of the judges and clerks said that the opinions sometimes do not show all the reasons behind the decisions, but generally added that this does not happen often or that they (or their judges) try to avoid letting it happen. On the other hand, a few rare judges do not seem to care that their opinions regularly show reasons different from those behind their decisions; one said, for example, that he often writes a first draft for himself and then rewrites it to make an opinion more acceptable to the other judges, circulating only the revised version.

There are a number of exceptions, probably applicable to every judge and every opinion, to the general rule that judges expect the opinions to reflect their reasoning. Several judges said, and surely all would agree, that they often leave out issues not needed for the decision or leave out less important lines of reasoning within the issues decided. An equally important exception, though seldom mentioned in the interviews, is that the citation of a precedent may represent (and leave unstated) a bundle of reasons that lie behind why the precedent is persuasive. There is, also, much unstated legal and social philosophy behind any decision. For example, when relying on precedent, judges virtually never say why precedent should be followed or whether the precedent is viewed as dictating or only allowing the result. Judges, moreover, rarely discuss why they decide what they decide—why they rule on some issues and not others and why a ruling is broad or narrow. In sum, judges and clerks exaggerate when they claim that the opinions reflect the reasons for decisions; every opinion involves exceptions such as these. But then, any reason given for any decision has other reasons behind it; the opinions would be extremely long if these were spelled out, and judges normally dislike long opinions.[14] (The Massachusetts and Ohio courts have traditionally emphasized short opinions more than the other four courts studied here.)

More important to this study, judges sometimes rely on certain types of information without mentioning them in the opinions. This is true of facts of the case that judges are not supposed to consider, for example, facts outside the record, facts that pertain only to the equities of the particular case (called "fireside equities" here), and characteristics of the litigants or attorneys that displease a judge but are not relevant to the issues. These will be discussed in Chapters 11 and 12, but they are of limited importance, at most.

That is not true, however, of policy arguments. It was said earlier that a third of the judges and clerks, when asked whether the opinions reflect the reasons for decisions, answered that some opinions do not. They usually said that this is so because passages are added or left out to satisfy colleagues, a topic to be discussed shortly, or because policy reasons are left out. One important type of policy reasons is the topic of later chapters—the social facts used in developing the law. Robert Leflar, a former Arkansas justice and a major scholar of appellate decision making, wrote:

Comparatively few judicial opinions, with the possible exception of those of the United States Supreme Court, undertake to go fully into all the reasons underlying the decision at the conference table stage. There is no dishonesty in this; it is only that these "real" conference table reasons do not read like law, and that they often are practical social and economic reasons rather than technical legal reasons, and that many opinion writers think their opinions ought to read like pure law undiluted by the facts of sociology and life. Some state court judges, and most United States Supreme Court Justices, realize that these "real" reasons are as much part of the law as are the legal rules and concepts that tie them together, and these judges try to put the whole combination of reasons into their opinions.[15]

Most of the judges were specifically asked whether their opinions contain the social facts important to the decisions. Less than half said they regularly do; most said they are not always aired.[16] In fact, a few judges said in one part of the interview that their opinions reflect their reasons, and in another part that social facts may be left out. Just how often these facts are not mentioned, however, is uncertain because the judges gave inexact answers, saying they are "not always" or "only sometimes" mentioned, for example. None said they are always left out. The Ohio justices are less likely than the others to mention the social facts, a lingering effect of former Chief Justice Weygandt's emphasis on stark opinions. In a related matter, the use of social science or other empirical data sometimes is not evidenced in the opinions.[17]

Over a dozen judges have written about whether reasons for decisions are placed in opinions, and the great majority believe they often are not, especially because policy arguments may be left out.[18] In fact, the difference between these writings and what was said in the interviews is quite startling. Some of the judges interviewed apparently answered in terms of what they believed was expected of them, rather than what they did in practice, as is evidenced by those who said they put their reasons in their opinions but elsewhere said they left out some social fact arguments.[19] Probably more important, however, is a recent shift in the judges' practices. "The great change in my lifetime in judicial opinion writing," said Justice Braucher of Massachusetts in a recent judicial conference, "has to do with the increase in candor."[20] And there was strong evidence in the interviews that opinions at two other state courts studied here, the focal and Ohio courts, now explain the judges' reasoning much more than they did a decade or two ago.

In general, the argument for not fully explaining why a decision is reached, and especially for leaving out policy arguments, are to limit the length of opinions and to preserve the respect and popular support given the courts, since otherwise the courts will be seen as lawmakers rather than law appliers (though by now judges routinely admit and accept the lawmaking role). Also, a full account of the author's reasoning may lead other judges to write separate opinions because they disagree with some of the reasoning. The reasons given for candid opinions are: They tell the bar and other judges how broad or narrow the ruling is. They tell counsel what sorts of information they should give judges in future cases. They make judges study more closely their reasoning and, thus, their decisions. Last and very important, they indicate the strength of the precedent created. If based on hidden (or admitted but unpersuasive) considerations, the precedent is less likely to influence other courts and may not withstand later attacks in the same court. A circuit judge, for example, told me about being overruled by the U.S. Supreme Court because the Court, as he later found out by talking to the Justice who wrote the opinion there, "hadn't seen the point that I had in mind, and I hadn't put it in the opinion; I had thought it was obvious." This and a few other similar disappointments, he said, taught him to state his reasons more thoroughly.[21]

TAILORING OPINIONS TO SUIT OTHERS. A major reason why an opinion may not reflect the writer's reasons is obviously that he may have in mind readers whom he wishes to impress, please, appease, or the like. This is a large topic, involving, first, the audience that judges have in mind when writing and, second, the bargaining process that opinions go through before publication.

The judges were asked who they would like to impress when writing opinions.[22] Half said they do not care—or at least are not conscious of caring—about impressing anybody but themselves. The other half mentioned a wide variety of groups, the bar and other judges being the most common by far, but most added that this is very secondary to the wish to please themselves. Judges, thus, view themselves as very self-willed and are not likely to abandon their own reasons for those they believe would impress others. This does not mean, however, that they write only for themselves, for they have in mind very definite audiences, which differ from case to case. They wish to give the losing parties the impression that the court has considered their arguments—wishes them "to feel they've had a good run for their money," as one judge said. Likewise, when reversing a lower court judge, they wish to show that his positions had been considered. On the lawmaking side, they try to make opinions and precedents serviceable to the lawyers and judges who must use them. The last may lead to opinions too short to explain fully the underlying reasons (because lawyers constantly complain about the burden that long opinions place on them), but otherwise writing for these audiences should not influence judges to write opinions that do not reflect their reasoning, provided the reasoning is based on considerations considered legitimate in legal circles. This is not the case, though, with some other audiences: the public, higher courts, and especially other judges on the same court.

The judiciary is traditionally viewed as the branch of government least answerable to or moved by the public. In fact appellate judges generally say that public opinion has no or very little effect on their decisions.[23] But this is far from the whole story. The public opinion that judges ignore is the public opinion about which side of an appeal should win; there are many other aspects of public opinion that do affect the judges. For example, they are greatly concerned about the courts' overall reputation, viewing that as the basis of the courts' strength and, thus, the strength of the legal system as a whole.[24] One outgrowth of this is the emphasis on showing the losing party that his arguments were considered; another is the view, probably not common now, that opinions should not overtly state that the court is making law. These two were mentioned earlier. A similar practice is keeping public reaction, especially press reaction, in mind when wording opinions (as opposed to when reaching decisions); judges may leave out language that could lead to attacks, or explain the holding with extra care so that the press does not misinterpret it.[25] This does not happen often, though, since the press pays no attention to the vast bulk of cases decided by courts below the U.S. Supreme Court level. Also, for public image—and not to hurt feelings —judges ordinarily do not vent their low opinion of work done by colleagues, trial judges, or attorneys.

A few rare opinions are written with an eye toward persuading another court upon appeal or collateral attack.[26] The opinion may even be considered a brief, and arguments may be added not because they are a basis for the decision but because they might persuade judges elsewhere.

By far the most important audience is the opinion writer's colleagues; he may tailor his opinion to get their votes or simply to please them. This can be done both before and after the opinion draft is circulated: the author might have the wishes of his colleagues in mind when writing the draft, or he might accede to suggestions they make after reading the draft. This incorporation of others' views is more likely when needed to gather a majority behind an opinion; few judges are indifferent about whether their opinions become precedents, whereas some care little about getting more than enough to form a majority (though others strongly desire a unanimous court).[27] In this process the opinion writer may add points to his opinion that are not his reasons for deciding the issues or, more frequently, delete reasons he believes important.

Whether the assigned judge attempts to incorporate the views of his colleagues in the initial writing depends largely on how thoroughly the issues are discussed in the postargument conference. The Rhode Island justices often give little more than their views about the outcome; so the opinion writer may not know what reasoning the others want. The focal court justices state their views at length, and the opinion writer can easily incorporate them when he wishes. The practice on the other four courts falls somewhere between these two. However, consciously tailoring opinions at this stage is not common, even on the focal court. One justice, who is probably typical, said he does this in only about 10 percent of his draft opinions; but the justice mentioned earlier who said he regularly rewrote his drafts with the others in mind is on the same court. Also, Judge Oakes of the Second Circuit said recently:

Courts of appeals, at least, have almost a built-in inexactness because they are committees. We necessarily compromise; at least the majority opinion represents a collection of thoughts and oftentimes compromises, indeed, sometimes some fudging. We work in time frames and with the pressure of statistics. We cannot always articulate all the major, let alone the minor premises. Of course, that's why it is more fun to write a dissent than a majority opinion.[28]

The Second Circuit, though, is a unique court. Between the arguments and the postargument conference each judge on the panel writes a memorandum in all substantial appeals; hence the assigned judge has before him a rather elaborate statement of the others' views to take into account when writing.[29]

In one extreme situation an opinion does not reflect the author's reasoning at all. A 1957 study[30] found that on several courts a judge might write a majority opinion for the court and then a dissenting opinion for himself. This practice was rare, however, on most of these courts, and it has probably been virtually abandoned by now. Massachusetts opinions do indicate once in a while that the author is stating the majority view, not his own, on a particular point, but judges no longer write majority opinions when they dissent. One focal court justice used to write per curium opinions for the court and then write dissenting or concurring opinions expressing his views. But this practice was quite rare.

After the assigned judge finishes his opinion draft, the others have a chance to suggest changes. Judges on the six courts, as is typical of appellate judges everywhere, pride themselves on the amount of attention given others' opinions. ''One man decisions'' is one of the most pejorative labels that can be applied to a court's work. (A few state supreme courts assign a second judge to check the work of the writing judge, and this may lead to two man decisions.) In fact, the bulk of the opinions in the six courts are hashed over at length; some opinions, though, do sail through without comment, particularly in cases considered clear-cut and particularly in June, when the judges rush to finish before the summer break. The circuit judges do not hold opinion conferences; they discuss the opinions on a one-to-one basis, mainly over the phone because their offices tend to be in different towns. Less of this sort of communication takes place in the state courts, since the bulk of the opinion discussion is in conferences, though the courts usually have specific pairs or sets of justices who do much informal talking, often in their offices or at lunch.

How often the drafts are changed at the suggestion of other judges varies greatly from court to court and from opinion writer to opinion writer. At five of the courts studied changes are made often, probably in most opinions, according to what the judges and clerks said. In Rhode Island, though, changes are much less frequent. Also, within the courts some judges make changes much more often than others, especially in the Sixth Circuit and the focal and Rhode Island courts. Many things lead to these differences. Opinions in unimportant cases are less likely to attract comments and require changes. The Rhode Island court issues many more such opinions than the others. Some courts and judges try harder than others for consensus opinions. This may simply mean that concurring judges go along with the majority opinion in spite of reservations; but, if they are not inclined to do that, it may lead the opinion writer to accept more freely suggestions from colleagues to prevent separate opinions. Some judges are thought by their colleagues to do especially thorough jobs on their opinions, leaving less to comment about. Also, a few judges dislike receiving any comments and are not prone to accept those given, though this attitude is limited largely to older judges, and the prevailing attitude is that comments on important matters are welcome and helpful and that changes should be made freely.

Suggestions about less important matters, however, are a different story. The major reason for the differences between judges and courts on how often draft opinions are changed is the attitude toward requests for small changes in language—"nit-picking requests," the judges call them—concerning, for example, syntax, clarity of sentences, or appropriateness of particular words. Judges usually consider these comments helpful. But they annoy some judges, who, therefore, are unlikely to comply with or receive them. The Massachusetts justices are especially free with nit-picking comments, and the Rhode Island justices especially wary of them. At any rate, minor changes far outnumber major changes. The latter are unusual on all six courts. The judges, though, vary a good bit; a few make major changes in as many as a fifth of their opinions, and a few more never make them.[31]

Interpersonal relations among the judges can also greatly affect the number of suggestions made and the general flow of information in the courts. As might be expected of small groups of men who must interact constantly, appellate judges greatly stress friendliness.[32] The job would be unpleasant, they say, if the judges could not get along. The judges do get along very well on the six courts, though several years ago strong animosities plagued the focal court. I was given secondhand accounts of feuds there (and at some other courts also) in which judges refused to communicate with each other; obviously, this limits the number of suggested changes and other comments about draft opinions. The reason judges might not get along, it was generally said, is personality clashes rather than ideological or other disagreements; judges should be able to disagree heartily and even heatedly without being personal enemies.[33] The typical view is: "Every single judge has marvelous faculties of agreeing and disagreeing—and disagreeing *vehemently*—without being disagreeable. I think that's a tribute to the personalities of the judges." Indeed, when asked if they felt they could say anything to their colleagues about the draft opinions, most said they could. Several, though, said they refrained from some comments, especially nit-picking comments, in order to maintain friendly relations. Justice Schaefer is of this view: "The relationship among judges is a personal one and a continuing one, and effectiveness can be blunted by excessive suggestions. The balance between complacent acquiescense and overassertiveness is delicate indeed.[34] This worry is not typical, though, at least among the judges interviewed. "I think it's absolutely important that people around you will let you know honestly what they think," said a circuit judge about both his clerks and his colleagues. "I think you do much better if you do that than if you spend your time soothing one another, saying how great everything is."

(A rather ticklish question in appellate courts is whether judges should vent in published opinions their full feelings about colleagues' views. Probably most courts have strong informal rules against this;[35] thus many opinions, especially dissents, hide the authors' feelings. At other courts, though, the judges bitterly attack each other in print; this happens at the focal court and at the U.S. Supreme Court.[36] Opinions of this kind, by the way, need not indicate ill will; they often indicate, rather, that the judges' relations are so secure that they are not damaged by public frankness.)

That an opinion writer adds or deletes things at the request of other judges does not in itself mean that the opinion fails to reflect his reasoning; he may agree with the request in that, upon reflection, it conforms with his reasoning. In fact, by far the major criteria given by judges for complying or not complying with a colleague's request is whether they agree with it.[37] A good number, however, especially in Massachusetts, said they also make some changes they disagree with or are neutral toward, especially if the colleague feels strongly about the point, as long as "it doesn't seem to do any particular damage to the opinion," as one judge phrased it. In these situations, then, the opinion contains material that is not a reason behind the author's decision or, when the colleague persuades him to delete things, does not show reasons he would like to announce.

Incidently, other than in the ordinary bargaining process described so far, there is no sign on these courts that any judge has enough influence to force another to phrase opinions (or, for that matter, vote) against his will. The judges are thought to be "individuals" in that they are not particularly influenced by any of their colleagues. There are some exceptions, though, to this statement. The judge assigned to write the opinion tends to be the most influential in that appeal because he does most of the work and can present more information to support his position. Also judges with expertise in the area of the case and, on some courts, one or two especially hardworking and respected judges are listened to with more deference than others.[38]

THE VIEWS OF CONCURRING JUDGES. An opinion is much less likely to reflect the views of those concurring with it than the views of the author.

Although the concurring judges tend to study the opinion fairly thoroughly and often make suggestions to the writing judge, they ordinarily go along with things they would prefer not to see in the opinion, rather than concur separately. Currently, but not several decades ago, judges on very few courts frown upon the idea of separate opinions, but in general they do like to limit them for the convenience of the bar. Thus, there is, as one judge said, "quite a lot of author's prerogative" in the opinion writing. If a concurring judge cannot persuade the writer otherwise, he will still go along with the length and writing style of the opinion, for example, and with the amount of authority cited and the use of secondary authorities. To a lesser extent, he will also go along with obiter dicta, narrowness or breadth of the ruling, and even the reasoning used to reach the result. Judges vary, of course, in their propensity to write separate opinions, though as a general rule they will do so more often when they feel strongly about a point, when they think the point is important to the development of the law, and when they are not pressed for time. These considerations apply mainly to separate concurrences, though on rare occasions, especially in Rhode Island and Massachusetts, some judges have signed majority opinions even when they disagreed with the holdings.

SUMMARY: OPINIONS REFLECTING REASONS FOR DECISIONS. This is an extremely complex subject. Opinions obviously do not reflect all, or probably even most, of the reasons why judges decide, in spite of the judges' and clerks' beliefs that they ordinarily do. Unconscious reasons are unknowable. Background philosophies are often left unstated. The inclusion of policy and practical factors are largely a matter of the writer's discretion. Various things are added to or, more often, deleted from opinions for the benefit of colleagues and others. Karl Llewellyn, who knew as much about appellate judging as anyone, championed the use of opinions to study how judges decide. The opinions are, he said, "rich ore, if worked with care." Nevertheless, he believed them largely adversary statements, directed toward colleagues, and said they do not accurately reflect more than a third of the "motivating stimuli" behind decisions. But he claims that this affects little one's ability to learn enough from opinions to predict how judges will approach and decide future cases.[39] Perhaps his upper figure of a third is accurate, but guesses here are risky. Whether opinions shed much light on how judges think is equally uncertain; judges probably do not know that themselves, and, as Llewellyn admits, one often cannot tell the relative importance of different arguments in opinions. Probably the most inscrutable parts of opinions are the use of precedent: the citation of a case may mean that the judge feels the precedent dictates or only allows the decision, and a citation is often a shorthand sign representing a large body of reasoning behind it.

In the following chapters, however, the opinions will be used as an indication of what information the judges use in making decisions, and seldom as evidence of how the information is used; thus many of these problems are not involved. As a general rule, the information mentioned in opinions are factors in the opinion writer's decision, except to the extent that things are added solely for the benefit of other judges.[40] But this exception is not common; judges do not often write with others in mind or make major changes in their draft opinions at others' requests, and even then they ordinarily agree with the changes. The interviews indicate, too, that tailoring opinions for other judges less often involves adding information to the opinion that restricts or clarifies the opinion by narrowing the holding, taking out dicta, and the like. Therefore, even if the opinion writer complies with a suggestion he disagrees with, the opinion is not likely to include information he did not use. Furthermore, even when things are added for the benefit of other judges, it is information that either the other judges think important or the writing judge believes they think important; thus they are still a good indication of what information judges on the whole use.

On the other hand, to say that the information mentioned in opinions is behind the decisions does not mean that all the information is there. It is not, for the many reasons just discussed, and because some types of information are more likely to be mentioned than others. When opinions do not reflect the reasons for decisions, it is a matter of omission; the reasons given are very unlikely to be bogus. The opinions contain the truth, but far from the whole truth. Therefore, during the next six chapters the information mentioned in the opinions must be considered as an accurate but incomplete indication of what information is used.

Part III

Five Types of Information

CHAPTER 8

Issues _____

The next six chapters discuss five types of information: issues, legal authority, facts of the case, social facts, and empirical data. One chapter is devoted to each type, and a sixth, Chapter 10, discusses the various categories of facts used in appellate decision making. The major concerns in these six chapters are: the importance of each type of information to the courts' dispute-deciding and lawmaking functions, how much the judges rely on the adversary system as a source for the information, how the judges find information when it is not brought forth by the attorneys, and how the judges deal with the problems of overload—that is, of having too much extraneous information given by counsel. In addition, Chapters 11, 12, and 13 look into how the judges evaluate the factual information they use. Part IV ties together the findings in Part III and discusses their implications for appellate decision making.

ISSUES—FOREWORD

Issues are the most important information attorneys give an appellate court. The courts decide issues, and determining what to decide is the sine qua non of any decision—an important truism. Rulings on the various issues in a case total up to a decision for the plaintiff or defendant (or, sometimes, for neither). Appellate courts create law by deciding issues, not cases; the ruling on an issue, not the whole case, is precedent for rulings on the same and similar issues in other disputes.[1] Unless equities peculiar to the case enter the judgment, issues determine what legal rules, facts of the case, and social facts may influence the court. Also, the briefs and opinions are ordinarily organized around issues; each issue is discussed in a separate section. A list of issues is placed at the very beginning of the briefs, before the statement of facts.

This basic point of this chapter is that appellate judges rely greatly on the adversary system to find issues and to weed out irrelevant issues, even though issues are such an important type of information. Judges largely abdicate to counsel the job of finding issues. They would like to be presented only the most substantial issues in a case, but lawyers do not always cooperate, thus adding to the court's work load.

An issue, as one writer said, is "incapable of any precise definition."[2] But judges and lawyers routinely use the word "issue" and its synonym, "question,"[3] without defining them; and I know of no debates about what the terms mean. A rough definition is an interconnected bunch of facts, legal rules, and interpretation of legal authority that presents the court with an opportunity to make a decision favoring one side or the other. Separate issues exist when they involve unrelated and dissimilar facts of the case or legal arguments.[4] If there is no dispute about the legal rules or the facts of the case, the issues are called fact issues or law issues, respectively.

A topic not covered here is the refining of issues, but it is important enough to deserve a brief mention. Much of appellate decision making consists of the judges' attempts to define and refine each issue they decide, delimiting the facts and legal authorities they must consider when making a decision. An important aspect of appellate advocacy is the presentation of issues in a manner allowing the court to understand quickly what must be decided and in a manner that leads the court to decide in one's favor. Likewise, the judges often complain that the attorneys do not define the issues well. One of the more common complaints in the judges' writings about appellate advocacy, discussed in Chapter 3, is that the issues should be stated clearly and specifically. Over 10 percent of the focal court justices' questions in oral arguments were attempts to get the attorneys to do this, especially by asking them to state their contentions more precisely.

FINDING ISSUES—LAWYERS

One of the basic jobs of a lawyer is to sift through the facts of a dispute to determine what issues may lead a court to rule for one side or the other. Ordinarily, issues are found long before the trial stage, and they become the framework for the trial proceedings. Sometimes, however, an unanticipated event at trial, such as a procedural ruling by the judge, produces an additional issue; the trial lawyer may spot the issue at the time, or the lawyer on appeal may later uncover it while reading the record.

When the lawyers were asked in the interviews how they found issues, they gave only very general answers (except prosecutors on appeal who did not find issues but only waited to see what the defense counsel threw at them.) Most lawyers said it was a question of legal ability and experience or knowing the law thoroughly. "It's a *creative* task," one said, "you have to be familiar with the law, and what I mean by the law is all the potential issues that have ever been raised in any appellate court in the country." Also, they commonly said that it is the basic task of a lawyer or the purpose of a law school education.

Q — How do you find issues in a case?
A — Well, that's what you spend three years in law school for.
Q — It's just the art of being a lawyer?
A — That's exactly correct. As I understand it, a lawyer's art is being able to find out where the problem is. The secondary part of it is to find the answers to the problem.

Several others said the issues just popped out or were found through intuition. "That's like asking me what qualities I find attractive in a woman. That's an impossible question. It's an intuitive thing—your intuitive intelligence." Lastly, they frequently said the issues must be found from studying the facts thoroughly. "You know the case; you know the facts. You have to sort out the issues from the facts." If there is a new attorney for the appellate stage, finding issues requires minute knowledge of the trial record, especially in criminal cases.

That was hell to read one thousand and twelve pages of transcript. What you do when you're an appellate counsel and you haven't tried the case—you don't know a god damned thing about what happened—you got to read it *over* a couple of times and get some brief ideas, and then you go back and look for what we consider to be points of error.

Thus, the ability to find issues depends greatly on the skill, knowledge, and industry of counsel; yet here the appellate judges rely on the adversary system more than for any other type of information, except the case facts in the record.

DECIDING ISSUES NOT RAISED

The adversary process is no more starkly challenged than when a court decides an issue not raised, for it actually decides something other than what the parties asked it to decide. Courts, it is often said, are rather passive organizations because they must await decision opportunities given them by outsiders, the attorneys. This is true not so much because courts cannot initiate law suits, for there is always a plentiful supply of those with which to make law, but because, as a matter of choice by the judges, they almost always stick to the issues presented by counsel; and even when they do not, it is ordinarily not to create law but to decide the specific case justly.

The judges on the six courts studied here generally said they are very reluctant to decide issues not raised; very few said they make a regular practice of it.[5] The main reason given was, not surprisingly, the wish to preserve the adversary system.[6] The losing attorney is unfairly deprived of the chance to present his views, and the court has received no help from counsel on the issue. One judge said about such issues:

We don't know enough about them. You're playing God then because you haven't had the benefit of the lawyers, the judge below, or the clients, or the evidence. You're just playing God without a record, and you have to assume a certain competence in your counsel. . . . I'm loath to do it. I have done it, I guess. I really don't like to because it's too dangerous. There's nothing worse than a lawyer being beaten by an assumption that simply is incorrect and wasn't raised.

These problems, however, can be mitigated by giving counsel a chance to argue the issue. The court can call for supplementary briefs, ask about the issue in the oral arguments, or look closely at the petition for rehearing. The Rhode Island court and the circuit courts insist, by and large, that the parties be given a chance to brief the subject, while the other three courts are more likely to decide on their own.[7] One Ohio justice said that the court does not ask for rebriefing because the time spent waiting for the supplementary briefs would affect the court's record of deciding cases quickly. On very rare occasions, if the new issue requires facts not in the record, appellate courts send cases back to the trial court for further testimony.

Another common reason given for sticking to issues in the briefs is a general rule (with, however, many exceptions) against reversing the trial court on issues not raised there. Decisive issues not raised on appeal are probably seldom in the trial record, for otherwise appellate counsel would be aware of them (though he may miss their significance). Judges dislike deciding issues not raised below for varying reasons. Some think it unfair to reverse a trial judge who has made no error. Some cite the traditional notion that an appellate court's sole job is to correct errors below. Other reasons are more practical: The trial judge and opposing attorney may have been able to cure the defect had it been brought to their attention, and trial counsel may have knowingly refused to raise the issue as a matter of trial tactics.[8]

Nevertheless, appellate judges do decide issues not raised by the attorneys. Nearly all judges interviewed said they had at one time or another. It is very difficult, though, to tell just how often it happens. Sometimes a dissenting opinion airs it, but probably only those who have read the briefs know in most cases. The practice is especially hidden on courts where it is such a common practice that it is not a grounds for dissent. Thus one must go beyond the opinions to study this topic; here I have compared the focal court opinions with the briefs and asked judges on the six courts about the practice.

Majority opinions in 16 of the 112 focal court appeals studied here ruled on issues not raised—19 issues in all.[9] No particular type of case predominated, and they included 3 of the most important decided by the court that year. Each judge wrote at least 1 of these opinions, but one judge wrote 7, far more than any of the other six judges. Examples are ruling that a statute is unconstitutional after the attorneys argued only about its interpretation or interpreting a statute in favor of an appellant who contested it only on constitutional grounds. Twice the court found that the record did not contain sufficient evidence to support plaintiff's claim, without any mention of this issue by the parties.[10] Only about half of the 19 issues were, in my judgment, strictly needed for the decisions. The rest were just alternative reasons,[11] though a number of them were probably decided because they would arise again on retrial. Still, even these alternative reasons were usually presented as a major basis for the decision. The court seldom gave the attorneys a chance to brief the new issues or argue them in rehearing. In three cases counsel were asked about the issues in oral arguments, but they gave the court very little help.

Thus the court decided an issue not raised in about 1 case in 7. The 19 issues represented 8 percent of all issues decided in the 112 cases studied (the average opinion decided two issues). In the vast majority of situations, then, the court decided only what was presented by counsel.

Even so, the number of issues not raised decided in these cases is probably atypically large—even for the focal court, judging by what the clerks and judges said about earlier and later periods. But, again, it is hard to tell how often judges decide these issues. In the interviews the judges and clerks gave rather inexact guesses, though all but a few judges said they had done it. The practice is the most common, according to what was said, at the focal and Rhode Island courts, and is about equally uncommon at the other four courts. In Massachusetts it is largely limited to criminal cases involving capital crimes; a statute allows the court to search for issues not raised in these cases.[12] The circuit courts are much more likely to decide procedural questions not raised than substantive ones. Also, there is considerable difference of opinion within all but the Massachusetts court and the First Circuit, and even some bitter debates, over the propriety of the practice, touching as it does the core of the adversary system. The rather frequent comment in the legal literature about deciding issues not raised suggests only that courts and judges around the country vary as much as those studied here.[13]

What determines whether a judge will decide an issue not raised? First of all, the issue must be found. Rarely do judges actually search for new issues; rather they just happen to notice them while doing research, reading the briefs and records, or hearing oral argument. Law clerks and staff attorneys also find some issues. Often, however, issues are found and ignored; at one extreme a law clerk said he noticed issues that the attorneys had missed in half the cases his judge was assigned,[14] but the court ruled on few of them.

Therefore, the second question is what determines whether the issue will be used. Judges have no qualms about deciding one class of issues not raised, those having to do with whether the court should decide the case—issues about jurisdiction, mootness, standing, and appealability.[15] Other than this it appears to be optional with the judge. The focal court rule, applied to issues not raised at trial as well as on appeal, is that issues not raised will be ignored unless doing so would result in an injustice. As was said in Chapter 1 when discussing the term "justice," this is a very uncertain standard, and it leaves the judges a good deal of discretion. A clerk said the rule meant that "if it really hits you, you will take it." Other courts often use "justice" or other elusive standards, such as "plain error" or "fundamental error," in determining when to decide an issue not raised.[16]

Because precedent is a ruling on an issue, not a whole case, the failure of counsel to raise, and of the court to decide, an important issue has no effect on the development of the law except the obvious fact that a precedent is not created. The decision whether to decide an issue not raised is ordinarily based on considerations of justice between the litigants; for example, the judges may have to decide if a litigant is to lose even though an established rule, missed by his counsel, supports his claim. Judges differ here, as is best illustrated by these two opposing views:

It's a perception of the function of what the appellate judge is supposed to do. It's easy to fall into the habit of trying to be everything, you know—to correct *every* wrong of every kind. And although that's awfully tempting always, obviously you can't do it. And everybody has a part of the system. The lawyer has, I think, perhaps the most siginficant part of the system for the administration of justice. The judges are certainly important, but their functions are and should be limited, and limited *largely* by their own appraisal of what their role is.

[I will decide issues not raised] at times, if manifest justice demands it. I think that's a view of an individual, and if I'm joined by three of my colleagues, it's the view of the court. . . . Sometimes you think the particular litigant is being badly served by his attorney for *not* raising issues [and you wish] not to punish the litigant because of the error of his attorney.
Q — Well, what does manifest injustice mean?
A — Well, manifest justice is that you know what the result should be, but it wasn't raised. So it would be an injustice to say, "You didn't raise it, therefore you stay in prison."

As the second passage suggests, judges are much more likely to decide issues not raised in criminal cases because the consequences of not doing so tend to be greater than in civil cases.

Courts may also point out a mistake made at the trial, even if not mentioned in the briefs, so that it will not be repeated upon retrial. The focal court twice gave this motive when deciding isues not raised, and it was probably important in two more cases.

Sometimes, though, judges have the lawmaking function uppermost in their minds when deciding issues not raised. Case-by-case adjudication can be a slow and an imperfect vehicle when developing the law, and judges may wish to cure quickly what they see as problems with the present law. The focal court seemed to be doing this in deciding several issues not raised. One opinion, for example, was a long treatise on the issuance of county bonds, aimed at helping the local governments by clarifying their powers. Another lawmaking consideration may be the wish to dodge issues presented by counsel, for example, by leaving tough constitutional issues for a later day. One of the judges interviewed pointed to a different sort of strategy; he disliked affirming summary judgments in tort appeals because he did not want to give the impression that the court favored summary judgments; thus he preferred to decide these cases on other issues, if necessary ones that were not raised.

The reasons for deciding or ignoring issues not raised often lead to a clash of both lawmaking and dispute-deciding considerations. Deciding issues not raised may produce a more comprehensive body of law, but the quality of the law may suffer for being made without the help of counsel. Deciding an issue not raised so that a litigant is not unjustly hurt by the mistakes of his attorney may lead the other side to believe it was unjustly deprived of victory and of its right to a day in court.

Incidentally, the attorneys did not like their cases decided on issues not raised. This was not one of the topics I questioned them about; yet half brought it up themselves, nearly always saying they disliked the practice. This was true even for those who won on the basis of the new issue; they said the cases should have been decided on issues they had argued. Perhaps they felt it did not reflect well on their advocacy. A good number of those who lost were very angry, for example:

The case became somewhat personal to me. I felt, one, [the client] got screwed. Two, I got screwed. He got screwed, that's *pretty bad. Me getting* screwed, that's an imposition up with which I shall not put.
Q — That's because the court decided upon something which you hadn't argued?
A — Yep, yep. I didn't think that was eminently fair treatment.

He said it was unfair because he had not been given a chance to argue the issue, a view several losing counsel gave.

INSUBSTANTIAL ISSUES

Although appellate judges can deal with counsel's failure to find important issues by simply refusing to decide issues not raised, they cannot so easily pass off the opposite problem, that of being overloaded with flimsy issues. In almost any litigation there are innumerable issues on which the attorneys and trial judge must take positions, but nearly always the answer is clear or the trial judge is given broad discretion. Rarely does an appeal contain more than a few issues that present much chance of reversal, and many contain none. Thus, besides finding issues, counsel must pick out those worth raising.

The work load of an appellate court is greatly affected by the attorneys' ability to judge which issues present little chance of success on appeal and by the attorneys' willingness to drop them. Of course, the judges can dispose of insubstantial issues more easily and quickly than tough issues; they need only write a few lines in an opinion to answer the appellant's arguments, or they may not discuss them at all, saying, for example, "We have considered the other issues raised by appellant and find them to be without merit." But, still, the time spent ensuring that the issues actually are insubstantial mounts up if there are a good many of them.

Courts without discretionary jurisdiction receive many appeals containing only insubstantial issues, especially, it is often said, in criminal cases because indigent defendants have nothing to lose by appealing. These courts are resorting, as was discussed in Chapter 2, more and more to summary procedures in these cases, for example, by relying greatly on staff memorandums, dropping oral arguments, and not issuing opinions.

When a court, such as the focal court, can choose the cases it decides, insubstantial appeals present no problem other than adding to the number of applications for leave to appeal or certiorari. Nevertheless, as in all courts, appellants sometimes raise insubstantial issues along with important ones. (When granting leave, courts can, but hardly ever do, limit the issues they want briefed.) A court must decide all issues presented, unless a ruling on one issue makes the others superfluous. The general, but often violated, rule is that if the trial court is reversed on one issue, the court does not decide other issues unless they will arise again on retrial.

The practice of throwing in a series of questionable issues hoping that one will catch the court's interest is variously called the shotgun, buck shot, bird shot, scatter shot, or garbage can approach. This is generally very unpopular with the judges. Of all the suggestions and complaints made by appellate judges in their writings on appellate advocacy, as was discussed in Chapter 3, by far the most common is that counsel should limit themselves to the most important issues and leave out insubstantial ones. Also, in the interviews the judges and law clerks typically said that the shotgun approach is a problem.[17] One focal court justice said:

Q — How often do the attorneys throw in a lot of flimsy issues—the shotgun approach? Does that bother you?

A — Yes, it does. And obviously they do it too often for my taste. Once is too often.

. . . My experience is half of the questions they raised on appeal shouldn't be raised at all.

This passage is typical of the judges interviewed, but probably overstates the problem in the focal court. Judging from the briefs, the shotgun approach does not seem to be that great a problem. Less than 30 percent of the focal court briefs presented more than three issues, and less than a tenth presented more than five. A rough guess as to the number of issues the court considered insubstantial can be derived from the number the court quickly affirmed in the opinions or did not mention even though needed for the decision.[18] This came to roughly a quarter to a third of the issues presented. The great majority of these issues came from cases with more than three issues raised and were, thus, the product of the shotgun approach. The interviews suggested that the circuit judges received substantially more shotgun briefs and more frivolous issues, especially in criminal cases (but civil and criminal cases in the focal court did not differ in this regard).

Judges discussing the shotgun approach commonly say it is a sign of poor advocacy; the lawyer, said one, is "a nit picker or lacks the balance to select out the really hot stuff." Furthermore, the shotgun approach, according to a number of judges both in the interviews and in the writings on advocacy, often detracts from the force of any substantial issues the appellant may have. Suspecting that the lawyer does not know his business, a judge may feel that he need not waste his time studying the briefs carefully; or after reading several flimsy issues he may approach the rest with a presumption that they are equally worthless.

Attorneys are also on the whole very much against the shotgun approach at the appellate level. I asked most of those interviewed whether they believe in this tactic, and nearly all said they do not—they try to present only issues they have a good chance of winning. There were a few exceptions: two defense counsel in criminal cases said they feel, as many elsewhere do, that they have a duty to bring up any possible issue; and one civil lawyer said he had to shotgun because he could not tell what issues might interest the court, citing a case he had just won on an issue he did not raise. The reasons that a number of attorneys volunteered for not using the shotgun approach jibe with the judges' feelings: Weak issues create a prejudice against parties advancing them. They give the impression that counsel does not understand or believe in his case. Or, as was greatly emphasized, they becloud the case and take away from one's strong points. "Courts are human and liable to misunderstand something," an attorney said in a typical comment, "and the more complicated something is, the more likely it is to be misunderstood and to be confused." Thus they agreed with the judges not only on the need to eliminate flimsy issues, but also on the reasons why such issues may hurt one's cause. What could be the natural inclination of counsel to increase his chances of winning by presenting a long list of issues, each with a small chance of success, is largely balanced, at least in civil cases, by other concerns of self-interest—the feeling that one's odds are better on the major issues when not accompanied by lesser ones.

But the lawyers' aversion to shotgunning far from eliminates weak issues, for they may be unable to tell whether the court will consider an issue weak. This involves the attorneys' basic ability as a lawyer, in much the same manner as the ability to find issues, along with their knowledge of the court and of what interests the judges, a problem described in Chapter 4. Probably the great bulk of insubstantial issues in the briefs results from this mismatching of minds between judges and counsel, another example of a major problem with the adversary system: the inability of counsel to determine what information the judges believe is needed for their decisions.

CHAPTER 9

Legal Authority

Legal authority is any source setting forth precedent, legal rules, or legal reasoning that judges may wish to use in deciding appeals. It comes in many forms—U.S. Supreme Court decisions, federal and state constitutions, statutes and agency regulations, local government rules, court rules, past decisions of the court (precedent), legislative histories, decisions of lower courts and courts in other jurisdictions, attorneys' general opinions, and various kinds of secondary authority such as texts and law reviews. These are listed roughly in order of their authoritative force; for example, American courts are much more likely to be persuaded by their own prior decisions on point than by suggestions in texts or law review articles.

This chapter will first discuss briefly the importance and uses of legal authorities in appellate decision making. Then the major topic is the match between legal authority presented by counsel and that cited in the focal court opinions—that is, the proportion of authority cited by counsel used by the court and the proportion used by the court that is cited by counsel. These indicate how well the adversary system works to present the useful, and to weed out the unuseful, legal authority. The last section is a discussion of an ethical provision requiring counsel to inform the court of important legal authority against his position if missed by opponents, an interesting attempt to suspend the adversary system.

THE IMPORTANCE AND USES OF LEGAL AUTHORITY

The tremendous importance of legal authority is beyond doubt, though it is often not in the traditional sense that it dictates a court's ruling. In the average case before the focal court, roughly half the briefs, oral arguments, and opinions were devoted to discussion of legal authorities and legal reasoning derived from them (but only a quarter of the justices' questions in arguments were in this category, a good deal less than questions about the facts of the cases). Judges almost invariably say that authorities, at least the more authoritative ones, are major components of their decisions. They feel, for example, that they must follow statutes on point; and nearly all feel that precedent should be given great weight, though they differ greatly in their willingness to overrule prior rulings (state justices are considerably more prone to do so than circuit judges).[1] The importance and uses of authorities, however, are immense and murky topics, and only a rough outline is possible here.

A major use, of course, is deciding issues, especially insubstantial issues, by applying the facts of the case to controlling authorities. The judge extracts a rule from the authorities and applies it to the facts before him, or he tries to match the facts in the case with the facts in various precedents. This is often a complicated process—where, for example, the rules are vague or only tangential to the issues being decided. A second important use is as a restraint: The judge determines how he would like to decide an issue, based on equities, practical considerations, philosophical notions, or the like, and he then studies the legal authorities to determine whether they prevent the outcome desired or, less strongly, fail to support the outcome. If the authorities are not such a hindrance, they can then become justifications reinforcing the decision. If they are a hindrance, the judge may change his mind, in effect allowing the authorities to dictate the result, or he may overrule or ignore them, both rare occurrences if the authority is important.

These two are not distinct and separate uses of legal authority; rather they are ends of a continuum. When deciding any one issue, a judge can treat authorities partly as steps in the reasoning toward a result and partly as boundaries within which the result must fall. Also, any one judge tends toward one style or the other in different issues, and judges seem to differ greatly as to which style they prefer. They have reputations for being "result oriented" or not depending on how often they seem to reach a tentative decision and then look for authority as support. It is not surprising that the focal court judges with greater reputations for being result oriented asked far fewer questions in oral arguments about legal authorities and legal argument (from 20 to 40 percent of each justice's questions were in this category). On the whole, however, it is futile to try to pinpoint how a judge is using legal authority in any one ruling because this type of thing is not often reflected in the opinions and the process is so deeply embedded in the judges' minds that they may not know themselves.[2] But it is enough to say that judicial decision making involves both, and that whichever way a judge uses legal authorities, with rare exceptions they are something he takes into account and, thus, are important pieces of information.

The major reasons why judges view legal authority, whether it dictates a result or is a restraint, as important are: First, judges hold with varying degrees of firmness the philosophy that their role is mainly to apply the law, especially when constitutions, statutes, agency regulations, and decisions of higher courts are involved. Second, decision making is more expedient if done by applying available authorities rather than studying the whole case for its particular equities or determining anew what is the wisest rule.[3] In this way courts are like any other organization in that rules and precedent are relied upon heavily because no one could rethink the organization's policies each time he had to make a decision.

Third and most important, judges believe authorities must be followed to make the legal system stable and predictable. They believe it unfair to change a rule relied upon by a litigant in his affairs, and citizens would have a tough time planning ahead if they thought the court might change the present rules. Thus the customary reason given by judges for the need to follow precedent is that otherwise the law would be too uncertain.[4] As is often said, judges are more reluctant to change the law in areas where they think people rely on the present law, like contracts, property, and wills, than in areas where they presume little reliance exists, such as tort, procedure, and evidence law. In the former areas, especially, judges sometimes subscribe to the old saying that it is more important that the law be settled than that it be settled right.[5] Incidentally, the attorneys interviewed were usually quite angry that the focal court was, in their eyes, constantly changing the law and leaving it in the state of flux, mainly because they found advising clients difficult.[6] Several of them added that they look ineffectual, or even foolish, when they can not give any definite advice or when their advice turns out to be wrong because the court later changes the law.

There are other important uses of legal authorities besides the two just mentioned. Authorities are a source of ideas about the reasoning behind the establishment of a rule; judges often study secondary authority or opinions of other courts to find reasons for announcing a rule in the case at hand. In fact, the court's own precedents are sometimes seen in this way; judges look at the reasoning in prior opinions to decide whether they should be overruled, narrowed, broadened, or given another of the almost unlimited treatments one can give precedent.[7] Lastly, authorities may be sources of social facts, a topic discussed in Chapter 12; social fact statements are often obtained from past opinions and secondary authorities,[8] and legal rules are sometimes used as evidence of what happens in society.

Legal authority is very important in both the dispute-deciding and the lawmaking functions of appellate courts. The decision between the immediate parties obviously depends largely on what rules and precedent the judges apply to the facts of the dispute. On the lawmaking side, those uses of authority discussed in the previous paragraph are, of course, very important. As for the other uses (applying rules or precedent to the facts and restraining possible decisions), the lawmaking implications arise mainly from the desire for predictability in the law. Information about legal authority is needed to keep the law coherent; if important authority is missed and an issue is decided contrary to that authority, the result is parallel authority. In the future, opposing parties facing this issue can each cite authority for their positions, leading to uncertainty, more litigation, and embarrassment for the court.[9]

Thus the consequences of missing authority are so drastic that the judges cannot very well rely on the adversary system to supply this information, and they conduct their own investigations for authorities. Also, they do not feel obliged to give opposing counsel a chance to comment on authority not briefed. The focal court made substantial use of legal authority not in the briefs, and it virtually never brought these to counsel's attention either in the oral arguments or in requests for further briefs. Unlike issues and, as we shall see, facts of the case, legal authorities need not be presented at the trial court before appellate judges will consider them. Moreover, appellate judges do not give legal rulings made by the trial judge the benefit of the doubt, as they do rulings about facts of the case, except that (1) on many matters of evidence and trial procedure, the trial judge has great discretion in interpreting the law, and (2) rulings by a highly respected trial judge are likely to carry some persuasive value at the appellate level. Thus, there are virtually no bounds, other than time limits, on the possible investigation for information about legal authorities.[10]

LEGAL AUTHORITY FROM COUNSEL

A little less than half the legal authorities cited in the majority and minority opinions in the 112 focal court cases studied here were mentioned in the parties' briefs or oral arguments, and but one-sixth of the authorities mentioned by the attorneys were cited in the opinions.[11] That is, the judges found more authority they believed worth citing than the attorneys presented, and they believed those authorities they found were more relevant than five-sixths of what the attorneys did present. At first glance, then, it seems that the attorneys poorly supplied the court with this type of information while giving it large amounts of unimportant stuff. However, these figures overstate things a bit. The next section will discuss the use of authorities by the court and will refine the figure of one-half; this section will discuss the extent to which the court used authorities given in the briefs and arguments.

Some of these authorities were cited only for issues not decided by the court, in which case they were virtually never used in the opinions. In fact, a quarter of the legal argument in the briefs was in the end wasted because the court did not reach the issues. Even after deleting citations in issues not decided, however, only one out of five of the attorneys' citations was used, as opposed to one out of six overall—not much of a reduction.[12]

The attorneys in a way attempted to weed out the less important authorities by stressing in the briefs a small minority that they considered especially important in the appeal. But the court cited only a third of these, still a startlingly small proportion.[13] Thus, by any measure, the attorneys did a poor job of restricting their presentations of authority to those the judges considered useful.[14] This is one of the major points made in the judges' writings on appellate advocacy. A substantial number ask counsel to limit themselves to the more relevant authority; especially galling to the judges is the long string of case citations to support a proposition, rather than a few apposite ones. Be that as it may, excessive authority from counsel is not awfully troublesome now that judges have law clerks and staff attorneys. Judges delegate to these aides the bulk of the work involved in checking out counsel's authorities; thus being overloaded with insubstantial authorities is not as great a problem as being overloaded with insubstantial issues, on which the judges must make decisions.

The attorneys, by the way, use the briefs much more than the oral arguments as the vehicle to present authorities. Though much of their oral argument is legal reasoning, few authorities in the briefs were also mentioned in the arguments (only some 10 percent of the case law, for example); and but 1 percent of the total was mentioned in the arguments and not in the briefs, largely authority out after the briefs were written.

LEGAL AUTHORITY FOUND AT COURT

As was said earlier, a little less than half the authorities cited by the justices had been mentioned by counsel.[15] This became exactly a half after adding other evident outside sources of information: authority cited by the lower courts in the case, authority cited by amicus briefs, and authority cited in briefs presenting similar issues in other cases before the court at the same time (the last two of these have been discussed in Chapter 5). The figure of one-half, however, is artificially low because a few opinions cited a large number of precedents not in the briefs. Actually, in half the opinions at least 60 percent of the authority cited had been brought to the court's attention from the outside, and in a quarter of the opinions all the authority cited was. The seven justices varied quite a bit; only 40 percent of one's citations were mentioned by counsel, while 65 percent of another's were, and the rest were spread evenly in between.

The opinions, of course, gave some authorities much more weight than others. Those emphasized by the justices—those quoted or relied upon for the positions taken[16]—were much more likely to have been brought to the court's attention from the outside. In all, over 60 percent were, and in most opinions at least two-thirds were. Also, upon looking at authorities emphasized in each issue (as opposed to each case) decided, it was found that in about a fifth of the issues none of these authorities were in the briefs or otherwise brought to the court's attention from the outside; in almost two-fifths of the issues some but not all were; and in over two-fifths of the issues all were.

Table 1

AUTHORITIES IN BRIEFS CITED IN OPINIONS			
	All Authorities (%)	*Authorities in Issues Decided by the Court (%)*	*Authorities Emphasized by Counsel in Issues Decided by the Court (%)*
Percent of authorities given in all briefs cited in opinions	17	20	34
Percentage in the median case	17	22	33

AUTHORITIES IN OPINIONS CITED IN BRIEFS		
	All Authorities (%)	*Authorities Emphasized by the Justices (%)*
Percent of authorities in all opinions cited in parties' briefs	48	61
Percent cited in parties' briefs, plus other briefs and lower court opinion	50	63
Percent cited (as above) in median opinion	60	67

Viewed in this light, then, the adversary system seems to do a better job of getting the basic authorities to the court. What little evidence there is suggests that the focal court is quite typical here, at least for those appeals that do not have easy, clear-cut answers (though there is probably a good deal of variation between courts).[17] A study of thirty Sixth Circuit civil cases in which opinions were published showed that 55 percent of the authorities cited (and 65 percent of those emphasized) were in the briefs.[18]

But these figures are an incomplete gauge of the attorneys' ability to present the court with useful legal authority because the amount of authority cited in the opinions beyond what the attorneys presented also depends on how much research is done at the court. The figures are as much an indication of the thoroughness of "independent research," as it is called, as of the thoroughness of the attorneys' work. In fact, the judges and law clerks on the six courts studied here said there is a good deal of library research to supplement the briefs. Some did more than others; for example, two focal court clerks said:

Depends on the case you've got. If it's a fairly minor case and the briefs *do* cite the proper cases, with the exception of Shepardizing it, you know, making sure we don't *miss* anything, I don't do much independent research. If it's a biggy case, then I try to read everything I can on the subject.

We *never* had a case where it didn't involve literally *hours* of research other than the briefs. We viewed the briefs as a starting point to look at the cites and see if the cases stood for what they said, and then we just, you know, stripped it right down. Took it from the start and did your own research.

Several clerks said that they used the briefs hardly at all or only as a place to begin the research when writing draft opinions or memorandums. The law clerks or, increasingly, the staff attorneys do the great bulk of the research. It is a major, if not the most important, part of their jobs. As can be expected, judges vary greatly in the amount of time they themselves spend doing research,[19] but on the whole they seldom do anywhere near as much as their clerks, though they often reach out of their memories for authorities missed by counsel. There is a tendency to do more research in difficult appeals, appeals with poor briefs, and appeals in areas unfamiliar to the assigned judge. In all, taking into account the variation in the difficulty of appeals, the six courts seemed to do independent research about equally, judging from the interviews; at most of these courts, however, the amount of research varies greatly from office to office. And courts elsewhere seem to do much research also, according to what has been written about the topic.[20]

Independent research tends to remain within the office of the judge assigned the case. The other judges rely on this research unless from their general knowledge and from the briefs they suspect they might disagree with the assigned judge's views; then they may have their clerks do considerable research. Thus to a large extent the assigned judge is delegated the responsibility of finding authorities missed by counsel.[21] When working on opinions, judges and clerks are sometimes told of authorities by judges and clerks elsewhere in the court, especially recent decisions that are not yet in the indexes. But this does not happen often, as has been discussed in Chapter 6.

BRINGING UP AUTHORITY AGAINST ONE'S POSITION

The Code of Professional Responsibility, Ethical Consideration 7-23, states:

The complexity of law often makes it difficult for a tribunal to be fully informed unless the pertinent law is presented by the lawyers in the cause. A tribunal that is fully informed on the applicable law is better able to make a fair and accurate determination of the matter before it. The adversary system contemplates that each lawyer will present and argue existing law in the light most favorable to his client. Where a lawyer knows of legal authority in the controlling jurisdiction directly adverse to the position of his client, he should inform the tribunal of its existence unless his adversary has done so; but, having made such a disclosure, he may challenge its soundness in whole or in part.[22]

Thus counsel must cite the most damaging authority he knows when his opponent fails to find it. The rule conflicts with a strict view of the adversary system and is an attempt to alleviate one defect in the adversary system— inadequate presentation by one side—by carving inroads in it. But, as a few clerks and judges said, damaging one's cause is simply against human nature.

The attorneys interviewed were generally asked if they felt obliged to follow this rule. All of the government attorneys other than public defenders said they did follow it, but half the rest said they did not. One attorney said he had followed the rule as a prosecutor, but now as a private practitioner he was under no such obligation. Perhaps many more felt they had no obligation, but did not want to admit that they in effect violated the law. Typical of the two views are these three statements by a government attorney, a public defender, and a private practitioner:

Sometimes we run into lawyers who don't bring out cases, and then you have to make a judgment as to whether as an officer of the court it's your duty to bring it to the attention of the court. You're not required to win the case for the other side. But it's a question of what's fair and just, particularly when you're in an office like this, where you represent all the people. You just don't represent an agency. If in private practice if the other side [fails to find] a case, you wouldn't cite it unless it was useful to you.

Q — What determines whether you think you should bring it up?

A — Well, it's a value judgment whether the court should be aware of it. Then you may try to distinguish it. A lawyer when he practices law in a public position particularly wants to have integrity so that in close cases he can be very influential in persuading the court. So then he has a duty to inform the court of everything. Or at least be able to explain to himself why he thinks it should be omitted.

Q — If the other side misses an important case for their side, do you feel obliged to bring it up?
A — No.
Q — Not at all?
A — No. I bring it up if I think the court would find it anyway or it would make me look good. But I don't feel any moral duty to bring it up.

Q — When your opponent fails to bring up a very important case for his side, do you feel obliged to bring it up before the court?
A — Hell no. This is an adversary system, not a search for justice.

The judges and clerks were asked how often the attorneys informed the court about important damaging authority missed by the other side, and most answered that it was not done very often.[23] Two circuit judges said government agency attorneys are much more likely to do it than private practitioners. Of course, as several pointed out, at the court one can only guess whether counsel purposely withheld the authority or simply did not know about it. In all, however, judges seem to consider this ethical provision only a minor element of appellate advocacy; almost none of the judges' writings on advocacy mention the specific topic (though several ask attorneys not to ignore adverse authorities, without reference to whether the other side brought them up).

Attorneys saying that they bring up adverse authority normally gave as one reason their ethical duties as officers of the court. However, most attorneys gave reasons of self-interest (usually in addition to ethical reasons): An attorney would lose the court's respect and trust if it found the authority and suspected the attorney knew of it, or it is better to have a chance to argue against the authority than to have the court find it later.[24] Also, a number of attorneys who said they did not feel obliged to bring up important contrary authority gave these as reasons for sometimes bringing it up. Therefore, the willingness to bring up contrary authority is based somewhat on counsel's fear that the court will find it. That is, the court's independent research can lead to more information from the attorneys.

Finding important authority an opponent has missed, however, does not happen often. In fact, two of the attorneys said they could not say whether they were obliged to mention such authority because they had never run into the problem. A few government attorneys said they faced the situation occasionally, but many more of the lawyers said they had only met a few rare instances. This is not only because their opponents would be likely to find any such authority they themselves would find, but also partly because many appellants believed it is advisable to meet all contrary authority in their briefs anyway. Moreover, attorneys occasionally interpreted the rule very narrowly to say that the authority has to be absolutely controlling.[25] One attorney, in fact, said he would never mention an adverse case missed by his opponent because he could always distinguish it from the present appeal. In sum, then, even though most attorneys say they adhere to this ethical principle, it is of little help in getting additional information to the court.

CHAPTER 10

Types and Uses
of Facts in
Deciding Appeals

It may sound paradoxical, but most contentions of law are won or lost on the facts. The facts often incline a judge to one side or the other. A large part of the time of conference is given to discussion of facts, to determine under what rule of law they fall. Dissents are not usually rooted in disagreement as to a rule of law but as to whether the facts warrant its application.[1]

Thus Justice Jackson of the U.S. Supreme Court, where lawmaking has a greater role than at any other court in the country, claims the facts are a prime element behind the decisions. As a practical matter, however, this passage is nearly meaningless because appellate judges use very different types of facts and use them for very different purposes, and Justice Jackson does not tell us which he is talking about.

Facts can be categorized along two dimensions: facts of the particular dispute in the case as opposed to facts elsewhere that might be used in many cases, and facts used only for deciding the dispute involved in the appeal as opposed to facts used for lawmaking purposes. The two dimensions form four categories:[2]

	USED IN DISPUTE DECIDING	USED IN LAWMAKING
Facts about the dispute only	1) Case facts	3) Case facts used as social facts
Facts pertaining to more than the dispute	2) Supporting case facts	4) Social facts

Case facts are the facts about the dispute before the court—about who did what, why, when, where, and how—and judges decide disputes by applying case facts to precedents, specific rules, principles, or their sense of justice. These are the facts one normally has in mind when referring to facts in legal decision making. Social facts are the polar opposite; they transcend the immediate case—they pertain not only to the parties—and are used to create rulings that will be precedent for future dispute deciding. They can be general facts about life in the world, or they can be specific occurrences that have taken place outside of the dispute in the appeal.

Between these two, with some features of each, are supporting case facts and case facts used as social facts. They are quite important, but they are not often evident from the judges' opinions and are not often mentioned in descriptions of appellate decision making. Supporting case facts, like social facts, pertain to more than the particular dispute being decided; but they are used by judges to determine what the case facts are, and not what the law should be. Case facts used as social facts are facts about the particular dispute but are used as evidence of what a just and workable rule should be for this case and for future cases presenting the same or similar issues.

The term "facts" does not imply that the facts are correct. They are merely assertions of facts by judges and attorneys or factual assumptions that otherwise enter the decision process. One of the main topics in the following chapters is how judges evaluate facts.

An example may help explain the distinctions among the four types of facts—a focal court case, chosen because it contains an interesting issue about appellate procedure. The labor board petitioned the state's intermediate court to enforce its order that a company reinstate an employee. The court refused, saying that there was not enough evidence on the record to support the board's finding that the employee had lost his job because of union activities. One judge, however, dissented on the ground that neither he nor his colleagues on the panel had read the record, and the court had relied upon a thirteen-page memorandum from a staff attorney. The labor board and the employee appealed, complaining about this procedure and claiming that the order was supported by enough evidence to be enforced. The case facts were the facts about the intermediate court's procedure in the case (none of which, incidentally, was in the record) and about why the employee had lost his job. For example, the labor board said that the intermediate court allowed it to submit a brief but not to present an oral argument. The only social facts mentioned in the case pertained to the first issue, mainly a description of the intermediate court's regular procedures. The briefs contained many pages describing the staff attorneys' general role in cases of this sort. For a more specific example, the employer's attorney said in the oral arguments that his law firm once considered hiring a young lawyer clerking for a federal circuit judge and that he told the judge that he was worried about a conflict of interest because the firm had pending before the court litigation that the clerk might be working on. The judge answered, "Don't worry, I'm deciding the cases and not he." This, the attorney said, is evidence that the intermediate court's procedures did not mean that the staff lawyers, rather than the judges, make the decisions.

The case facts about the intermediate court's procedure in this appeal were also used as social facts. The judge dissenting below described the procedure in this case as an example of what his court often did, and the focal court looked upon the case largely as an example of general procedures that it was asked to rule permissible or not for future cases. Thus, the specific facts of the dispute can be used as lawmaking information, in much the same manner as social facts that are specific occurrences not part of the dispute, such as the story about the circuit court clerk.

An example of supporting case facts occurred in the second issue. When the employee's lawyer was asked about testimony that his client had said he was quitting since he was not given a raise, he answered that this was just ordinary bargaining and, thus, not an excuse for the company to say that his client had resigned and was not fired. Then to bolster this case fact argument, the attorney gave a supporting case fact analogy: This situation is like attorneys arguing over damages in a negligence case, one side often rejects the other's offer even though he wants bargaining to continue. Here a general fact of life is used to explain a specific fact in the dispute. The general fact about bargaining would have been a social fact had the attorney been arguing that the court should rule that whenever an employee says he resigns after his pay demands are refused, this cannot be used as evidence that the employee actually did resign. But here the attorney was only arguing that his client did not resign in this particular situation. (The court, incidentally, sent the case back to the intermediate court to be decided again, but the opinion was so cryptic that one cannot tell whether the intermediate court was ordered to consider appeals of this kind more thoroughly.)

Virtually all facts used by appellate courts fall into at least one of these four categories.[3] Often, though, the same fact falls into two categories at the same time because it is used for both dispute deciding and lawmaking. And, as is the case for law or social science definitions in general, the boundaries between the four are not always clear. The major uncertainty is that one cannot enter a judge's mind to discover whether he is using a fact, especially a case fact, for dispute deciding or lawmaking. These distinctions, however, are necessary because they have important implications for how appellate judges obtain and evaluate fact information, the topics of the following chapters. The rest of this chapter will explain in more detail just what these various types of fact are, how they are used, and their importance in appellate decision making.

CASE FACTS

The importance of case facts is indicated by the great attention they receive in the appellate process. In the 112 appeals studied at the focal court, roughly a third of the briefs, oral arguments, judges' questions in oral arguments, and majority opinions were devoted to case facts, much more than the portion given social facts, as Table 2 shows.[4] The attention given case facts in the arguments is surprising because the justices prepared for arguments and were familiar with the facts; thus virtually as much time was spent on case facts in the appellees' arguments (and, for that matter, their briefs) as in the appellants', where the facts are traditionally expounded at length if the judges enter the arguments cold.

Table 2

ATTENTION DEVOTED TO CASE FACTS AND SOCIAL FACTS AT THE FOCAL COURT

	AVERAGE PERCENT OF THE PARTIES' BRIEFS	AVERAGE PERCENT OF ORAL ARGU- MENT TIME	AVERAGE PERCENT OF JUDGES' QUESTIONS	AVERAGE PERCENT OF MAJORITY OPINIONS
Case facts	29	33	35	36
Social facts	5	9	11	4

On the other hand, the attention given case facts varied greatly from appeal to appeal, and they were barely mentioned in many of the more important appeals. In fact, as a general rule, the more far-reaching the lawmaking implications of an appeal, the less important are the case facts relative to other types of information. The focal court has discretionary jurisdiction and, thus, concentrates on lawmaking questions rather than the fact issues often before courts that must take every case appealed. Therefore, the great attention given case facts by the court is probably atypically low.[5]

The appellate judges writing about appellate advocacy, as has been discussed in Chapter 3, give further evidence of the importance of these facts. Half either asked the attorneys to know the facts well or asked that they state the facts thoroughly (though a greater number warned that the statement of facts should be succinct and to the point); many more emphasized the facts in this manner than emphasized legal argument or any other type of information.

Case facts are important to dispute deciding in two ways: by applying the facts to precedent or specific rules, and by developing what is here called "fireside equities." When judges say, as they often do, that their job is primarily deciding cases by applying facts to the law, they are referring to case facts (though in the process of applying the facts to the law they may actually be creating law, refining it such that similar fact patterns in the future will be decided the same way). Case facts used in this manner are mainly specific occurrences or motives, such as evidence about how fast a car is moving. But the implications from these facts—what they add up to— often enter the uncertain zone between law and factual judgment, such as determining whether the driver was negligent. In all, however, the process of applying case facts to legal rules or precedent is very complicated and is beyond the scope of this book.

Although applying facts to the law is far and away the most important dispute-deciding use of case facts, another, fireside equities, is an interesting and rather mysterious use. For this reason, and because fireside equities are easily confused with using case facts as social facts, they will be given a rather lengthy discussion here. Fireside equities (a term used by Karl Llewellyn) are the equities of the particular case that propel a judge toward a desired result directly from the case facts, mediated only by his sense of fairness and not by any consideration of present or future law.[6] One judge interviewed called it "the widow and orphan kind of equities" and "justice of the peace style justice." Another said:

I think most of the judges regardless of what party they come from are—whether you classify them as liberal or conservative—most of them have a human interest. And if there's a widow with children and she's poor, we're more apt to find that there is a law which *helps* her than otherwise.

Fireside equities are at most only one of many elements entering a decision; they alone probably never dictate a result. Should they enter a judge's consideration, they lead him to search for a rule or a way to bend a rule so that he can reach the desired result—but a result desired for this case only, without attempting to use the facts behind the equity considerations as a foundation for creating law. In fact, the rule or precedent used to decide the case is probably completely unrelated to the equities. For example, a judge may feel that a defendant's jail sentence is too long; so, lacking legal authority to lessen the sentence, he may be more likely than otherwise to reverse the conviction on a technical evidentiary issue. The labor board case used as an example earlier may have contained some elements of fireside equities; perhaps the court did not openly prohibit the intermediate court's decision process for fear of hurting the feelings of the judges there (appellate judges often worry about hurting the feelings of lower court judges).

Fireside equities are difficult to study. When judges speak or write about the subject, it is often hard to distinguish between using case facts as a basis for deciding fireside equities and using them as an aid in formulating the law. The commonly mentioned goal of "justice in the particular case" may refer to either, and its meaning must be discovered from the context.[7] Also fireside equities are not placed in the opinions, and are even likely to be an unconscious element of decision making. Thus one can get only a rough idea of how important case facts are in this sense.

A number of judges were asked whether they used fireside equities (generally in the form of the question that follows); nearly all said these equities entered some decisions, though the emphasis given them varied greatly. One of the stronger statements was:

Q — When you decide a case, do you try to reach justice in the particular case—are you concerned with that or more with concentrating on the broader effects of the opinion?

A — Well, that's always a problem for judges, because you're human and you hate to be deciding a case that's going to be an injustice in the particular case just because it's good law in the long run. What our *duty* is is to decide a case according to the law. We're not supposed to do perfect justice. If we can accomplish substantial justice, we've done our duty. But the answer to your question is, yes, any judge who's human, and every judge is, when a decision is going to be *good* law generally speaking but an injustice in a particular case, you try like the devil to do something about it if you can. Most of the times you can. Sometimes you can't.

Q — If you think a defendant is probably—good chance of not being guilty. . . .

A — Oh, no, if you think a defendant's not guilty, that's the end of it. If he's not guilty, you're never going to write a decision, no matter what the law is, [affirming the lower court].

With only a few exceptions, the judges said there are conflicts in some cases between fireside equities and the legal rules or other broader considerations. However, they generally placed more emphasis on the latter than the judge just quoted, for instance, "If you can *achieve* justice in that particular case and still do no violence to the law, I'm willing to go along."[8]

The most commonly discussed example of firesides equities in appellate courts is the judges' impressions about a defendant's innocence or guilt in criminal cases.[9] If they strongly suspect innocence, they may well, based on what several clerks and judges said, search for an excuse to order a new trial. "If we get one around here that looks like it has been railroaded or something," one federal judge said, "we'll stretch things a bit." The opposite feeling is probably just as likely. A few state justices volunteered comments similar to this:

You look at the case sort of as a whole, and it's just as clear as a bell that this fellow is guilty as sin. There isn't any *doubt* about that. Well, that doesn't quite justify using illegally obtained evidence or whatever against him, unless you can say that beyond a reasonable doubt that the error was harmless, and so forth. Well—those cases, there is some result orientation. And we've had them where we've tried like hell to say, "Well, this one really ought to be upheld. It's an outrage to go and make them try this case over again."

He went on to say that he tried to fight this feeling, though judges probably differ greatly in that. The facts about innocence or guilt are fireside equities because they are not supposed to be relevant to the ruling (with some exceptions not involved here), and the decisions are based on other issues, especially procedural issues.

At the focal court the justices' opinions and questions in oral arguments rarely showed obvious concern for fireside equities, though it is impossible to say how much concern existed below the surface. The attorneys, on the other hand, brought out facts that seemed aimed at fireside equities in a number of cases, usually in the briefs. These were generally prosecuting attorneys who emphasized the bad character or clear guilt of the defendant and plaintiffs' attorneys who told the court how badly off their clients are. Normally, these were just short side remarks; only a half-dozen attorneys expounded fireside equities at length. The judges usually made no comment when presented these in the arguments, but a number of times they told the attorney to stop. Whether the attorneys thought the judges would be persuaded by the equities is uncertain; perhaps they were only unable to control their feelings (most of the attorneys interviewed gave me fireside equity arguments for why they agreed with their side of the case, usually attacks on the motives or character of the opposing parties).

Counterbalancing fireside equities, and limiting them, is the notion of objectivity. This term has many meanings, but judges generally use it in the sense that certain case facts should not affect their decisions, for example, personal characteristics of the litigants and their lawyers, possible personal gain to the judge himself, or simply considerations of fireside equities in general.[10] There is a very fine line, if any, between fireside equities and the lack of objectivity—for instance, between favoring widows or orphans and favoring labor unions or the Democratic Party—and guessing where any particular judge draws the line would be foolish.

CASE FACTS USED AS SOCIAL FACTS

The search for justice in the particular case also may have a powerful impact on lawmaking; appellate judges use case facts to determine what the law governing the case should be, as opposed to determining only an equitable outcome through fireside equities. Judges often get an impression, by studying what happened in the instant dispute before them, about what a just and wise rule should be for the litigants' situation and, additionally, for similar situations involving others in the future. This is probably what Judge Lumbard of the Second Circuit meant by:

[The statement of facts] is by all odds the most important part of the brief from the standpoint of the judges. If the facts are well marshalled and stated, the facts themselves will develop the relevant and governing points of law. . . . A well written statement of facts is by itself the strongest argument of the law.[11]

The old maxim *ex facto jus oritur*—the law arises out of the facts—contains much the same idea.

It is impossible, as a practical matter, to tell how important case facts are in lawmaking. One cannot read the judges' and attorneys' minds when they discuss and study facts, and they do not often say they are doing anything more than applying facts to the law. In only a few focal court appeals did it seem obvious, as it did in the labor board appeal given as an example earlier, that the case facts in the opinions or the questions about facts from the bench were a major input in lawmaking. The attorneys gave only slightly more emphasis to case facts as lawmaking information; most of this was, again as in the labor board appeal, presenting the situation involved in their case as an example of a problem that the court should solve by making new law.

Nevertheless, there is considerable evidence elsewhere that judges do quite often use case facts in lawmaking, though by and large without acknowledging it. Several respected scholars and appellate judges have emphasized that court-made law is often created, refined, and tested through the influx of new fact situations, from which judges get a sense of what the law should be.[12] Although I did not ask the judges about this topic in the interviews, a few mentioned it on their own. A state justice said, "It is the facts that make the law. The law will sprout from the seed of the facts," and a circuit judge said: "I think the legal process is particularily dependent on facts, and some of the strength of our legal process is that it does continually feed back into real honest-to-goodness facts, and I think that's where you get some of your best input." Also a reason several judges gave for overruling precedent is that the precedent, if followed, would lead to an injustice in the instant case. Similarly, the justice of the litigants' situation probably plays a major role when a precedent is distinguished on its facts; here the judges use case facts to create a new, interstitial law, though not often admitting that the distinction is fostered by the justice of the result.

In using case facts for lawmaking, judges are using them for a purpose for which they were not developed below. In the lower tribunal the parties presented evidence relevant to their dispute and relevant under the law as it stood then (except for the rare case in which social facts are developed at the trial level). Hence the appellate court receives only a narrow view of the problem area. This is one reason, as will be explained in later chapters, why judges prefer to make narrow decisions.

A similar point—and another indication of the importance of case facts in lawmaking—is the doctrine of ripeness, or the courts' aversion to deciding cases in which the facts are not clearly developed. Especially, courts dislike deciding a case when the exact facts of the dispute must await future occurrences. One of the two major reasons for the doctrine (the other is to conserve judicial time) is that courts find it difficult to decide issues that have not been clearly outlined in the presentation of facts.[13]

Likewise, as has been discussed in Chapter 3, courts dislike giving advisory opinions and deciding cases when one party lacks standing (that is, has no direct stake in the outcome) for reasons related to the lawmaking role of case facts. In order to formulate a decision in an advisory opinion that would cover the contingencies left hanging because the case facts are incomplete, the judges often must make a broad ruling that may adversely affect other situations they are not aware of. And a major reason given by the U.S. Supreme Court for insisting that parties have standing is to help ensure that the parties will thoroughly develop the case facts needed in the Court's lawmaking role.

The lawmaking importance of case facts is not limited to their effect on the ruling in the case, for they may, in effect, become social facts for later appeals. Although the facts of one appeal are a rather meager sample upon which to develop law, the facts of many cases added together lead to a considerable background knowledge of life, which can provide a judge with a substantial social fact foundation for making law.[14] An interesting example of this is that Judge McGowan of the D.C. Circuit felt qualified to write a long tract on the regulation of police behavior, even though his "range of vision is confined to the cold records of criminal trials," which he had read over several years as an appellate judge. These records, though, may not provide complete information, as he admits: "Although I have seen what seems like an infinite number of them, my observation point is both fixed as to angle and remote in space and time from the actual happenings and from the people involved in them."[15]

These background facts come not only from cases a judge has heard himself but also from opinions written elsewhere (one value of thorough fact statements in opinions) and from applications for leave to appeal and for certiorari (one argument against removing the Supreme Court's certiorari duties). Thus judges are more likely to create broader rules the more an area has been litigated, incorporating the fact situations of many cases previously decided. Or they may take fact questions away from the jury once they receive enough cases to understand what happens in a particular type of situation.[16] Or after seeing the same problem in many cases, they may become convinced it is widespread enough to justify judge-made corrective measures. Lastly, a court with discretionary jurisdiction can delay tackling an issue area until enough fact patterns have been decided in lower courts in order to have greater knowledge of the facts of life in the area.[17]

A tangential use of specific facts in the development of the law is the use of hypothetical fact situations, either questions about what the law should be in a hypothetical situation differing slightly from that in the appeal being decided, or questions about what would have happened in the present dispute had somebody acted differently. Both are rather rare; they constituted only 4 and 2 percent, respectively, of the justices' questions at the focal court, and the attorneys virtually never discussed them except when answering the justices. First, questions about the law in hypothetical situations, which are not really fact questions, seem aimed at broadening the court's view of the fact picture. The judges wonder about other situations that must be considered when making law. The second category of hypothetical fact questions ask how a change in one event would change the overall fact picture. For example, in a quest passenger case a focal court justice asked whether the car driver would have stopped speeding if the passenger, his wife, had asked him to (and the attorney answered that he believed the husband would not have listened). Just what the judges use this sort of information for is not clear, though they may be trying to learn more about the situation so that they can frame a more sensible rule.

All in all, then, case facts seem to be quite important for lawmaking in addition to their primary role in dispute deciding. They lead to an impression of what a fair and workable result would be in the situation and, thus, to precedent embodying that result; and fact matters presented in numerous cases help provide information for developing a comprehensive body of judge-made law. The extent of this use, however, is uncertain because it is not often evidenced in the opinions or oral arguments.

It must be kept in mind, also, that the case facts are not always accurate or complete and, thus, may be a slippery foundation for lawmaking. Using facts of the immediate appeal results in only limited damage here, because the precedent can be restricted to the fact pattern actually presented and decided. A meager fact base, though, can prevent judges from forming a clear idea of where justice lies in the dispute, greatly restricting the lawmaking value of the case facts. A greater danger is systematic errors and omissions in fact patterns received continuously during a judge's work; to the (unknown) extent that this happens, the judges' background knowledge based on this information is a poor foundation for lawmaking.

SUPPORTING CASE FACTS

Supporting case facts in themselves have nothing to do with the dispute before the court; they are brought in to establish the case facts in one's mind.[18] Their most frequent use is as a link between one fact and another—to surmise one from another. This happens routinely in every appeal, yet it is rarely explicit. By and large supporting case facts are assumed, unstated, and probably unconscious steps in a judge's reasoning. The most basic example is determining the meaning of words in the record. The raw case facts are just printed words, and in order to give them meaning a judge must draw upon his assumptions—supporting case fact assumptions—about the meanings people in general attribute to the words. Another common use is to gather various case facts together to form an ultimate fact from which legal consequences flow: For example, background knowledge about how people in general act is used when deciding if a defendant's actions amount to negligence; in condemnation cases testimony about the value of other property is used to determine how much should be paid for the property involved in the litigation; and a medical malpractice case is likely to have testimony about normal medical practices with which to judge the doctor's actions. Much of the expert testimony given at trials falls into this category. A similar factual background is needed to decide whether evidence is admissible in a case; for instance, the relevance of evidence must be determined by applying background assumptions about how things affect other things in the world. Supporting case facts are also used to evaluate the accuracy of facts in the record. This may be openly stated in the record, such as testimony of character witnesses, or more likely it may lie in the back of one's mind, such as assumptions that halting speech indicates deception or that police, ministers, and disinterested witnesses are less likely to lie than most others.

At the appellate level, especially, supporting case facts hardly ever come to the surface. They were mentioned in less than half the focal court briefs and oral arguments and rarely in the opinions. Less than 1 percent of the justices' questions were in this category; there were fifty times more case fact questions than supporting case fact questions. The only appeals where they were given more than a quick mention were a few in which expert testimony was presented at the trial level. But, as the examples given previously show, this slight attention evidenced belies the great importance of these facts.

SOCIAL FACTS

Everything is grist for our mill. We draw or ought to draw upon the whole range of human knowledge.[19] (Justice Cardozo)

If your case turns on an issue of substantive law, [the black letter] rules derive from economic and social factors, and these determine whether or not a particular doctrine of law is going to be extended to include your case or is going to be shut off, cut off short of your case. Shortly stated, the law does not live in black letter rules. It lives in the conditions of actual life that have given birth to those rules.[20] (Justice Schaefer)

Those who have worked long with legal problems know that not all "law" is to be found in the books. There is much of it to be found in experience, seasoned contacts with practical affairs, insight into the whole of society, appraisal of political realities. One who reads a statute often needs more than a dictionary if he is to have understanding. He needs insight into the nature of the organism with which the statute deals. The problem is different only in degree when one construes a Constitution written in general terms for an indefinite future.[21] (Justice Douglas)

Social facts are factual statements and assumptions that apply to more than just the controversy between the parties, and that are used to fashion legal rules and precedent. They are statements about what has happened or is happening in the world or about what might happen as a consequence of a court ruling. They can be facts about virtually anything—scientific data, public opinion and mores, behavior of police or trial attorneys or jurors, and so on. They may be specific incidents or general facts; the latter are more common. The overriding criteria are that they are fact statements, rather than ideological statements, that they are used in lawmaking and not merely in dispute deciding, and that they are not facts of the dispute being decided. Again, the term does not imply that the facts are correct.

TERMINOLOGY. There is no convenient word for this concept; "social facts" is only the least unsatisfactory term. (In spite of the word "social," the definition includes scientific and technological information.) No term is routinely used by judges and lawyers just for this concept. Different people recognize different terms, and any one person is likely to use the same term for several different concepts.

"Policy" and "public policy," which are largely interchangeable, are the terms they most often use by far when referring to social facts. But these are indefinite words and often include more than social facts. They almost always refer to reasons for deciding issues other than by applying legal rules or precedent;[22] however, this is a broad area including both social facts and nonfact policy considerations. Some judges and lawyers use the words "policy" or "public policy" in a sense that appears pretty well restricted to social facts, as in this famous statement by Holmes:

In substance the growth of the law is legislative. And this in a deeper sense than that what the courts declare to have always been the law is in fact new. It is legislative in its grounds. The very considerations which judges most rarely mention, and always with an apology, are the secret root from which the law draws all the juices of life. I mean, of course, considerations of what is expedient for the community concerned. Every important principle which is developed by litigation is in fact and at the bottom the result of more or less definitely understood views of public policy; most generally, to be sure, under our practice and traditions, the unconscious result of instinctive preferences and inarticulated convictions, but none the less traceable to views of public policy in the last analysis.[23]

Thus public policy is "considerations of what is expedient for the community." This necessarily implies knowledge about how communities operate, or social facts. On the other hand, policy may refer to goals, such as ideologies, moral considerations, and the purposes of legal rules, all of which are called "ideals" here.[24] Whenever a judge says that the legislature, not the courts, makes policy, he is probably using the term in this sense. Also, to many policy means both ideals and social facts; they use policy to describe one or the other or both.[25]

(Ideals are outside the scope of this study and will be discussed only briefly. Rarely are they openly expressed;[26] only 30 percent of the focal court opinions contained any statements about ideals, and these statements seldom comprised more than a tiny part of the opinions.[27] Equally little attention was given ideals in the briefs and oral arguments—for example, only 1 percent of the justices' questions from the bench were in this category. Most of the statements about ideals referred to policies presumed to be behind statutes or constitutional provisions, especially statements about what a provision was intended to accomplish. Incidentally, ideals mentioned by counsel were rarely used in the opinions, and ideals mentioned in the opinions were rarely brought up by counsel. All this does not indicate that ideals are unimportant in judicial decision making; it only indicates that they are rarely made explicit. Obviously, ideals enter at many points in a judge's deliberations in any appeal, if only his views on the weight that should be accorded precedent or statutory rules.[28])

Besides policy, the most frequently used term to describe social facts is "practical considerations," along with numerous variations such as "practicalities" and "practical aspects." These nearly always refer to social facts and never, as far as I know, to ideals.[29] But since they imply the consequences of rulings, they might not encompass many social facts: Social facts are generally about past and current states of affairs rather than speculation about what the result of a ruling might be. Practical considerations, then, include how much a proposed criminal procedure ruling would hinder the police and prosecution, but it may or may not, depending on the speaker, include facts about the current police and prosecution practices a judge is considering when deciding if changes are needed.

"Social facts," the term used in this book, is the third most common term, but, again, those using it may not intend to include matters within the realm of the physical sciences. Lawyers and judges use many other terms. Some are as vague as "policy" and may also refer to elements of decision making other than social facts, for example, justice, equity, fairness, underlying facts, extralegal reasoning or facts, common sense, pragmatism, and even philosophy. Other terms describe specific types of social facts, usually just narrow categories—public needs, experience, customs, workability, and constitutional facts. In addition, three important scholars have coined terms to describe factors in appellate decision making that, to varying degrees, seem close to social facts: Kenneth Davis's "legislative facts," Justice Cardozo's "method of tradition" and "method of sociology," and Karl Llewellyn's "situation sense."[30]

This uncertainty concerning terminology often makes it hard to understand judges' writings in this area and, especially, to interview judges and lawyers. In my early interviews, including nearly all those with attorneys, questions about social facts were phrased in terms of "policy," since that was the word used most often to describe social facts. But I had trouble determining whether the person answered in terms of social facts, ideals, or both. Reading excerpts from Holmes's statement quoted earlier did not help because most judges then said they did not agree with that definition and proceeded to use their own. Later "practical considerations" was used, either alone or as "policy and practical considerations." But practical considerations is too narrow a concept. Moreover, a few people simply said they did not understand what these terms meant and, thus, could not answer the questions, as, for example, in this exchange with a very polite judge:

Q — How often are policy or practical considerations important in decisions on the ——— Court?
A — *Whose* policy? The court's policy?
Q — Just. . . .
A — or public policy?
Q — Public policy, yeah.
A — I guess I'm with Voltaire in if you would converse with me, define your terms. I don't know what you mean by practical considerations, you know, because if for instance you have a case that—it's *easier* to answer specifically if you have it in a specific factual context.

Unfortunately, presenting examples of social facts did not help because it was difficult to broaden the discussion beyond the issues in the examples. I also tried using words the judge had used in opinions and articles to describe social facts, but even this often did not work because the words could be used in other contexts as well.

Finally, and most successfully, questions were designed with a whole battery of expressions, such as social facts, facts of life, and what people actually do. This generally worked eventually to arrive at some basis for communication. The following judge had used the term "policy" in many different ways in the interview:

Q — How important is knowledge of how things work in general? Knowledge of what people actually do, practical wisdom, workability of rules. This type of thing. How important is this in making decisions?
A — I'm not sure I know what you mean.
Q — Well, when you consider a legal rule—when you consider changing it or upholding it, how important is the consideration of how the rule actually works in practice? How important are the practical aspects of life? How rules work, rather than just consideration of the legal rules themselves?

A — Well, if I understand you correctly, and I'm not sure I do, the validity of any rule is its *practical* efficacy in accomplishing what it's supposed to do.
Q — So it's important? Practical efficacy?
A — Oh, yeah, it's of primary importance.

Thus further questions about social facts in this interview could be phrased in terms of "practical efficacy." A few other judges also supplied their own terms—for example, "fallout effect" or "realities of the case," but more often they chose a term from the question or accepted the question as a whole.

It may seem odd that an important and often written-about factor in judicial decision making does not have an agreed upon label. But judges do not often discuss decision-making techniques among themselves or with others (though judicial seminars are increasingly providing a setting for this) and, thus, have little need to define the various elements. Consequently, interviewing was difficult in this area. With a few judges, especially those interviewed early in the study, no satisfactory agreement was made on a label to be used; hence little was learned about their views on social facts. Also, in several interviews, especially when lawyers answered questions about "policy," it was never clear what the person had in mind. These problems must be kept in mind throughout the discussion of social facts here.

THE IMPORTANCE OF SOCIAL FACTS. A rather incomplete indication of the importance of social facts is the amount of attention given them in written opinions, incomplete because, as was explained in Chapter 7, the opinions may not include influential social facts. In any event, nearly half the majority and minority opinions at the focal court contained at least some social fact statements, though in a few the social facts seemed of little importance to the lines of reasoning used. In only 15 percent of the opinions did the social facts appear necessary to the reasoning behind the decision (in a fourth of the opinions the social facts were alternative lines of reasoning presented in addition to reasoning based solely on legal rules and precedent). Also, social facts were used in only a quarter of the issues decided by the court, though these strongly tended to be the most important issues. As can be seen from Table 2 (on page 142), on the average only 4 percent of a majority opinion was devoted to social facts. Most of their use occurred in only a half-dozen cases.

This somewhat meager attention given social facts results partly from some judges' reluctance to place this type of information in the opinions.[31] In fact, the judges gave two or three times as much attention to social facts in the oral arguments as they did to those in the opinions (see Table 2). Even so, much more attention was given to case facts than to social facts in the arguments (and in the briefs). In less than a third of the arguments was 10 percent or more of the time spent on social facts, and in only a sixth was 20 percent or more of the time spent on them. Even less attention was given to social facts in the arguments at the other five courts studied here.[32]

The greatest use of social facts was in the few appeals with equal protection issues, as might be expected. Chapter 13 will discuss the frequent use of statistical and social science materials to establish or refute social fact contentions that a plaintiff has been denied his constitutional equal protection rights. Excluding these cases, however, there was not much difference in the amount of attention given social facts over broad categories of cases in the focal court: statutory and common law issues involved almost as many social facts as criminal procedure issues and constitutional issues besides equal protection. It may seem strange that statutory construction would involve social facts, since judicial lawmaking is more often associated with the common law and constitutional law. But, as Justice Breitel once wrote, "In an ever increasing degree, courts have looked to surrounding economic and social data in construing statutes and making them intelligently purposive."[33] In other words, social facts help determine which interpretation will further the ideals attributed to the legislature or, perhaps, simply desired by the judge.

The judges interviewed varied greatly in their attitudes about the importance of social facts—as with many other matters, they varied both within and between courts—though on the whole they considered social facts quite important. There is considerable evidence that this is typical of appellate judges throughout the country. Judges writings often say, for example, that decisions should "reflect good sense," that courts should "keep the law in tune with the needs of society," and that judges should "bring the court from the ivory towers of scholastic pedantry to the realities of just decisions affecting everyday people." And many political scientists have interviewed judges on this point, finding widespread, but varying, use of social facts.[34] In the present study, the within-court differences were the greatest at the Sixth Circuit; it contained the only two judges who claimed they never use social facts—never consider, for instance, the facts of life or the workability and practical implications of proposed rules—whereas several of their colleagues greatly emphasized them; for example one said:

What are you deciding? If it's just writing paper, anyone can write paper. You're dealing with people. I don't know that our system is ever designed to address itself to anything but people. I mean we're not satisfying *law review* articles. We're not trying to fill *books*. We're trying to solve *problems* and to *adjust* differences between people; so consequently the more you know about what the country is, the deeper your experience, the more able you are to *create* laws which *work*, do what you want them to. . . . The practical application has to be important. You simply can't set out on your horse like Don Quixote and fight the battle in the abstract.

Most judges on each court considered social facts important, but the tendency was strongest at courts with discretionary jurisdiction. The circuit judges and Rhode Island justices gave more emphasis to deciding cases by applying settled law to the facts before them.

Judges often say that only certain kinds of cases call for social fact considerations. A First Circuit judge said the reason for these differences is not always clear, but:

I suppose in areas of law where there's a great deal of precedent and things have settled down into fixed patterns, the tendency of the courts is to hold people to arguing things within those patterns. When you're dealng with constitutional and administrative law, particularly in frontier areas or in subject matters that don't come to court very often, I think you're pretty much more open to the whole spectrum of argument, if only because you're not as clear in your own mind as to what is relevant and what isn't relevant.

Quite obviously, since social facts are used in lawmaking, they are used more by judges who see greater lawmaking opportunities in the appeals before them. Discretionary jurisdiction means that a higher proportion of the court's case load falls in that category. And the more a judge views his job as only applying the facts to existing law— the more conservative his judicial philosophy—the less likely he is to find lawmaking opportunities and to use social facts. This was pretty much the case among the judges interviewed, mainly because the very conservative judges said they never or seldom used social facts. In all, the judges seem to consider from 50 to 90 percent of their appeals as determined by existing law.[35]

OVERRULING PRECEDENT. As might be expected, social facts are very important in overruling precedent. When asked what leads them to overrule precedent, the great majority of the judges gave as one reason that times have changed since the precedent was formulated,[36] and this reason was mentioned far more than others—mistakes in prior decisions, the development of the law in other jurisdictions, and the injustice produced by applying the old precedent to the case at hand. The changing-times basis for overruling precedent is a pure social fact basis: Social conditions, customs, public opinion, or technologies underlying the old rule have changed, or knowledge about these things has advanced. Examples of this are numerous. A clear-cut statement is found in an opinion written some time ago by one of the judges interviewed: "But *stare decisis* in its most rigorous form does not prevent the courts from correcting their own errors, or from establishing new rules of case law when facts and circumstances of modern life have rendered an old rule unworkable and unjust." This decision took away governmental immunity from liability for damages caused by employees' negligence, and the following reasoning in the opinion is a good example of using social facts in deciding that times have changed:

Each brief speaks of the crushing weight of negligence awards which might bankrupt a small governmental unit. Most of the briefs filed to support appellee city avoid mention of public liability insurance as if it were a new and barely tried invention of which the courts could not possibly have knowledge.

No such scheme for prepaying and sharing risk did exist in any common form at the time when the courts of this country adopted the doctrine of governmental immunity. The probabilities are strong that this fact, and the possibility of a crushing liability falling upon a small governmental unit, had as much to do with adoption of the rule as did *stare decisis* and the fact that Kings had no inclination to be liable in damage to their subjects.

In 1961, however, liability insurance is no new and untried device. We take judicial notice that it serves private citizens and private corporations as a means of prepaying and sharing just the sort of unexpected burden with which we deal in this case.[37]

Liability insurance enters into many common law liability issues, for example, whether holding doctors to promises of complete cures would lead to more malpractice suits and increase malpractice insurance rates, and whether the liability of charitable organizations or landowners can now be safely expanded because liability insurance is more common.

SOCIAL FACT ASSUMPTIONS BEHIND DECISION-MAKING METHODS. Many appellate court decision-making methods are grounded on—or justified by —social fact arguments, which are nearly always left unstated in the opinions. Some of these have been discussed in earlier chapters: Standing and mootness rules and the judges' reluctance to write advisory opinions are partly based on the assumption that counsel will be less motivated to inform the court without immediate tangible gains or losses contingent on the outcome, and the most important justification for *stare decisis* is the supposed unsettling effects on society of uncertainty in the law. Others will be discussed later: Appellate judges are reluctant to overturn lower court case fact findings because trial judges and juries view the witnesses' demeanors and, thus, can better judge the truth of their statements; the rule against using case facts outside the record is partly based on the assumption that appellate judges cannot determine which of contradictory case fact statements by counsel are true; and judges often advocate judicial restraint because they believe courts are less able than legislatures to gather information about what a good law would be or because courts may lose the support of the public if they venture outside their traditional domain. Therefore, social fact assumptions (along with ideals, it should be added) form a large part of the underpinning behind important appellate court decision-making traits. However, these social facts, like social facts used by judges in general, are really not proved or undeniably true;[38] rather, the judges simply assume they are true based on their own experiences.

CHAPTER 11

Case Facts

This chapter explains how judges obtain and evaluate the three types of case facts; social facts are left for the following two chapters. The different types of facts were distinguished in the last chapter largely because they are gathered and evaluated differently. For the most part, however, there is little discernible difference between case facts and case facts used as social facts in the topics discussed in this chapter, and the term "case facts" refers to both unless stated otherwise.

Finding and evaluating facts can be done either through the adversary system—that is, the attorneys present their own facts and contest their opponents—or by the court, using either the judges' knowledge based on past experiences or actual investigation of the facts. Case facts virtually always come in through the adversary system by means of the record, which contains the pleadings and other papers and exhibits filed in the tribunal that originally heard the case, along with a transcription of what was said there, including the testimony.[1] As will be seen, though, the attorneys surprisingly often tell the courts about facts outside the record. The great bulk of supporting case facts comes from outside the adversary system and outside the record, supplied by the judges' background knowledge. The problem of overload, the problem of receiving an inconveniently large amount of information from counsel, is much greater for case facts than for other types of facts. The often excessive amounts of case facts and the courts' attempts to deal with this problem will be the last topic of the chapter.

DECIDING CASE FACTS

As a general rule, American appellate courts try to leave case fact decisions—the finding and evaluation of case facts and supporting case facts—to the trial court or administrative agency that originally heard the case. But appellate judges, especially on intermediate courts, are often faced with issues in which they are asked to make a decision about the facts of the case.

Because they virtually never take testimony or otherwise gather case facts, the judges must decide these issues on the basis of the record.[2] Thus a dispute over what actually happened in the case is unlikely at the appellate level. I asked a number of judges how often they and their colleagues disagreed about what the facts of the case are, and all said it was very seldom, though disagreements over inferences drawn from the facts are, of course, much more common. In spite of all this, as will be seen presently, appellate judges often make decisions on the basis of case facts in much the same manner as the trial court fact finders.

Appellate courts face two very different kinds of fact issues, those in which a finding has been made in the lower tribunal and those in which one has not. A case fact determination made below is given the benefit of the doubt. Appellate judges will not overrule a jury's or trial judge's finding of fact simply because they disagree with it; rather, they review the evidence to see if the finding is "clearly wrong," or they use some similar test that gives great weight to the finding of fact made below, and also is so elastic that appellate judges have considerable discretion.[3] One reson for this deference is the case load and time problems: A close review of the facts requires judges to spend much time studying the record, and it prompts more appeals. But this probably is not the main reason, for the one almost universally given by appellate judges is that they cannot view the witnesses' demeanors as the juries and trial judges can.[4] One judge said:

The trier of the facts has had the advantage of *seeing* the witness on the stand, *hearing* him, seeing the averted glance, the hesitancy, the apparent forthrightness, *all of these things*, and they're very much better equipped to deal with questions of fact than somebody who is reading this from the cold record. A record may say *"no"* when you look at the answer, and what actually happened in the court below, the fellow says "hum, hum, hum, ah, *no.*" [As he said this he rubbed his lower lip with his thumb and forefinger.] Well, you can't put that in the record.

In a similar vein, appellate courts often say they are reluctant to overturn fact findings of government agencies because the agencies' expertise gives them better knowledge than the courts with which to evaluate the facts.[5] Thus the judges attribute an important substantive decision-making rule, the deference to fact decisions below, to their means of receiving information. Their source of information, the record, does not contain information that may be crucial to evaluating the case facts; so they leave the bulk of the fact decisions to those having access to that information. In this way, by delegating fact decisions, appellate courts go a long way toward solving the problem of evaluating case facts. In a few rare cases, on the other hand, they do overturn fact findings below when they believe them to be clearly wrong. Here the judges must draw on their background knowledge for supporting case facts to evaluate the facts in the record.

A surprisingly large number of appeals contain the second category of fact issues—those that appellate judges decide without the benefit of a finding below. They are almost always questions about what happened in the lower court, for example, when appellate courts choose to decide questions about the procedure of a trial even though no objection was made at the time. Also the incompetence of counsel issue is a fact issue of this type: Here a criminal defendant's appellate lawyer claims that the trial lawyer presented an incompetent defense and thus deprived the defendant of effective representation by counsel, and the appellate court must determine whether the apparent mistakes by trial counsel were actually mistakes rather than trial tactics or something else excusable. Probably the most common example, however, is the issue of harmless error. When an appellate court decides that an error was committed below, it must then determine whether that error might have made a difference; if not, the court will not upset the lower court decision. Often the error is obviously harmful or considered harmful by law, but judges sometimes must study the record thoroughly and apply the court's harmless-error test, for example, whether there is a good chance that the error affected the jury verdict.[6] This requires a fact determination, albeit a probability rather than the existence or absence of a fact.

Many other, less common issues require a fact determination from the record unaided by a ruling below. Because the focal court has discretionary jurisdiction, it seldom decides incompetency of counsel and harmless-error issues; yet in quite a few of the 112 cases studied the judges had to interpret the record to find out what had happened without the benefit of a trial court ruling, though these issues were seldom the most important issues in the cases. A good number were questions about whether an attorney had objected to some point at trial or had made a particular motion.[7] Other examples are whether a litigant was given certain files he had requested in an administrative hearing and whether a trial judge, sitting without a jury in a criminal case, read the preliminary examination transcript. In each case the record was ambiguous and opposing counsel either differed about, or admitted they did not know, what the facts were, and the judges had to make a guess about what had happened.

FACTS OUTSIDE THE RECORD

The question of how appellate judges obtain fact information is largely a question of how often they go outside the record. In general, case facts do come from the record, whereas supporting case facts do not and are supplied by the judges' background knowledge. There is an almost flat rule against going outside the record for case facts; insofar as the rule is followed (and the departures will be discussed presently), the source of this type of information presents little problem. This does not mean that appellate judges always get sufficient case facts; they do send cases back to the trial level on rare occasions for more facts or, under the ripeness doctrine, refuse to decide the merits because the facts are not certain enough. Also, as one focal court judge complained several times, the facts may be too skimpy to help in developing the law, even though the case must be decided. But at least the judges know where they are supposed to go for the case facts. A problem much more important than obtaining case facts is, as will be discussed later, weeding out the irrelevant facts from the mass of materials in the often lengthy record. The record, then, is all important for case facts. Probably nothing throws a cog in the wheel of the appellate process more than when important parts of the record are garbled or missing; that problem must be solved before the court can proceed.[8]

Independent investigation at the appellate level for case facts is virtually nonexistent.[9] And disputes are rarely so notorious that judges might learn of the facts from newspapers or friends. Thus if judges depart from the record, they must either obtain the facts from the attorneys or guess at what the facts are using their background experiences to read between the lines of the record.

THE PROHIBITION AGAINST USING FACTS OUTSIDE THE RECORD AND JUDICIAL NOTICE. The general and strongly espoused rule is that case facts either must be in the record or must be indisputable such that judicial notice is possible.[10] The judicial notice standards, which are far from clear-cut, allow courts to use case facts outside the record only if there is little doubt about their accuracy and only if the facts are either generally known or can be found in some trustworthy reference book.[11] Under these restrictions, however, judicial notice of case facts at the appellate stage does not really exist; facts about the immediate dispute are highly unlikely to qualify. In fact, I ran across only a couple of examples in all my study of the six courts. As a practical matter, then, the record is expected to be the sole source of case facts.

What is the reason for the severe restrictions on the source of case facts? Most of the judges interviewed were asked why it is important to decide cases solely on the basis of facts in the record. They usually answered that appellate courts are not set up to find case facts: The record is the only means the judges have of knowing what has occurred; any information they receive outside the record is not subject to the safeguards of cross-examination, and if the attorneys were allowed to introduce new facts upon appeal, there would be never-ending disagreements between counsel that the court could not resolve. For example:

Good man, I can't think of anything more fundamental than that. You can't have people coming into court and saying "Well, that's what the record says, but actually this is what *happened* down below.'' If you depart from that, you're in grave danger. That's fundamental. . . . How do you *know* what happened? You may have—one fellow says ''This is what happened down there,'' and the other fellow says ''Oh, no it didn't.'' So then you say ''Well, what's the record show?'' You've *got* to stand by the record. You'd have judicial *chaos* if you did anything else.

Thus the courts' difficulties in gathering information are seen as a reason for tightly restricting the source of the information. Furthermore, some judges worry about fairness to litigants, as they do in many aspects of appellate courts operations; a number said that they should not use facts that the parties have not had a chance to contest:

Well, I suppose the reason is that the parties themselves would not be able to address themselves to points on which you are deciding the case. I guess there's a general feeling that the parties are entitled to have notice of what the ball bark is and what to talk about. If the judge suddenly goes home and talks to his wife and gets some slant that no one knows anything [about] or some set of assumed facts, of course the parties have no opportunity to criticize it.

This reason, of course, applies only to facts assumed by the judges themselves and not brought out at the arguments.

Whether supporting case facts are expected to be in the record is very uncertain. The general consensus among scholars is that the judicial notice restrictions either do not apply to them or are relaxed considerably.[12] The reason is that making decisions without these facts is impossible and requiring them to be in the record would lead to extreme inconvenience.[13] That is not to say that supporting case facts are never in the record when they fall outside the judicial notice restrictions; but just when they are is unclear. The record is most likely to contain these facts when the subject matter falls outside the general knowledge of the average layman; that is the basic rule as to when expert testimony is allowed in jury trials.[14] But this does not mean that the judicial notice restrictions are followed, because the general knowledge used as supporting facts is often of doubtful accuracy—often based on generalizations derived from experiences unique to the individual judge. Judicial notice restrictions are not applicable to ''the wide variety of background knowledge, prejudice and misinformation about people and things necessarily relied upon by jurors and judges in evaluating evidence through the use of hypotheses and generalized knowledge.''[15] On the other hand, the great bulk of supporting case facts does fall within the judicial notice restrictions, especially when the actual fact deciding is left to the lower tribunal and the supporting case facts are used at the appellate level only to interpret the record, for example to determine the meaning of the printed words.

An interesting example of the uncertainty in this area concerns the use of technical advisers to help appellate judges understand the record in patent, environmental, antitrust, and similar cases involving complicated technical data. At present law clerks and staff attorneys in the Court of Customs and Patent Appeals have technical training, often advanced degrees in the physical sciences. They help the judges interpret engineering, chemical, and other types of evidence in the record; that is, they supply supporting case facts.[16] Various suggestions have been made that other appellate courts be given similar advice when handling technical information that is above the judges' heads. So far these suggestions have come to nothing; the judges are badly split over whether technical assistance of this sort should be in the record and, especially, whether counsel should be given a chance to answer the experts' contentions.[17]

In all, the net result of the uncertainty in this area is probably that appellate judges have and use considerable discretion as to whether they will use or ignore supporting case facts not in the record and falling outside the judicial notice restrictions.[18]

READING BETWEEN THE LINES OF THE RECORD. Because the record is only printed words, appellate judges often describe it as "cold" or "dead." But it need not be completely so; many judges, especially those with much trial court experience, enliven the transcript considerably while reading it.[19] Their imaginations and memories allow them to embellish the printed words. Two judges said, for example:

A good transcript is a very alive thing. I think it was Justice Frankfurter who said "you can't read from a deadly transcript and get it," but to *me*—I can live the whole life of the people in that transcript.

You can picture what's happening, and it's the best way to try to understand the case and try to picture the judge sitting on the bench, and the lawyers arguing and the jury and the people. You get a picture of it.

Judges generally go a step further; they read between the lines and smell out facts beyond the actual words of the transcript.[20] They use knowledge gained from their trial experience to impute motives to the trial judge and attorneys and to guess the effects of happenings in the courtroom on the jury. One state justice explained:

[When reading the record] sometimes an instance may trigger an experience I had, and you see something and say, "That sort of takes me back," you know, without verbalizing all of that. It triggers the personal recollection. We're all products of our experiences. Since we've had experience as trial lawyers, we perhaps respond to recognize a situation. We can see between the lines when a judge says certain things in a certain way or a lawyer says things in a certain way.

He then gave an example: The way a trial judge talked to a lawyer indicated that the judge was irritated because the lawyers did not settle the case, a situation in which the appellate judge himself had been as a trial lawyer. And, when asked if he gets a feeling for what happens beyond the written words of the record, a circuit judge said:

Yes, yes, I do. And I *believe* that this is the great advantage that the trial judge generally has *over* the man who has not been a trial judge. This is the *great* advantage. . . . my law clerks are smarter than I ever was, but they don't have that experience. It's very hard to convey why I would *view* the facts in a certain way when the *briefs* are so *beautifully* written the other way, but there's the record and if you read it with objectivity, but with an understanding of all the nuances, I think you're just more— you can more accurately assess what took place if you've had the experience yourself.

Also, Karl Llewellyn, who knew appellate judges well, said they have an "experienced 'feel' for what may lie, unspoken, underneath the record." Then in a footnote he continued, "We know that the court's 'smell' for the 'facts' beneath the officially given 'facts' is frequently, not just semioccasionally, a factor in the deciding."[21]

The examples of this practice given by judges involved issues of fact without a fact finding below. In issues of incompetency of counsel, judges read between the lines of the record by attributing to counsel motives about trial tactics to explain away apparent mistakes. In harmless-error issues, they try to read the jury's mind, using their trial court experience to determine whether a particular error made by the trial judge was prejudicial in this case. And on a wide variety of questions they ascribe motives to trial judges and attorneys from the written record.

The nature of these issues makes reading between the lines necessary. The points were not contested or decided below; therefore, there is no evidence developed specifically aimed at the issues and no finding of fact by the trial judge or jury to rely on.

Here the judges decide issues on the basis of case facts not in the record— that is, the probability that a criminal defense counsel was concerned with trial tactics or the probability that the jury was affected by the trial judge's error—and these case facts are determined largely by supporting case facts, which also were not in the record, for example, the judges' impressions of defense attorneys' trial tactics in general or their impressions of how juries decide. Facts used in these situations certainly do not fall within the allowable limits of judicial notice.

Since the supporting facts come from the judges' experiences in the trial court, that experience is extremely important. In the interviews the judges nearly always said that experience as a trial lawyer or trial judge was important for an appellate judge (the exceptions were judges who had had little such experience), and the usual reason given for this importance was that the experience provided the supporting facts needed to make many appellate-level decisions.

SUPPORTING CASE FACTS OUTSIDE THE RECORD BY COUNSEL. As has been noted in the preceding chapter, supporting case facts are not often openly discussed during the decision-making process; as a practical matter, therefore, they are supplied by the judges' background knowledge, such as that gained from trial experience, rather than from the adversary system. In a number of the focal court cases the attorneys did mention supporting case facts, but generally just one or two; in only a half-dozen cases were they discussed at length. Except fot the latter cases, the attorneys' supporting case facts were rarely in the record. For an interesting example, the record in a criminal case contained a letter to the defendant from his lawyer saying that the prosecutor had offered to drop a second suit pending against the defendant if the defendant did not appeal the conviction in the present case. Since there was nothing else on this point in the record, at oral arguments the court asked the prosecutor's appellate counsel what had happened. He answered that he had had the same thing done to him when he was a private defense attorney; whereupon two justices quickly asked how often and who did it. Counsel said it was done to him once by a trial judge and then said "I don't disbelieve" it happened in the present case, since it had happened to him before. In the end, the court gave the prosecution's offer as a major ground for reversal; that is, the court assumed the offer was made on the basis of defense attorney's letter and, very likely, but without mentioning it, the supporting fact admission by the attorney from the prosecutor's office.

The supporting case facts were not in the record even in most of the few cases containing a lengthy discussion of them. When they were, they were expert testimony taken below at the trial court. Both the focal court and the Rhode Island court during this study reviewed, apparently for the first time in both courts, sentences given by trial judges. Both courts used sentences given for similar crimes to judge the sentence in the immediate cases, and in each case these supporting case facts were supplied by counsel only at the appellate level and, thus, were outside the record.[22]

CASE FACTS OUTSIDE THE RECORD. Except when a judge uses supporting case facts to make an educated guess at a case fact, the only likely source outside the record for case facts (called simply "facts" in this subsection) is the attorneys. Although the record is by far the main source of these facts, they do also come in through the briefs and, especially, the oral arguments. The attorneys mentioned facts clearly outside the record in the great majority of the 112 appeals studied, and at least one justice asked about facts clearly outside the record in half the appeals.[23] Fourteen percent of the justices' questions about facts (and 5 percent of all questions) asked for facts outside the record; the percentages for the individual justices varied from 8 to 23 percent. A third of the attorneys' statements of fact outside the record in the arguments were in response to questions asking for such facts.

Generally, however, facts outside the record were only a small part of counsel's presentations, and in the average case only four such facts were mentioned. All told, much less than 1 percent of the facts received by the judges were outside the record. On the other hand, the arguments in 3 appeals seemed more like evidentiary hearings than appellate arguments; between them the judges asked 65 questions, and the attorneys made almost 100 statements, about facts not in the record. In all this the focal court is probably typical; at least that is my impression from listening to oral arguments in other courts.[24]

Thus counsel and the court quite often violated the rule that the attorneys' presentations should be limited to facts in the record. Despite this rule, counsel rarely refused to answer the justices' questions requesting this type of information by saying it was outside the record. Quite naturally, a few times they admitted that they did not know the answer. Occasionally, when an attorney strayed from the record, a justice told him not to; each justice did this at least once during the year. But they never warned their colleagues, at least in open court. The adversary system did little to hinder discussion outside the record; the attorneys rarely objected to their opponents' introduction of these facts, and they often continued the discussion. They objected only twice when facts were introduced at oral arguments, but appellees commonly objected when appellants' briefs went outside the record.

This is an intriguing topic: Why do judges and attorneys wander off the record so much, when they clearly know it is prohibited by rules of appellate practice, and what role do these facts play in the judges' decisions? This gets into the difficult area of the judges' and attorneys' motives. The written opinions are of no help, since judges would not be expected to announce that they were influenced by such facts.[25] Moreover, a staff attorney checks all the focal court opinions to make sure the facts are supported by the record, as is done at many appellate courts.

Judges seem moderately concerned, at most, about facts outside the record. When asked in the interviews about the attorneys' bringing up these facts, the judges generally said it is not a problem, mainly because, they added, the judges simply told them to stop. Furthermore, in the judges' writings on appellate advocacy (which have been discussed in Chapter 3) only 30 percent of the nearly sixty judges who discussed the presentation of facts warned counsel not to depart from the record. The judges interviewed who talked about questions from the bench outside the record usually acknowledged that they or their colleagues did knowingly ask them:

Some members of the court ask a hell of a lot of questions that did go beyond the record. I don't think they make much difference in the final analysis, but it's subjective, and I can't be sure about it.

You do it to satisfy your personal curiosity. Make the job a little more entertaining. But you don't do it for the purpose of reaching a decision.

The few giving reasons for going outside the record usually said it was simply for "curiosity" like this second judge. But the others were not as confident that it had no effect on the decision, saying that there was no way to tell.[26] There is no way I can tell either, not being able to enter the judges' minds. There was no discernible pattern in the type of cases or facts involved, except that cases in which more attention was given case facts tended to involve more facts outside the record. One might think that procedural questions would predominate, but less than half the facts outside the record had to do with procedure at any stage. On the whole, though, the facts outside the record, in my opinion, seemed important to the issues raised in only several focal court cases, but the judges and attorneys may have intended differently.

The importance of facts outside the record seemed greatest, as might be expected, in the few appeals involving many of these facts. The issue in one appeal, for example, was whether residents of a home for emotionally disturbed children were under the guardianship of the home's president such that they could attend the local public schools. In the oral arguments, the court was very interested in the details of the home's operation, the children's relations with their parents (who usually lived far away), and the children's relations with the home's president. None of these facts outside the record showed up on the court's opinions, but it is hard to believe that the justices' interest in them was for naught.

In other cases the court seemed to ignore the facts outside the record. For example, the court reversed a criminal conviction for lack of speedy trial, largely on the ground that the record showed no reason for the delay—even though the prosecutor had explained (outside the record) that the delay was caused by an influx of cases following a riot. And, in arguing that the prosecution did not search thoroughly enough for a witness, a defense counsel claimed that the witness had recently been quickly located for another trial. One justice, however, said in the arguments that the court could not consider this fact, and the opinion just said there was no indication in the record that a diligent search for the witness was made.

For the most part, as in these examples, the facts outside the record did not seem to be aimed at anything other than finding out what happened in the dispute so that the facts could be applied to the law. Perhaps some were also used as social facts, that is, for lawmaking. Since facts were developed at the trial level for dispute-deciding purposes only, the judges and attorneys may have felt them inadequate to understand the situation for lawmaking purposes on appeal. But, again, one cannot read their minds, and only several facts outside the record seemed obviously aimed at lawmaking. In one case, counsel argued that his client had a constitutional right to a preliminary examination after a grand jury indictment; he was asked what the defendent would gain from a preliminary exam in this case. In another appeal the court was asked to change the state's insanity defense rule in criminal cases, and a justice asked what would eventually happen to the defendant here if found insane, adding that he was obviously dangerous to society. Later, the defense counsel said that prisons do not have the facilities to treat his client. It is really only happenstance that statements such as these were classified as case facts, since they could just as well have been phrased in terms of social facts—in terms of preliminary examinations in general and in terms of what typically happens to those found not guilty by reason of insanity.

Some of the facts outside the record seem to have been introduced solely for the purpose of fireside equities. For example, a plaintiff demanded specific performance of a contract to buy defendant's house, and suggested in his brief that the defendant would not sell because plaintiff was black. The defendant answered that there was nothing in the record to support that, and in fact the neighborhood is now black and the defendant still wants to live there. And a retired city employee sued for benefits under the city's retirement plans and said in the arguments that the city was doing everything it could to defeat the plaintiff's rights under the pension plan. The attorney for the city said they had nothing against the plaintiff, as shown by the fact that they had just given him a raise. This inveighing against one's opponent's motives was typical of the fireside equities outside the record. In several other cases counsel tried to emphasize the difficulties or unfairness of his client's present plight. A plaintiff's injury was still so severe at the time of oral arguments that his wife had to turn him over in bed every few hours. A few criminal lawyers mentioned parenthetically in the arguments that their clients were still in prison (as opposed to being on parole); this had nothing to do with the issues presented, but perhaps counsel thought it would make the court more reluctant to affirm the verdicts.

However these facts outside the record were used, one must keep in mind that they comprise a small portion of the case facts received by the judges and that they still come in through the adversary system when counsel presents them in the briefs and oral arguments.

WEEDING OUT IRRELEVANT CASE FACTS

A dispute brought to the courts is likely to involve an extremely large number of fact details, but only a tiny portion is relevant to a trial court decision and even fewer to an appellate decision. The work load and efficiency of appellate courts depend greatly on the ability of counsel to condense and winnow the facts, a process that takes place all during the history of a particular litigation. The great bulk is done before the appellate level;

the lawyers select the facts they think will help their sides at trial, and the trial judge further limits the facts by applying the rules of evidence and, in general, trying to retain only facts that make a difference under the law and that help him or the jury decide the case. Even so, the record made there and sent to the appellate court is often very long, usually over 2 inches thick. At the Sixth Circuit, I was told, about 10 percent of the records are from a carton to several cabinets full.

Appellate judges, then, are overloaded with factual information; they do not have time to read the record in each case they hear, and they must rely on others—on counsel, colleagues, and the court staff—to condense it. The major question here is: How well does the adversary system operate to condense the case facts such that the relevant facts in the record, and only those, are presented to the judges? The answer is, not very well.

The word "relevant" means information the judges may wish to use in reaching their decision; in general, that is information presented at trial with respect to the issues the appellant raises on appeal, which often involves the whole record and often involves only a few pages. But the judges may want more information than that from the record, for example, when studying fireside equities, using case facts as social facts, or deciding issues not raised. This can lead to great uncertainty about what portions of the record are relevant, an uncertainty that probably cannot be cured by any method of presenting facts to an appellate court.

There are four successive waves of fact condensing by counsel. First, many courts allow the appellant to leave behind parts of the record if the appellee consents. Rule 10b of the federal appellate rules provide for this, but counsel seldom oblige. Attorneys in Rhode Island make a little more use of a similar provision there.[27]

The major fact condensing by counsel is done in the other three waves: the appendixes and the statements of facts in the briefs and oral arguments. Appendixes are excerpts from the record.[28] The appellant is supposed to include all parts of the record touching on the issues he raises, including all facts unfavorable to his side. Appendixes at the focal court vary from about 10 to over 1,000 pages, and they are sometimes much longer in the federal courts.

The statements of facts in the briefs and arguments are shorter distillations of facts, generally from one to ten pages in the briefs and one to ten minutes in the arguments. They are in narrative form, while the appendix is copied verbatim from the record. The statements of facts are also supposed to be fair presentations of the facts; for example, the focal court rule is: "The statement of facts shall be presented without argument or bias and in such a manner as to fairly present the facts, both favorable and unfavorable."

Thus, the courts attempt to suspend the adversary system by requiring the appellant to represent both sides when presenting the facts in the appendixes and statements of facts. On the other hand, they also use the adversary system to ensure complete information by allowing the appellee to contest and add to the appellant's versions. In the federal courts the appellee can require the appellant to include material in the latter's appendix, resulting in a joint appendix. The focal court has no such rule, and joint appendixes are very infrequent; the appellee files his own appendix if he disagrees with his opponent's version. In the briefs or arguments, the appellee can make corrections or additions to what the appellant said or, as often happens, he can submit a complete separate statement of facts.

There is considerable dissatisfaction with the appendixes, especially at the focal court. The judges complained in the interviews that the appendixes included too much extraneous material, that many important parts of the record are omitted, and that when two opposing appendixes are filed, they have trouble piecing together the two versions and following the testimony.[29] The focal court, during the year its cases were studied, occasionally ordered supplemental appendixes because the originals were inadequate. Also, half the appellees filed their own appendixes, apparently believing the appellants had not fairly presented all the facts. The Sixth Circuit appendixes, on the other hand, were considered better, probably due to, as was sometimes said, the provision for joint appendixes.

Similar problems arise in the statements of facts. In the judges' writings on appellate advocacy, the great majority who discussed the presentation of facts cautioned against bias or excess argumentation, particularly in the briefs. For example, Judge Tuttle said, "Nothing more quickly generates in the minds of the judges complete confidence in the lawyer's advocacy than an accurate, well-documented statement of facts—facts that hurt as well as facts that help his cause."[30] On the other hand, the several judges and clerks I talked to about the subject claimed that the facts are seldom badly biased. They generally expected that the facts would not be completely fair—that an attorney would naturally put his best foot forward—and they were not bothered by this unless too extreme.

The lawyers interviewed were split evenly between those who believed their factual presentations should be unbiased and those who attempted to slant them (e.g., by emphasizing fireside equities) without being blatantly biased. Government counsel strongly tended to be in the first category. No attorneys, quite naturally, claimed to write completely one-sided statements of facts, though a great many said that opponents had done so in the past.

An indication of how neutral appellants' statements of facts are, at least in the eyes of the appellees, is that only a fifth of the appellee briefs accepted them in the 112 appeals studied. The great majority wrote their own or, occasionally, made a few corrections and additions. Quite a few appellees complained bitterly that the appellants' statements of facts were biased or inaccurate.

A substantial number of judges who discussed, both in the interviews and in the writings on appellate advocacy, the problem of biased fact presentations added, as did Judge Tuttle earlier, that the forthrightness of the statement of facts reflects on the rest of the attorney's presentation or on his general reputation for candor. "You get a magnifying glass out for everything he says," said one judge interviewed about attorneys who mistate facts. The attorneys seemed aware of this attitude, commonly giving it as a reason for tempering advocacy when presenting facts.

READING THE RECORD AT COURT. The best indication of how little judges rely on the adversary system to condense case facts is how often they resort to reading the record and, thus, going beyond the appendixes and attorneys' statements of facts. To begin with, at the six courts studied the record is kept in the court clerk's office until oral arguments and then nearly always given to the judge assigned the case. The judge or his law clerk typically read at least part of it. Beyond that there is no standard practice; the handling of the record differs greatly between courts, between judges on the same court, and even between clerks of the same judge.[31] In about half the offices the judge or his clerk read the whole record (including the transcript of testimony) in each case, though often skimming or passing by material clearly outside the issues raised. Here the adversary system clearly is not trusted to pick out the important facts.

In the remaining offices, the judges lean more heavily on counsel. In several the record is studied only when the appendix seems inadequate on its face (as it often does) or only when the facts in the opposing briefs seem to conflict. In several more offices, especially in Massachusetts and Rhode Island, the judges and clerks tend to read only portions that the attorneys have designated as falling within the issues raised. The overall attitude here was given by a circuit judge:

That is one place where you depend upon the lawyers to an extent because if they can't point to something in their briefs that you *ought* to read, unless you feel that the lawyer is so poor that it wouldn't be fair to his client to rely on him, why, you would usually take the position, "Well, if he can't find anything in the record, I've got better things to do than hunt myself."

This position is less common, though, in criminal cases; judges tend to check the attorneys work more thoroughly there, and statutes in a few states require the judges to read the record in some types of criminal appeals.[32]

Apportionment of the record-reading task between a judge and his law clerk also varies greatly. Some judges feel that they themselves should read the transcript:

If you've got important factual questions I think that's one thing a judge is likely to do better than a clerk. The clerks are often better on some of the legal points and things, cause that's the kind of training you get in law school. If your experience means anything as a judge, generally it lies in things like reading over the transcripts and figuring out what went on.

More often, however, the judges only read selected parts, if any, of the transcript, relying largely on the clerks to check the facts against the record.

The reason for giving so much attention to the record is mainly, of course, that the briefs and appendixes may not include all the important facts. Beyond that, several judges and clerks mentioned that the transcript itself gave them ''a better feel,'' as it was usually phrased, for what happened in the trial court, even though much of it may not be directly related to the issues presented. Also, as was mentioned in the last chapter, delving into the transcript helps judges keep up to date with what is happening in the trial courts and in society generally.

Only the assigned judge and his clerk, however, pay much attention to the record; the other judges are very unlikely to send for and study it unless they have some doubts about the facts after reading the draft opinion. They do not have time to do any more, and the bulky record is likely to be miles away in the assigned judge's office. The nonassigned judges rely, in the first instance, on the adversary system—on the briefs, arguments, and appendixes—to bring the relevant facts forward, and then they delegate to the opinion writer and his clerk the job of making sure counsel accomplish this. One clerk said he read the whole transcript of every case assigned his judge, but wondered about what happened in other offices: ''You had to rely on the clerks and other judges, and if you had some guy dogging it, you were screwed up. You know, that's how you start writing bad opinions.'' In Massachusetts the justices were especially careful to check out the attorneys' factual allegations when writing opinions, because the nonassigned judges often did not read even the briefs and thus relied very heavily on the assigned judge for the facts.

CHAPTER 12

Social Facts _____

In the present state of our knowledge, the estimate of the comparative value of one social interest and another, when they come, two or more of them, into collision, will be shaped for the judge, as it is for the legislature, in accordance with an act of judgment in which many elements cooperate. It will be shaped by his experience of life; his understanding of the prevailing canons of justice and morality; his study of the social sciences; at times, in the end, by his intuitions, his guesses, even his ignorance or prejudice. The web is tangled and obscure, shot through with a multitude of shades and colors, the skeins irregular and broken. Many hues that seem to be simple, are found, when analyzed, to be a complex and uncertain blend. . . .

Many things must be learned as facts in law as in other sciences. They are the coin which we must have in our pocket if we are to pay our way with legal tender. Until we are provided with a plentiful supply of it, we shall do better to stay at home and not go forth upon our journey.[1]

The definition and importance of social facts have been discussed in Chapter 10. The present chapter is about finding and evaluating social facts, a key and difficult problem for appellate judges in their lawmaking role, as Justice Cardozo emphasizes in the preceding passage. Although the term "social facts" as it is used here includes scientific and technical material, the great bulk of those used by courts are facts about human behavior, that is, areas typically studied by sociologists, political scientists, psychologists, and historians. They are areas of great uncertainty; hence appellate court lawmaking involves many possible social fact contentions of questionable accuracy. Judges can go to scholars or to empirical studies for information about social facts, and that will be the topic of the next chapter. Much more often, though, social facts come from the lawyers' contentions, from the judges' background knowledge gained from experience, and from fact patterns and legal sources met in normal appeals-deciding activities.

FINDING AND EVALUATING SOCIAL FACTS—THE ATTORNEYS

The amount of attention given social facts in the focal court briefs varied greatly. In six appeals the attorneys submitted Brandeis briefs—briefs with lengthy discussions of empirical data—which will be discussed later. Most of the parties' briefs, however, offered little social fact information: A third gave none at all, and 70 percent had less than one page of it. The average percent of the briefs devoted to social fact argument was only 4 percent.[2] Proportionally two or three times more attention was given social facts in oral arguments; though the briefs contained half again as many social fact statements as the arguments, for more information overall can be placed in the briefs. The overlap between the briefs and arguments was surprisingly small: Less than a third of the social facts in one were also mentioned in the other. The arguments, therefore, are an important vehicle for this type of information, in contrast to legal authorities and case facts, which are rarely mentioned for the first time in the arguments. But, as will be seen later, the court was much more likely to use the social facts from the briefs than from the arguments.

In spite of the somewhat sparse social fact information in the briefs and arguments, nearly all the attorneys interviewed believed it a good idea to make these arguments (or rather policy arguments, the term used in the attorney interviews). Several said that courts should leave lawmaking to the legislature and, thus, should not consider this sort of information; but they did realize that the court does in fact use it, and all but a couple said they would make these arguments to better their chances of winning. The two exceptions insisted on presenting their appeal as they believed it should be presented—they insisted on playing the game their way and not the court's —but this position was so unusual that it resulted in little information loss to the court.

There was not much of a match between the information given by the attorneys and that mentioned in the court's opinions. Only 12 prcent of the social facts given by the attorneys wound up in the opinions—15 percent of those mentioned in the briefs and 7 percent in the arguments. Less than 5 percent was used if one excludes the three cases that involved the greatest use of social facts. The social facts used in the opinions came almost exclusively from the briefs: The great majority were given in the briefs and not the ar- guments, and nearly all those used in the opinions that were presented in the arguments were also presented in the briefs. Thus the arguments, though often used by counsel to present their social fact contentions, are not really a source for this type of information actually mentioned by the court, any more than they are for legal authority or case facts.

The judges, therefore, appear to have used an astonishingly small portion of the social facts presented by counsel. But, as was said earlier, judges may not put this type of information in their opinions even if important to the decisions; thus the attorneys' social fact information is probably more im- portant than these figures suggest. In any event, however, no matter how few of the social fact contentions in the briefs and arguments the judges consider valuable, one cannot say that counsel overload the courts with useless information in this area, simply because it constitutes such a small part of their presentation.

On the other side of the coin, only a quarter of the social facts in the opinions had been mentioned by counsel, though this figure becomes one-half if one excludes those social facts that, in my opinion, were not used to support the holding.[3] Usually when an issue was decided by using social facts in the opinion, none of them had been mentioned by counsel, and less than a fifth of the time had all those used in the opinion been mentioned by counsel. The social facts obtained from outside the adversary system were probably arrived at during the stages of independent research and opinion writing; at any rate, the justices rarely asked counsel in the arguments about those social facts it used that counsel did not mention on their own. That is, counsel were given no opportunity to speak to this information.[4]

Much more of the amicus briefs than of the regular briefs was devoted to social facts—partly because they typically concentrated on social facts more than the parties' briefs and partly because they were more common in the more important cases. But less than 1 percent of the social facts in the opinions were in the amicus briefs but not first brought out by the parties.

For all that, the judges usually do not evidence much concern that counsel fails to inform them on these matters. Unlike legal authority and case facts, for example, courts place counsel under no obligation to provide important adverse information about social facts.[5] More important, the judges' writings on appellate advocacy give little attention to social facts. About one judge in seven mentioned that the attorneys should include this type of argument. Justice Vanderbilt of New Jersey, for example, told counsel to "tie law with its social environment and show its relation to the assumptions of the age in which we live."[6] The remaining judges ignored the topic; none said that counsel should not make these arguments. Perhaps they believed that counsel do present social facts adequately as it is and need not be reminded to do so; but more likely they do not expect attorneys to be a major source of this type of information, or they do not believe (or do not want to admit) that social facts are an important enough factor to mention.

The judges and law clerks interviewed differed greatly in their views about how thoroughly counsel presented social facts.[7] Within most of the six courts about an equal number said that the attorneys were and were not adequate in this regard, but those interviewed at the Ohio court were strongly disappointed by counsel's overall social fact presentations. One justice there gave this reason:

An advocate could get nailed by some judge. He'll say from the bench "Counselor, is that in the record?" And he'll make some snide remark, "Well, why don't you stick to the record?" So again, some of these guys don't want to know. And others will ask "Well, what's the local situation? What is the local practice?" That may not have anything to do with the record, but it gives a background on what's going on.

Q — You mean judges differ on this?

A — Yea, and you can't get a consensus, and one judge by some smart remark like that from the bench will just close off any more discussion because the counsel's afraid to tread on that ground too much, because he's really speaking off the record.

Q — But in conference do these judges who object to it in argument talk about these?

A — [Yes.] These guys think they're smarter than—some judges think they're smarter than the lawyers, so they can talk about it, but they don't want counsel to talk about it on a theory that counsel will lie; but they won't. But I don't think anyone really deliberately lies. It's just a question of what part of the truth you want to bring out.

Several others at the Ohio court gave this explanation for why attorneys do not often mention social facts (though there was no evidence of the problem at the other courts). A clerk said, for example, that the attorneys "hardly ever" bring out social facts "because they'd be chastised by the judges." Social facts, however, are as important in decision making at the Ohio court as at other courts generally. And, as will be explained later, not many judges require that social facts be in the record.

The only other reason given for why attorneys may not present social facts adequately is that they are interested in their immediate case and, thus, do not discuss the broader implications. Several made statements to this effect, for example: "An attorney wants his client to win. That's his chief job. That's why he's there. He isn't there *primarily* trying to do a public service to improve the law or to get the court to improve the law." However, there are several objections to this line of reasoning. First, it assumes that the attorneys are so obtuse that they do not recognize the court's lawmaking activities and do not realize that their success may depend on presenting arguments about the broader implications.[8] This is unlikely, no matter how ill-informed the attorneys are about the court. Thus the attorneys interviewed said that policy arguments are a useful tool. Second, most attorneys seem interested in the broader aspects of their cases apart from their views of the court's interest, very likely because this made their appeals and their jobs appear more important. "Lawyers in general are kind of egotistical" a Rhode Island law clerk said in explaining why counsel usually supply the social facts, "and like to think they're going to make something new" in their appeal. In fact, the attorneys interviewed usually volunteered that their cases were important because, in their opinion, the decisions would have wide implications (even though few seemed strongly motivated by the desire to establish a particular legal principle). Furthermore, when talking about the merits of their appeals in the interviews, they generally gave social fact arguments, concentrating on them considerably more than in their briefs and oral arguments.[9] So, in all, the attorneys tend to have their minds focused on the broader, social fact type of justification for their positions.

That, however, does not mean that they are any more able to find and evaluate social facts than the judges. Even though there was a high degree of subject area specialization among the attorneys, their social fact contentions were not often based on any specialized knowledge, and thus probably added little to what the justices already knew. Also, counsel gave the court little help in evaluating the accuracy of social fact statements: Very few such statements by one side were challenged by the other side in the briefs or arguments, and when they were, it was often by simply asserting the opposite facts rather than giving reasons why the opponents' contentions were wrong. Each side, then, just threw out social facts supporting his view of the law, paying little attention to what the other side said. The major exception to this is some vigorous battles over social facts in the few rare cases in which empirical data were introduced at the trial level.

On the other hand, counsel's social fact information seemed to help the court in a few appeals. The Brandeis briefs, discussed in the next chapter, are one example. Another is a few cases involving attorneys with a good deal more practical experience in the area than the judges. To give an illustration, two cases argued at the same time contained the same issue—whether a criminal defendant is entitled to a preliminary examination hearing after indictment by a grand jury—and both were argued by prosecutors on one side and ex-prosecutors, now criminal lawyers, on the other side. A large portion of the judges' questions and of the attorneys' presentations were devoted to social facts. The defense attorneys claimed that the grand jury, being a tool of the prosecutor, did not adequately protect defendants and that grand jury secrecy made it difficult to plea bargain intelligently and to prepare fully for trial. The prosecutors, on the other hand, said that defense lawyers used preliminary examinations to delay trials and that grand jury secrecy was necessary to protect witnesses who might be murdered to prevent their testimony in the forthcoming trial. The justices bore down on all four attorneys, trying to find out just what the practical problems were; and the attorneys answered from their experiences, largely by giving specific past cases as examples. The following excerpt from one prosecutor's argument is typical of what judges attempt to gain (but do not necessarily succeed in gaining) from knowledgeable attorneys:

Q — What are the considerations for going this route [the grand jury route as opposed to a preliminary examination]?
A — To be perfectly frank, the reason we used the route, and the reason that we make the choices in using this route, is in *my* opinion, for the better administration of criminal justice. For example—
Q — In what way?
A — For example, [one recent gambling conspiracy case going through the grand jury] was *processed* through the courts in a five month period. Went to trial, the

individuals were convicted, and they were sentenced in three to five months. Now I submit to this court—

Q — Couldn't they have done that just as well using a preliminary examination?

A — No they could not, your honor, based on—

Q — Why not?

A — Based on the past experiences that we've had, the average time to handle a *gambling* conspiracy case runs about a year to a year and a half—

Q — How long does it take to have a preliminary examination?

A — In a gambling conspiracy case? I think the one before this particular case took about nine months.

Q — For the preliminary exam?

A — Over a nine month period. It didn't take nine months of full time. It took nine months—

Q — How many days of trial time?

A — Of trial time?

Q — Hearings.

A — Oh, hearings.

Q — In court.

A — I would think that in that particular case I'm thinking of—the one proceeding the grand jury—I would think—

Q — Six weeks would be a long one, wouldn't it?

A — Nope. Not in our jurisdiction. I would think it would be—it might be a *long* one, but it's not *unusual* to have a six week preliminary examination, and I'm not exaggerating because when you have ten or fifteen defendants, eight or ten counsel, you're going to get *a lot of* examination, a lot of time. And we made a judgment—

Q — Is that what you're trying to eliminate?

A — To some extent I am, yes. I'm trying to eliminate some of the *long delays* in getting these cases to court and trial. To be perfectly frank, that's what I'm intending to do in many of these cases. . . .

Q — Do you process [the cases] through the grand jury, or does the grand jury exercise some independent judgment?

A — Well, they exercise some independent judgment, but I'd say when we go into a grand jury, to be perfectly honest, I suspect we'll come out of there with most cases with an indictment. We will not go in there without *at least* what we consider a case where we *could*—if a warrant could be issued, like in a narcotic case, that we could have issued—

Q — I mean, you go in there with your case, you don't go in there—

A — Many times—

Q — You don't go in there to make it.

A — *Many times* we do go in there with our case, but for another reason than making it—and that is we're processing a case. In the area of narcotics we have been able to cut in half the time period between the *time* of arrest and the *time* of trial of these individuals, as distinguished from going through the preliminary examination.

The court, however, was not persuaded by the prosecutor and ruled for the defendants.

In another case the result depended largely on an uncertain social fact, about which counsel differed but were of little help to the court. Two people in one car were injured by the driver of another car who had no insurance, and the injured each had insurance policies giving themselves plus one other person in their car $10,000 if injured by an uninsured motorist. The policies also contained a clause limiting recovery under the uninsured motorist provision to $10,000 a person, but the plaintiffs claimed $20,000 each based on a recent statute requiring that insurance policies include the $10,000 per person uninsured motorist protection. The social fact question was whether the insurance companies based their premiums for uninsured motorist coverage on the $10,000 limit in the policies or on the assumption that there may be "stacking" up to twice that figure. The court's decision was largely based on a finding that the latter was the insurance company practice, and thus for the companies to take premiums and then not provide the coverage violated legislative policy. But in deciding this fact, the court received little help from the attorneys. Even though they were negligence lawyers with long experience in dealing with insurance companies, each flatly stated opposite versions, with no further support other than court opinions in jurisdictions elsewhere deciding the social fact point their respective ways. Thus, as is typical, the adversary system was of little help in evaluating this information.

JUDICIAL NOTICE AND STIPULATION OF SOCIAL FACTS

That the attorneys are not relied upon to supply social facts is to be expected because the judges cannot very well rely on the parties to provide information used to create precedent that affects future disputes involving other people. Likewise, judges cannot very well use only the information in the record or falling under the stringent judicial notice restrictions.[10] Every once in a while, an appellate judge does talk in these terms. But since nearly every judge uses background fact assumptions of uncertain accuracy, this leads to some striking inconsistencies. The situation at the Ohio court described earlier is one example. The focal court justices in a few appeals applied the judicial notice restrictions to social facts, while routinely using social facts obviously outside these restrictions elsewhere. Social facts are not often in the record—that is, introduced as testimony or exhibits at the trial level. This happened in only five focal court appeals during the year studied, and even that is probably an unusually large number for a state supreme court. Therefore, the great bulk of the social fact information introduced by counsel is outside the record.

Furthermore, appellate courts do not feel bound by the parties' stipulations of social facts; doing so would go a long way toward allowing the parties to stipulate the law governing future disputes involving other parties.[11]

The following exchange about social facts took place in the focal court arguments:

Q — I have one question for you. You're the prosecuting attorney, and in this case you have represented the people of the state of ————?
A — Yes.
Q — How come you entered into a stipulation such as I see here right in front of me? What *effect* is *your* agreeing to a set of facts on a high court of a state when it's about to make a precedent of some importance?
A — I don't think it has any effect—
Q — Is it *worth* anything at all?
A — [He said that the social facts were uncertain.]
Q — Of course that's true. Then why stipulate facts when it affects a whole lot [more] in the way of people than you and those you immediately represent?
A — Well, those facts were stipulated to—I imagine, I didn't try the case—they were stipulated because as a matter of trial tactics and strategy at the time the case was being tried. Some of those stipulated facts are helpful to us and some are *not* helpful. That's probably the real reason they were stipulated to.

Needless to say, the court went beyond the stipulated social facts; it could not allow a matter of trial tactics between the two parties to control a major legal principle. Likewise, it is unlikely that an appellate court would give a presumption of correctness to a trial judge's findings of social facts such as is given to case fact findings; if that were the case, different trial court districts could be subject to different laws.[12]

FINDING AND EVALUATING SOCIAL FACTS—
THE JUDGES' EXPERIENCES

Since the attorneys may not thoroughly present social facts and seldom contest their opponents' social fact contentions, the judges often must rely on their own resources to find and evaluate this information. The most important resource is their experience—their knowledge gained from their work before becoming an appellate judge and from their study of many disputes while on the bench. They also, as will be discussed elsewhere, do library research for empirical data, get advice from outside experts, use social facts mentioned in published opinions, or use legal rules as evidence of social facts; but these are relatively minor sources of information.

Obviously, judges are, as one put it, "the sum total of our many parts, and we bring it to the bench." Their experiences shape their decisions by providing a storehouse of background attitudes and information used to judge the information presented in a specific appeal. The judges interviewed often emphasized the importance of their past experiences, and did so in a variety of contexts. As was seen in the preceding chapter, past experience supplies supporting case facts used in making decisions about the facts of a case. Also, of course, past experience provides background knowledge of the law, and it provides, as the judges often said, various philosophies and biases.[13]

For this chapter, however, the important point is the major role of experience when finding and evaluating social facts, a role that the judges generally mentioned in some context or another in the interviews.[14] The experiences believed important were anything from the general "experience with people" and "experiences in life" to the more specific and specialized experiences based primarily on their work before becoming appellate judges. As lawyers they gained experience in handling clients' problems and learned about the practical aspects of, for example, tort claims or business operations. Probably the great majority of appellate judges have had considerable trial experience, either as lawyers or trial judges. These experiences, then become an important part of the judges' appellate decision making. To give an example, when explaining why trial court experience is important, a number of judges said it helped them understand the practical effects of decisions on the conduct of trials or it taught them that trial judges had the difficult job of making many snap judgments, so that appellate courts should not be quick to second-guess their rulings.

Most of the judges were asked how they evaluate social fact contentions made by counsel or others. A good many found this a hard question to answer; words like "judgment," "intuition," and "what strikes you" were common, and several just did not answer. But in the end the majority said they tested the contentions against their own experience, for example:

You apply your best judgment. You can't tell whether they're correct unless you've got a pretty definite idea based on experience that what you're saying is so. As I say you apply your best judgment to them. That's all anyone can do.

In all candor, I suppose we're a *bundle* of our own experiences—prejudices, I guess. *Ideally* what we should do is *find what* the effect—that is, it is represented to us that this thing doesn't work. Okay, we investigate, and find out the instances of how often it doesn't work, and find out how often it *does* work. I don't know that we do that probably as much as we should.
Q — How could you?
A — Well, I suppose we could, if we wanted to take the time. But I think most of us tend to fly by the seat of our pants, and as they say, "Well, hell, when I was practicing law—"

Several other judges also said they might investigate the social facts, either by reading on the subject or by consulting experts. Interestingly, only two mentioned the arguments of opposing counsel as an aid in judging social facts.

The central place of the judges' experience, especially in the development of the common law, has long been emphasized. Thus Holmes said, "The life of law has not been logic: it has been experience," and Pound, "The traditional legal reasoning represents the experience of generations of judges in the past. It is in some sort a traditionally transmitted judicial intuition founded in experience." When evaluating social fact arguments, a judge, said Cardozo, gets his knowledge "from experience and study and reflection; in brief, from life itself," and Llewellyn said judges use "general and balanced but rather uninformed horse sense."[15]

The importance of experience in finding and evaluating social facts showed up very clearly in the clerks' interviews.[16] They generally felt that their judges' experiences before becoming appellate judges are an important part of the decision making—important, the clerks typically said, in determining what the social facts are. When asked how they themselves judge the merit of social fact contentions, the clerks had an even harder time answering than the judges—in fact, none really answered the question other than by giving vague criteria, like "common sense" and "judgment," or by simply listing examples of social facts. Most specifically said they really did not know how to judge social facts. And in stark contrast to the judges, none mentioned their experiences as helpful here (though several mentioned using empirical data). Typical answers were:

I don't know. I guess the process is—the best I can say is you just sort of think it out yourself, and try to see which side makes sense.

There's a tendency, I guess, by lawyers generally to exaggerate. The flood-gates argument is sort of a—you know, the judges are all men of experience and sense and reason, and you know, they can take arguments like that and accept them at face or laugh them off. I guess, being more naïve there were times when, you know, I see an argument like that and say, "Well, gee," you know, and discuss it with the judge, and he'd say, "All that's nonsense. He's grandstanding," or whatever.

Most of the clerks added, like the second one just quoted, that their judges, because of their greater experience, were much more qualified than themselves to make these judgments. On the other hand, clerks may help provide information about current customs in society, something judges tend to be cut off from. Justice Rutledge, for example, reportedly felt "cloistered in the Supreme Court" and in need of law clerks because he "felt out of contact with the world, and particularly, with young people and their opinions."[17]

The judges' experiences are, of course, spotty. They tend to have much more background knowledge about trial courts and law firms, for example, than about most other organizations in society. One circuit judge complained that because he knew nothing about how prisons are run, he could not evaluate wardens' arguments that expanding prisoners' rights would interfere with the operation of prisons. There was no tendency at the focal court, on the other hand, for opinions to mention social facts more often when discussing issues about court operations than at other times.

The position of appellate judge is, for two reasons, a difficult one from which to gather and absorb new experiences that may help in social fact questions. First, judges engage in little outside work or other activities because they are restricted by time problems and ethical rules.[18] Thus they have little chance to gain direct experience about the facts of life. The appellate judge's job is often referred to as being "cloistered" or "monastic." Several social scientists have asked appellate judges about the drawbacks of their positions, and the most frequent response is the isolation, which judges dislike partly because they may become out of touch with the surrounding world and partly because they have little companionship.[19] And several judges have written about this problem. "There is no doubt," said Justice Hiscock of New York earlier this century," that life in an appellate court does tend to separate a judge from contact with many if not most kinds of activity and does tend, if he is not careful, to make him something of a theorist and metaphysican."[20] Judge Breitel, also from New York, said that because ethics restrict his interaction with others, "the judge is ever removed more distantly from the maddening scene. This entails a loss of contact with the greater environment, and for many men, a loss of sense of the movements of their time."[21]

Even so, appellate judges far from lose all contact with the outside world. Continuing with the New York judiciary, Chief Justice Fuld said that the judges do not really live in a cloistered cell because:

There is no field of technical knowhow, no borderline profession or calling, no fugitive diversion, but invites our attention at one time or another. Astrology and fortune telling in all its forms, gambling games, such as Gee Far, Policy, and the casting of dice, do not long remain mysteries to men who sit on our bench. Worldly we soon become.[22]

That is, as was discussed in Chapter 10, judges obtain knowledge about the world from the constant diet of fact patterns presented in appeals, in applications for leave to appeal, and in published opinions. This is a huge amount of information. But it is a scatter-shot sample, unorganized and likely to be incomplete—incomplete especially in the first wave of cases in a new area, where the lawmaking role is exceptionally important.[23]

Another exception, mentioned by several judges interviewed, is work on the administrative side of an appellate judge's job, which has grown enormously in recent years at many courts. Here the judges must keep in touch with the workings of lower courts, learning about the problems there and, thus, about practical problems their decisions may cause. Judges can also, of course, learn from simple observations of everyday life, learn some things from their clerks (and even from their secretaries, as one judge said he did), and, if they have time, learn through general reading of newspapers, magazines, and books.

A second reason why the position of an appellate judge is a difficult one from which to obtain background social fact information is the feeling against specialization on appellate courts, which was explained in Chapter 7. On one hand, a major argument against specialization is exposure to a wide range of cases giving judges background knowledge needed to make law.[24] On the other hand, lack of specialization means that judges cannot easily build up concentrated background knowledge about the practical aspects of specific areas of the law. One circuit judge interviewed said:

But maybe *fundamentally* a judge should be a generalist, because he's concerned with the interrelationships of all the institutions of society—its people and all of its institutional aspects—and he's got to know a little bit about *all* of the things that will come before him. And so he has to be a generalist. And I guess the best judge who ever lived, of course, would be the ultimate generalist. But then he has to have a capacity for specialization to go into *considerable* depth in *individual* cases in individual areas of human knowledge.

This, needless to say, is not an easy task and requires a full life of experience and study, along with an extensive effort in each case decided.

However, specialized knowledge can be very important in the social fact area, particularly experience gained from prior jobs. A number of judges said that when they had little experience with a topic, they found advice about social facts from colleagues who had previously specialized in the area very helpful, though a few others said that advice of this sort was of little or no importance.[25] Also, several judges added that appellate courts should have a good mix of judges from varying backgrounds to provide a wide range of experiences. This is a fairly common viewpoint among judges.[26]

The importance of the judges' experiences in determining social facts makes the connection between a judge's background and his decisions tremendously complicated. For example, one might think that a former prosecutor would tend to favor the prosecution in criminal cases; however, his knowledge of prosecution and police practices may lead him to understand problems there better than his colleagues and, thus, to be more likely to create new procedural safeguards. A judge's decision making must be greatly affected by his background—his upbringing, training, professional experiences, and so on—but much of this effect is due to the details of experiences in his life that result in odd bits of social fact information, making it improbable that any broad generalizations about the connection between a judge's background and his decisions will explain very much.[27]

SOCIAL FACTS DERIVED FROM ORDINARY WORK AS A JUDGE

Social fact information comes to appellate judges in several ways simply during their ordinary study of legal authority. One was just discussed: the fact patterns in published opinions. Judges also use social facts stated in prior opinions, and they use legal rules as evidence of what actually happens in life.

At the focal court one of every seven social facts mentioned in majority opinions (though almost none in minority opinions) was in a quotation from a prior opinion, generally an opinion of the U.S. Supreme Court or the focal court itself. These were seldom brought up by counsel; thus ordinary legal research in the law library is a fairly important source of social facts used—or at least openly used—by the court. Social facts found in opinions very likely have an aura of authenticity that leads judges to accept them more readily and that makes them more presentable in opinions. The attorneys' briefs, likewise, often presented social facts in quotations from precedents—more than a fourth of the social facts, excluding the Brandeis briefs. The attorneys possibly believed their social fact statements carried more weight if found in prior opinions; but an interesting point is that most of the attorneys' quoted social facts were in opinions from other states and lower federal courts, whereas the judges seldom quoted social facts from such opinions, probably because they are considered far less authoritative than its own or Supreme Court opinions.[28]

Appellate courts sometimes use legal rules to determine social facts; a rule is taken as evidence of what people actually do—it is assumed that people follow the law—and what people do is used as a social fact for making law. Here the rule does not serve as a legal proposition in any traditional sense. The focal court, for example, ruled that hearings are not needed in a parole revocation when the revocation is based on a felony conviction, because such a conviction is not supposed to (and, therefore, does not) occur without the right to a trial. The constitutional principle was used to establish a fact. As a practical matter, it is hard to tell how many social facts fall into this category because often only an expert in the particular field of law can tell whether a social fact statement is also a legal rule, especially when the operations of government agencies are described. In my opinion, however, less than 5 percent of the social fact statements at the focal court were obviously legal rules.

CONCLUSION

The problem of finding and evaluating social facts is a major problem for appellate courts, probably the major information-gathering problem they face in their lawmaking role.[29] The adversary system, as this chapter has discussed, is of limited help, and judges rely largely on their past experiences for this information, aided by the materials they routinely come across during ordinary legal research. Some judges also actively investigate social facts, getting advice from experts and using empirical data, especially from scholarly texts. But this is a dangerous and relatively minor source of social fact information, as will be discussed in the next chapter.

The practice of not placing influential social facts in opinions is, in my opinion, a bad policy. If judges make conscious efforts to explain the social facts underlying their lawmaking decisions, they are more likely to rethink their assumptions and not rely on those they are unsure of. And the social fact bases will be there for others to attack; the decision can be more easily overturned if the social facts are incorrect or change over the years, and courts elsewhere can more easily judge the strength of the ruling. Appellate courts, I believe, are not moving in the correct direction, as has been discussed in Chapter 7.

A further point of great importance, which will be a major topic in Chapter 15, is that many judicial decision-making techniques mitigate against the problems of finding and evaluating social facts. Examples are the exercise of judicial restraint, which means leaving social fact decisions to the legislature or executive, and the propensity to decide cases narrowly, which ties lawmaking more to the facts of the case than to broad social fact assumptions.

CHAPTER 13

Empirical Data and Investigating Social Facts

There is always an area not covered by legislation in which [courts] must revise old rules or formulate new ones, and in that process policy is often an appropriate and even a basic consideration. The briefs carry the first responsibility in stating the policy at stake and demonstrating its relevance; but if they fail or fall short, no conscientious judge will set bounds to his inquiry. If he finds no significant clues in the law books, he will not close his eyes to a pertinent study merely because it was written by an economist or perhaps an anthropologist or an engineer.[1]   (Justice Traynor)

If an appellate judge wishes to find or evaluate social facts through means other than those described in the preceding chapter, he must leave the legal milieu and learn from experts in other fields—that is, he must use scientific, social science, behavioral science, statistical, or other technical information about what happens in the world. (This wordy concept will be called "empirical data.") Appellate judges can obtain this information in several ways: (1) from the record through testimony or exhibits by professors and other experts introduced at the trial level or in an administrative hearing, (2) from arguments made in the briefs but outside the record, (3) from books and articles written by experts, and (4) by writing or talking directly to experts. The major topics in this chapter are the importance of empirical data information, how well the adversary system provides it, how the judges find it, and how they evaluate it.

THE USE OF EMPIRICAL DATA

The concern here is empirical data as social facts, not as case facts—that is, empirical data used in lawmaking rather than in dispute deciding. The latter is much more common in appellate courts, both empirical data as regular case facts (e.g., descriptions of a patented object or the future effect of an injury in a tort case) and as supporting case facts (e.g., background information needed to understand technical concepts in a patent case or medical knowledge about the aftereffects of injuries similar to the plaintiff's).[2] The circuit judges interviewed seem to get many more appeals involving empirical data as case facts than the state justices, and they often talked about scientific materials presented as case facts. On the other hand, the state justices, above all the focal court justices, tend to make greater use of empirical data for social facts.[3]

Empirical data are potentially very important information in appellate court lawmaking, for much lawmaking is based on social fact assumptions. This is especially true of the social sciences, because as one focal court judge said about them:

I think they're essential because to my way of thinking the law—if you had to put it in a niche—is a social science *itself.* So most research in the social sciences has a *bearing* on the law, because you're dealing with people, and you're dealing with raw emotions in many cases; and you're dealing with tempers and you're dealing with human outlooks and so forth. So I think *social sciences* are *closely* related to law.

Even so, courts in practice do not often use social science findings or other empirical data when making law.

Five majority and eight minority opinions, in 10 of the 112 focal court cases studied over a year, mentioned empirical data, representing 7 percent of all opinions; but in most there was just a quick reference to one or two sources.[4] As with social facts, however, the opinions gave only a rough indication of the attention given empirical data because its use may not be acknowledged.[5] In most of these cases much more empirical data were in the briefs or uncovered by the judges than were mentioned in the opinions; and attorneys in fifteen more cases presented some empirical data, though generally not much, which was not mentioned in the opinions.[6] But I do not know how much reliance was placed on this unmentioned information. In any event, the use of empirical data to support social facts was fairly limited. Only one-sixth of the opinions containing social facts as an important link in the reasoning mentioned empirical data, and social facts elsewhere were rarely supported by data presented to or found by the justices but not in the opinions.

Even this infrequent use of empirical data to support social facts is probably greater than usual. The focal court used it less in other years, according to the judges and clerks, though still more than the other five courts studied here. None of those interviewed in Ohio had run across empirical data used as social facts, and the circuit judges and the Rhode Island and Massachusetts justices, based on what was said in the interviews, use it in only one or two cases a year on the average. Also, from what has been written about courts elsewhere, empirical data are rarely if ever used except at the U.S. Supreme Court and a small number of circuit courts and state supreme courts.[7] This slight use, though, understates the importance of this material because it is used in the more important cases.

The use of empirical data varied greatly among the judges within the courts studied, except the Ohio court, of course. One circuit judge with long appellate experience had never used it. The maximum use was by a few state justices who made an effort to see when empirical data might be relevant and searched for such data. At this extreme, one justice said:

You try to get down on the *underside* and find out what *impact* the decision has, you know, on the people who use it. Now, naturally you can't tell before, but when you're deciding on precedential lines, as you do, you can find out from *lay journals* what's happening. And I did that . . . in nearly every kind of a case that I didn't have some feel for. If it had any complexity, I'd go to the lay journals first. If it was *planning,* I'd go to the *planning officers'* journal and the municipal officers' journal. . . . I mean, this was kind of a religion with me on things I didn't have a good feel for. There were some kinds of law I had better knowledge of than others, and I knew *what happened* because I'd practiced that kind of law; but I mean, you know, take a pirating of assets case in a big corporation. I had no experience in that. I don't know what they were talking about. I can always *write* it from the language. But, I mean, *what happened?* . . . One in particular, I just got all immersed in *Harvard Business Journal* and other things of that kind before I even got into the law to find out *what happens,* and *then* go into reading the facts and then the rules, and then of course I thought I could write a better opinion because of that.

But the vast majority of the judges had far different habits, making no substantial efforts to incorporate empirical data into their thinking. Most gave reasons why they did not use this material more often, the usual one being that the attorneys do not often bring it up. This includes those judges, to be discussed presently, who believed they should not use empirical data unless placed in the record. Many probably just did not notice that empirical data might be applicable to the problems, though only several made this explicit, for example: "It hasn't been either relevant or pinpointed to the extent that you had to [read empirical materials] many times. I say relevant and pinpointed because many times it may have been relevant but not pinpointed, and I didn't realize its relevance."

Another reason commonly given why empirical data are not used more often is simply that not many cases call for this type of information. The Massachusetts justices, for example, said they are extremely reluctant to rule statutes unconstitutional, and thus they do not often consider (or get) empirical data in that regard. Lastly, as will be discussed later, there is considerable skepticism about the value of some types of empirical data, especially social science research, along with a fear that judges cannot evaluate the material.

Just as social facts are used in a wide variety of issues, so are the empirical data used to support these facts. Empirical data, though, have become associated with some types of issues more than others. Two of these—equal protection and the admissibility of scientific techniques—will be given as examples. In equal protection issues a litigant claims that a law is unconstitutional because it unjustly discriminates against him and his category of persons. He must persuade the court that the legislation does not further any purpose the court believes to be a legitimate purpose—does not further it at all or does not further it efficiently, the test varying between judges and types of classification in the statutes. Here empirical data are often used to determine whether the plaintiff's group is actually treated differently to its disadvantage or whether the law is furthering the purposes attributed to it. In this category fall the numerous racial segregation cases, including Brown v. Board of Education.[8]

The second example is rules about whether a scientific technique of proof can ever be admissible, applied to, for example, polygraphs, drugs, and voice recordings to indicate whether someone is telling the truth, blood tests in paternity suits, breath tests as evidence of drunkenness, and accident reconstruction techniques in automobile negligence cases.[9] This type of evidence is not allowed unless the technique is shown to be at least fairly accurate, and the most common standard used to determine accuracy is whether the technique is generally accepted in the particular field to which it belongs. But the strictness of this standard varies greatly; for instance, breath tests but not polygraph tests are admissible even though the former are probably no more reliable. An interesting issue, on which appellate courts now differ, is whether voice-print tests can be used as evidence that a recorded voice is that of a specific person. Several courts have recently ruled the test either admissible or not after studying the extent of controversy among experts about its accuracy, using testimony and exhibits by police and by phonetics and linquistics professors submitted at the trial level, along with scientific journal articles read at the appellate level.[10]

THE ATTORNEYS AND EMPIRICAL DATA

The rest of the chapter discusses how appellate courts can obtain and evaluate empirical data. This is among the most difficult and controversial issues of appellate procedure, and dozens of judges and scholars have written about it over the past half-century.[11] The bulk of this literature concerns the extent courts should use the adversary system as a source for empirical data; thus the logical place to begin here is the attorneys' practices and attitudes about the use of empirical data.

On the whole, the focal court attorneys had only a moderate interest in presenting empirical data to support social facts. They gave at least some in 25 of the 112 cases, though nearly half the time it was merely ancillary—just quick references to one or two sources and constituting a very small part of their arguments. One or more attorneys emphasized empirical data in 13 appeals, 5 of which had equal-protection issues (out of 10 such cases that year). In 6 cases counsel filed full-fledged Brandeis briefs—briefs with page after page of empirical information, mainly medical, social science, and statistical materials. However, the court opinions generally did not cite any of the empirical data offered in a case, even when the attorneys emphasized it.[12]

Most attorneys interviewed said they had never used empirical data to support "policy arguments," as the question was phrased, and but a few had used it in more than a couple of cases. The reason almost always given for the slight use of empirical data was that their cases or type of practice did not call for this material.[13] It is difficult to second-guess them about how often, in fact, relevant empirical material was available; but in my opinion it was more often than the attorneys used it, and a couple of them said they kept an eye out for possible uses and found many. Perhaps a more important underlying reason for the limited use of empirical data is, as a few attorneys added, that their thinking is not geared toward using this material to support arguments of law.[14] Though the attorneys surely knew about the use of empirical data by the U.S. Supreme Court, the focal court had only just begun citing this material regularly; thus the attorneys may not have believed it to be very influential. It cannot be said, however, that the attorneys are in general unfamiliar with empirical data, since they often run across it at the trial level as case facts—for example, medical testimony in tort cases and economic data in antitrust cases. But this is altogether a different type of use, not geared to developing the law. Another reason attorneys may not place empirical data in their briefs—a reason volunteered by several—is that they believe that the data must be placed in evidence at the trial level, and they cannot later on appeal decide to submit it.[15]

There are, in fact, two ways attorneys can present empirical data to appellate courts: through the record and through the briefs and arguments. Judges often consider the latter permissible, in spite of what some attorneys believe. The attorneys' empirical data came solely from the record in only one focal court case, and very little data were involved in that case. Empirical data were in the record in four other cases, three equal-protection cases with Brandeis briefs, two of which had massive amounts of empirical data in the record. Four medical doctors, two sociologists, and a psychologist testified at length in one case about the effects of various drugs; and in the other each side retained statisticians, who then filled 3,000 pages of transcript with exhibits and testimony about the state's educational system. But generally all the empirical data submitted by counsel in a case came as statements in the briefs supported by citations to scientific and social science writings, law review articles discussing empirical data, government reports, or even newspaper articles. Virtually none came in at the oral arguments without first being mentioned in the briefs.

I asked the attorneys who had much experience with empirical data as social facts how they located this material. They normally relied on the advice of experts—experts they happened to know or experts employed by their clients—for this information and for what publications to read or what other experts to contact. (They were generally able to obtain this advice free of charge.) Also, a good number did library research on their own, but only two relied on this completely.

The likelihood that opposing counsel will present adequate empirical data to the court varies greatly from attorney to attorney and from case to case. It depends on, among other things, the attorneys' interest in presenting data, the time and money they have, and their ability to find experts or publications supplying the information. Thus there is a good chance that the court will not receive adequate empirical information and that one side will present much less than the other. And as Professor Kadish has said, "It is truer here than in the legal argument that the more persuasive, if not more valid, case will be made by the side with the biggest research team of scholars."[16] Only one side presented empirical data in most of the focal court cases in which attorneys used that material; only several times was there anything resembling a balance between the amount, at least, of empirical data given by the adversaries. A study of the U.S. Supreme Court cases involving empirical data also found that there was normally an imbalance of this sort.[17]

SEARCHING FOR EMPIRICAL DATA AT THE COURT

The question of whether judges should be able to search for and use empirical data not given by counsel is hotly debated, though the trend is strongly toward permitting it. Judges, as will be seen, are of different minds about the question, as is the literature on the subject.[18] The arguments are similar to those involved in other aspects of information gathering: The court should not investigate social facts because it is unfair to the losing party to use information he has not had a chance to answer. Information derived from the adversary process, especially information subject to cross-examination at the trial level, is more likely to be accurate than information found by judges (a contention that will be discussed later). On the other side, it is said that lawmaking in important cases should not depend on counsel's often incomplete information.

Several procedures have been suggested to mitigate these conflicting considerations. If judges believe that one or both counsels have inadequately presented empirical data, they can ask them for more help, either by requesting new briefs containing the material or by sending the case to a master or back to the trial court for expert testimony. And if the judges do conduct independent research and find useful material, they can send it to counsel for comment before deciding the case, or they can put it in the opinion and allow it to be attacked in a rehearing petition. These suggestions are often made, but the procedures are rarely if ever used at the courts studied and apparently at other courts as well.[19]

About a fourth of the judges (at least one from each court but the Rhode Island court) felt that any empirical data used must be in the record, mainly because they believe that the materials should be subject to trial court adversary fact-finding procedures, particularly cross-examination. However, the great majority said they use empirical data sources not in the record, and almost all of them have done their own research for empirical data.[20] At most of the courts, especially at the focal and Massachusetts courts, there was considerable disagreement about the propriety of independent research for empirical data and, additionally, about whether this information should be used even if in the briefs or records.

Although the judges seldom gave specific figures about how often they actually did research for empirical data, they clearly varied greatly within each court, and overall the focal court obviously did more research than any of the other five. Several of its justices did research of this type for at least 10 percent of their opinions, and no judge at the other courts approached this figure. The Rhode Island justices were the next most likely to search for empirical data, and, of course, the Ohio justices did no such research. The reason for this great variation in the amount of research is simply the variation in the amount of attention given empirical data; those using it more tended to be those who did more research. The judges, incidentally, delegated this research to their clerks substantially less often than traditional legal research; several focal court judges, however, did rely on their clerks' endeavors and only looked at the materials selected by them.

Much of the empirical data in the focal court opinions was found by the court. Only one-third of the references to publications involving empirical data were cited in the briefs.[21] Half of these were in amicus briefs and not the parties' briefs; so here at least the amicus briefs seemed to add something.[22] In addition, however, about a fourth of the empirical data in the opinions came from the record in two cases. All together, over 60 percent of the social facts supported by empirical data were supported by empirical data in the record or briefs, including amicus briefs.

HELP FROM OUTSIDE EXPERTS. It has been said in Chapter 6 that most of the justices in the state courts studied, except the Ohio court, get advice from experts off the court, though not often. From the examples given of this practice, at least at the focal and Rhode Island courts, it appears to have been used largely to obtain information about empirical data, though this source of information is rarely evident from the opinions.[23] A number of focal court justices contacted the state's prison officials either to obtain figures on how many prisoners would be freed if the court made a ruling retroactive, or to obtain figures on the length of sentences given for a specific crime to see what constitutes an unconstitutionally excessive sentence. The Rhode Island and focal court justices and law clerks quite often asked science or social science professors for advice simply to get a list of things to read. Probably less often, they also asked experts for their opinions about the substance of empirical questions. For example, one justice said that he talked to his doctor during an annual physical examination about what practical effect a proposed ruling would have on surgeons' dealings with their patients. It should be made clear, however, that outside experts are not a major source of information about empirical data; probably few judges in the country go to them for any kind of advice, and even on the Rhode Island and focal courts advice on empirical matters was rarely or never sought by most justices.[24] Also, the advice, always, as far as I know, involves little effort on the part of the outside expert or agencies contacted. They are never paid for their efforts; their advice is typically verbal rather than in written reports; and they never do any actual empirical research or, probably, even much library research for the judges.

An often suggested but apparently never adopted means of meeting the problems of finding and evaluating empirical data is that appellate courts use a staff of nonlawyer experts located either within the court or in organizations established to advise appellate courts around the country.[25] The major problem with these proposals is, in my view, that the staff would have to be very large—and very expensive—if it were to include expertise in more than a small percentage of the areas in which courts use social facts. A more feasible approach may be to hire professors or other experts to study and advise the court on specific problems as they arise, rather than hiring full-time scholars and rather than using the informal arrangements presently used.[26] The advice would be in writing and, thus, could be made available to counsel for comment. But even here the expense is likely to be a handicap (one benefit of the adversary system is that the information it supplies comes to the court free of charge), and to mitigate against the likely event that an expert will exaggerate his knowledge, courts should obtain studies from two or more experts before relying on what they receive.

EVALUATION OF EMPIRICAL DATA

The main problem with using empirical data for social facts is that the material may not be accurate.[27] Reliance on mistaken social fact findings affects future disputes, whereas mistaken case facts have little impact beyond the immediate dispute and thus cause less damage. How, then, can and do judges tell whether empirical data are accurate? Advice directly from experts outside the court is not a likely source of help here, as we have seen. Thus the judges must rely either on the adversary system—on expert testimony presented by the parties or counsel's arguments on appeal—or on the judges' own independent research or background knowledge.

TRIAL COURT ADVERSARY PROCEEDINGS. The usual method in the court system for testing the accuracy of technical information is through testimony by expert witnesses at trial. When case facts, especially supporting case facts, are outside the general knowledge of ordinary people, trial counsel may place experts on the witness stand and cross-examine opponents' expert witnesses. A small number of appellate judges and scholars believe that this process should be required for empirical data used as social facts, as was said earlier, because the adversary proceedings at trial help determine the accuracy of the data.[28] Certainly, expert testimony and cross-examination can help appellate judges evaluate this type of information. At the focal court, for example, by far the most argument about empirical data was found in the few rare appeals containing substantial amounts of expert testimony. There was conflicting expert opinion and, in one case, debate about statistical methodologies; my impression, though, based on a quick reading of the records, is that even in cross-examination trial counsel tried mainly to establish separate facts supporting their respective sides, rather than to attack or contradict opponents' contentions.

There are many problems with the view that empirical data must come in from the record, problems that require a broad discussion of trial court testimony as a source for social facts. The problems greatly limit the effectiveness of using this traditional means of evaluating information supplied by experts.

To begin with, the present use of expert testimony and the adversary system to present case facts does not work well. According to McCormick, it "is widely considered a sore spot in judicial administration,"[29] and he gives two reasons. First, lawyers tend to choose experts who will be the best witnesses for their positions, rather than those who know the most about the subject. An adversary, being such, does not want to present empirical data damaging to his case. The main problem, which is applicable to social facts and case facts alike, is that a litigant may fail to present his side thoroughly or to discover the opponent's weaknesses, and the opponent is not likely to make up the deficiency. An often suggested but little used answer is that the trial judge himself call expert witnesses; but the neutrality of an expert far from ensures his accuracy.

McCormick's second reason is much less applicable to social facts: The adversary method of presenting empirical data, with direct and cross-examination, is not dispassionate enough and overemphasizes conflicts in scientific opinion, which the jury is unable to resolve. The trial courts, according to Judge Frank, "witness daily the sorry spectacle of hired, partisan experts disagreeing with one another."[30] But emphasizing conflicting views is beneficial when judging social facts; the court is much freer to conclude that a social fact question has no answer than is a jury to dodge a case fact question. On the other hand, this is not a strong reason for restricting empirical data to testimony in the record, since a judge can just as easily learn of conflicting views from the briefs or from independent research. Whether the cross-examination of experts on the stand helps attack their views above the presentation of opposing views is questionable. Judge Leventhal, for example, has noticed that on "broad technical issues and policy determinations," as opposed to ordinary factual disputes, lawyers rarely accomplish anything devastating when cross-examining experts in administrative hearings.[31]

Further objections to relying on trial testimony for empirical data and for the evaluation of empirical data are numerous.[32] First of all, trial court testimony is an inconvenient way of getting the information. The question-and-answer format is longer, less well organized, and more difficult to follow than written materials such as Brandeis briefs. At the focal court, at least, much of the trial records containing social fact testimony consisted of discussions about, and rulings on, technical evidentiary objections of the sort normally associated with case fact testimony; these serve little purpose when dealing with social facts except when attacking the qualifications of an expert to speak on a subject.[33]

More important, the ever-present problems of inadequate presentation by counsel and the imbalance of counsel are very likely to be damaging here because of the great amount of time and money needed to put the best experts on the stand when the empirical data are at all elaborate. Trial counsel may believe that the chances of getting into the court of last resort are too slim to justify the expense of presenting empirical data testimony, or he may simply not see the need for this information at the time of trial. The cost of paying experts may restrict the quality of information in the record. With a given amount of funds a litigant can probably gather more and better data in a Brandeis brief than he can by obtaining expert testimony. If the attorneys use experts who volunteer their services, as those before the focal court generally did, they may well not get the best experts. Also, experts answering questions on the witness stand have less opportunity to contemplate their answers and to check source materials than when writing a book or article. The appeal process often takes so long that empirical data in the record are out of data by the time the court of last resort decides the case. And the parties may present data relating to only a limited issue or limited set of outcomes they are interested in, whereas the judges may want broader knowledge of the area.[34]

The attorneys used expert testimony for social facts in only five of the focal court cases studied, and in three not a great deal of information was placed in the record. The other two involved massive amounts of empirical data, but I interviewed counsel in these cases and one attorney from each said he doubted the accuracy of data relied on by his opponents, and neither pursued the point because of time and money problems. One with exceptionally heavy financial backing said he thought his opponent's data had been sloppily collected,

> but we would have had to have five years to prepare the case if we were going to go into all that stuff. So we made a decision that probably, you know, overall, those statistics are *basically* accurate. The variation would be *insignificant* in terms of the overall context of the case. So we decided, you know, there are limits to what can be done, both human and financial; so we decided not to go beyond those figures.

His objections seemed persuasive to me at least; but by not raising them he, in effect, admitted that the figures were correct. The two sides then selected aspects of the figures favorable to their respective positions, and neither they nor the court questioned the accuracy of the underlying figures.

Hence, especially in view of the lawmaking implications of social facts, the judges typically believe they cannot safely rely solely on the testimony of the parties' experts to evaluate empirical data, although it can partly serve that need. Therefore, the judges must look to counsel's appellate arguments and to their own research and background knowledge for evaluating this type of information.

EVALUATION BY THE ATTORNEYS. Another way the adversary system may help appellate judges evaluate empirical data is through counsel's criticism and critical filtering of the information. I asked the attorneys who had had some experience with empirical data as social facts—less than half those interviewed—how they evaluated this material. Most gave as one means the caliber or reputation of the expert involved. (The lawyers often touted the qualifications of their experts in the interviews and to the court, and much of the experts' trial testimony was about their qualifications.) A good number said they simply assumed that data compiled by government agencies were correct. Lastly, three younger attorneys said frankly that they did not care whether the material was accurate; they presented whatever supported their position. Only one lawyer said that he himself judged the substance of the materials; he could do so because he had a good deal of experience in the particular field outside his law practice.

Possibly because the attorneys rely on these surface features to judge empirical data, the data in the focal court briefs and arguments, even in the Brandeis briefs, were seldom challenged or contradicted by the opponents. By and large, each side simply presented the facts supporting his position, leaving untouched the facts presented by the other sides. And quite a few of the challenges that were made were done only by questioning the credentials of the expert who supplied the information. (By challenging empirical data,

I do not mean arguments that the legislature, not the courts, should make decisions based on the data—an argument routinely made in these cases.) Also, as will be discussed later, when the judges were asked how they evaluate empirical data, none answered that they use counsel's arguments for this purpose—except one judge who said he was more prone to accept empirical data agreed to by counsel and except, of course, the small minority who said the data should be subject to trial court adversary proceedings.

EVALUATION BY THE JUDGES. The adversary system, then, is of limited help in presenting information about the accuracy of empirical data. How, then, do the judges evaluate it?

Appellate judges have varying degrees of background knowledge about the social or physical sciences, though probably few have enough to help them evaluate the conclusions of experts. Many obtained some familiarity with this type of information before joining the appellate bench, especially in trial courts and in government jobs. And then even in their present position some must deal with a steady dose of empirical data. Federal judges, especially, decide cases with massive amounts of technical material as case facts. Judge Wright from the District of Columbia Circuit Court, which receives an unusually large amount of this material, wrote:

Review of regulatory agency decisions . . . certainly taxes the generalist skills with which federal judges are said to be endowed. Just during the past year I have received a compulsory education in a variety of subjects of considerable economic and technological complexity. To name just a few, I now have more than a nodding acquaintance with some of the intricacies of nuclear breeder reactor development, pipeline construction through the Alaskan tundra and its possible ecological implications, the effect of different gasoline grades on automobile engine performance, the future of air transport between the small cities of New England, and the differing methods of producing sulphuric acid.

While the view of America's future, that a seat on the court reviewing a wide variety of agency decisions gives, is nothing short of kaleidoscopic, I must confess that on occasion I wish I had taken more math, science and economics courses.[35]

Many judges also have some contact with statistics, the use of computers, or the social sciences in the administrative side of their jobs—studies of the court system and the like. Outside reading supplies some background knowledge. High case loads and the constant heavy reading of briefs and opinions tend to limit appellate judges' appetite for serious reading at home. Surprisingly, though, a good number of judges said that they do quite a bit of reading in the sciences or, mainly, the social sciences.[36] This is either general reading in books or journals aimed at laymen, for example *Scientific American* or *Transactions*, or fairly concentrated reading in a specific area that interests the judge, such as one judge who was interested in illegal drugs.

Even so, the judges' overall exposure to empirical data is necessarily spotty and probably seldom helps actually evaluate the material. It may, though, help them understand the literature or testimony. When asked if his reading in the social sciences helped him evaluate the materials, one judge said: "Oh, I think it helps you comprehend the experts. It doesn't make me an expert. I mean, I know what he's *talking* about. I've become acquainted with the vocabulary, what some people would say, pejoratively, the jargon." Moreover, the law clerks do not often have much background knowledge useful to their judges here. They lack the judges' practical exposure to empirical materials, though many had substantial doses of social science courses in college or law school.

The judges who had used empirical data as social facts were asked how they evaluate it. The most common method, given by about a third of them, was to study the overall state of expert opinion on the subject, either by reading as much material as possible in the area to see whether the experts agreed or by simply using materials the judges believe generally recognized as reliable. For example: "Obviously if you go to as many sources as you can of that nature, and if they fall into a *pattern*, you have no reason to believe that you're *not* right." This is the same type of test described earlier often used to determine whether proof by means of scientific techniques, such as polygraph tests, can be admitted into evidence. This standard "assures that those most qualified to assess the general validity of a scientific method will have the determinative voice,"[37] in theory not burdening the judges with the technical decision. Also, it is very close to one of the judicial notice criteria—whether the fact is readily ascertainable from a reliable source. There is little direct indication, however, that the judges interviewed had either of these tests in mind; only two judges mentioned them in this context. Also, the judges usually indicated that they do not adhere to a strict standard here: Either this was only an alternative evaluation method sometimes not used, or the test is not very strict, for example, determining the "preponderance of evidence."

Several judges said that in evaluating empirical data they relied, at least partly, on the expert's reputation or credentials, a standard used to a greater extent by the attorneys. For example:

Q — How do you tell whether this evidence is correct when it comes to you?
A — Well, you never do. I mean you never know *certainly*. I guess you look at the qualifications of the person who testifies. You look at the extent of his studies, and you're impressed by this. And, for example, you never really know whether the people who tell us that, oh, say a planet like Saturn is essentially gaseous. I can't prove it. I suspect you can't either. But I guess you accept statements of astronomers and physicists about this because you're impressed by their credentials and maybe by the uniformity of opinion on it.

Another test that was mentioned by the attorneys is the assumption that the government is a reliable source. A few judges said or implied that they were more likely to believe government reports and statistics or empirical data supplied by high government officials. A good number of the authorities cited for empirical data in the focal court opinions (and in the briefs) were state or federal government materials.

None of these means of evaluating empirical data involves the judges' actual evaluation of specific studies; rather, the judges evaluate the source of the study or the overall beliefs of experts in the field. In fact, a number of judges volunteered that they had no means to evaluate the materials and had to rely on these extrinsic indicators. On the other hand, about a third of the judges said they had attempted to evaluate the substance of the data, usually along with one of the previously mentioned methods. Half of these used an emotional, indescribable test, for example:

Whenever you get into a discipline that's not your own discipline, you lack a firm basis for judgment, and I think it probably is something you pick up through the pores. That's a feeling. It's a prejudice. It's not an intellection at all. It's a reaction or feeling.

But others, who had had an unusually large amount of contact with the social sciences, said they use their own knowledge of the area or looked to see whether the expert's reasoning is internally consistent or supported by ample data. Justice Traynor claims that judges' experiences render them capable of evaluating empirical data:

We need not distrust judicial scrutiny of such extralegal materials. The very independence of judges, fostered by judicial office even when not guaranteed by tenure, and their continuous adjustment of sight to varied problems tend to develop in the least of them some skill in the evaluation of massive data. They learn to detect latent quackery in medicine, to question doddered scientific findings, to edit the swarm spore of the social scientists, to add grains of salt to the fortune-telling statistics of the economists.[38]

But confidence to this extent was rarely expressed by the judges interviewed.

On the other hand, Justice Traynor's suspicious and deprecating attitude toward the caliber of much empirical data is typical of the judges interviewed.[39] This feeling is based on their past experiences with experts and is largely directed toward the social sciences. Two typical comments are:

I'm rather skeptical on experts generally since—this is another advantage of having been a trial judge—you know you can buy an expert on anything. All you have to do is try about two dozen product *liability* cases, and you see just exactly how many Ph.D.'s you can line up on any issue.

I ran into political sci people all through state government for twenty years. I've never known one that knew anything about it.

Several said, as in the first statement above, that one can find expert support for almost any point one wishes to make. Circuit Judges David Bazalon and Jerome Frank, who probably know as much about the social sciences—and certainly about psychology—as any appellate judges, have been extremely skeptical of, and actually annoyed at, the quality of social science work. Bazalon has called psychiatry the "ultimate wizardry"; Frank has denounced "the students of society" at length because they "have delivered little that the courts can use."[40]

CONCLUSION

Roscoe Pound in 1923 wrote that judicial lawmaking is partly based on the judge's "intuition founded in experience" which "continually leads him to the right results" even though the reasoning used in opinions may not be sound.[41]

The instinct of the experienced workman [the judge] operates with assurance. Innumerable details and minute discriminations have entered into it, and it has been gained by long experience which has made the proper inclusions and exclusions by trial and error until the effective line of action has become a habit.[42]

Then in 1942 he wrote:

In the simple social and economic order of [the early nineteenth century], the law-maker could find in his own experience, or in the general knowledge of his neighbors, all that he needed beyond what was in his law books. Mostly it was patent to the observation of an intelligent man without special training or special effort. Today lawmaking suffers from the assumption that a lawmaker may find in his own experience of life or general knowledge of men and things all that is needed to make for a due functioning of the legal order. . . . It is futile to expect that the needed preliminary work of searching for, organizing, and making available the data required for law-making or judicial rule-making or for judicial notice of the background of fact upon which judgments of reasonableness must be made, will do itself spontaneously. . . . More than one unhappy feature of American administration of justice is a result of short-sighted or ignorant application of lay common sense to difficult problems of law and of judicial organization and administration which called not for common sense but for the trained uncommon sense of experts.[43]

Pound then advocated the use of statistics: "No one believes more firmly than I in the importance of bringing together authentic information as to exactly how legal precepts and doctrines and institutions are functioning.[44]

But he added a long, angry attack on the quality of statistics available and said that the use of statistics in appellate court decision making had made little headway because of this poor quality.[45]

This is still the issue as it stands today: As long as appellate judges insist on deciding appeals by considering the wisdom of the rules made—that is, by using social facts—to what extent should they rely on their background knowledge gained from experience and to what extent on empirical data? The answer requires balancing the ease of obtaining information from the different sources against its probable accuracy and completeness.

Judges expend virtually no effort and time when drawing upon their background experience for social fact information, but the information gained is likely to be parochial, outdated, influenced by one's desires, or simply absent.

Empirical data are gathered and evaluated by appellate judges with great difficulty. The adversary system is not a satisfactory tool here. Rarely are both sides of an appeal interested enough, knowledgeable enough, and paid enough to present the relevant information adequately and to attack the weaknesses of the opponent's material. Incomplete and imbalanced presentation is probably so common that more often than not information gained from counsel leaves the judges no better off than when they started. Judge J. Skelly Wright, having been presented much statistical data by counsel in a school case, complained that the experts differed over basic assumptions, that each party engaged in "data shopping and scanning to reach a preconceived result," and that the lawyers inadequately explained the technical materials. Therefore, he said:

Lest like a latter day version of Jarndyce v. Jarndyce this litigation itself should consume the capital of the children in whose behalf it was brought, the court has been forced back to its own common sense approach to a problem which, though admittedly complex, has certainly been made more obscure than was necessary.[46]

If judges use empirical data, then, they must go beyond the record and the briefs. But they have limited expertise, time, and staff with which to find and evaluate the empirical data sources. The possible use of outside experts involves substantial problems, as has been discussed.

This is a perplexing situation; judges have two risky tactics—two risky sources of social fact information when making law. One option, of course, is to limit lawmaking, and indeed information-gathering problems are a reason behind judicial restraint, as will be shown in Chapter 15. But when judges do make law, there is no satisfactory solution to the dilemma. In practice, judges nearly always take the more expedient road; they seldom use empirical data to substantiate social facts.

My own opinion is that, in general, this is the correct road, particularly when social science information would be used to determine social facts about what actually happens in life (by far the most common type of social facts used in judicial lawmaking). Often the issue of whether empirical data should be used is phrased according to one's feelings about the probable accuracy of the judges' background knowledge and of empirical data. For example, a social scientist has written, "The Court's use of social science in the Brown [school segregation] case confirmed the success of efforts . . . to have constitutional law propounded in the light of reliable extralegal data rather than of arbitrary judicial biases,"[47] and a law professor has stated, "A canny judicial guess, unsupported by evidence, might be more reliable than a finding of fact based on pseudo-scientific surveys."[48] Surely, much social science work, along with other types of empirical data, is not accurate; but one cannot say with any certainty just how much is. At any rate, more important issues than the accuracy of empirical data are whether judges can find and, especially, evaluate this information. Whether accurate and relevant information exists is beside the point if judges cannot find it or determine that it actually is accurate. The judges lack the resources, as was just said, to perform these tasks adequately, especially in disorganized fields such as most social sciences. Lastly, and probably more important, the infrequent replication of social science studies means that, no matter how much library research is done, one can rarely actually establish the accuracy of a social science finding. Overall, then, the odds of uncovering empirical data about social life sufficiently trustworthy to act as a social fact basis for appellate decisions are so remote that the search for empirical data to be used for such a purpose is not worth the effort.[49] An exception might be some extremely rare situations in which judges' background knowledge is almost totally absent, where the issue is important enough to justify an extraordinary amount of time researching the literature, and where the issue falls into one of the very few areas that have been researched over a long period of time by many social scientists so that the judges have the benefit of thorough criticism within and between social science specialties. Offhand, I can think of no such situations.

These arguments are less applicable to some other empirical data sources. A judge's background knowledge is less likely to supply background information in physical science areas, and findings there are much more likely to have been replicated and, thus, are more reliable. Perhaps simple descriptive writings, as opposed to research studies, would help in areas of life judges know nothing about, as long as the material is selected with care. Hence, the practice of the judge quoted earlier who read business journals to learn about the pirating of corporate assets may not be objectionable. Also, it may be safe to use statistics from government agencies that have no obvious ax to grind, but only if rough approximations are enough, such as figures supplied to the focal court by the state's prison authorities. However, the great bulk of social facts used by appellate courts fall within the traditional realm of the social sciences, especially facts about what motivates people and what causes what in social life. These are the traditional uses of empirical data in opinions, and they should be greatly restricted.

The discussion so far has been about empirical data used to establish social facts about what happens in life. But empirical data can be used in other ways, where it can have an important role. It can be used merely to show the existence of certain scholarly views without implying their accuracy. This was the purpose of the original Brandeis briefs early in the century; they only attempted to show that a body of expert opinion supported the need for the legislation attacked as being unconstitutionally arbitrary. Another example is using the fact that psychiatrists' views differ when making standards for insanity defense in criminal cases. When used in this way, the problems of finding and evaluating empirical data are greatly lessened. Judges need not make a thorough search of the scholarly work in the area, for a moderate sample will do. And they need not decide whether the empirical data are correct, except that once in a while they must decide whether a particular view is so tenuous that it should be ignored. (Judges often use presumptions that a law will or not be changed—e.g., presumptions for or against the constitutionality of statutes—that limit the areas in which they consider empirical data and allow them to decide when empirical data are skimpy. But, unless this presumption is very strong, the judges must do more than simply learn the views of the experts, since they must determine the accuracy of any empirical data considered whenever they believe there is a chance that the presumption might be overcome.)

Lastly, and very important, judges can—and should—use the views and research findings of nonlaw experts to restrain their social fact assumptions based on past experiences. Empirical data and background knowledge can work together in social fact questions, not by establishing social facts, but by creating doubts and uncertainty. A judge's preconceived notion about the facts of life can be attacked through information from the social sciences and other nonlaw fields. He need not determine that the information is correct—only that it is entitled to some respect. The empirical data would not really add to the information used in the decision; rather they would "unsettle a preconception which a judge might otherwise employ without reservation."[50] Hence empirical data may mitigate the dangers of using social facts based on background knowledge. How often judges actually use empirical data this way is hard to tell because they would be very unlikely to mention the material in the opinions, but the judges interviewed gave virtually no evidence of this use.

One thing seems certain, however: Counsel are unlikely to supply empirical data with this purpose in mind, for they are unlikely to know the judges' social fact assumptions ahead of time. Judges may not be self-constrained and industrious enough to do independent research aimed at attacking their assumptions. Judges should, therefore, notify counsel, at least in important appeals, of social facts they think important to their decision, giving counsel a chance to present empirical data attacking these assumptions.[51] The judges could even give counsel a tentative draft opinion that specifies the important social facts; counsel would then know not only what facts are important but how the court proposes to use them.[52]

Part IV

Epilogue

Summary and Comparison: Sources of Information

The concluding remarks are divided into two chapters, which present some new material as well as summarizing the book. This chapter reviews briefly what has been said about how and where appellate courts obtain information, and estimates the relative importance of information received from within and outside the adversary system. The final chapter, Chapter 15, is devoted to several speculative questions: why judges obtain different information from different sources, how information-gathering problems interrelate with appellate court decision methods, and how judges deal with the uncertainty caused by decision making with incomplete information.

In all this, one must realize that appellate court information gathering, like most areas of social life, is an uncertain and complex subject. The fact that the information-gathering activities are more accessible than other aspects of appellate decision making only partly mitigates the uncertainty. The complexity means that each topic tends to interrelate with many others, requiring the intricate organization of this book. The temptation is strong in both social science and law to impose simplified order by concentrating on a few aspects of a subject area and on theories proporting to tie them together. But taking a few aspects out of their setting strips them of much of their meaning and gives an incomplete picture of their interrelations. Also, if one emphasizes matters of theoretical concern, he is strongly biased toward finding patterns of theoretical interest and may be constrained to find them, while disregarding important aspects of the area that have not been incorporated into theories.

In this book, therefore, the search for patterns has been secondary. If they arise, they are noted, but the main objective has been simply to describe the information-gathering activities of appellate courts, a broad and important topic. Likewise the purpose of this summary is largely, by giving an abbreviated version of what has been said earlier, to present appellate court information gathering as a complex and sometimes murky subject that cannot be organized neatly.

INFORMATION FROM COUNSEL

Appellate judges get information from four basic sources; two are through the adversary system, the record and counsel's argument on appeal, and two are outside the adversary system, independent investigation and the judges' background knowledge based on experience. Information from counsel is, with rare exceptions, tightly restricted to only a few channels. The record consists of the papers and testimony presented below, and it is condensed in the statement of facts and, ordinarily, appendixes. Virtually all of counsel's argument on appeal is in the briefs and oral argument, and little comes in after the arguments. Applications for rehearing almost always lead nowhere. Informal contact between counsel and the court is restricted because fairness requires that each advocate be able to answer whatever information his opponent gives. Nevertheless, a few attorneys do send letters after the arguments, and on very rare occasions the judges meet informally with opposing counsel during the opinion-writing stage. The briefs are by far the most important source of information from counsel; little is presented in the oral arguments that is not already in the briefs. Judges and attorneys, though, believe the arguments are important for other reasons, especially for presenting a concise picture of the case and for giving judges a chance to question counsel.

Information from the adversary system strongly tends to come from only the two opposing parties. In a good number of appeals, especially the most important ones, the focal court did receive three or more briefs from different sources, that is, from amici, intervenors, separate parties, or counsel briefing similar issues in different cases. But, on the whole, these extra briefs added little to the information presented by the two basic parties. On the other hand, the briefs themselves generally include input from two or more cooperating attorneys.

The value of information received through the adversary system, of course, depends greatly on the quality of the attorneys' work. The great majority of appellate judges are disappointed by the help they receive from counsel; yet they have done little to improve it other than give speeches telling the bar what it should do. For their part, appellate counsel tend to be better than average lawyers, and there is a good deal of appellate specialization. All agree that the quality of the briefs and arguments varies greatly, and evidence strongly suggests that the imbalance of counsel affects the outcome of appeals.

Adverseness is a backbone of the adversary system, based as it is on the assumption that counsel's self-interest will propel him to present thoroughly the information supporting his position. Partly for this reason, judges are reluctant to decide appeals lacking opposing parties who stand to gain or lose directly by the outcome of the dispute—that is, lack of standing, friendly suits, moot cases, and requests for advisory opinions. On the other hand, the attorneys' incentives to win appear, on the whole, to be rather mild; as opposed to their clients, they often have little stake in the outcome other than sympathy with their side and a general desire to win.

In spite of the assumption of adverseness, judges try to dampen adverseness in some areas, asking counsel to supply information favorable to opponents. A major emphasis in judges' writings about appellate advocacy is that counsel should be candid about the weaknesses of his position—for instance, he is expected to provide a fair description of the facts in the appendixes and briefs, and he is expected to bring forth important adverse authorities missed by his opponent. These, however, are not large inroads on the adversary system; on the whole they are not very successful, and attorneys are not obliged to bring up some important types of adverse information, especially issues and social facts.

Another major aspect of the adversary system is the extent counsel limit their presentations to the relevant information; they help the court little when relevant information is buried in large amounts of other material. An unlimited amount of information is available, but little of it has a bearing on any decision the court may wish to make. Thus the judges' work loads depend greatly on counsel's ability and willingness to weed out the excess information. One of the major means of forcing attorneys to concentrate on the key elements of their appeals is the oral arguments, where time limits require that counsel only mention a small part of the information in the briefs.

The overload problems differ considerably for the different types of information. Although the focal court opinions used only a small portion of the legal authority and social facts brought up by the attorneys, the overload is not particularly damaging. Judges sometimes do complain about excessive citation of authority, but checking the citations can be delegated to law clerks. Social facts (and also supporting case facts) comprise such a small portion of the attorneys' presentations that, no matter how irrelevant, they do not take much of the judges' time.

On the other hand, excessive issues and case facts are major problems. Probably the biggest complaint judges have of attorneys is that they present too many insubstantial issues—that is, too many appeals with scant hope of reversal and too much shotgunning, throwing out numerous issues even though one or two at most have any merit. Courts with discretionary jurisdiction can refuse appeals that have little substance, but they still must deal with the shotgun approach (although that approach was not the usual one at the focal court and was unpopular among the attorneys interviewed). The amount of case facts is limited in the first instance by restricting the facts to those in the record (with some exceptions). Still, the record is often lengthy, containing much that is not relevant to the issues being decided. The attorneys abbreviate the record in the appendixes and in the shorter narrative statement of facts. The judge writing the opinion or his clerk, however, very often study the record thoroughly, though the other judges do rely largely on counsel's abbreviation of the facts.

One incentive prompting an attorney both to limit the amount of less useful information and to give information opposed to his position is that, if he does not, the judges might doubt his competence or forthrightness and depreciate the worth of other information he submits. That judges often feel this way is evident from the interviews and the judges' writings on appellate advocacy, especially in reference to the shotgun approach and to biasing the statement of facts in the briefs. Many attorneys are aware of this effect on the judges and, thus, temper what otherwise would be the full adversary tactic of indiscriminately presenting all information that might favor one's side while disregarding that which favors the opponent.

INFORMATION FROM OUTSIDE THE ADVERSARY SYSTEM

Information from outside the adversary system comes in through investigation or through the judges' background knowledge based on experience. Virtually all the investigation is done within the court; informal advice from outside experts is rare. Much of the investigation within the courts is delegated; the bulk is done by law clerks and, increasingly, staff attorneys. In addition, little research is done in the offices of concurring judges. The task of checking the facts in the trial court record is also delegated in somewhat the same manner. The law clerk's job is mainly to search for information and to present it to his judge in memorandums or draft opinions, and the clerks are encouraged to speak freely with their judges. Therefore, they have considerable influence in the sense of providing judges with information that goes into the decisions.

The source of information used by judges varies greatly from one type of information to another, as is indicated in the accompanying table based on the discussion in Chapters 8 through 13. Because of numerous uncertainties involved, the table is approximate, especially in apportioning the information between the two sources within the adversary system and between the two outside.[1] The question of why different types of information come from different sources is left to the next chapter.

The issues come from the briefs in the sense that judges are reluctant to decide issues not briefed. (In addition, they are also reluctant to decide issues not raised below.) Less than a tenth of the issues decided by the focal court were not in the briefs, and even that is probably an atypically large portion. New issues can crop up during any phase of a judge's work on an appeal.

Legal authorities in the table are those emphasized in the opinions (about half of all legal authorities in the focal court opinions were not mentioned by counsel). The portion of authorities derived from the judges' background knowledge is conjecture, for little was obtained in the interviews about this topic, though assigned judges did not often learn of important authorities from their colleagues.

Case facts in the table include case facts used as social facts, since distinguishing the two is often impossible. The main source of case facts by far is the record, but a surprising number outside the record were mentioned in the briefs and, especially, the arguments. Also, the judges decide some fact issues by reading between the lines of the record, using their past experiences to guess what went on there. Supporting case facts are not often brought to light in the appellate process, but without question they virtually always come from the judges' background knowledge.

The social facts in the table are those that seemed important to the holdings in the focal court opinions (only a quarter of all social facts in the opinions were mentioned by counsel). "Empirical data" is a subcategory of social facts; and the social facts from the record, from independent investigation and some from the briefs are empirical data. Most empirical data cited by the focal court had been presented in the record or the briefs, though the judges did some independent research. Judges occasionally believe that the empirical data must be in the record, though the record is too uncertain a source to justify complete reliance on it.

The term "information" all through the book has not implied that the information is correct, and a major problem, of course, is its evaluation. I have only looked at how judges evaluate factual information, for the evaluation of issues and legal authority is based on complicated considerations of legal reasoning, a type of information not studied here. The evaluation of case facts is, by and large, left to the fact finders in the lower tribunal, although some fact issues—a surprisingly large portion of them—have not been decided below, and here the judges must use their experiences. Social fact questions are not left to the lower court, and evaluation is a major problem appellate judges face. Here again they rely on their past experiences, though sometimes using empirical data. Empirical data itself is evaluated several ways: by studying the consensus of expert opinion, by looking at the reputation of the source of the data, by emotional reaction, and only occasionally by judging the validity of the work itself. In all, the adversary system gives the judges very little help when they evaluate social facts and empirical data.

A striking point is the amount of discretion appellate judges have as to where they get information and what information they use. In spite of the general rule against deciding issues not raised, judges do decide these issues if they feel like doing so. Also, to varying extents, they can pick and choose among the issues presented them: Discretionary jurisdiction, of course, allows this; standing and mootness rules give some discretion; and when only one of several issues will decide an appeal, the judges can choose those

SUMMARY TABLE OF SOURCES OF INFORMATION

SOURCE OF INFORMATION	TYPE OF INFORMATION					
	Issues	Legal Authorities	Case Facts	Supporting Case Facts	Social Facts	Empirical Data
The adversary system						
From the record						
From the briefs and arguments						
Outside the adversary system						
From independent investigation						
From background knowledge						

Nearly or virtually all (85% +)
Most (55-70%)
About half (45-55%)
Substantial minority (30-45%)
Small minority (15-30%)
Almost or virtually none (15% −)
None or small trace

they wish to decide. The amount of independent research for legal authorities varies and, as will be seen in the next chapter, is not subject to any set criteria. Outwardly, the most binding restriction on information gathering is that case facts be in the record; yet the judges are sometimes rather bold about asking counsel for facts outside the record. The source of supporting case facts, social facts, and empirical data is largely discretionary (disregarding the restrictions on going to people outside the court for advice). Judges freely go beyond the adversary system for this information when they wish, while at other times they refuse to consider the information if not in the record. Probably, decision makers everywhere are reluctant to bind themselves to mandatory rules governing how they do their job, since they cannot foresee situations that might arise. (Information-gathering sources are far from the only area where appellate judges exercise discretion in their decision methods, for example, in the handling of precedent or statutory construction techniques, as Llewellyn has emphasized.[2] Appellate court procedural rules, for another example, often contain provisions expressly allowing the judges to depart from the rules when justice demands it.)

Another important point is the overall lack of congruence between the information supplied by counsel and that used in the opinions—that is, the excess information from counsel compared with that found at court. Social facts present the extreme case: The focal court seldom used social facts given in the briefs and arguments, and the great majority of those used came from the judges' experience or empirical data research. Likewise, only a small minority of the legal authority in the briefs was cited in the court's opinions, whereas about half the authorities cited were not mentioned by counsel. The congruence is greater for information emphasized by counsel or the court, but it is still quite small. As for case facts and issues, the judges often complain about excessive unneeded information; and though often said to be obliged to stick to the information in the briefs and records, they do go beyond it to a surprising extent.

This lack of congruence may be due to poor work by counsel or to an inherent impossibility of predicting what information the judges believe important. Which predominates is uncertain. Although probably the latter does in the area of social facts, the former may be more important in finding authorities and issues, traditional realms of lawyers. Differences about how to approach a case arise quite often even among the judges themselves;[3] so one should not expect a competent counsel's thinking to always mesh with the court's. In any event, the lawyers interviewed often indicated that they could not understand the judges' thinking: They knew little about what arguments would interest specific judges; at times they did not know why the court was interested in the case; lawyers in civil cases were quite inept at predicting how the court would rule; and a number of lawyers complained that the judges' questions did not seem important in light of their own view of the issues.

Appellate court procedures are not adapted to take into account this lack of a meeting of the minds between court and counsel. For the most part counsel must present his information without feedback about what specifically interests the judges in the case. The major exception is the judges' questions in oral arguments, but counsel must answer quickly and may not have the information he needs at his fingertips. Requests for rebriefing are rare, as is other communication between the court and counsel after arguments. In my opinion, as is discussed in Appendix B, the adversary system should be much more flexible and should include more interaction between court and counsel.

On the other hand, the impact of the adversary system on the judges' decisions is obviously substantial. The table at the beginning of this section gives an overall impression about how much of the information is supplied by counsel. It indicates that the vast bulk of the information does come from counsel (though one must bear in mind that some types of information are not listed there, especially legal reasoning from the authorities). Also, much was said in the preceding chapters about the importance of the various types of information; and, though comparisons are difficult, there tends to be more use of the adversary system for the more important types of information, especially issues, case facts, and legal authorities.

This impression jibes with two broader but less exact indications of the impact of the adversary system. One is the apparently substantial relation between the quality of counsel's presentations and the outcome of the appeals, discussed in Chapter 3. The second is based on how often judges change their tentative votes made in the postargument conference.

As has been said in Chapter 5, judges receive little information from the attorneys after the oral arguments, provided that they read the briefs beforehand as they do on most courts and on five of the six courts studied here. Also, the vast bulk of the independent research by judges and their staff takes place after the arguments.[4] Hence the close of the arguments marks the end of the information received from the adversary system and the beginning of that found by investigation; thus how often judges change their views after the first stage gives a rough idea of the importance of the two sources of information. Judges, it should be added, often know a good deal about the issues before receiving a case, suggesting that this measure may overstate the importance of counsels' arguments. On the other hand, and somewhat counterbalancing this, the judges may be influenced by rereading the briefs and studying the record after arguments (but probably only the assigned judge does this with any regularity); and judges sometimes change their minds because their colleagues have persuaded them or because they have rethought the problems, rather than because they have received new information.

A judge's postargument position changes in some 5 to 25 percent of the appeals, varying somewhat between judges and courts, but usually the figure is around 10 to 15 percent. These are only estimates; judges do not keep track of these figures, and often they cannot give exact percentages. The estimates are based on statements by half the judges and clerks interviewed, and they are substantiated by statements in the legal literature by judges at most other state supreme courts and circuit courts.[5]

The figure of 10 to 15 percent, however, overemphasizes the importance of the attorneys' presentations. First, judges may not state their positions in the postargument conference because they have not been persuaded one way or the other and feel that further research is needed before giving even a tentative vote. This is especially likely in close, difficult cases. Perhaps 10 percent of the appeals are in this category, though more are in Massachusetts because the briefs are not read before arguments. Secondly, any new material uncovered by investigation at the court is nearly as likely to support the judges' tentative votes as to suggest the opposite result. Thus if the judges find authority leading them to change their minds in 10 percent of the cases, they probably find important authority missed by counsel in close to 20 percent of the cases (but not a full 20 percent because an imbalance of counsel may have led to the original tentative vote). Taking all this into account, in roughly one-fifth to two-fifths of the appeals the decisive information is not supplied by counsel and is found by the court itself.

CHAPTER 15

Summary and Conclusion:Information Gathering and Decision Making

Appellate judges must make decisions on the basis of incomplete information, as all who hold important decision-making positions must. The adversary system often poorly supplies the information needed, judges' background knowledge is not always helpful, and investigation at the courts is limited. Moreover, information about facts may not be available from any source, and legal authorities may provide only meager guidelines.

Judges have limited time for gathering information because of case load and administrative pressures, and they still have few aides in spite of the recent proliferation of law clerks and staff attorneys. Therefore, they must apportion their information-gathering resources among the various types of information: They must choose among the several means of getting information and must decide when lesser amounts of information are sufficient. Why, then, do judges use the different sources of information in different areas? What determines the limits of their investigation? And what are the consequences of the resulting decision making with incomplete information? These questions are the most engaging aspects of the information-gathering topic. But they deal with the judges' motives and, thus, with how their minds work; hence the empirical grounding for any answers cannot be as firm as one would like.

Much has been said earlier about the distinction between dispute deciding and lawmaking. Dispute-deciding aspects of a decision simply settle the litigants' dispute; lawmaking aspects create precedent that can be applied to other disputes. In dispute deciding the adversary system serves not only to provide the court with information, but also the purpose of persuading the parties, especially losing parties, that the court has dealt fairly with them. Thus the emphasis in dispute deciding is to use only information supplied by the adversary system so that both sides are given a chance to discuss the information used. In lawmaking the courts rely less on information supplied by the litigants, for the law created also applies to others not before the court.

These explanations, however, are far too neat and too simple. The same information is often used for both lawmaking and dispute-deciding purposes (although each type of information is more important for one function or the other). Moreover, a competing explanation, which is at least as important, is the ease with which the various types of information can be gathered from the different sources. The attorneys happen to be the most convenient source of information closely tied to the particular dispute and, thus, information used mainly in dispute deciding.

Much of this chapter centers around the fact that no matter how information is obtained, it may be incomplete or wrong. Appellate courts have developed many mechanisms that help skirt this problem. Some are obviously designed for that purpose; others probably just fortuitously do so. These mechanisms differ greatly between information used for lawmaking and that used for dispute deciding. Nevertheless, information problems still lead to considerable uncertainty when deciding appeals, especially when making law. Judges should recognize and acknowledge the uncertainty.

CASE FACTS AND ISSUES

Case facts, supporting case facts, and issues are akin in that their dispute-deciding roles overshadow their lawmaking roles, and in that the judges use much the same method to handle uncertainty due to incomplete information. On the other hand, they vary in the ease with which they can be obtained. Thus they have different primary sources: the adversary system for case facts and issues, and the judges' background knowledge for supporting case facts.

Case facts and supporting case facts are obviously crucial to dispute deciding, whether through applying the facts to the law or through fireside equities. In addition, case facts may be lawmaking information: Judges may study the facts to determine what a fair and wise rule should be in the situation, and exposure to the facts of numerous disputes gives judges some background knowledge of life in general. But nothing definite can be said about how important these lawmaking uses are, since one cannot read a judge's mind to determine how he is using the facts. The lawmaking impact of case facts used as social facts, however, is more limited than the impact of legal authorities or social facts themselves; poor information about case facts does not result in poor precedent to the degree that poor information about social facts and legal authority does. Much lawmaking involved in using case facts is tied closely to the fact pattern in the dispute, and the precedent can later be restricted to the facts actually used. Moreover, if the facts are too nebulous for lawmaking purposes, the judges often can refuse to decide the case for lack of standing or ripeness. On the other hand, continually poor information about case facts may give judges poor background knowledge about an issue area, leading to poor law.

The problems of finding and verifying case facts would be enormous if the judges went outside the adversary system. Neither their experiences nor library research would supply the facts, and actual investigation by questioning witnesses would be very time consuming. As it is, studying case facts—for example, reading the record—takes up much of the judges' and law clerks' time. Consequently, when asked why they should not use facts outside the record, most judges said they would have trouble getting the facts any other way. Surprisingly often, judges do ask counsel about facts outside the record, but that involves very little effort on their part. Also they are still obtaining information from within the adversary system. Judges' guesses about what happened by reading between the lines of the record and by extrapolating from the record require only information obtained from judges' background knowledge, again requiring little effort.

Although both factors, the dispute-deciding use of the information and the difficulty of obtaining it, strongly push toward limiting case facts to those supplied by the adversary system, they pull in opposite directions for supporting case facts. These are background facts used when interpreting and determining case facts, and by definition they are used only in dispute deciding. But they are innumerable and often hard to establish; the adversary system would be swamped and the courts mired in inaction if the information came from the record or otherwise from counsel. Also, judges' background knowledge is ordinarily as good a source for these facts as trial testimony or attorneys' contentions. Perhaps because the two factors pull in opposite directions, appellate judges are sometimes uncertain about how they should get this information. As a practical matter, nevertheless, they strongly tend to use their background knowledge, the handiest way of obtaining it, rather than the adversary system or investigation at the court.

Information about issues affects both the lawmaking and dispute-deciding functions, but mainly the latter. The appellant's recognition and selection of issues greatly affect his chances of winning the dispute, and the issues presented give the court an opportunity to make law in the area. However, counsel's failure to find an issue affects lawmaking only to the extent that law is not made on that issue in that appeal. The issue may still be, and if widespread surely will be, tackled in a later appeal. Hence incomplete information about issues affects the timing of law development, not the quality of the precedent made.

Problems of gathering information also suggest that judges would leave issue finding to the adversary system. While judges sometimes do notice issues not raised by appellant during the ordinary course of deciding the issues raised, the actual search for issues requires a thorough reading of the record. Although many judges and clerks do this, it takes a great deal of time. More important, tackling an issue not raised often requires information about legal authority and case facts that counsel has not given the court. That, along with the feeling that fairness demands that losing counsel be given a chance to deal with the issue, is the most common reason given by judges for sticking to issues raised in the briefs.

The argument that losing counsel should be given a chance to answer information used against him applies to the case facts as well as to the issues. This argument presents a clash between the two major rationales for the adversary system—a means of gathering information and a means of making losing parties feel they have been dealt with fairly. When the second is emphasized, the adversary system actually works to restrict information gathering; it rules out information gathered in other ways (except to the limited extent that judges inform counsel of the new information before the decision). Fairness to the parties is much less a factor when legal authorities or social facts are involved and is restricted to two areas: Judges tend to give it as a reason for not consulting outside experts, and it may be an important reason why some judges believe that empirical data should be in the record (though the predominant consideration here is using the trial court adversary procedures as a way to evaluate the information).

Of course, appellate judges' reliance on the adversary system for issues and case facts does not ensure complete information. Since issue finding depends greatly on the knowledge and capabilities of counsel, it is safe to assume that important issues are often missed. The facts in the record and findings of fact below may be very inaccurate, as Judge Frank's *Courts on Trial* explains at great length, because of witnesses' lack of knowledge, faulty memories, biases, and perjuries.[1] Yet appellate judges freely, and with little apparent worry, decide appeals with this suspicious information. They do it by passing the problems off on the adversary system and on the trial court fact finders. It is the adversaries' fault, not the judges', that important facts were not put in evidence or that important issues were not raised. Since it is the job of the appellate court to review, issues and facts not presented below are not really its business. Evaluation of evidence is the job of the trial judge or jury, largely because they alone view a witness's demeanor.

Supporting case facts are often the most nebulous factor in a decision. This information, when used at the appellate level, is rarely obtained from the adversary system. However, appellate judges do often free themselves from having to use the more uncertain supporting case facts by strongly presuming the correctness of fact conclusions made below.

By and large, therefore, appellate judges manage to stave off uncertainties that might result from bad information whenever the information has a limited effect on lawmaking and is difficult to obtain by investigation. The major exceptions to this general rule, as were discussed in earlier chapters, arise when judges search for issues not raised and when they decide fact decisions without a fact finding below. But the general rule applies to the great bulk of appeals.

LEGAL AUTHORITIES AND SOCIAL FACTS

Both the lawmaking importance and the effectiveness of possible sources of information suggest that legal authorities and social facts should not be restricted to those supplied by the adversary system. Poor information about legal authorities leads to inconsistent law, and poor information about social facts leads to unfair and impractical law. Precedent affects many people not before the court; its form cannot very well depend on the characteristics, capabilities, and industry of counsel and trial court decision makers. Thus, appellate judges do not limit legal authorities and social facts to those in the record or mentioned in the briefs and oral arguments. Also they do not give a presumption of correctness to pronouncements made below about social facts or legal rules. They do not pass the buck to the adversaries and the lower tribunal.

Judges have as much access as counsel to the sources of legal authorities. They or their law clerks can do research in law libraries. Social facts come largely from background knowledge based on experience; judges can ordinarily supply this information at least as well as counsel. Empirical data information (i.e., the investigation of social facts) is rarely used, probably because it is not often useful. The courts' ability to obtain and evaluate this information is quite limited. But counsel's ability is limited also, and trial court hearings are not an efficient source. Thus, judges generally feel free to look for empirical data. On the other hand, several judges believe that empirical data should come only from the trial court record; even though the information's importance lies in the lawmaking function, these judges believe that the courts' ability to find and evaluate this material is so inadequate that it should be exposed to trial court fact-finding techniques.

MITIGATING INFORMATION PROBLEMS. Going beyond what counsel presents does not ensure that judges are fully (or even adequately) informed when making law. Legal authority may be missed. More likely, the judges may have insufficient background knowledge about social facts. Since they cannot leave these problems to the lower court or the adversary system, the judges face a good deal of uncertainty in their lawmaking, uncertainty about the quality of the precedents they create. Many appellate decision-making methods, however, mitigate this uncertainty by limiting the amount of information needed or by lessening the importance of past decisions that may have been made with incomplete information. These will be discussed over the next several pages. Many of them are closely related to others, and their categorization must be somewhat arbitrary.

Applying the Facts to the Law. The most common, most obvious, and most mundane means of limiting the search for lawmaking information is simply deciding issues by applying the case facts to what is considered a controlling precedent or rule. This is a traditionally espoused decision method and is most common in routine issues before courts with little discretionary jurisdiction; but opinions expressed in these terms may hide more complicated reasoning behind the decision. When judges label an issue as one that can be treated this way, they eliminate the need to consider social facts, and they can limit the search for legal authorities to those that contain what they consider to be the controlling law.

Presumption of Correctness of the Law. Ordinarily there is a strong presumption that precedent, statutes, agency regulations, and other laws are correct. They will not be upset without a strong showing—especially a strong social fact showing—that the rule needs changing, is unconstitutional, or violates a statute. This presumption is implied whenever a court uses one of its precedents. In other areas it is more openly expressed; for example, in equal-protection issues courts often presume that the legislation attacked is valid. In administrative law the courts often stress that agency rules are presumed valid because the agency has greater knowledge of the social facts behind the rule.[2] These presumptions do not obviate the need to find and evaluate social facts because social facts may be required to determine whether the presumptions are overcome, but they do cut down the number of attacks on the validity of laws (and, thus, the number of times when social facts are necessary information) and provide the courts with a clear path when the social facts are very uncertain.

Judicial Restraint. Similar to the presumption of correctness of a law is the notion of judicial restraint. This is an inexact term—most topics in this book were discussed by at least one judge interviewed in terms of restraint or activism—but the major meaning, and the one used here, is a feeling that certain decisions should be made by the legislative or executive branch rather than the courts. Under the idea of separation of powers, judges will not make decisions they believe are outside the province of the judiciary. The role of the judiciary is, of course, a hotly debated subject. The more activist judges believe they should go further in fostering certain goals—for example, protection of individual or minority rights—that conflict with legislative and executive actions. But each judge has a point beyond which he will not go in practically every issue area.

Quite obviously, when lawmaking is left to other branches of the government, judges need less lawmaking information and, thus, need not find and evaluate that information. But this in itself does not mean that information-gathering problems are a reason for judicial restraint. The judges interviewed were asked about their reasons for judicial restraint, and they gave three types of answers:

1. Most emphasized the separation of powers doctrine in and of itself; the constitutions delineate the spheres of each branch, and judges (in some jurisdictions) are far removed from popular control.

That isn't our function. We're not elected by the people like the representatives and the senators. They're *accountable* to the people. We're not. . . . But the *main* reason is that the courts are not set up to legislate. That isn't their function. That isn't their purpose. That isn't the scheme of things. We're here to decide cases and controversies.

Because the constitution restricts [the court's role]. We have prerogatives in certain areas, and the legislature in others and the executive in others. We should stay within the bounds of constitutional limitations.

However, only a small minority of the judges, largely Rhode Island justices, gave this as the only reason; others gave more practical ones.

2. Several said that the courts had to preserve the support of the legislature and the people if they are to retain their power. Should the courts embark into areas traditionally reserved for the legislative sphere, respect for the courts, and thus the courts' power, would lessen. The most elaborate statement in the interviews was by a fairly activist judge:

I just think there are certain things that we *can* do and certain things we can't do.
Q — In terms of philosophy?
A — No, in terms of power. The public sees the difference. The public's a lot smarter than we give them credit for being. They can see the difference between a political question and a legal question. I think that's where the courts are getting such a bad name. It isn't that we're *changing* things. It's that the courts are getting into the area of what's properly legislative, properly political. . . . And the court is *properly* being *judged*, in my opinion, to the extent it intrudes into political questions on a political basis. The court can't ask deference for a political decision (I don't mean political with any pejorative sense) that it is entitled to for its traditional areas of responsibility. And the court enters the political thicket—when it gets into questions such as obscenity, abortion, bussing, educational financing—areas of this kind, it must accept the fact that it is going to be attacked by those who are unhappy with the decision. And properly so, I think, because the court is entering areas which are essentially political, and it cannot expect to insulate the result that is reached from public comment by saying "This is a judicial decision and we are deciding it according to law and how dare you question our decision that's made according to law."

3. The third type of answer is the crucial one here. Most judges said judicial restraint is important because the legislature is better equipped to gather information upon which new laws can be based (although several of them said it was of secondary importance to one of the other two reasons). They usually elaborated, saying that the legislative hearings can obtain views

of a much larger number of people than is possible in the adversary context, or that the court does not have the staff or powers to investigate that
the other branches have, or that the courts cannot easily make systematic
rules covering an area because information arrives in bits and pieces through
the individual appeals. Typical comments are:

I feel very strongly that the legislature has a most important function, and it has a
way to put in a crucible, if you will, the experiences and feelings and wishes of the
whole of [this state] or the United States as the case may be. They can do all these
things.
Q — The court can't do that?
A — And we can't do that. No. We just have to say, "Well, now this was the law in
such and such a case, and this, and this, and this."

The point is that the judicial fact-finding process is geared to find out who killed
Cock-Robbin. It hasn't *anything to do* with whether the Cock-Robbins of the world
are taking grain out of the fields.

For a healthy commonweal is only that in which all its parts vigorously perform
their own functions. The courts are not all-purpose problem solvers. They cannot
approach a problem programmatically; they feed only on the specific causes that
have come to their doors. Their perspective is limited to the record of the case before
them. They are severely limited in manpower, staff, and range of information presented to them.[3]

Therefore, to a rather large extent judges view judicial restraint as a decision-
making mechanism designed to mitigate against the courts' inability to
gather information, especially social fact information. And the legal literature, especially judges' writings, confirms this point.[4]

Narrow Decisions. Appellate judges strongly tend to decide cases narrowly, using reasoning applicable to little else but the situation before them,
so that the precedent will apply to a limited range of issues beyond what was
decided in the dispute. Nearly all judges who talked about this subject in the
interviews believed narrow decisions to be the best strategy overall.[5] (Some
decisions, of course, are quite broad, especially in the U.S. Supreme Court.
Several judges interviewed mentioned that they sometimes wrote broadly,
especially to set out guidelines for the bar and lower courts in areas where
the law was uncertain and where the judges had had experience.)

The reason given for narrowness was almost always prudence: The judges
want to save their options.[6] They cannot foresee all the situations affected
by a broad ruling. They can put more thought into the factual situation
before them than is possible for the many hypothetical disputes that may
fall under a broad rule. "If you decide more than you have to" a Massachu-

setts justice said, "you will wish you kept your fool mouth shut." In other words, the judges are afraid of making mistakes because they lack information required for a broad ruling. One of the more elaborate statements was:

Courts are asked to decide controversies between litigants, and legislatures are asked to make rules that will cover a lot of people. As someone expressed it once, courts make law retail and legislatures make it wholesale. And so that necessarily means the narrowest possible grounds, because you don't know just what the next case will be, and you preserve more of your options the narrower it is. And you should preserve them, because you may not perceive all of the relevant factors. If I can decide a case by just going from one to three, why should I go all the way to five, because I may not perceive appropriately what exists between four and five? No one here cares, because it doesn't matter, and they haven't really argued that. And if I go all the way to five, I might get a case the next time that involves this space from four to five, and the people would indicate that I'd just done exactly the wrong thing. Then I'm faced with the problem of reversing the court, and this sort of thing, which is better avoided.

Moreover, the judges commonly said that the adversary system was a cause of this danger. The attorneys may not present adequate information about matters not bearing directly on their appeal: "When you get into these fringe areas, you're getting into areas that have probably not been fully briefed and argued, and so you're liable to be talking about something that you don't have all the available authority on." A few even said that broad decisions are unfair to litigants in future disputes that would fall under a broad rule:

It's easy enough to make some broad generalization without seeing that there may be some very large exception; so indeed it shouldn't go any further than it has to. And I don't think it's even fair to future parties. If I have to decide that you are wrong, that doesn't really make it right to decide that some other fellow was wrong where there was a different case that I *hadn't* adequately thought about.

In all, then, judges are able to mitigate against some aspects of their information-gathering problems by restricting the scope of their decisions. They need worry less about the existence of situations that may fall under a broad rule, which is one type of social fact information; and they need not worry about legal authority and social facts necessary to make a good precedent for those other issues. Deciding narrowly means greater reliance on using case facts as social facts; the case facts can indicate what a wise and just precedent is for the situation in front of the judges, without the need to study other speculative situations existing in society. The case facts are there in the record, and this information, even though sometimes skimpy or subject to the inadequacies of trial court fact finding, is almost certain to be more available and more accurate than social fact information about other possible disputes. However, once many disputes involving similar issues have been decided, the judges may feel they have information about enough situations to chance a broad rule covering the area.

The narrow decision strategy, incidentally, means that courts tend to change and create law slowly, a small step at a time; though this tendency probably is not as great as it is traditionally thought to be. Narrow decisions, of course, are more likely than broad ones to leave the law in surrounding areas intact, until met in later appeals. On the other hand, an issue may, although decided narrowly, make major changes in the law, either because it is a seminal decision in a new area or because it actually decides many other issues containing less extreme fact situations. So the speed at which court made law changes depends greatly on the type of issues that attorneys present to the courts, as well as the scope of decisions made.

The Precedential Value of Dicta. Obiter dicta are language in an opinion not used to support the outcome of the case, or some would add, not needed to support the outcome. They may be parenthetical remarks or views on how issues similar to the one before the court should be decided. Without getting into the problems of defining dicta, the point of interest here is that dicta have weaker precedential value than the actual ruling on an issue. They are not part of the stare decisis doctrine, which holds that past court decisions provide the basis for deciding disputes now before the court.

Dicta are closely related to the frowned-upon broad opinions, because both involve discussions not needed to decide the case. Consequently, when judges were asked why dicta are not considered precedent,[7] some of the answers were similar to reasons for making narrow decisions: The dicta were not produced by adversary arguments, or the judge writing the dicta is not likely to think through the problem as well as the holding in the case. One said:

Because they're fairly *hypothetical.* The judge is sitting in his ivory tower, trying to conceptualize a problem. Maybe he's talking to himself. Maybe he's talking to his law clerk. Maybe he talks to one of his colleagues. And they dope it out the best they can in sort of a think-tank, and they can come up with an awful lot of answers. But when they're all done they still are likely to only have part of the pieces to the puzzle. It's just that our experience is too limited.

Thus dicta are less likely to be based on sufficient information than the actual holding, and according it less precedential value mitigates against this problem.

But this is not the whole story, for most judges gave other reasons. The most common was that dicta are only the views of the opinion writer; perhaps the concurring judges did not agree with the statements, and thus they are not the view of the majority of the court.

You put seven different justices to work on the same case, and you're going to get *seven different* explanations, and, as one of my colleagues said recently, you have to ingest a great deal of dicta if we're not all going to write separate opinions in every case the way the English do.

And several said dicta are not precedent just because that is the way things are done—that is the tradition.

Well, because the doctrine of stare decisis requires us to do so. Is that too big a circle for you to go around in? It's just one of those things. A memory of man runs not to the contrary, and it just seems to me that it's fundamental that the court decides only what it had to decide.

Leaving Issues Undecided. Appellate courts leave undecided many of the issues presented them, mainly because they are reluctant to decide those not needed to resolve the dispute. When a lower court ruling is reversed, the judges need only decide one of the alternative grounds for reversal given by the appellant, unless the other issues will arise again upon retrial. Probably the main reason for this is to save time. But Justice Weintraub of New Jersey has emphasized other reasons: It is best to "avoid unnecessary excursions into the unknown or unforeseeable"; the judges and attorneys may not give the alternative issues sufficient attention; and deciding alternative issues makes agreement among the judges more difficult.[8] Most of these reasons are the same as those typically given for why issues are decided narrowly.

Also, judges can refuse to decide an issue that involves a good deal of uncertain information if deciding a less far-reaching issue will decide the appeal. Why judges dodge issues is too intricate a subject to explore here, but a likely reason why they, for example, tend to decide statutory issues instead of constitutional issues when both are presented is that the practical consequences are less uncertain. Likewise, courts with discretionary jurisdiction, most notably the U.S. Supreme Court, can delay addressing an issue until lower courts and scholars have had a chance to explore the area fully.

Ensuring Adverseness. Courts attempt in a half-hearted way to make sure there is true adverseness in the litigation before them; presumedly the parties will give better information if they care about the outcome of the case. As was seen in Chapter 3, one reason, but often only a minor one, behind the friendly suit, standing, and mootness rules and behind the aversion to adversary opinions is that litigants may not be motivated to present the lawmaking information adequately.

Giving Discretion to the Lower Court. Appellate courts often have a choice as to whether they treat a subject as a social fact question or a supporting case fact question. This gives them the option either to incorporate the facts into a flat rule, making them controlling in all future cases containing the same issue, or to leave them to the trial judge or jury, allowing the fact determination to vary from case to case. Thus Holmes claimed that appellate judges make broad tort rules when they have little practical experience in the area, leaving the jury with wide latitude to decide what type of conduct is negligent.[9] Also courts may create presumptions rather than flat rules when the facts are uncertain, allowing the parties to present case fact evidence in the trial court to overcome the presumption.[10] An example is scientific tests introduced in evidence: As a general rule courts have made a social fact determination that blood tests to determine paternity are very accurate, thus making the results of a validly conducted test conclusive; on the other hand, the courts are not convinced that breath tests to determine drunkenness are always accurate, so that a defendant can attempt to show that the test was wrong as applied to him.

Similarly one of the major reasons why appellate judges give trial judges discretion in many areas is that the appellate judges do not have sufficient information to make detailed law in the area.[11] The factors an appellate court would have to take into account in fashioning rules may be so complicated and varying, such as in questions of admissibility of evidence, that the appellate judges feel that they cannot tackle the problem, at least until after they have decided many cases in the area.

Lawmaking Techniques Requiring Little Information. There are several more ways that judges can make law without needing much information, especially social fact information. At one extreme is the notion that it is better that the law be settled than that it be settled right. As has been discussed in Chapter 9, not many judges subscribe to this idea; but when they do, they need not worry about information to determine whether the law is wise or just. Also, judges can restrict the need for information if they interpret statutes by using rules of statutory construction or, to a lesser extent, by looking only at legislative intent; in practice, however, these are often uncertain standards. Two other examples, which are probably rare in this country, are creating rules by using only logical deduction from existing rules and creating rules directly from what in Chapter 10 were called ideals, that is, goals and moral prescriptions, without any concern for practical considerations.

Overruling Precedent. Lastly, as a final measure, if a court makes law based on poor information, it can always overrule the precedent later.

The bulk of these ways of mitigating problems of finding and evaluating lawmaking information amounts to restraining influences; they restrict the kind of decisions an appellate judge is likely to make. In fact, restricting the information needed to decide almost necessarily restricts the possible decision outcomes. Whether the information-gathering problems lead to the restraint is a much more complicated point, and there is a great deal of variation from one area to another. But, on the whole, these problems can be said to contribute substantially to the restraint, at least according to the judges' views of their own motives.

Another point about these ways of mitigating information-gathering problems is that they give judges a wide range of discretion. None of them, except perhaps the assumption of correctness given existing law, provides anything approaching a hard and fast rule governing the process by which judges make law. This jibes with the point made in the preceding chapter that judges retain for themselves considerable discretion in their information-gathering activities.

DEALING WITH UNCERTAINTY. Although this long list of decision-making methods (along with those discussed earlier concerning case facts and issues) helps mitigate problems of finding and evaluating information, it falls far short of eliminating uncertainty or of providing judges with the belief that certainty exists. This is especially true in the lawmaking area, where an appellate judge will always be, in Judge Friendly's words, "a legislator exercising powers over generations yet unborn—a legislator dealing with many subjects as to which he has little familiarity."[12] Justice Cardozo said the following about the few cases in which the judge is a "lawgiver"—in which there is a creative element in his job:

> I was much troubled in spirit, in my first years upon the bench, to find how trackless was the ocean on which I had embarked. I sought for certainty. I was oppressed and disheartened when I found that the quest for it was futile. . . . As the years have gone by, and as I have reflected more and more upon the nature of the judicial process, I have become reconciled to the uncertainty, because I have grown to see it as inevitable.[13]

The judges on the six courts were asked to read and comment on this passage.[14] Nearly all agreed with Cardozo that there was uncertainty (the few exceptions said Cardozo overdramatized the amount of uncertainty); so, not surprisingly, it seems to be taken as an assumption of appellate decision making. In fact, two judges said they suspected that Cardozo knew of the uncertainty before becoming a judge and was exaggerating here to create an effect on the reader. Cardozo's disheartening experience, though, is not typical. The judges typically said they found the uncertainty not at all disheartening, mainly because it is just an accepted part of the job. A few added that it presents the most interesting and enjoyable aspects of their work.

The normal reason given for the uncertainty was, and Cardozo is here referring to, the changing nature of the law and the need to decide issues falling outside the realm of settled law. The judges usually added that a major cause of the uncertainty here is social fact type material, especially the complexity of human affairs with which the courts must deal when making precedent. One said that a judge "fails in his purpose if his law doesn't relate to people, and there's three billion of them out there, and how can we possibly be certain?"

The uncertainty is also shown by the general lack of standards as to when a judge should stop his search for information. Even though the decision-making methods listed earlier allow judges to limit their independent research, there is still a large amount of information applicable to deciding many issues or helpful in shaping the written opinion and the rule produced. The judges were asked what determined when they had done enough research for an opinion,[15] and not many gave definite answers. Typical replies were that one determines whether enough has been done by gut feeling, judgment, common sense, or experience—all vague criteria.

Q — What determines when you feel that you have done enough research for an opinion? How do you *tell* whether you've got enough information?
A — It's very hard to say. How does a doctor decide when he's got the right diagnosis. Stop testing the guy; it's time to operate. It's a matter of judgment based upon your experience, and basically you know you should have stopped a long time ago, and other times you should keep going.

It's feel. When I stop fighting with myself. And it's an innate thing. There's obviously no end to the research you can do. It's when you finally have the feeling that—it's just—it's innate.

A number simply said they stopped when they were "satisfied" that they had enough information, though several more said specifically that they often were not satisfied with the amount of research done.

Occasionally, the judges did give more definite criteria: Enough research has been done if one's colleagues accept the opinion or, more often, if it does not appear that more research will affect the result reached on the issue, for example:

There's some limit to the amount of independent research one can do. The case load is usually the most effective controller of this. But you have to at least be reasonably *satisfied* that you have the right *result*, even though you might have a more polished . . . *document* if you spent more time.
Q — How do you determine when you have done enough?
A — Well, I think you're pretty much certain that this is the way it's going to *come out.* That no matter how deeper you go, you're not going to change directions, and that's really what you're interested in.

Case load and time limitations are, of course, very important restraints on the amount of research at the courts, as this and a good number of other judges mentioned. Only two judges said they tried to exhaust all the authorities that may exist on point.

The judges here are talking about research for legal authorities; that is the subject of virtually all their independent research. Criteria for when one stops trying to imagine social fact considerations would be even more vague, since the judges do not have well-organized law libraries as a guide.

In the face of the often incomplete information, the vagueness about when to stop looking for information, the time problems, and the general uncertainty, do judges worry that they have not done an adequate job? I asked them if they worry about their opinions after sending them out.[16] About half said they never did, for example:

Q — How often, if ever, do you worry that an opinion isn't adequate after you've finished it?
A — I never do.
Q — You never do?
A — Once I've finished it, it's behind me.
Q — Huh, you go on to the next one?
A — Go on to the next one. Drive you crazy if you had to worry about opinions, whether they were right or wrong.

This statement is typical: If a judge worries about things already done, he would not be able to do his job. Yet just as many judges said they do worry, either in a few types of cases or in general:

Q — Do you worry after you've gotten an opinion out that it might not be adequate?
A — Well, if I said no to that it would be an implication that I had massive self-confidence. There may be some things that go out that are in specialized areas where I am concerned with the implications of it in other situations than the one that was before me. And I can be nervous in that respect. How are people going to treat it? Are they going to misuse it? Are they going to suggest we meant something when we *really didn't know enough about the field* to really mean any other than what we were deciding. . . . You can be somewhat nervous about it, but you cannot waste much time about it; you've got to go on and decide the next case.

Q — How often do you worry that the opinion isn't adequate after you've sent the drafts around?
A — Oh, always.
Q — Always?
A — Yeah, and I've said this any number of times. This is no job for a perfectionist. . . . If you wait until you're satisfied with an opinion, you simply would never get things done. The volume of work *simply* doesn't permit it. And there's never an opinion that goes out that, you know, I wouldn't like to go over one more time, and do a little polishing on it and all that.

The differences among the judges, though, are not as great as this discussion implies because most of those who said they may worry seemed, like the two just quoted, to be referring to the time when the opinion was sent off rather than afterward. In other words, there is little evidence that the judges are overcome with worry. (Judges quite often are disappointed with themselves upon noticing mistakes in their old opinions long after publication, but this seems to be accepted as an unavoidable part of appellate work.[17])

There is a theory abroad that judges (and presumably others in important decision-making posts) cannot and should not face the self-doubts that would result from full recognition of the uncertainties involved in their decision making. One of the clerks interviewed said that to be a Justice,

you have to think you're *always* right, or you'd go *crazy*. And that's what happened [to two Justices; one is] *very* insecure. He thinks he's not up to the work. He *agonizes*. [And the other] went crazy. He simply couldn't handle it. That's not to say that they aren't good men. That may mean they're better men. They recognize their doubts very strongly. You can't do that and be a Supreme Court Justice. You just can't.[18]

Perhaps, as common sense suggests, there is a tendency for one who must make important decisions with inadequate information and with a wide range of discretion (as judges often have when engaged in lawmaking) to believe he has some sort of superhuman ability to reach good decisions; otherwise he might succumb to the uncertainty with the resulting debilitating effects—the anxiety, the inability to come to a decision, the protracted decision making in the face of heavy case loads, and the drain of enjoyment from the job. In fact, some judges tend to think very highly of their ability to decide issues. An appellate judge has written, "Every occupation has its peculiar vice. The vice of judges is arrogance," because, he said, a judge may come to believe he deserves the power he wields and, thus, "that he really must be quite a fellow."[19] Two judges said in the interviews:

The judicial office is a very *powerful* office, and *power* has a tendency to make the person wielding it think he's God and that the power's somehow due to him, and obviously it isn't. And I think I'd be a liar and a hypocrite if I told you that I didn't think a lot of judges have in their minds smudged the distinction between God and themselves. . . . In fact that is what *I* think we have to fight against all the time. That's what I *try* to fight against most of the time.

Most judges have a very high opinion of themselves, and it's always too bad to have the bubble pricked, you know [by showing them transcripts of their interviews].
Q — Yeah, that's what the clerks say, the judges all have big egos.
A — Many of them are—I should say many of *us* are, I don't mean to exclude myself. No, it's a judicial syndrome that can be very bad for you. You think you've been chosen by God to tell everybody else what's what.

But this is probably not that great a problem among appellate judges, based on the clerks' impressions of the judges as well as my own. In spite of what I told the second judge, the clerks did not say that all the judges have big egos—only some judges.[20] They usually named one or two judges as having big egos (or as being prima donnas), by which they generally meant that the judges always believed they were right, magnified their capabilities, or overly disliked criticism. My vague impression from interviewing the judges, in addition, was that they were often quite modest about their capabilities. Most of them somewhere in the interviews stressed that judges are simply human beings or that they themselves had limited capacities. Also, it is unclear whether this trait, limited as it apparently is, is a reaction to the uncertainties in a judge's job; most likely an equally large proportion of the population at large would be seen by others as having big egos.

Nevertheless, there is a danger in arrogance—tending to think one is always right—in that the judges may rely too much on their initial impressions and their intuitions in the face of incomplete information without admitting that the necessary information actually is absent, without rethinking their position on the basis of what little information they can obtain, or without considering information adverse to their initial judgment. The main danger here is in the use of social facts when making law (and perhaps also supporting case facts when deciding facts issues without the benefit of a lower court ruling), since these facts come from the judges' background knowledge based on experience, the only readily available source but one that may be a poor foundation for an intuitive judgment. These problems underlie the type of decision making described by Judge Hutcheson:

The successful ones are those who, when a tight question's up for decision, calling upon the spirit, give their imagination play. They wait brooding over the cause for the feeling, the hunch, the intuitive flash of understanding which, when it comes, makes the jump-spark connection between question and decision, and at the point where the path is darkest sheds its light along the way. "'Tis no paradox to say that in our most theoretical moods we may be nearest to our most practical applications." It is that tiptoe faculty of the mind which can feel and follow a hunch which makes the best gamblers, the best detectives, the best lawyers, the best judges, the best doctors, the materials of whose trades are most chancey because most human, and the results of whose activities are for the same cause the most subject to uncertainty and the best attained by approximation.[21]

That is, in the face of incomplete information a judge may rely on emotional hunches and arrive at decisions that he cannot explain. But there is no real check on the emotions, and in the extreme a judge may come to believe, as one clerk said, that "by some majestic infusion of knowledge, once he takes the oath, becomes unto himself some type of a superintelligence—that because of the particular calling because of his qualifications, has been ordained to speak on everything and anything with authority.'' The clerk was talking about two judges who refused to consider social science studies on a particular issue, but, as I have argued, empirical data offer little help in dealing with uncertainty caused by problems of finding and evaluating social facts.

Several judges have written very strong warnings against these dangers. For example, Judge Clark of the Second Circuit wrote, with his law clerk, about "the dangers of elusive certainty":

For the judge the consequences are twofold. First is the danger created by a false faith in judicial objectivity. If judges are easily convinced that they possess the key to objectivity, or a sixth sense for right and justice, will they not gain a false confidence in their own conclusions—conclusions that are in fact based on the humble stuff of subjective preference? Cardozo knew the inevitable impact of subjectivity; and he reports that it filled him with awe whenever he stumbled—or leaped—into the heart of legal darkness where the lamps of precedent and of the common law tradition flicker and fade: "What am I in these great movements onward, this rush and sweep of forces, my petty personality should deflect them by a hairbreadth?" He recognized that judges must struggle to transcend bias and prejudice. If, however, a judge is convinced that he possesses a special sense of things, which can lead to the one right rule, or that the human stuff he shapes and forms is "neutral" and "objective," will that judge struggle quite so hard? That, we submit, is a paramount danger of too quick a grasp at certainty.[22]

The second consequence, according to Judge Clark, is that a judge will not "face the responsibility of judicial freedom" and will "avoid the necessity of facing the consequences of his own decisions." However, this is largely an ideological note, since, as he says, "a natural consequence of stress on certainty is to put a premium on judicial conservatism." Similarly, Justice Traynor of the California Supreme Court has said:

Regardless of whether it is attended by abundant or meager materials, a case may present competing considerations of such closely matched strength as to create a dilemma. How can a judge then arrive at a decision one way or the other and yet avoid being arbitrary? . . . He is painfully aware that a decision will not be saved from being arbitrary merely because he is disinterested. He knows well enough that one entrusted with decision, traditionally above base prejudices, must also rise above the vanity of stubborn preconceptions, sometimes euphemistically called the courage of one's convictions. He knows well enough that he must severely discount his own predilections, of however high grade he regards them, which is to say he must bring to his intellectual labors a cleansing doubt of his omniscience, indeed even of his perception.[23]

In fact, several important state appellate and federal circuit judges have written in a similar vein, that judges should practice humility, tame judicial arrogance, or the like, when making law.[24] These writings are concentrated in time at about 1960; perhaps—but this is only speculation—not until then had appellate judges labeled themselves as lawmakers long enough to think through the implications of that role.

The judge's job probably mitigates against the development of feelings of omniscience more than it fosters it. On the one hand, appellate judges have substantial prestige and many trappings of authority, such as the black robes, the dais, and the imposing courtroom. Also, the attorneys are very deferential, almost kowtowing to the judges. On the other hand, there are aspects of judicial decision making not often found in other organizations that may lessen judges' feelings of omniscience and feelings that their intuitive reaction is the last word. First, written opinions can make them take a second look at possible reasons behind their decisions[25] and leave them open to criticism for the reasons announced; on the whole, though, judges are rather thick-skinned about others' views of their opinions, as has been noted in Chapter 7. Second, in Chapter 7 it has also been said that there is a norm among judges that one should not make up one's mind until late in the decision-making process—one should keep an open mind when considering the arguments of others. Third, an appellate judge is only one of three to nine people of equal power having a hand in the decision; thus his views are continuously subject to disagreement, and even attack, by others with equal rank and in close contact. Then there are the law clerks, who by and large are encouraged and feel free to criticize their judges, as has been discussed in Chapter 6. Lastly, the use of the adversary system as a major source of information ensures that a judge will be presented with arguments—though often incomplete arguments—against his initial impressions of the issues. However, a judge could dampen or seal himself against these forces; as a final word, then, much depends on whether he believes that "by no means does the doubt that has been referred to as 'the agony of decision' indicate weakness in a judge"[26] and on whether he "learns that make-do is the way of an appellate court's quest for justice."[27]

Style and Research Procedure

This appendix has three sections, discussing the basic research strategy, the style of presentation of data in the text, and the specific research methods. In these areas the study often differs from common practices in social science work (a term used here to refer mainly to sociology and political science). The basic assumption is that social scientists should face and openly admit the uncertainty and complexity of social life, and they should adopt methods suited to them. In this regard social scientists are no different from appellate court judges.

RESEARCH STRATEGY

The overall approach and research methods were shaped by attempts to deal with what I consider to be three major problems in the social sciences. These problems are probably unsolvable, but they should be mitigated as much as possible.

1. One cannot know what to study about any social matter without first knowing a great deal about it, because one cannot know what data can be found, how accurate the data are, and what they mean in relation to other aspects of the organization or setting one is studying. This knowledge must be gained largely through actual research, for the literature is likely to be very incomplete. Unless the study is a narrow one in a well-tread area, one cannot simply select a theoretical framework, set up a research design, compose and pretest a questionnaire, and so on, without first deeply immersing one's self in the thing to be studied. Moreover, even with considerable advance preparation, many unforeseen complications and ramifications are bound to appear only after the research is well along. An important illustration of this problem is composing questionnaires: If one tries to write questions without extensive research to determine what the questions mean to those studied, answers to all but the simplest questions will be worth little.

For these reasons, before choosing a topic, I spent a year conducting research at the courts, mainly listening to arguments, reading briefs and opinions, and interviewing and chatting with the people around the courts. The information-gathering topic was then chosen, partly because it is relatively free of the constraints of judicial secrecy and the judges' inability to describe their thinking processes. It was also chosen because it contained several subjects that had interested me, for example, the continual complaints about poor advocacy, attention given facts outside the record, and the amount of independent research and reading of the records. The first year also provided the necessary background understanding of what people do around the courts and what terminology they use. Even so, long afterward, new aspects of the topic and new problems in studying it cropped up, leading to a constant revision of the study, especially the interview questions.

One result of this method of study, of course, is that information about each topic could not be obtained from each person interviewed (another reason is the great variation in time allowed for interviews, to be discussed later). Many were reinterviewed, but that was not possible in every case. This is a typical trade-off: obtaining incomplete interview data that are understandable, as against complete but largely meaningless data.

2. The second problem is: Why would any reasonable person believe what I have written? The great bulk of social science research is irresponsible in the sense that there is little check on its quality or honesty other than what appears in the final published product. Replication, the check relied upon in the physical sciences, is of little use because research is rarely replicated such that the author of one study cannot credibly claim that differences found in another study are due to differences in time or the subjects studied. Because prestige and position are largely determined by how many and how impressive one's publications are, social scientists have a strong incentive to be less than forthcoming about the shortcomings of their works. There is no way of knowing how many actually fudge data or hide discrepancies; but that is the point: There is the incentive and the opportunity to do so, but the reader is very unlikely to know what has gone on behind the scenes. This problem is exacerbated by the great attention given theory; one must stretch his data more if he wishes to test or find theory than if he simply describes what he is studying. A theoretically oriented research study, therefore, is especially suspect.

The problem is a very difficult one to deal with, but several ways to mitigate it are: downplaying theory, which will be discussed later; dropping the pretense of exact findings, also discussed later; and making one's data available to others. Though this last is probably the most important method available, it has severe limitations. In the present study the material relating to the focal court cases can be given to anyone interested. (I promised the justices I would not name the court in anything published, but otherwise I can name the court.) The interviews are a problem because they are strictly confidential, and the judges can often be identified even though substantial parts are deleted. But I have transcribed the interviews verbatim (when tape-recorded) and have arranged the material so that passages pertaining to a specific topic are grouped and can be copied for anyone interested in a topic. Anything identifying a speaker has been deleted. All of this required years of work and was done mainly because of this second problem. However, freeing data is not, in general, a total solution to the second problem because what the subjects actually say is not the data made available; rather, data are filtered by the researcher. But arranging tape-recorded passages probably constitutes less filtering than taking notes during interviews or coding interview responses and putting them on computer tape.

3. The third problem is the difficulty of learning anything about causation in

human affairs above and beyond what is intuitively obvious. It is trite to say, but nonetheless true, that there are simply too many possible interacting forces to understand easily what leads to what. Even so, the current and strongly embedded custom in the social sciences is to concentrate on "theory," a term with no definitive commonly accepted meaning but that by and large refers to causal statements. The two main methods used to study causation in the social sciences are studying relationships and studying peoples' motives. The problems with the former are that life is too complex for statistical correlations and the like to portray even roughly what really happens; the data used are ordinarily too imprecise to justify the statistical techniques used; and researchers using this method tend to delegate the actual gathering of data to others and, thus, have little knowledge of what the figures they are working with actually represent. The second method, peoples' motives (i.e., the reasons they give for their actions), suffers from the problems that people may not know their true motives and may not wish to recount accurately those that they do know.

The present study from its beginning was intended to be a discriptive study, shying away from causation for these reasons and because, as was mentioned earlier, dealing with theory creates a bias. And the bulk of the book is simply descriptive. However, causation is often an interesting aspect of a general topic, interesting enough to attempt studying, though one must acknowledge the uncertainty involved. Some of the book, therefore, especially that summarized in the last chapter, does deal with causation. With few exceptions, the method of studying causation has been using peoples' motives. But they may well have other motives besides the ones they gave; I suspect that the judges' case load and time problems—or perhaps, pejoratively, laziness—are stronger factors than acknowledged. Also, using written opinions as evidence of information used runs into the problems of using motives, for opinions are essentially statements of motives. Thus although the information-gathering topic was chosen largely because much can be studied without delving deeply into the judges' minds, it sometimes leads to this difficult area.

METHOD OF PRESENTATION

This is a quantitative study, but in presenting data in quantitative studies one should be careful to indicate the degree of exactness one has achieved. There is a misleading practice in the social sciences of giving exact percentages, even with decimal points, when the author knows (or should know) that the figures are only approximations because of numerous errors in determining them—for example, errors due to poorly worded questions asked subjects, inexact or incorrect answers, problems of interpreting answers by interviewers, coders, and others reading the results. The problem of incorrect answers alone is substantial; as is discussed at the end of the appendix, over a tenth of the factual statements given are clearly wrong. Several other things that cause inexactness in this study are: the small and nonrandom sample, incomplete information from those interviewed, and difficulties in classifying answers to open-ended questions, the type used here. For this reason various adjectives, adverbs, and other quantifying words were used, as are listed in Table 3.

Table 3

DEFINITION OF QUANTIFYING WORDS USED IN THE TEXT

All, every, always, uniformly, invariably, each	100%
Virtually all, every, etc.	95-100%
Nearly or almost all, every, etc. Vast majority	85-95%
Great majority A great many, a great deal Generally Customary Typically Normal, normally	70-85%
Most, mostly, most often The majority More than half, over half Usual, usually Frequent, frequently Mainly	55-70%
A little more than half Half, about half Almost half, nearly half	50-55% 45-55% 45-50%
A number, a good number, a substantial number or amount Less than half A substantial minority At times Common, commonly	30-45%
Several, several times Quite a few A small minority Occasionally, on occasion	15-30%
Few, a few, a few times, a very few Seldom Unlikely Unusual Infrequently	5-15%
Rare, rarely, a few rare Virtually or almost never, none, no	0-5%
Never, none, no	0%

These exact definitions were not used when quoting or paraphrasing people interviewed or when it was otherwise obvious that the definitions were not appropriate.

When I did not know the percentage figures, I used other words, especially "many," "often," "some," "little," "the great bulk of," and "ordinarily."

Fractions and percentage figures were given with respect to the focal court cases and, rarely, to interview results. These figures were rounded off (except in the tables, which should also be considered approximations), percentage figures to the nearest multiple of five and fractions to the nearest fraction comprised of small integers. The qualifiers "about," "almost," and "nearly" meant that the "true" figure was within two percentage points from the rounded figure; and "over," "more than," and "less than" meant the rounded figure was one to three percentage points from the "true" figure. Near zero and one, of course, I was much more exact. An exception to all this was "a half," which is in the preceding table.

Several other facets of the presentation of data need to be explained. Because of the research strategy used here, rarely did all judges, clerks, or attorneys speak to a topic. I indicated in the footnotes or text how many did, except when nearly all did. Expressions like "most judges and clerks" mean most in each category. Also, the judges or others quite often spoke to the various topics without being asked questions, but I did not differentiate between the volunteered statements and others unless, as often happened, it seemed to make a difference in the discussion, in which case I said the judges, and so on, "volunteered," "added," or "mentioned" certain things.

Quotations from the interviews were used for two purposes: to give one of many similar statements as an example or to emphasize a point with what I considered an astute or colorful statement. Examples are clearly labeled as such, especially by saying "for example" or by saying the statement was "typical"; all other quotations fall in the second category. It should be noted that the presentation of typical statements constitutes little evidence for the point made, though probably one reason for giving the quotations is to present an air of authenticity. More important, though, the quotations give a feel for what the judges and others think and they enliven the text. Choosing quotations for examples was somewhat arbitrary because statements in the interviews differed so greatly in their details that there was no possible criteria for picking one out of a number of statements that said essentially the same thing. I did tend to choose the more coherent passages and virtually always used statements from tape-recorded interviews; this often narrowed down the selection considerably, but it also meant that some judges were quoted much more than others. The tape recordings were transcribed exactly, except that anything identifying the speaker or his court is left out, and repetitious phrases and all the "ah's" and "er's" are deleted for the sake of readability.

RESEARCH METHODS

Because a full discussion of the research methods would require too much space here, only some of the more important topics are discussed. My dissertation contains a much more detailed discussion, though it was based on only a portion of the data used in this book (*Appellate Courts and the Adversary System: Information-Gathering and Appellate Decision-Making*, 256-279 (1976)).

The six courts were selected mainly on the basis of convenience. Random sampling is of little use with such a small sample, though the courts are in the industrial north-eastern part of the country and very likely differ from courts in southern and rural states. The focal court is considered one of the more "liberal" and "activist" courts in the country, and the ideological differences among its members are probably greater than on the average state court. More important, as is discussed in the text, its justices seem to use some types of information not supplied by the adversary system more freely than most.

The interviewing was done from late 1971 to late 1975. I tried to interview each judge who had been on the courts for at least a year during this period, including senior circuit judges, plus judges who had retired from the focal court after 1965 (three were in this category), except for one judge who lived too far away to be interviewed conveniently. They were interviewed only after they had had at least one year's experience; an atypically large percent, about 30 percent, were in their second year at the time of the first interview.

Most of the law clerks were from the focal court. I tried to interview all clerks there during the study's first year and a half, and at least one clerk of each judge who was on the court during other periods encompassed by the study. At the other courts, I interviewed two clerks from each court (five at the Sixth Circuit), chosen on the basis of convenience. As for the remainder of the court staff, I interviewed the court clerks, the staff attorneys at the focal court, and several staff attorneys at other courts. The attorneys interviewed all argued cases before the focal court during the year the briefs and arguments were studied. I only interviewed those within an hour's drive for me, an area that included three-fourths of the state's bar members. Otherwise, they were selected to get a representative portion of those with various characteristics that seemed important, especially type of practice, experience, and location. Those interviewed were typical of all attorneys who argued that year except that a larger proportion were from medium-sized cities or suburbs and argued more than one appeal during the year. In order to get more attorneys who handled empirical data, five were selected in part because their cases involved this material; but this does not affect the quantative terms used in Chapter 13. Most attorneys were interviewed within a month of their arguments, though several were interviewed at least three months afterward.

In all, 132 people were interviewed—46 judges, 33 law clerks, 17 staff members, and 36 lawyers. The judges were at the following courts: focal court, 12; Rhode Island court, 6; Massachusetts court, 10; Ohio court, 4; Sixth Circuit, 10; First Circuit, 4. Ten judges refused to be interviewed: focal court, 1; Massachusetts court, 1; Ohio court, 6; Sixth Circuit, 2. Fourteen of the judges, mostly at the focal court, were interviewed two or more times. The average interview time (excluding interruptions) was over 100 minutes, though the amount of time the judges granted varied greatly. Interviewing appellate judges, by the way, is not an uncommon research technique— there have been over 100 studies using interviews or questionnaires resulting in publications or dissertations— and the judges by and large have been very cooperative. (Bibliography D contains a list of studies in which judges were interviewed or sent questionnaires.) Three clerks and one attorney refused to be interviewed, and interview time with them averaged about two hours. A number of clerks were interviewed twice, and the attorneys, with a few exceptions, were telephoned later.

The interviews were very unstructured. I had long lists of questions that were continually revised. Because people, especially the judges, varied greatly—by a factor of ten—in how long they took to answer questions, as well as how much time they would allot for interviews, more often than not the questions were not all covered. The questions were given varying degrees of priority, and the most important were asked early in the interview.

A tape recorder was used whenever possible because it is more accurate, because a great deal more ground can be covered in a given time period than when one takes notes, and because it frees the interviewer to contemplate what is being said. Almost two-thirds of the judges, all of the clerks, and the great majority of the attorneys allowed a recorder. The most obvious disadvantage of tape recorders is that people may not be frank, but the questions I asked were rarely about controversial subjects, and the judges in recorded interviews did not seem less open than those not recorded; for example, they were just as likely to criticize other judges or talk about pending cases.

The accuracy of interview responses is always a problem, and a couple of attempts were made here to gauge it. The focal court judges, clerks, and attorneys often described specific cases and courtroom events about which I could gather independent information from the opinions, briefs, or oral arguments. There were over 800 such separate fact contentions in tape-recorded interviews (so there was no question about what was said). Some 80 percent were clearly correct; a great many of the rest were clearly wrong, but for others there was some question of interpretation. In the few fact statements in which the person said "I think" or made some other indication that he was not sure he was correct, the statements were wrong over 40 percent of the time. Excluding these, almost 85 percent of the statements were correct. A second way to gauge accuracy occurred when people I reinterviewed spoke about the same subject on more than one occasion, allowing for a comparison. There were 120 such incidents, and about 85 percent of the time there was, in my judgment (for they never spoke twice in exactly the same words), very close agreement between what was said both times. Most of the rest were clearly contradictory statements, but at times it was uncertain as to whether there was a contradiction even though there was not close agreement. These two gauges give a rough indication of what the interview answer error is; that the two arrived at very similar results should not be taken to mean the error was determined that exactly. The errors, it should be emphasized, are probably greater when the judges gave more subjective answers, especially their explanations for why they did certain things.

The 112 focal court appeals studied here are all cases argued or (which rarely happened) submitted without argument at the focal court over a year's period in the early 1970s. The cases do not include summary dispositions, cases affirmed because leave should not have been granted, cases not decided for various reasons, or administrative and nonjudicial matters. The arguments were tape-recorded. The notes in Chapters 8 through 13 describe how specific subjects were analyzed and describe the spotty study of oral arguments, briefs, and opinions at the other five courts.

Some Suggestions for Appellate Court Decision–Making Procedures

This appendix will suggest several appellate court decision-making procedures that are not commonly used or discussed. The overall plea is for more flexibility than present procedures permit and for more use of counsel and the adversary system. Few of the suggestions are original, but the reader is unlikely to be familiar with most and at first glance will probably think some of the more radical ideas a bit outlandish.

The great increase in appeals over the past several decades has led to much discussion and debate about how appelate courts should function. For the most part, however, I will not enter the major areas of discussion and debate. The suggestions here are independent of whether and how staff attorneys are used, whether law clerks draft opinions, whether attorneys are given a chance to file briefs or make oral arguments, whether attorneys should attend prehearing conferences with judges or staff, and whether opinions should be written or published. These topics are fully discussed many places elsewhere. Several of the suggestions made here, though, help alleviate the problems caused by some of these practices. On the other hand, I do assume at times that cases are assigned by rotation early in the appellate process and that judges read the briefs before oral arguments. Most appellate courts follow these two practices, though not all judges or commentators think them the best practices. Federal courts, especially, prefer that cases be assigned by the presiding judge after they have been discussed in conference.

SEVERAL GOALS

At the outset it is best to have as a foundation a list of goals for appellate court decision-making procedures. The major, overriding problem is how best to inform the judges so that they can decide cases as well as possible within the time constraints. This involves numerous subsidiary goals, but the list that follows is limited to those that have traditionally been troublesome in appellate courts.

1. The judges should receive as much relevant information about the case as possible. It is more important that information pertaining to the court's lawmaking function be complete than that pertaining only to the dispute-deciding function, for lawmaking decisions ordinarily have a greater impact on society. But the information, however used, should be as free as possible from time-wasting extraneous material.

2. Each judge sitting on a case should know enough about it to make his own

informed, independent decision. He should delegate as little as possible to the judge assigned the case and to law clerks and staff attorneys. This, of course, is a matter of degree; time problems make delegation of independent research and study of the record necessary, and delegation of the search for information necessarily means some delegation of decision making.

3. Similarly, each judge should participate in the content of any opinion, especially if published, with which he concurs (except for the details of writing style). A number of minds can produce an opinion more serviceable to the bar than can one mind alone. So, again, each judge must understand the case, and he must study and comment on draft opinions as thoroughly as time and the preservation of friendly relations at the court allow. Also, the author of an opinion should be receptive to his colleagues' suggestions.

4. A judge should be open-minded in that he should withhold his final decision until he is fully informed and should weigh carefully arguments presented to support the opposing sides.

5. Appeals should be decided quickly, and judges should save time whenever possible without lessening the quality of their work. Judges' time is in short supply at many courts because of increased case loads and administrative duties.

6. Judges should get as much help as they can from counsel, both to save time and to improve their decisions and opinions. Judges believe that the quality of much appellate advocacy is low, and the trend now is to rely less on counsel and more on staff research. But, at the least, judges should use counsel as much as they can if only to check the work done at the court.

These goals are obviously very interrelated, and the categorization must be somewhat arbitrary. But they do provide a background for comparing present procedures with the procedures suggested here. In doing so, I shall try to present a balanced picture, explaining the major problems behind the suggestions along with their benefits.

RECOMMENDED PROCEDURES

The first suggestion is a prehearing judges' conference similar to that used by most California courts of appeal and by the New Jersey Supreme Court under Chief Justice Vanderbilt:[1] Well before the oral arguments the judges circulate thorough memorandums or draft opinions and discuss the cases in conference. In more detail, I recommend the following. As soon as it is possible to work on an appeal, ordinarily right after the two main briefs arrive, a judge is assigned to prepare a "tentative draft." This is a thorough discussion of the issues and includes the bulk of any independent research the case seems to require. But its conclusions as to how the issues should be decided are very tentative, except when an issue appears to have a clear-cut answer. It is not as polished in style or clarity as the typical draft opinion now circulated in appellate courts, and it may leave tough issues unresolved, indicate areas of doubt, or explain some arguments more fully than a final opinion would. The judges should consider it a working paper and not, as is the case with draft opinions now, a document ready for publication. Law clerks or staff attorneys might write the tentative draft, but the judge must edit it and make sure it contains no major departures from his thinking.

The tentative draft is circulated to the other judges, who read it alongside the briefs (preferably by reading the facts in the briefs, then those in the tentative draft, and then each issue in the briefs and draft in turn). In important cases they may circulate memorandums stating their differences with the assigned judge. If the case seems frivolous to all the judges, that could be the end of the appeal. But the vast majority of cases would be discussed in conference—a telephone conference, perhaps, if the judges' offices are scattered. Whenever it becomes clear that the assigned judge is in the minority, another would be assigned to rewrite the disputed parts of the tentative draft.

At the conference the judges discuss the tentative draft, and each would be expected to suggest changes or, at least, point out areas of uncertainty. From there the judges could take any of a number of tacks. They could decide the case if they believe they have all the information and have done all the study needed. They could direct the staff attorneys or law clerks to do more research on specific points. The most important options, however, concern ways to get counsel involved in the case again. The most obvious option is whether to hold oral argument, at least on those courts that do not allow it as a matter of right. When the assigned judge first studies a case, he should order arguments if he believes they will be helpful; in other cases any of his colleagues could ask, either at or before the conference, that the case be argued. The length of arguments would be determined in the conference at those courts that vary the length of arguments. And, very important, the judges can decide what points they wished discussed in the arguments and then inform counsel right away, giving them time to prepare. Likewise, the judges could ask counsel for further briefing on specific points.

Furthermore, the tentative draft should be sent to counsel for comments (unless considerations of judicial secrecy prevent it, a point discussed later). This is not as farfetched a suggestion as most judges will believe. Judge Thompson of the California Court of Appeal has made virtually the same suggestion and made it for many of the reasons discussed later in this paper.[2] (As it is, at least one California Court of Appeal routinely tells counsel at the beginning of oral argument how the court is leaning in the case.[3]) Judge Leventhal of the D.C. Circuit Court of Appeals has suggested that proposed opinions be circulated to the attorneys for comment in complicated environmental cases.[4] Judges Thompson and Leventhal also discuss situations in which counsel are given proposed opinions at the trial level. There is now some support for letting counsel comment on staff memorandums,[5] and the Iowa Supreme Court used to, at least, do that.[6] And several courts earlier this century had what amounted to the procedure suggested here: The judges did not confer about the cases before the opinions were issued, but the concurring judges then took a closer look at them when sent petitions for rehearing, which they were quite likely to grant.[7]

The court could decide in conference whether to distribute the tentative draft to the attorneys, or, preferably, to save time the assigned judge could circulate it to the judges and attorneys at the same time. He could even circulate it to counsel first so that his colleagues can read it and counsel's written comments, if any, together. The attorneys should be given the option of commenting on the tentative draft in written memorandums, oral arguments, or both. Except in difficult cases, counsel need not be given much time to submit memorandums—perhaps a week for the tentative loser and another week for his opponent to answer. If arguments are held, the opponent's answer could be made there. At any rate, appellate courts could do away with the reply briefs allowed under present procedures.

After the conference, if no argument is held, the judges would study anything further counsel submitted and any further memorandums from within the court. Often the case could be decided without another conference. If arguments are held the judges would confer afterward, as is the custom now, and they would decide many cases then and agree on an opinion, if one is to be issued. Of course, deciding from the bench is possible, too, if the judges like that practice. Some cases contain issues too tough or controversial to decide this quickly, and in others the arguments or supplemental briefs will raise doubts about the earlier position. For these there must be additional discussion and circulation of opinions, though the regularly scheduled opinion conference now held at most state supreme courts probably would not be necessary, since these cases could be discussed and decided in later preargument or postargument conferences.

COMMENTS AND FURTHER DETAILS

This is the core of the proposal made here, though many specific additions, often independent of the core, will be added later. It is time now to discuss the advantages and disadvantages of this general scheme; but two important and complicated factors, the judges' ability to keep an open mind and judicial secrecy, are reserved for later separate sections.

A key benefit is that the judges' attention given a case would be concentrated into a shorter time period than under present procedures (except, of course, summary procedures). The arguments would ordinarily follow the circulation of the tentative draft by about two weeks, and in most cases everything the nonassigned judges do would take place in that period. Some cases would require further work after the arguments; still that would seldom take more than a week or two. As it is now, the judges read the briefs, hear arguments, and confer in a short time span; but they often must wait one, two, or many months before the draft opinion is circulated. Thus the proposed procedure would enable the concurring judges to make more informed final decisions because the case is still fresh in their minds. And, similarly, they would be in a much better position to bear down on the contents of the draft opinions and suggest improvements.

There is a substantial possibility, however, that some judges would put so little effort into the case when studying the tentative draft that these goals would not be accomplished and that the preargument discussion would not be worthwhile. The California courts of appeal apparently have this problem sometimes.[8] But it is no more of a drawback than that concurring judges under present procedures occasionally put little effort into their decisions. The amount of work done by a concurring judge does not depend on when that work is supposed to be done; rather it depends on the work load and on what the judge thinks he ought to do and what he believes his colleagues expect of him. If there is a preargument conference, at least, it would be obvious that a judge does not prepare if he routinely accedes to the tentative draft, thus making effective any informal rule that all judges fully inform themselves about each case; while under present procedures he may be able to get by in the postargument conference on what he picked up in the arguments. Also, as Judge Thompson emphasizes, the circulation of the tentative draft to counsel would give counsel a chance to contest and bring to the judges' attention mistakes made by the assigned judge or staff attorney writing the draft.[9]

Appeals would be decided more quickly under the proposal (assuming, perhaps unrealistically, that the court's backlog is small), mainly because it makes use of the time between scheduling oral argument and the argument itself, time now largely unused. Also, the decisions would take less judge-time. The proposal would save whatever time the judges now spend rereading the briefs when the draft opinions arrive. Also, because the screening process is incorporated into the overall deciding process, it would save whatever time is now spent on screening. Several more time-saving features will be discussed later, especially saving time by relying more on counsel.

There are, however, two possible time-wasting features of the proposal. The first occurs when the assigned judge is in the minority. At present a case can be assigned or reassigned to a judge in the majority after the judges' positions are announced in the postargument conference. But under the proposal the assigned judge would circulate his tentative draft before the others' positions are known, so that some of his work must be duplicated by a colleague. However, their differences would usually involve only a portion of the tentative draft, and in any event a minority judge should spend considerable time studying his position under any procedure.

A mechanism that could lessen this problem, though it serves other purposes also, is to assign a check judge. At least four state supreme courts now assign a second judge to check the opinion writer's work thoroughly,[10] a procedure that is somewhat suspect because it may lead to two-judge decisions. But if a case contains an important and controversial issue, the concurring judges are unlikely to defer to the assigned and check judges. As soon as the assigned judge realizes that he has received such an issue, he should inform the chief judge, who would assign a second judge to write a second tentative draft on the issue. The two drafts would be circulated to the remaining judges, providing them with more information than one alone would. The check judge should be someone who is likely to disagree with the originally assigned judge, and he would skip a place in future rotations to even the work load.

A second possible time-wasting feature is that the assigned judge would prepare the tentative draft without the benefit of this colleagues' help. Perhaps they could quickly answer questions that trouble him, or they might later persuade him that he need not have tackled a certain issue or argument. Because of this, the assigned judge should be free to admit in the draft that he is temporarily stumped by a problem and free to omit full discussion of points that the court might not need to decide.

A great benefit, and the major purpose, of the proposed procedure is the chance to get more help from counsel. At present the attorneys have a rigid two-shot chance to persuade the court, the briefs and oral arguments, with but a rare use of supplemental briefs or rehearing. The major problem here is the lack of communication back and forth between counsel and the court to iron out exactly what points interest the court so that counsel can give information the court needs. All but the simplest cases contain numerous possible issues, points, angles, and so on; one cannot reasonably expect an attorney to forecast with much accuracy which of them will especially interest one or more of the judges. Thus the briefs and arguments often miss areas in which the judges would like help and, equally important, are often loaded with matters the judges do not feel are needed for their decision. Present procedures do not conveniently permit the judges to inform counsel in advance of the points they would like covered more fully. They very seldom ask counsel for supplemental briefing on specific subjects. A few courts tell counsel at the beginning of arguments what areas the court wants covered, and, of course, the judges ask questions in the arguments. But they often do not know enough about the case at argument time to focus on the points that will later prove to be crucial to their decisions. More important, the attorneys have no advance knowledge of the areas the court is interested in and of the specific questions asked; hence they often are not prepared to help the court. Therefore, more effective communication between court and counsel requires that the judges put a good deal of work into a case early, in time to tell counsel of their concerns and to give counsel a chance to prepare answers.

Thus under the proposed procedures courts could greatly expand the use of supplemental briefs and could tell counsel a week or so before arguments what specific topics should be discussed there. Forewarned that the judges are concerned about the topics—that the outcome is likely to hinge on them—the attorneys would be motivated to prepare more thoroughly. They would better apportion their time and, perhaps, be prompted to put more overall effort into the appeal. Giving the attorneys copies of the tentative draft would accomplish this purpose especially well because the attorneys could focus on the details of at least the assigned judge's thoughts.

Oral arguments would be much more efficient under the proposed procedures than they are now. During this century the arguments at most courts have changed from long, uninterrupted speeches by counsel during which the judges learn about the case for the first time, to shorter presentations with frequent questioning. The proposed procedures would carry this trend even further. Because counsel knows what is on the judges' minds, and because the judges understand the case fully, the arguments would be more of a conference discussion than a presentation by counsel. Judges would use the arguments as a final check on their conclusions, rather than an opportunity to learn about the case. Argument time would be used to greater advantage: Counsel would stick closer to points that interest the judges without the often fruitless attempts by judges to focus the discussion; counsel need waste no time stating the facts and outlining the issues, which take up a good portion of the arguments now; and counsel would be better prepared and much more likely to provide helpful answers to the judges' questions. If the tentative draft is circulated, the tentative loser should argue first; this may leave the other side with little to say, shortening his argument. Indeed, the other argument can be eliminated altogether if the judges' views remain unchanged and they do not mind making decisions from the bench. These benefits would not be gained without penalty, however. The major problem, which will be discussed later, is that the judges' advanced preparation may make them so fixed in their decision before the arguments that they would not consider counsel's contentions as carefully as they should.

Handing out the tentative draft for counsel's criticism has many advantages beyond those already mentioned. It would be a check on the possible overinfluence of staff attorneys and law clerks when they write the tentative drafts, and it would assuage the lawyers' suspicions of such an overinfluence. It would go a long way toward solving the problems involved in not allowing briefs, as a few intermediate courts do; counsel would have their say later when commenting on the tentative draft. Likewise, if counsel were allowed to mail in comments on the draft, there would be less objection to the growing practice of refusing oral arguments.

The problems involved in not publishing would also be lessened. Courts now, when they do not publish an opinion, either (1) write an opinion for the parties only, leading to the hot debate over whether such opinions can be cited, or (2) write no opinion, in which case the losing counsel has no assurance that the judges considered his arguments, and no judge has gone through the valuable test of seeing his thoughts written down. The writing and circulation of the tentative draft accomplishes these two purposes, while few would question a noncitation rule, since these opinions are not final. The case would, of course, be decided by a simple order.

In addition, the published opinions could be stripped of all but the important law-making materials. Much of the discussion in many opinions at present is there only to show losing counsel that the court has considered all his arguments and authorities. Under the proposal, this would be in the tentative draft, but not in the published opinion. Anything that shortens opinions, of course, is very valuable.

A perennial problem in appellate courts is the shotgun approach—a lot of weak issues thrown in by appellant, often not argued thoroughly. Courts now either decide these issues on the basis of the scanty material given in the briefs and arguments or they spend time doing research and checking the record to make sure the issues are in fact weak. Under the proposed procedures the court could tell counsel in the tentative draft, or simply in a memorandum, that from the information in the briefs certain contentions seem without merit, and that the court will decide them for the appellee and not mention them in a published opinion, unless the appellant gives more persuasive arguments. This would throw the onus back on the attorney who raised the issues, telling him, in effect, to put up or shut up. And it will give the attorneys time to prepare answers; at present the judges often ask in the arguments whether counsel has any authority for a particular point, but the off-the-cuff answer is less likely to be reliable. This suggestion is a means of relying more on counsel in dispute-deciding rulings, where any mistakes a court makes only affect the litigants. It involves a value judgment, which only each judge can make for himself, namely, whether the client should suffer for his lawyer's mistakes. Judges who believe this unjust (and judges are especially likely to feel that way in criminal cases) should not use this mechanism.

A similar suggestion, and one involving the same questions about justice to the parties, is that the court use only the briefs as the source of facts in the tentative draft and then tell counsel that the facts in the tentative draft are the settled facts unless they have anything to add beyond what is in the briefs.[11] This probably must be done in a tentative draft, rather than a memorandum containing nothing but the facts, because counsel would have trouble determining what additional facts might persuade the judges without knowing in detail how the facts are used. Moreover, the now common, but unwieldy, expensive, and time-consuming, appendix system of presenting the record can be done away with, leaving the briefs and the original record as the sole sources of facts for the judges. Virtually the only reason for appendixes is to give the nonassigned judges a convenient source of facts (the assigned judge has the only copy of the record, and the parties could just as well designate pages for him to read as give him an appendix), but they would not need the appendixes if they can rely on the briefs, the tentative draft, and the attorneys' answers as the source of facts. The most important reason for this suggestion, however, is to cut down the enormous amount of time judges and staff now spend checking the facts in the record. That can be left to the attorneys, and the judges need resort to the record only when the attorneys disagree about what it contains. At the very least, when a judge wants to know whether a certain fact is in the record, he should ask counsel to look for it and report back later in a memorandum or in the oral arguments. At present, either the judges or their clerks comb the record for such facts, or the judges ask counsel about them in the arguments, often getting ill-prepared answers. The major objection to this proposal, to my mind, is that reading the record is a valuable educational tool for appellate judges; it keeps them in touch with how the lower courts are operating and with what is going on in society, somewhat counteracting the ivory tower life of appellate judges. Another objection, as was mentioned earlier, is that judges may feel that litigants, especially criminal defendants, should not suffer because their lawyers miss important facts.

Judges are wary of doing—and many refuse to do—a number of things they believe to be inroads on the adversary system, but that would be less so if tentative drafts were circulated. The ambiguous and exception-ridden rule against deciding issues not raised in the briefs could be safely dropped because the parties would have their say once they viewed the tentative draft. (Searching for and deciding issues not raised would be especially valuable in criminal cases to lessen the chance of further attacks on convictions.[12]) Advice from law professors, which some judges would like more of, would be safer and ethical if described in the draft.[13] And so would the use of empirical data obtained from scholarly texts and articles rather than from the briefs and records. Many judges now take the inconsistent position that these practices are unfair because they involve arguments and materials not brought forth by counsel, although they freely use authorities or law review articles not in the briefs under the fiction that the latter are available to counsel if he does his research well enough. Distributing the tentative draft would give counsel the opportunity to answer anything used against them, even legal authorities.

Along this same line, courts routinely use social facts when developing the law even though the facts are not in the briefs or record and even though they are often of uncertain accuracy. Kenneth Davis has argued that courts should inform counsel when they propose to take judicial notice of social facts to give counsel a chance to contest them,[14] a valuable suggestion because these facts are often important in the courts' lawmaking function. Placing them in the tentative draft, of course, would accomplish Davis's goal; and it would accomplish it much better than in a memorandum stating these facts because, like the facts of the case, counsel need to know how the facts are used. Social facts are often put in final opinions now, but counsel can only contest them in a rehearing petition, an unsatisfactory alternative.

One last benefit of allowing the attorneys to comment on the tentative draft is that the court could prohibit rehearing petitions (except en banc requests) unless the final decision is based on grounds substantially different from those put forth in the tentative draft. As it is now, rehearing petitions are allowed as protection against the rare case where decisively important information is missed. But since the judges have already committed themselves and are loath to change their minds, their efforts in reading the petitions and the attorneys' efforts in drafting them are virtually always wasted. This energy and time would be much more productive if the judges were still in the process of deciding the case and writing the final opinion.

All these procedures designed to engage counsel more actively in the later stages of an appeal might tempt them to do less work in the earlier stages. They might feel that their time is better spent writing the supplemental briefs or preparing for oral arguments then writing the original briefs. Also, their briefs might ignore adverse authority, under the assumption that, should their opponent or the court find it, it can be explained away later. However, these strategies would be risky because a judge's first view of a case tends to carry through to the final decision; a contention might have a greater impact if brought up in the briefs than if brought up later. This gets into the question of the judges' open-mindedness, which will be discussed presently. Also, in many cases—probably most civil cases—the issues on appeal were argued thoroughly at the trial level, so that the briefs represent little additional work anyway. And, of course, if the case was decided by a lower appellate court, the attorneys would ordinarily have studied the issues closely there.

OPEN-MINDEDNESS

How the proposals would affect the judges' ability to keep an open mind is uncertain; but the greatest objections probably occur in this area. Judges greatly prize the ability to keep an open mind to the arguments of counsel and of their colleagues, and they routinely emphasize that their initial thoughts about a case and their votes in the postargument conference are purely tentative. Yet there is always a danger that initial impressions will be held too strongly. This danger is greater if the judge has announced his position to others, and greater still if he has presented his position as the result of his best efforts. The latter is what happens with draft opinions under the present procedures; thus judges rarely change their minds about the outcome after circulating drafts, and some are almost impervious to suggestions that their opinions can be improved. The proposed procedures would alleviate these problems because the tentative draft is not presented as a final, polished document.

On the other hand, the tentative draft would be circulated at an earlier stage in the proceedings than draft opinions are now. The assigned judge would prepare it before he has received any input from his colleagues and may be less receptive to their suggestions than to those now made in the postargument conference. If the tentative draft is circulated to the attorneys, moreover, the assigned judge has broadcast his position even more widely and, thus, may become even more entrenched. All the judges, in addition, would study the case and present their views in conference early in the proceedings; thus counsel's presentations in supplemental briefs or oral arguments may meet tough resistance. Hence there must be a strong feeling among the judges that they should continue to leave their expressed views open to doubt. As a practical matter these problems are not much of a disadvantage when compared with the present procedures because no matter what procedures are used, the judges will make tentative decisions based on the first information they receive, tending to make that information more important than later information. Thus under the proposals the briefs would be studied by the assigned judge much more thoroughly before the arguments than is presently done, placing more importance on the attorneys' main presentations and less on the oral arguments, which are not as thorough as the briefs and which include things like the demeanor of counsel that may, but should not, influence the judges. Likewise, under the proposal independent research would be done at an earlier stage, and, thus, the authority found would be more likely to affect the decision and less likely to be used simply to justify a decision reached earlier, for example, in the postargument conference under the present procedures.

Sending the tentative drafts to the attorneys cuts both ways in this question of open-mindedness. On the one hand, the assigned judge may be defensive, assume that the attacks on the draft reflect on him, and thus be loath to admit that changes are needed. On the other hand, the tentative draft would be sent to the attorneys with an explanation that it is tentative and that the judges are fully open to persuasion. If that is not what happens in practice, it would quickly become obvious to the bar. The judges would be seen as being less than open-minded, not the sort of reputation appellate judges desire. Moreover, the judges must fairly frequently change the results and reasoning contained in the tentative draft if they wish to obtain much help from the attorneys' written comments and oral arguments. Should counsel believe that the draft is almost always the final word, they would be unlikely to waste much time attacking it. Therefore, the judges' self-interest and their wish to get help from the bar may prompt them to keep an open mind.

In sum, the proposals would tend to make judges more open-minded than they are under present procedures in some respects, and less so in others. The major handicap is probably that the judges would go into oral arguments with much firmer positions than they do now. For the proposals to work, the judges must change their concept of the draft opinion from a polished document to a working paper; otherwise decisions would be made too hastily and counsel would give the court little help after the draft is circulated. If the judges are unable to do that, they should substitute a memorandum without conclusions for the tentative draft.

JUDICIAL SECRECY

A major objection to circulating the tentative draft (and, perhaps, to other communication sent from the court to counsel) is that it violates the confidentialness of decision making. Appellate courts strictly prohibit the dissemination of internal discussions; unless this is changed, the tentative drafts could not be sent to the attorneys. But the secrecy should be carried no further than its justifications support. Virtually every decision-making organization desires secrecy and uses various rationalizations to justify it. In recent years secrecy in the legislative and executive branches has been attacked severely, and the tendency has been to look closely at the reasons for the secrecy and then limit it to situations where the reasons actually support it. The judicial branch should do the same. To date, attacks on judicial secrecy have been relatively infrequent; but the case load and time problems may force judges to take a closer look at their practices.

There are a number of reasons for judicial secrecy. One was just discussed: If judges' tentative thoughts are made public, they may be less open-minded thereafter. A second is that judges and others at the courts should be free to express whatever is on their minds, and the wider the audience, the more cautious they will be. The question here is what effect would airing the tentative draft have on its content, or, more bluntly, what factors relevant to the decision would a judge want to tell his colleagues but not the attorneys? I hope there are not any. Even if judges do decide because of prejudices or unsubstantiated suspicions, which they do not want known outside the court, they probably would not tell their colleagues anyway. It is important to note that in recent years judges have emphasized more and more the need to put the real reasons for decisions in their published opinions; if they can do it there, they can do it in the tentative drafts. Even if there is something the assigned judge wishes to hide from counsel, he could bring it up in the conference or could put it on a memorandum apart from the tentative draft and not given to the attorneys, but these practices should be rare.

Three more reasons for judicial secrecy, on the other hand, require some precautionary measures. The tentative draft must be kept confidential in the very small number of cases where advance knowledge of a decision may enable someone to profit on the stock market. Likewise, if one party learns before his opponent of a tentative decision, he might settle the case to his benefit; therefore, the court must require that any settlement made after the circulation of the tentative drafts be accompanied by statements by all concerned that they have read the tentative draft. In the few rare cases (below the U.S. Supreme Court level) of public notoriety giving the tentative drafts to the attorneys may lead to rumors in the press about what is happening on the court. Judges, who tend to be very sensitive about the public's perception of the courts, may feel that press speculation degrades the courts and, thus, that the tentative drafts must remain at the courts in these cases.

In all, these reasons for judicial secrecy would prevent giving the drafts to the attorneys in but few appeals. There are probably other reasons why judges like their activities kept secret. Karl Llewellyn has said that the courts make a "fetish of secrecy" and that the secrecy, he suspects, "represent[s] partly a closing of ranks to protect the court from criticism or attack."[15] A judge's job, like that of any decision maker, is certainly more pleasant the more he can isolate himself from disapproving eyes. But judges should not base their procedures on considerations of convenience to themselves only. In England, it should be added, cases are decided at the close of oral arguments, so that the judges' deliberations take place on the bench and their opinions are oral and tentative, to be edited later if published. Even in this country judges often air their tentative views in oral arguments, at least on courts where they prepare well beforehand and question heavily.

ADDITIONAL SUGGESTIONS

In cases falling under a court's discretionary jurisdiction, the application should be accompanied by full briefs, and as soon as a case is taken, it should be sent to the assigned judge (or a staff attorney) to write the tentative draft. This would cut several months off of these appeals, and study of the case when granting leave would be fresh on the judges' minds when deciding the merits. If the court hears appeals from intermediate courts, at any rate, this procedure would ordinarily present no hardship for the attorneys, because as it is now the briefs on the merits are usually almost the same as those filed below, adjusted to include new authorities and to meet the lower court's opinion. This procedure assumes substantial staff participation in the leave granting process, for the judges do not have time to read full briefs if the court's discretionary jurisdiction is at all large.

In tough cases, especially those involving complicated or technical facts, the judges should confer with the attorneys at any time they want help. This can be done in conference at the court, in a judge's office, or simply over the phone. All counsel must be present, of course, and the phone call must be a conference call. Also, the court could bring law professors or other outside experts into these discussions. These procedures are all used now by a very few appellate courts[16] and seem to be valuable means of getting more help.

Draft opinions should be sent to staff attorneys for a thorough going over before they are issued as an extra check against mistakes.[17] This used to be one of the major functions of law clerks, but has gone by the wayside in as much as the clerks draft the opinions themselves. It would provide an interesting variation to the staff attorneys' jobs, and it would allow for frank criticism without damaging the judges' interpersonal relations; but the staff attorneys may be wary of attacking their employers. If staff attorneys originally draft the opinions, this function could be given to the reporter's office, which would then go beyond the fact and citation checking duties typically lodged there now.

SCHEDULING PROBLEMS

A court adopting the proposed procedures would have to revamp its schedule. Unless it has a light case load, it would have to skip a month's arguments while the tentative drafts are written and the old opinions are finished. This would increase any backlog of briefed but unargued cases the court may already have. The overall scheduling would be easiest at those courts that sit a few days each week. But most courts prefer to sit one week a month or two weeks every other month; such a schedule is probably necessary if the judges' offices are not all at the court. The following schedule is suggested for a court that sits one week every month. During the first two weeks (or three weeks when there are five weeks between sittings) the judges work separately on their tentative drafts, writing from two to ten of them depending on the court's case load, the difficulty of the cases, the amount of staff or law clerk help, and the size of the court or panel. The tentative drafts are circulated as soon as finished. Any case in which the tentative draft is not finished within the two weeks would be carried over to the next month. During the third week the judges hold conferences, perhaps over two mornings to allow time to study some cases in the afternoon of the first day. Also during the third week, the judges do further research and writing on the cases assigned them, write separate opinions in others' cases, and work on tentative drafts for the next month's cases. In the fourth week the judges hear arguments and confer after each sitting. There should be a day or two left in that week—because the arguments would be shorter than now—in which to finish the opinions and to work on tentative drafts. A few opinions, though, would not be finished until the following, or even a later, month.

Soon after the assigned judge starts on the tentative draft he must determine the week in which the case is to be argued. He must, also, predict accurately that he will finish the tentative draft by the end of the second week if he orders arguments for the fourth week, though perhaps it would not be too much of a burden on the attorneys if arguments were postponed with almost two weeks notice. Scheduling arguments at large intermediate courts that sit in rapidly shifting panels would be intricate, and the total length of arguments held by a panel would vary greatly because of chance variation in the difficulty of cases. Therefore, for the system to work it is probably necessary that the same panel sit for several days at a time. The preargument conferences could be arranged informally by the panel and could be held over the phone.

CONCLUSION

These proposals are not aimed at any particular category of appellate court; they could be tailored to fit any court, except probably the U.S. Supreme Court. The proposals, also, are designed to mesh into an overall decision-making procedure, but most are largely independent of the overall procedure and could be adopted alone. Any one of the most important suggestions, the tentative drafts, the preargument conferences, and the circulation of draft opinions to counsel, could be adopted without the others; but for various reasons given previously each would be less effective alone.

Past efforts to make appellate judges more productive have focused on staff help and on dropping parts of the appellate process, especially oral arguments and opinions. The suggestions here focus on greater productivity and quality of decisions through more efficient use of judges' time and through greater use of counsel's efforts. That is, the judges should make their working hours count as much as possible, and they should wring every bit of help they can out of the attorneys. "Appellate courts do not always demand of the adversary system the assistance it is capable of providing."[18] Judges often complain about the quality of advocacy. But they should not put all the blame on the other side of the bench; they can do much to help counsel prepare better and provide more helpful information.

Appellate Court Internal Decision-Making Procedures

These writings discuss in some detail the internal decision-making procedures of state appellate courts and U.S. Circuit Courts of Appeals, but not those of the U.S. Supreme Court. Only descriptions of decision-making procedures are included, and not discussions limited to possible or proposed procedures. Every effort has been made to find writings published from 1950 on, and only some of the more important earlier ones are listed. Also, the bibliography includes only the major writings about staff attorneys and screening procedures; an enormous literature on this subject has developed in recent years, too much to include here. When the same material is published in more than one place, I have included only one citation, except where a hard-to-locate description is partly reproduced in an accessible journal. Appellate courts in many states, it should be added, are now in the process of preparing handbooks for attorneys; these will probably contain descriptions of the courts' internal procedures.

GENERAL COURT SURVEYS

American Bar Association, *Methods of Reaching and Preparing Appellate Court Decisions* (1942) and *Internal Operating Procedures of Appellate Courts* (1961).

Council of State Governments, *The Courts of Last Resort of the Forty-eight States* (1950) and *State Court Systems* (rev. 1976). (The latter is revised every other year.)

E. Curran and E. Sunderland, The Organization and Operation of Courts of Review, in *Third Annual Report of the Judicial Council of Michigan* 51 (1933).

A. Frantz, *How Courts Decide* 7-14 (1968).

G. Hazard, After the Trial Court—The Realities of Appellate Review, in *The Courts, the Public, and the Law Explosion* 60 (H. Jones, ed. 1965).

L. Hyde, Appellate Court Decisions, 28 A.B.A.J. 808 (1942).

Institute of Judicial Administration, *Appellate Courts. Internal Operating Procedures. Preliminary Report* (1957) and *Appellate Courts. Internal Operating Procedures. 1959 Summary and Supplement* (1959).

R. Leflar, *Internal Operating Procedures of Appellate Courts* (1976).

G. Lilly and A. Scalia, Appellate Justice: A Crisis in Virginia? 57 Va. L. Rev. 3 (1971).

S. McConkie, *Environmental, Institutional, and Procedural Influences in Collegial Decision-Making: A Comparative Analysis of State Supreme Courts* (unpublished Ph.D. dissertation, Washington State University, 1974), partly reproduced in S. McConkie, Decision-Making in State Supreme Courts, 59 Judicature 337 (1976).
J. Parker, Improving Appellate Methods, 25 N.Y.U.L. Rev. 1 (1950).
G. Smith, The Appellate Decisional Conference, 28 Ark. L. Rev. 425 (1975).
A. Vanderbilt, *Minimum Standards of Judicial Administration* (1949).
F. Wiener, *Effective Appellate Advocacy* (1950) and *Briefing and Arguing Federal Appeals* (1961).

DESCRIPTIONS OF A LIMITED NUMBER OF COURTS

American Judicature Society, Queries Concerning Methods of Work in Supreme Courts, 8 J. Am. Jud. Soc'y 101, 165 (1924, 1925), 9 J. Am. Jud. Soc'y 20, 49, 115, 152 (1925, 1926), and 10 J. Am. Jud. Soc'y 57 (1926).
Federal Judicial Center, *Comparative Report on Internal Operating Procedures of United States Courts of Appeals* (1973).
C. Haworth, Screening and Summary Procedures in the United States Courts of Appeals, 1973 Wash. U.L.Q. 257.
J. Howard, *Decision-Making Procedures in the U.S. Courts of Appeals for the 2d and 5th Circuits* (Federal Judicial Center 1973).
D. Karlen, *Appellate Courts in the United States and England* (1963).
D. Meador, *Appellate Courts, Staff and Process in the Crisis of Volume* (1974) and Appellate Case Management and Decisional Process, 61 Va. L. Rev. 255 (1975).
J. Wold, *Internal Procedures, Role Perceptions and Judicial Behavior: A Study of Four State Courts of Last Resort* (unpublished Ph.D. dissertation, Johns Hopkins University, 1972).

DESCRIPTIONS OF SPECIFIC COURTS, BY STATE

ALABAMA

R. Frye, *The Alabama Supreme Court: An Institutional View* (1969).
National Center for State Courts, *The Appellate Process in Alabama* (1973).
J. Goodwyn, The Supreme Court at Work, 21 Ala. Lawyer 5 (1960).

ARIZONA

C. Bernstein, The Disposition of Civil Appeals in the Supreme Court, 5 Arizona L. Rev. 175 (1964).
J. Cameron, Internal Operating Procedures of the Arizona Supreme Court, 17 Ariz. L. Rev. 643 (1975).

ARKANSAS

L. Brown, The Handling of Supreme Court Cases—Processing, Practice, and Procedure, 22 Ark. L. Rev. 679 (1969).
G. Smith, A Primer of Opinion Writing, for Four New Judges, 21 Ark. L. Rev. 197 (1967).

CALIFORNIA

E. Bishop, An Appellate Department at Work, 26 Calif. St. B.J. 419 (1951).

W. Goodman and T. Seaton, Foreword: Ripe for Decision, Internal Workings and Current Concerns of the California Supreme Court, 62 Calif. L. Rev. 309 (1974).

W. Hepperle, *People* v. *Sharp*: A Look Behind the Court's Blue Velvet Curtain, 1972 Calif. J. 221.

P. Johnson, Foreword: The Accidental Decision and How It Happens, 65 Calif. L. Rev. 231, 249-251 (1977).

J. Masuda, *The Politics of a State Intermediate Appellate Process: The California Court of Appeal*, 25-54 (unpublished Ph.D. dissertation, University of Iowa, 1976).

J. Molinari, The Decisionmaking Conference of the California Court of Appeal, 57 Calif. L. Rev. 606 (1969).

National Center for State Courts, *The California Courts of Appeal* (1974).

R. Peters, Five Years of the Conference System, 19 Calif. St. B.J. 399 (1944).

R. Peters, A Judge's View of Appellate Advocacy, in *California Civil Appellate Practice* xv (California Continuing Education of the Bar, 1966).

R. Thompson, One Judge and No Judge Appellate Decisions, 50 Calif. St. B.J. 476 (1975).

R. Traynor, Some Open Questions on the Work of State Appellate Courts, 24 U. Chi. L. Rev. 211 (1957).

DISTRICT OF COLUMBIA

District of Columbia Court of Appeals, *Internal Operating Procedures* (1978).

D. Meador, *Proposals for the Use of Screening Procedures and Legal Assistants in the District of Columbia Court of Appeals* (Criminal Courts Technical Assistance Project, American University Law School, 1974).

A. Stevas, Monitoring and Tracking Procedures in the District of Columbia Court of Appeals (District of Columbia Court of Appeals, 1975).

The District of Columbia Court of Appeals and the A.B.A. Standards of Judicial Administration, A Study Report (D.C. Judicial Planning Committee 1977).

FLORIDA

T. Boyer, Appellate Mystique: What Goes on Behind Closed Doors? 51 Fla. B.J. 506 (1977).

A. England and M. McMahn, Quantity Discounts in Appellate Justice, 60 Judicature 442 (1977).

H. Whitaker, The Florida Supreme Court Internal Procedures, 4 Fla. St. U. Gov. Research Bull. 1 (Dec. 1967).

J. Wigginton, General Aspects of Appellate Practice, 33 Fla. B.J. 421 (1959).

IDAHO

Report of the Supreme Court Appellate Committee, *An Investigation into the Problems Created by the Growing Appellate Caseload in Idaho* (1977).

ILLINOIS

O. Carter, Methods of Work in Courts of Review, 12 Ill. L. Rev. 231 (1917).
F. Thompson, Practice in the Supreme Court, in *Appellate Jurisdiction and Practice in the Courts of Illinois* 23 (W. Dodd and P. Edmunds 1929).

INDIANA

A. Ashman et al., *Examination of the Administrative Operations of the Court of Appeals of the State of Indiana* (Criminal Courts Technical Assistance Project, American University Law School, 1974).

IOWA

J. Beatty, *An Institutional and Behavioral Analysis of the Iowa Supreme Court* (unpublished Ph.D. dissertation, University of Iowa, 1970).
Institute of Judicial Administration, *The Supreme Court of Iowa* (1971).
M. McCormick, Appellate Congestion in Iowa: Dimensions and Remedies, 25 Drake L. Rev. 133 (1975).
F. Miller, Mechanics of Appellate Decision—Iowa, 28 A.B.A.J. 578 (1942).
D. Rendleman and P. Pfeffer, Appellate Procedure and Practice, 19 Drake L. Rev. 74 (1969).

KANSAS

S. Jackson, The Over-Worked Supreme Court of Kansas, 26 Kansas St. B. Ass'n J. 190 (1957).
Report of the Kansas Judicial Study Advisory Committee, 13 Washburn L.J. 271 (1974).

KENTUCKY

B. Martin, Kentucky's New Court of Appeals, 41 Ky. Bench & B. 8 (April 1977).

LOUISIANA

Institute of Judicial Administration, *A Study of the Louisiana Court System* (1972).

MAINE

R. Fellows, Practice Before the Supreme Judicial Court of Maine, 43 Me. St. B. Ass'n 85 (1954).
Institute of Judicial Administration, *The Supreme Judicial Court and the Superior Court of the State of Maine* (1971).
D. Webber, Appellate Advocacy with Maine Flavor, 18 Maine L. Rev. 59 (1966).

MASSACHUSETTS

P. Reardon, The Internal Operations of Appellate Courts, in *Proceedings, Eighteenth Annual Meeting of the Conference of Chief Justices* 19 (1967).

MICHIGAN

H. Kelley, The Michigan Supreme Court, Some Random Observations, 33 U. Detroit L.J. 381 (1956).

T. Lesinski and N. Stockmeyer, Prehearing Research and Screening in the Michigan Court of Appeals: One Court's Method for Increasing Judicial Productivity, 26 Vand. L. Rev. 1211 (1973).

J. Dethmers, Improving Procedures for Appellate Review, in *Proceedings, Nineteenth Annual Meeting of the Conference of Chief Justices* 19 (1967).

MINNESOTA

Minnesota State Court Report, 1976-1977 5-9 (1977).

National Center for State Courts, *Study of the Appellate System in Minnesota* (1974).

MISSISSIPPI

S. Robertson, Recent Changes in Mississippi Supreme Court Rules and Procedure, 38 Miss. L.J. 547 (1967).

NEW JERSEY

M. Conford, The Appellate Division, New York and New Jersey: Varying Problems in Organization and Advocacy, 26 Record 301 (1971).

J. Francis, Post-Argument Procedures, 52 F.R.D. 70 (1971).

J. Francis, Joseph Weintraub—A Judge for All Seasons, 59 Cornell L. Rev. 186 (1974).

A. Vanderbilt, Our New Judicial Establishment: The Record of the First Year, 4 Rutgers L. Rev. 353 (1950).

A. Vanderbilt, The Record of the New Jersey Courts in the Fourth Year Under the New Constitution, 7 Rutgers L. Rev. 317 (1953).

A. Vanderbilt, Improving the Administration of Justice—Two Decades of Development, 26 U. Cin. L. Rev. 155 (1957).

J. Weintraub, Writing, Consideration and Adoption of Opinions, 83 N.J.L.J. 477 (1960).

NEW MEXICO

M. Nobel, The Law Clerk, 7 Trial Judges' J. 4 (Oct. 1968).

NEW YORK

A. Brennan, Looking Through the Periscope of an Appellate Tribunal, 15 Fed. Ins. Counsel Q. 44 (1965).

M. Cuomo, The New York Court of Appeals: A Practical Perspective, 34 St. John's L. Rev. 197 (1960).

H. Gamso et al., Highlights of Appellate Division Practice, 26 N.Y.Co.B. Bull. 18 (1968-1969).

J. Hopkins, The Winds of Change: New Styles in the Appellate Process, 3 Hofstra L. Rev. 649 (1975).

J. Hopkins, The Appellate Division, New York and New Jersey: Varying Problems in Organization and Advocacy, 26 Record 306 (1971).

J. Loughran, The Argument of an Appeal in the Court of Appeals, 12 Fordham L. Rev. 1 (1943).

B. Shientag, The Appellate Division, First Department, Its Jurisdiction, How It Functions in Conference, Briefs and Oral Arguments Presented to It, 5 Record 377 (1950).

OKLAHOMA

J. Williams, Oklahoma Supreme Court: The Mechanics of the Decision-Makers, 2 Tulsa L.J. 148 (1965).

OREGON

R. Kester, Tailoring Appellate Arguments, 43 Ore. L. Rev. 135 (1964).

PENNSYLVANIA

Institute of Judicial Administration, *The Appellate Courts of Pennsylvania* (1972).
R. Jacobs, The Judge's View, 42 Pa. B. Ass'n Q. 119 (1970).

RHODE ISLAND

E. Beiser, Decision-Making in the Rhode Island Supreme Court: Judicial Behavior, Attitudes, Norms, and Role Perceptions (paper delivered to the Annual Meeting of the Am. Pol. Sci. Ass'n, 1971). This is partly reproduced in: E. Beiser, The Rhode Island Supreme Court: A Well-Integrated Political System, 8 L. and Soc. Rev. 167 (1974).
T. Kelleher, The Anatomy of the Judicial Process, 24 R.I.B.J. 4 (1976).
National Center for State Courts, *The Appellate Process in the Rhode Island Supreme Court* (1977).

SOUTH CAROLINA

Institute of Judicial Administration, *The Judicial System of South Carolina* (1971).

TENNESSEE

W. Hall, Comment on "One-Judge Opinions," 21 Tenn. L. Rev. 383 (1950).
Institute of Judicial Administration, *The Judicial System of Tennessee* (1971).
L. McAmis, The Lawyer and the Court of Appeals, 24 Tenn. L. Rev. 279 (1956).

TEXAS

P. Burleson, Practice in the Court of Criminal Appeals, 23 Texas B.J. 103 (1960).
R. Calvert, The Mechanics of Judgment Making in the Supreme Court of Texas, 21 Baylor L. Rev. 439 (1969).
J. Greenhill, Presentation of a Case to the Supreme Court of Texas, 38 Texas L. Rev. 538 (1960).
C. Smith, Appellate Procedure and Method of Review of Causes in the Supreme Court of Texas, 1 So. Texas L.J. 121 (1954).

UTAH

National Center for State Courts, *Utah Supreme Court Project Report* (1977).

VIRGINIA

L. I'Anson, How the Supreme Court of Appeals of Virginia Functions, 71 Rep. Va. St. B. Ass'n 221 (1960).
T. Morris, *The Virginia Supreme Court, An Institutional and Political Analysis* (1975).

WASHINGTON

National Center for State Courts, *Washington Appellate Court Project* (1975).

WISCONSIN

G. Broadfoot, How I Go About Making Up My Mind, 31 Wisc. B. Bull. 30 (Aug. 1958).
J. Martin, The Mechanics of Hammering Out the Decision: Assignment of Cases, Individual Study, Conferences, the Opinion, 31 Wisc. B. Bull. 27 (Aug. 1958).
National Center for State Courts, *Wisconsin Appellate Practice and Procedure Study* (1975).
T. Ragatz and J. Shea, Supreme Court Law Clerks, 35 Wisc. B. Bull. 33 (Aug. 1962).
H. Wilkie, Supreme Court Practice, 36 Wisc. B. Bull. 27 (Dec. 1963).

U.S. COURT OF APPEALS FOR THE:
DISTRICT OF COLUMBIA CIRCUIT

J. Langner, Description of the Operating Procedures of the United States Court of Appeals for the District of Columbia Circuit (Federal Judicial Center 1973).

FIRST CIRCUIT

J. Langner, Description of the Operating Procedures of the United States Court of Appeals for the First Circuit (Federal Judicial Center 1973).

SECOND CIRCUIT

Committee on Federal Courts, The Association of the Bar of the City of New York, *Appeals to the Second Circuit* (1975).
J. Lumbard, Appellate Advocacy (unpublished paper, Institute of Judicial Administration 1962).
C. Clark, The Role of the United States Courts of Appeals in Law Administration, in *Conference on Judicial Administration* 87 (University of Chicago 1956).
H. Medina, The Decisional Process in the United States Court of Appeals, Second Circuit, 149 N.Y.L.J. Feb. 18, 1963, p. 4; Feb. 19, 1963, p. 4; and Feb. 20, 1963, p. 4. This is partly reproduced in H. Medina, The Decisional Process, 20 N.Y.Co.B.Bull. 94 (1962).
Note, The Second Circuit: Federal Judicial Administration in a Microcosm, 63 Colum. L. Rev. 874 (1963).
M. Schick, *Learned Hand's Court* (1970).
W. Whittaker, Description of the Operating Procedures of the United States Court of Appeals for the Second Circuit (Federal Judicial Center 1973).

THIRD CIRCUIT

United States Court of Appeals for the Third Circuit, *Internal Operating Procedures* (1974).
W. Whittaker, Description of the Operating Procedures of the United States Court of Appeals for the Third Circuit (Federal Judicial Center 1972).

FOURTH CIRCUIT

S. Flanders and J. Goldman, *Screening Practices and the Use of Para-Judicial Personnel in the U.S. Courts of Appeals: A Study in the Fourth Circuit* (Federal Judicial Center 1974).
J. Langner, Description of the Operating Procedures of the United States Court of Appeals for the Fourth Circuit (Federal Judicial Center 1973).

FIFTH CIRCUIT

J. Coleman, Appellate Proceedings in the United States Court of Appeals, 38 Miss. L.J. 554 (1967).
I. Goldberg, Preparing for Hearing Oral Argument, 63 F.R.D. 499 (1974).
G. Rahdert and L. Roth, Inside the Fifth Circuit: Looking at Some of Its Internal Procedures, 23 Loyola L. Rev. 661 (1977).
D. Sweeney, Law Clerkships—Three Inside Views: III. In United States Court of Appeals, 33 Ala. Lawyer 171 (1972).
United States Court of Appeals for the Fifth Circuit, *Internal Operating Procedures Manual* (1976).
W. Whittaker, Description of the Operating Procedures of the United States Court Appeals for the Fifth Circuit (Federal Judicial Center 1973).

SIXTH CIRCUIT

Cincinnati Chapter of the Federal Bar Association, *Practitioners' Handbook for Appeals to the United States Court of Appeals for the Sixth Circuit* (1977).
G. Edwards, Exorcising the Devil of Appellate Court Delay, 58 A.B.A.J. 149 (1972).
J. Langner, Description of the Operating Procedures of the United States Court of Appeals for the Sixth Circuit (Federal Judicial Center 1973).

SEVENTH CIRCUIT

J. Langner, Description of the Operating Procedures of the United States Court of Appeals for the Seventh Circuit (Federal Judicial Center 1973).
P. Tone, United States Court of Appeals for the Seventh Circuit, 53 Notra Dame L. Rev. 395 (1978).

EIGHTH CIRCUIT

F. Gibson, Some Observations on Our United States Court of Appeals, 35 U.M.K.C.L. Rev. 261 (1967).
J. Langner, Description of the Operating Procedures of the United States Court of Appeals of the Eighth Circuit (Federal Judicial Center 1973).

United States Court of Appeals for the Eighth Circuit, *Practice and Procedures of the Eighth Circuit Handbook* (1978).

NINTH CIRCUIT

J. Langner, Description of the Operating Procedures of the United States Court of Appeals for the Ninth Circuit (Federal Judicial Center 1973).

Statement of O. Trask to the Commission on Revision of the Federal Court Appellate System, April 16, 1975, p. 940.

United States Court of Appeals for the Ninth Circuit, *Internal Operating Procedures* (1977).

TENTH CIRCUIT

J. Langner, Description of the Operating Procedures of the United States Court of Appeals for the Tenth Circuit (Federal Judicial Center 1973).

J. Talesnick, Understanding the United States Court of Appeals for the Tenth Circuit: A Guide for the Practitioner, 52 Denver L.J. 375 (1975).

Judges' Writings on Appellate Advocacy

What follows is a list of eighty law review articles and books written by eighty-two judges. They were published from 1950 through 1977, though a few were actually written before 1950. Nine judges wrote more than one piece on appellate advocacy, and two articles contain writings by several judges. The list does not include writings on aspects of appellate advocacy other than the briefs and oral arguments; much has also been written about the records and appendixes, jurisdiction, and so on.

Nearly all the articles are advice to lawyers about how to write briefs and argue orally; these are generally speeches made to bar groups and then published in local law journals. A few are reviews of books about appellate advocacy, in which the judge concentrates on giving his version of what appellate advocacy should be like.

The writings vary greatly in length and thoroughness. Most contain five to ten pages of discussion about appellate advocacy. Only four are over twenty pages long. Seventeen judges made fewer than a dozen different points, and thirty-two judges wrote about just the oral arguments or the briefs.

Twenty-three of the judges were on courts with discretionary jurisdiction (including two U.S. Supreme Court justices). Twenty-five were on state supreme courts without discretionary jurisdiction; nineteen were on the U.S. circuit courts; and fifteen were on state intermediate courts. The writings tapered off during the end of the period; there were only sixteen in the past ten years. But on the major topics, at least, there is little difference between the later and earlier articles.

Exact percentages are not used when discussing these articles in the text for a number of reasons. The judges are obviously not a random sample of appellate judges, so that exact percentages may not reflect the percentages among appellate judges as a whole. Sometimes, though not often, there is a problem as to how different comments should be categorized (in all there were 239 categories, though a few were later combined, especially those dealing with the same topic but referring to the briefs or oral arguments only). Most important, the frequency of any category depends largely on the breadth of the category—for example, the category "clarity is important" would have been much more common had it included comments about literary style, the need to rewrite briefs, and the use of good grammar (that category included only judges' statements using essentially the words quoted). Thus, as is often the problem with content analysis in the social sciences, comparisons of the frequency of different topics is tricky unless the topics are very similar. When comparing the frequency of comments about the need to know the facts and the need to know the law, exact figures are more meaningful than when comparing, say, the importance of conciseness with suggestions that counsel use charts and exhibits in oral arguments. Also, of course, that a judge does not mention a category or make a specific suggestion does not mean he disagrees with it. Every judge would probably agree with almost everything said. But it is assumed that the frequency with which the various suggestions are made gives a rough indication of their importance in the eyes of the judges.

If the reader would like a list of references for a specific point, I would be glad to supply them under the same arrangements as those for interview material.

L. Bejach, Presenting a Case Before the Court of Appeals, 30 Tenn. L. Rev. 337 (1963).

J. Bell, Oral Arguments Before the Supreme Court of Pennsylvania, 24 Pa. B. Ass'n Q. 133 (1953).

C. Breitel, Summing Up, in *Counsel on Appeal* 195 (A. Charpentier ed. 1968).

M. Bright, The Changing Nature of the Federal Appeals Process in the 1970's, 65 F.R.D. 496 (1975).

T. Brown, The Argument; Objective, Persuasive Enlightenment, 31 Wisc. B. Bull. 21 (Aug. 1958).

W. Carswell, The Briefing and Argument of an Appeal, 16 Brooklyn L. Rev. 147 (1950).

T. Chadick, An Effective Appellate Brief, 26 Texas B.J. 923 (1963).

M. Conford, The Appellate Division, New York and New Jersey: Varying Problems in Organization and Advocacy, 26 Record 301 (1971).

G. Currie, What Happened; Stating the Facts, 31 Wisc. B. Bull. 19 (Aug. 1958).

G. Currie, Some Aspects of Appellate Practice Before the Wisconsin Supreme Court, 1955 Wisc. L. Rev. 554.

A. Denecke et al., Notes on Appellate Brief Writing, 51 Ore. L. Rev. 351 (1972).

W. Doyle, Some Observations on Brief Writing, 33 Rocky Mt. L. Rev. 23 (1960).

W. Ethridge, How to Win a Case on Appeal, 34 Miss. L.J. 363 (1963).

C. Fahy, Observations from Appellate Experiences, 34 Wisc. B. Bull. 52 (April 1961).

C. Fahy, Book Review, 3 J. Legal Ed. 471 (1951).

T. Fairchild, Setting the Stage, the Synopsis, and Issues Stated, 31 Wisc. B. Bull. 14 (Aug. 1958).

R. Fellows, Practice Before the Supreme Judicial Court of Maine, 43 Me. St. B. Ass'n 85 (1954).

J. Fontron, Troublesome Areas in Appellate Practice, 37 J. Kansas B. Ass'n 173 (1968).

J. Fournet, The Effective Presentation of a Case to the Supreme Court in Brief and in Argument, 3 La. B.J. 95 (1956).

T. Garfield, Workshop Outline, in *A. Vestal and P. Willson, Iowa Practice*, sec. 62.01 (1974).

J. Godbold, Twenty Pages and Twenty Minutes—Effective Advocacy on Appeal, 30 Sw. L.J. 801 (1976).

H. Goodrich, A Case on Appeal—A Judge's View, in *A Case on Appeal* 1 (4th ed. 1967).

J. Greenhill, Presentation of a Case to the Supreme Court of Texas, 38 Texas L. Rev. 538 (1960).

V. Griffith, Suggestions for the Preparation of Briefs, 29 Miss. L. Rev. 413 (1958).

F. Hamley, Appellate Advocacy, 12 Ark. L. Rev. 129 (1958).

J. Harlan, What Part Does the Oral Argument Play in the Conduct of an Appeal? 41 Cornell L.Q. 6 (1955).

C. Harris, The Advocate on Appeal: What to Do and What Not to Do, 19 Ark. L. Rev. 67 (1965).

R. Harwood, What I Expect from an Appellate Lawyer, 25 Ala. Lawyer 357 (1964).

W. Huxman, Book Review, 7 Kansas L. Rev. 396 (1959).

L. Hyde, Book Review, 1953 Wash. U.L.Q. 478.

R. Jackson, Advocacy Before the United States Supreme Court, 37 Cornell L.Q. 1 (1951).

R. Jacobs, The Judge's View, 42 Pa. B. Ass'n Q. 119 (1970).

F. Kenison, Some Aspects of Appellate Arguments, 1 N.H.B.J. 5 (Jan. 1959).

R. Kester, Tailoring Appellate Arguments, 43 Ore. L. Rev. 135 (1964).

O. Knutson, Oral Argument Has Power to Influence Tentative Advance Decision Made by Court, 26 Hennepin Lawyer 115 (1958).

E. Lampron, Observations on Appellate Advocacy, 14 N.H.B.J. 105 (1973).

D. Lay, Oral Argument on Appeal—"Where the Action Really Is," 63 F.R.D. 508 (1974).

H. Leventhal, What the Court Expects of the Federal Lawyer, 27 Fed. B.J. 1 (1967).

H. Leventhal, Cues and Compasses for Administrative Lawyers, 20 Ad. L. Rev. 237 (1968).

J. Lumbard, Appellate Advocacy (unpublished paper, Institute of Judicial Administration 1962).

L. McAmis, The Lawyer and the Court of Appeals, 24 Tenn. L. Rev. 279 (1956).

T. Marshall, The Federal Appeal, in *Counsel on Appeal* 139 (A. Charpentier ed. 1968).

P. Merrill, Appellate Practice, 25 Ala. Lawyer 33 (1964).

O. Moore, Some Observations on Oral Argument, 33 Rocky Mt. L. Rev. 30 (1960).

O. Moore, Some Observations on Colorado Appellate Practice, 34 Dicta 363 (1957).

J. Norvell, The Case on Appeal, 1 So. Texas L.J. 229 (1954).

J. Palmore, The Brief, 42 Ky. Bench & B. 8 (July 1977).

R. Peters, A Judge's View of Appellate Advocacy, in *California Civil Appellate Practice* xv (California Continuing Education of the Bar, 1966).

J. Pope, Argument on Appeal, 14 Prac. Law. 33 (Dec. 1968).

E. Prettyman, Some Observations Concerning Appellate Advocacy, 39 Va. L. Rev. 285 (1953).

W. Roberds, Some Suggestions as to Oral Arguments and Written Briefs in the Supreme Court of Mississippi, 29 Miss. L.J. 404 (1958).

G. Rossman, Appellate Practice and Advocacy, 16 F.R.D. 403 (1955).

G. Rossman, Appellate Court Advocacy: The Importance of Oral Argument, 45 A.B.A.J. 675 (1959).

W. Schaefer, Appellate Advocacy, 23 Tenn. L. Rev. 471 (1954).

W. Schaefer, The Advocate as a Lawmaker: The Advocate in the Reviewing Courts, 1956 U. Ill. L.F. 203.

G. Seidenfeld, Professional Responsibility Before Reviewing Courts, 25 DePaul L. Rev. 265 (1976).

B. Shientag, The Appellate Division, First Department, Its Jurisdiction, How It Functions in Conference, Briefs and Oral Arguments Presented to It, 5 Record 377 (1950).

J. Simeone, Views of an Appeals Judge, 19 St. Louis B.J. 43 (summer 1972).

R. Simons, Effective Appellate Advocacy, 48 N.Y.St.B.J. 18 (1976).

C. Smith, Appellate Procedure and Method of Review of Causes in the Supreme Court of Texas, 1 So. Texas L.J. 121 (1954).

G. Smith, The Introductory Portion of the Appellant's Brief, 15 Ark. L. Rev. 357 (1961).

S. Sobeloff, Book Review, 40 N.C.L.Rev. 822 (1962).

R. Steinle, The Oral Argument; Its Purpose and Importance, 31 Wisc. B. Bull. 23 (Aug. 1958).

P. Stevens, The Court of Appeals Looks at the Lawyer, 24 Ohio B. Ass'n Rep. 617 (1951).

A. Tate, The Judge as a Person, 19 La. L. Rev. 438 (1959).

A. Tate, On Questions from the Bench, 7 La. B.J. 128 (1959).

A. Tate, The Appellate Advocate and the Appellate Court, 13 La. B.J. 107 (1965).

G. Thompson, Oral Arguments in the Supreme Court of Iowa, 38 Iowa L. Rev. 392 (1953).

E. Tuttle, Book Review, 33 Miss. L.J. 147 (1961).

H. Ughetta, The Appellate Brief: Some Observations, 33 Brooklyn L. Rev. 187 (1967).

U.S. Court of Appeals for the Third Circuit, In the Matter of Oral Argument, 1 Prac. Law. 12 (Jan. 1955).

P. Vallee, Book Review, 24 So. Calif. L. Rev. 140 (1950).

A. Vanderbilt, *Forensic Persuasion* (1950).

A. Vanderbilt, Book Review, 25 N.Y.U.L. Rev. 933 (1950).

W. Wertz, Preparation of Abstract and Brief for Appellate Court, 30 Kansas Jud. Council Bull. 3 (1956).

D. Webber, Appellate Advocacy with Maine Flavor, 18 Me. L. Rev. 59 (1966).

W. White, Presenting a Case Before the Supreme Court, 30 Tenn. L. Rev. 333 (1963).

J. Wigginton, General Aspects of Appellate Practice, 33 Fla. B.J. 421 (1959).

H. Wilkie, Supreme Court Practice, 36 Wisc. B. Bull. 27 (Dec. 1963).

R. Wilkins, The Argument of an Appeal, 55 Mass. L.Q. 115 (1970).

Words of Advice to Attorneys from Members of Appellate Courts of Alabama, 4 Ala. L. Rev. 207 (1952).

See also comments by judges interviewed for the following studies:

F. Cooper, Stating the Issue in Appellate Briefs, 49 A.B.A.J. 180 (1963).

J. Harley, *Establishing Criteria for Effective Oral Argument Before a Court of Appeals* 138-176 (unpublished Ph.D. dissertation, Case Western Reserve University, 1976).

C. Palmer, The Practical Way to Prepare a Case for an Appellate Court, 59 W. Va. L. Rev. 56 (1956).

A. Partridge and G. Bermant, *The Quality of Advocacy in the Federal Courts* 209-225 (Federal Judicial Center, 1978).

A. Scanlan, Effective Appellate Advocacy in the Court of Appeals of Maryland, 29 Md. L. Rev. 126 (1960).

In addition, the Winter 1978 issue of *Litigation* is devoted to appellate advocacy. This was published after the cutoff date for the writings used in this book.

Law Clerks' Duties

This is a bibliography of publications that contain more than a fleeting description of law clerks' duties in appellate courts.

COURT SURVEYS BASED ON QUESTIONNAIRES FROM JUDGES

American Judicature Society, Law Clerks in State Appellate Courts (1968).
P. Barnett, *Law Clerks in the United States Courts and State Appellate Courts* (American Judicature Society, 1973).
Council of State Governments, *State Court Systems* 85-89 (Rev. 1976). (Also earlier editions from 1950 to 1974).
Institute of Judicial Administration, *Appellate Courts. Internal Operating Procedures. Preliminary Report*, appendix 28-33 (1957).
Institute of Judicial Administration, *Appellate Courts. Internal Operating Procedures. 1959 Summary and Supplement* 36-42.

STATE COURTS AND U.S. CIRCUIT COURTS—SYMPOSIUMS

A. DiLeo and A. Rubin, *Law Clerk Handbook* (Federal Judicial Center, 1977).
Judicial Clerkships: A Symposium on the Institute, 26 Vand. L. Rev. 1125 (1973), containing: P. Baier, The Law Clerks: Profile of an Institution; E. Wright, Observations of an Appellate Judge: the Use of Law Clerks; R. Braucher, Chosing Law Clerks in Massachusetts; G. Smith, A Primer of Opinion Writing for Law Clerks; F. Hamley, Sample Instructions to Law Clerks; R. Aldisert, Duties of Law Clerks.
Law Clerkships—Three Inside Views, 33 Ala. Lawyer 156 (1972), containing: A. Fite, In Alabama Supreme Court; D. Sweeney, In United States Court of Appeals.

STATE COURTS AND U.S. CIRCUIT COURTS—
OTHER ARTICLES AND WRITINGS

J. Beatty, *An Institutional and Behavioral Analysis of the Iowa Supreme Court, 1965-1969* 38-45 (unpublished Ph.D. dissertation, University of Iowa, 1970).

N. Bedell, The Good Law Clerk, 56 A.B.A.J. 1167 (1970).

G. Braden, The Value of Law Clerks, 24 Miss. L.J. 295 (1953).

J. Brown, Letter to Senator Joseph D. Tydings, 42 F.R.D. 305 (1967).

G. Edwards, Exorcising the Devil of Appellate Court Delay, 58 A.B.A.J. 149, 153 (1972).

S. Flanders and J. Goldman, *Screening Practices and the Use of Para-Judicial Personnel in the U.S. Courts of Appeals: A Study in the Fourth Circuit* (Federal Judicial Center 1974).

W. Hastings, Chief Justice Wilkins—A Law Clerk's Perspective, 55 Mass. L.Q. 107 (1970).

F. Hamley, Condensation of Remarks to Ninth Circuit Law Clerks Schools, 63 F.R.D. 478 (1974).

N. Johnson, What Do Law Clerks Do?, 22 Texas B.J. 229 (1959).

J. Lee and R. Maloney, The Kentucky Court of Appeals Apprentice Law Clerk Program, 21 Ky. St. B.J. 90 (1957).

J. Lumbard, Current Problems of the Federal Courts of Appeals, 25 N.Y.Co.B. Bull. 210, 219, 220 (1967-1968).

D. Meador, *Appellate Courts, Staff and Process in the Crisis of Volume* 15-17, 112-120 (1974).

H. Medina, The Decisional Process in the United States Court of Appeals, Second Circuit, 149 N.Y.L.J., Feb. 18, 1963, p. 4, Feb. 19, 1963, p. 4, Feb. 20, 1963, p. 4 (partly reprinted in H. Medina, The Decisional Process, 20 N.Y.Co.B. Bull. 94 [1962]).

National Center for State Courts, *The Appellate Process in Alabama* 151-157 (1973).

National Center for State Courts, *Wisconsin Appellate Practice and Procedure Study* 15, 22, 40, 58, 100 (1975).

M. Nobel, The Law Clerk, 7 Trial Judges' J. 4 (Oct. 1968).

T. Rabatz and J. Shea, Supreme Court Law Clerks, 35 Wisc. B. Bull. 33 (Aug. 1962).

N. Stockmeyer, *Michigan Court of Appeals, Manual for Law Clerks and Prehearing Research Attorneys* 4-6 (1972).

C. Wisch, An Inside View of Appellate Clerkships, 2 Briefcase 12 (Spring 1976).

B. Witkin, Appellate Court Opinions—A Syllabus for Panel Discussion, 63 F.R.D. 515, 547-550 (1974).

UNITED STATES SUPREME COURT CLERKS

H. Abraham, *The Judicial Process* 237-241 (3rd ed. 1975).

D. Atkinson, Opinion Writing on the Supreme Court, 1949-1956: The Views of Justice Sherman Minton, 49 Temple L.Q. 105, 112, 113 (1975).

V. Brudney and R. Wolfson, Mr. Justice Rutledge—Law Clerks' Reflections, 25 Ind. L. Rev. 455 (1950).

N. Dorsen, Law Clerks in Appellate Courts in the United States, 26 Modern L. Rev. 265 (1963).

C. Falk, Legal Springboard: High Court Law Clerks Rarely Sway Decisions, but Job Is Prestigious, The Wall Street Journal, July 22, 1971, at 1, col. 1.

J. Frank, *The Marble Palace* 116-119 (1958).

R. Hills, A Law Clerk at the Supreme Court of the United States, 33 L.A.B. Ass'n Bull. 333 (1958).

C. Newland, Personal Assistants to Supreme Court Justices: The Law Clerks, 40 Or. L. Rev. 299 (1961).

D. Meador, Justice Black and His Law Clerks, 15 Ala. L. Rev. 58 (1962).

W. Rehnquist, Who Writes Decisions of the Supreme Court? U.S. News & World Report, Dec. 13, 1957, p. 74, and Another View: Clerks Might "Influence" Some Action, U.S. News & World Report, Feb. 21, 1958, p. 116.

W. Rogers, Do Law Clerks Wield Power in Supreme Court Cases?, U.S. News & World Report, Feb. 21, 1958, p. 114.

R. Smith, Clerks of the Court, Patomic Magazine, Washington Post, Aug. 29, 1976, p. 14.

The Bright Young Men Behind the Bench, U.S. News & World Report, July 12, 1957, p. 45.

J. Wilkinson, *Serving Justice* (1974).

(In addition, I have been referred to, but have not been able to locate, Sarshikl, The Supreme Court and Its Clerks: Bullets or Blanks for the Hired Guns?, 4 Juris Doctor 40 (March 1974). See also, M. Herman, Law Clerking at the Supreme Court of Canada, 13 Osgoode Hall L.J. 279 (1975).)

Studies Involving Interviews with or Questionnaires Sent to Appellate Judges

This bibliography includes only published writings and dissertations, not unpublished papers, of which there are many. Only one citation is given for each study, even though the same study may lead to several publications. It does not include studies in which there is doubt as to whether the judges are appellate judges and studies about subjects unrelated to being an appellate judge or to the appeals-deciding aspects of their jobs. This bibliography is not totally complete; I have seen references to five or six studies that may involve interviews or questionnaires but that I was unable to locate. The key for the symbols is as follows:

Column 1 Q — questionnaire (or letter in a few studies)
I — interview

Column 2 P — political science study
L — study by a law professor or law student
C — study by a court reform organization (even though done by a political scientist or law professor)
O — other (as indicated after the citation)

Column 3 the court or judges studied

Column 4 the number of judges who were interviewed or who returned questionnaires

Column 5 percent of those sent questionnaires or asked for interviews that returned questionnaires or were interviewed (often this figure must be approximated from the publication; this is indicated by saying "about" or the like). Unless otherwise indicated, I assumed that the researcher tried to interview or receive questionnaires from all judges on the court in question.

	1	2	3	4	5
D. Atkinson, Opinion Writing on the Supreme Court, 1949-1956: The Views of Justice Sherman Minton, 49 Temple L.Q. 105 (1975)	I	P	U.S. Supreme Ct. Black, Warren	2	?

	1	2	3	4	5
A. Ashman et al., *Examination of the Administrative Operations of the Court of Appeals of the State of Indiana* (Criminal Courts Technical Assistance Project, American University Law School, 1974)	I	C	Indiana Court of Appeals	9	100
P. Baier, The Law Clerks: Profile of an Institution, 26 Vand. L. Rev. 1125 (1973)	I	L	not stated	?	?
J. Beatty, *An Institutional and Behavioral Analysis of the Iowa Supreme Court—1965-1969* (unpublished Ph.D. dissertation, University of Iowa 1970)	I	P	Iowa Supreme Ct.	9	100
T. Becker, Surveys and Judiciaries, or Who's Afraid of the Purple Curtain? 1 Law and Soc. Rev. 133 (1966)	Q	P	Hawaii Supreme Ct.	3	75
E. Beiser, The Rhode Island Supreme Court: A Well-Integrated Political Process, 8 L. and Soc. Rev. 167 (1974)	I	P	Rhode Island Supreme Court	5	100
M. Berry, *A Study of Judicial Role Orientations in Fifteen Western States* (unpublished Ph.D. dissertation, Washington State U. 1974)	Q	P	appellate judges in 15 western states	about 110	80
M. Bright, The Changing Nature of the Federal Appeals Process in the 1970's, 65 F.R.D. 496 (1975) (appellate judge)	Q	O	chief judges of U.S. circuit courts	8	probably 73
E. Beiser, et al., Judicial Role in a Non-Judicial Setting, 5 Law and Soc. Rev. 571 (1971)	I	P	N.Y. and Md. appellate judges	10	at least 90
S. Cann, Social Background and Dissenting Behavior on the North Dakota Supreme Court, 50 N.D.L. Rev. 773 (1974)	I	P	N. Dak. Supreme Ct.	4	80
R. Carp, The Scope and Function of Intra-Circuit Judicial Communication: A Case Study of the Eighth Circuit, 6 L. and Soc. Rev. 405 (1972)	I	P	C.J. of Eighth Circuit	1	?
P. Carrington, Crowded Dockets and the Courts of Appeals, 82 Harv. L. Rev. 452 (1969)	I	L	U.S. circuit judges	?	?
W. Cook, The Rehearing Evil, 14 Iowa L. Rev. 36 (1928)	Q	L	state C.J.'s	48	100
F. Cooper, Stating the Issue in Appellate Briefs, 49 A.B.A.J. 180 (1963)	Q	L	?	"a number"	?
Council of State Governments, *The Courts of Last Resort of the Forty-eight States* (1950)	Q	C	state C.J.'s	46+	96+

	1	2	3	4	5
Council of State Governments, *State Court Systems* (12 editions every other year from 1954 to 1976)	Q	C	state C.J.'s	normally over 90% reply	
E. Curran and E. Sunderland, The Organization and Operation of Courts of Review, *Third Annual Report of the Judicial Council of Michigan*, 51 (1933)	Q I	C	?	?	?
J. Daly, *The Use of History in Decisions of the Supreme Court:* 1900-1930 (1954) (historian)	I	O	U.S. Supreme Ct.—Burton and Frankfurter	2	?
B. Daynes, *Congestion and Delay in the State Appellate Courts* (American Judicature Society, 1969)	Q	C	sample of state supreme court and intermediate court judges	133+	?
T. Farrer and C. Jacob, *The Appellate Process and Staff Research Attorneys in the Appellate Division of the New Jersey Superior Court* (National Center for State Courts, 1974)	Q	C	N.J. intermediate court judges	13	87
Federal Judicial Center, *Selection and Tenure of Chief Judges of Federal Courts* (1974)	Q	C	circuit judges and senior judges	97	about 75
P. Fish, *The Politics of Federal Judicial Administration* (1973)	I	P	U.S. circuit judges	7	?
S. Flanders and J. Goldman, Screening Practices and the Use of Para-Judicial Personnel in the U.S. Courts of Appeals: A Study in the Fourth Circuit (Federal Judicial Center, 1974)	I	C	Fourth Circuit	6	86
R. Frye, The Alabama Supreme Court: An Institutional View (1969)	I	P	Ala. Supreme Ct.	at least one	?
W. Gemmill, Report of Committee E, 3 J. Crim. L. 566 (1912)	Q	C	all appellate court C.J.'s	?	?
W. Gibson, Literary Minds and Judicial Style, 36 N.Y.U.L. Rev. 915 (1961) (English teacher; more description of study is in R. Leflar, Some Observations Concerning Judicial Opinions, 61 Colum. L. Rev. 810 (1961))	?	O	state supreme court and circuit judges in a seminar	25	?
H. Glick, Policy-Making and State Supreme Courts, 5 Law and Soc. Rev. 271 (1970)	Q	P	state C.J.'s	42	84
H. Glick, *Supreme Courts in State Politics* (1971)	*I*	*P*	La., Mass., N.J., and Pa. courts of last resort	26	93

	1	2	3	4	5
J. Goldman, *Attitudes of United States Judges Toward Limitation of Oral Argument and Opinion-Writing in the United States Court of Appeals* (Federal Judicial Center, 1975)	Q	C	circuit judges and senior judges	50	36
J. Goldman, *An Evaluation of the Civil Appeals Management Plan: An Experiment in Judicial Administration* (Federal Judicial Center 1977)	Q	C	Second Circuit	16	probably high
S. Goldman, Conflict and Consensus in the United States Courts of Appeals, 1968 Wisc. L. Rev. 461	I Q	P	circuit judges	23(I) 4(Q)	?
D. Grey, Interviewing at the Court, 31 Public Opinion Q. 285 (1967) (journalism student)	I	O	U.S. Supreme Ct.; Circuit Ct.	8 3	89 ?
F. Hale, The Court's Perception of the Press, 57 Judicature 183 (1973) (journalism student)	I	O	Wash. Supreme Court	9	probably 82
J. Harley, *Establishing Criteria for Evvective Oral Argument Before a Court of Appeal* (unpublished Ph.D. dissertation, Case Western Reserve University 1976) (speech communication)	I	O	Court of Appeals of Ohio, Eighth Appellate District	6	100
S. Hatting, *Judicial Interpretation and Review of Legislative Action in the American States: An Exploration in Role Theory and Analysis* (unpublished Ph.D. dissertation, Duke University, 1975)	Q	P	State supreme court C.J.'s Justices on 12 state supreme courts	42 47	84 47
B. Henderson and T. Sinclair, *The Selection of Judges in Texas* (1965)	Q	P	Tex. Supreme Ct.	9	90
J. Howard, *Role Perceptions on the U.S. Courts of Appeals for the 2D, 5TH, and D.C. Circuits* (Federal Judicial Center 1973)	I	P	Second, Fifth, and D.C. Circuit Courts	35	95
Institute of Judicial Administration, Expediting Appeals, *A Study of the Supreme Court of New Mexico* (1963)	I	C	N.Mex. Supreme Ct.	5	100
Institute of Judicial Administration, *Appellate Courts. Internal Operating Procedures. Preliminary Report* (1957), and *Appellate Courts. Internal Operating Procedures. 1959 Summary and Supplement*	Q	C	one judge on each circuit court and state intermediate and supreme court	93	86
IJA, *The Supreme Judicial Court and the Superior Court of State of Maine* (1971)	I	C	Me. Supreme Ct.	some	?
IJA, *The Supreme Court of Iowa* (1971)	I	C	Iowa Supreme Ct.	9	100

	1	2	3	4	5
D. James, Role Theory and the Supreme Court, 30 J. Pol. 160 (1968)	I	P	Douglas of U.S. Supreme Ct.	1	?
Y. Kamisar and J. Choper, The Right to Counsel in Minnesota: Some Field Findings and Legal-Policy Observations, 48 Minn. L. Rev. 1 (1963)	I	L	Minn. Supreme Ct.	2	?
I. Kaufman, A Response to Objections to the Second Circuit's Proposed District Court Admission Rules, 61 A.B.A.J. 1514 (1975)	Q	C	Second Circuit	?	?
R. Kluger, *Simple Justice* (1976) (journalist)	I	O	retired U.S. Supreme Ct. justices —Clark, Fortas, Douglas, Warren	4	?
J. Lake, *The Appellate Process and Staff Research Attorneys in the Supreme Court of Nebraska* (National Center for State Courts 1974)	Q	C	Neb. Supreme Ct.	7	100
J. Langner and S. Flanders, *Comparative Report on Internal Operating Procedures of U.S. Courts of Appeals* (Federal Judicial Center 1973)	I	C	circuit judges	"a few"	?
G. Lilly, *The Appellate Process and Staff Research Attorneys in the Supreme Court of Virginia* (National Center for State Courts 1974)	Q	C	Va. Supreme Ct.	probably 7	100
D. Louisell and R. Degnan, Rehearing in American Appellate Courts, 44 Calif. L. Rev. 627 (1956)	Q	L	circuit courts and state supreme courts (one letter to each)	?	"almost all"
J. Lucas, *The Appellate Process and Staff Research Attorneys in the Illinois Appellate Court* (National Center for State Courts 1974)	Q	C	Ill. Appellate Ct.	13	100
W. Mack, Settlement Procedures in the U.S. Courts of Appeals: A Proposal, 1 Justice System J. 17 (March 1975) (a lawyer)	Q	O	all circuit judges	?	?
J. Masuda, *The Politics of a State Intermediate Appellate Process: The California Court of Appeal* (unpublished Ph.D. dissertation, University of Iowa, 1976)	I / Q	P	as in title I—presiding judges Q—all judges	4 / 25	? / 49
G. Mason, *Judges and Their Publics: Role Perceptions and Role Expectations* (unpublished Ph.D. dissertation, University of Kansas 1967)	I	P	Kans. Supreme Ct.	5	63
S. McConkie, Decision-Making in State Supreme Courts, 59 Judicature 337 (1967)	Q	P	state supreme court C.J.'s	47	94

	1	2	3	4	5
D. Meador, *Proposals for the Use of Screening Procedures and Legal Assistants in the District of Columbia Court of Appeals* (Criminal Courts Technical Assistance Project, American University Law School, 1974)	I	L	D.C. Court of Appeals	6	prob-ably 67
T. Morris, *The Virginia Supreme Court, An Institutional and Political Analysis* (1975)	I	P	Va. Supreme Ct. sitting judges retired judges	5 2	63 ?
S. Nagel, Off-the-Bench Judicial Attitudes, in *Judicial Decision-Making* (G. Schubert ed. 1963)	Q	P	state and federal supreme court judges	119	about 40
National Center for State Courts, *Caseload, Backlog and Delay in the Fourth District Court of Appeals of Florida* (1973)	I	C	as in title	"some"	?
NCSC, *Report on the Appellate Process in Alabama* (1973)	I	C	Alabama appellate courts	"some"	?
NCSC, *The California Courts of Appeal* (1974)	I	C	as in title	48	100
NCSC, *Study of the Appellate System in Minnesota* (1974)	I	C	Minn. Supreme Ct.	"some"	?
NCSC, *Wisconsin Appellate Practice and Procedure Study* (1975)	I	C	Wisc. Supreme Ct.	7	100
NCSC, *Washington Appellate Courts Project* (1975)	I	C	Wash. appellate courts	some	?
NCSC, *Court Reporting Services in Maryland* (1976)	Q	C	Md. appellate courts	17	90
NCSC, *Utah Supreme Court Project* (1977)	I	C	as in title	5	100
NCSC, *Minnesota Supreme Court Automated Caseflow Management and Docketing Feasibility Report* (1977)	I	C	as in title	9	100
NCSC, *Court Reporting Services in South Dakota, Findings and Recommendations* (1977)	Q	C	S.D. Supreme Ct.	4	80
National Document Commission Formed, 8 The Third Branch 5 (Sept. 1976)	Q	C	all federal judges	?	?
Note, The Second Circuit: Federal Judicial Administration in a Microcosm, 63 Colum. L. Rev. 874 (1963)	I	L	Second Circuit	5+	?
M. Osthus and R. Shapiro, *Congestion and Delay in State Appellate Courts* (American Judicature Society 1974)	Q	C	appellate courts in the states and D.C.	363	48

	1	2	3	4	5
M. Palley, *The Appellate Division of the New York State Supreme Court, First Department: A Study in Role Behavior* (unpublished Ph.D. dissertation, New York University, 1966)	I	P	N.Y. Appellate Div., 1st Dept.	8	100
C. Palmer, The Practical Way to Prepare a Case for Appellate Court, 59 W. Va. L. Rev. 56 (1959) (a lawyer)	I Q	O	scattering of state and federal appellate judges	4+	?
A. Partridge and G. Bermant, *The Quality of Advocacy in the Federal Courts* (Federal Judicial Center 1978)	Q	C	active and senior circuit judges	98	75
Queries Concerning Method of Work in Supreme Courts, 8 J. Am. Jud. Soc'y 101, 165 (1924, 1925), 9 J. Am. Jud. Soc'y 20, 49, 115, 152 (1925, 1926, and 10 J. Am. Jud. Soc'y 57 (1926)	Q	C	state supreme courts (one questionnaire to each)	10	21
Report of the Study Group on the Caseload of the Supreme Court (Federal Judicial Center 1972)	I	C	U.S. Supreme Ct.	9	100
F. Rich, *Role Perceptions and Precedent Orientation as Variables Influencing Appellate Judicial Decision-Making: An Analysis of the Fifth Circuit Court of Appeals* (unpublished Ph.D. dissertation, University of Georgia, 1967)	I	P	Fifth Circuit	13	87
A. Sager, *An Evaluation of Computer Assisted Legal Research Systems for Federal Court Applications* (Federal Judicial Center 1977)	Q	C	judges on five U.S. circuit courts	?	?
A. Scanlan, Effective Appellate Advocacy in the Court of Appeals of Maryland, 29 Md. L. Rev. 126 (1969) (a lawyer)	Q	O	C.J. of Md. Court of Appeals	1	?
M. Schick, *Learned Hand's Court* (1970)	I	P	Second Circuit	7+	?
G. Schubert, Jackson's Judicial Philosophy: An Exploration in Value Analysis, 59 Am. Pol. Sci. Rev. 940 (1965)	I	P	Jackson on U.S. Supreme Ct.	1	?
Section of Judicial Administration, American Bar Association, *Methods of Reaching and Preparing Appellate Court Decisions* (1942)	Q	C	all state appellate and circuit court judges	?	less than half
W. Shafroth, Survey of the United States Courts of Appeals, 42 F.R.D. 247 (1967)	I	C	circuit court: C.J.'s other judges	10 about 50	91 ?

	1	2	3	4	5
C. Sheldon, Contrasting Judicial Roles: Trial vs. Appellate, 11 Judges' J. 72 (1972)	Q	P	supreme courts of Vt., Me., N.H., Nev., and Utah plus a N.Y. Supreme Ct. Appellate Div.	26	74
E. Slotnick, Who Speaks for the Court? The View from the States, 26 Emory L.J. 107 (1977)	Q	P	all C.J.'s of state supreme courts	45	90
G. Smith, The Appellate Decisional Conference, 28 Ark. L. Rev. 425 (1975) (an appellate judge)	Q	O	state supreme court C.J.'s	49	95
A. Smith and A. Blumberg, The Problem of Objectivity in Judicial Decision-Making, 46 Soc. Forces 96 (1967) (study by Blumberg and Winick —sociologists)	?	O	appellate courts: federal and state "superior" courts	30	? prob-ably low
N. Totenberg, Behind the Marble, Beneath the Robes, N.Y. Times Magazine 15 (March 16, 1975) (reporter)	I	O	U.S. Supreme Ct.	some	?
T. Ungs and L. Baas, Judicial Role Perceptions: A Q-Technique Study of Ohio Judges, 6 Law and Soc. Rev. 343 (1972)	Q	P	Ohio appellate courts	20	53
J. Uppal and R. Brun, *Judicial Planning in the States* (The Council of State Governments, 1976)	Q	C	chief justices of all states and Puerto Rico	51	100
M. Wall, What the Courts Are Doing to Improve Judicial Opinions, 32 J. Am. Jud. Soc'y 148 (1949)	Q	C	C.J.'s of all federal and state appellate courts	66	57
R. Watson and R. Downing, *The Politics of the Bench and the Bar* (1964)	I	P	Mo. appellate courts	16	67
H. Whitaker, The Florida Supreme Court Internal Procedures, 4 Fla. St. U. Gov. Research B. 1 (Dec. 1967)	I	P	Fla. Supreme Ct.	some	?
W. Whittaker, Differentiated Case Management in United States Courts of Appeals, 63 F.R.D. 457 (1974)	I	C	circuit courts	"nu-mer-ous judges"	?
F. Wiener, *Effective Appellate Advocacy* (1950) (a lawyer)	Q	O	one judge on each state su-preme court and circuit courts	about 47	about 80
F. Wiener, *Briefing and Arguing Federal Appeals* (1961)	Q	O	one judge on all circuit courts	about 10	about 91

	1	2	3	4	5
B. Wilcox et al., Justice Lost—By What Appellate Papers Cost, 33 N.Y.U. L. Rev. 934 (1958)	I Q	L	N.Y. appellate courts at all levels	?	?
B. Witkin, Appellate Court Opinions, A Syllabus for Panel Discussion, 63 F.R.D. 515 (1974)	Q	C	all appellate judges	?	?
J. Wold, *Internal Procedures, Role Perceptions and Judicial Behavior: A Study of Four State Courts of Last Resort* (unpublished Ph.D. dissertation, Johns Hopkins University, 1972)	I	P	Del., Md., N.Y., and Va. courts of last resort	22	92
G. Yuhas, Statewide Public Defender Organizations: An Appealing Alternative, 29 Stan. L. Rev. 157 (1976)	Q	L	Ill. intermediate court judges	13	38

Notes

CHAPTER 1

1. The strategy of studying decision making in organizations by looking at what information is used and how it is gathered is fairly common in the social sciences. See, for example, R. Bauer, I. Pool, and L. Dexter, *American Business and Public Policy* (1963); R. Cyert and J. March, *A Behavioral Theory of the Firm* 44-67 (1963); H. Wilensky, *Intellectuals in Labor Unions* (1956) and *Organizational Intelligence* (1967); J. Robinson, Decision-Making in the House Rules Committee, in *The Making of Decisions* 315 (W. Gore and J. Dyson, eds. 1964); K. Entin, Information Exchange in Congress: The Case of the House Armed Service Committee, 26 Western Pol. Sci. Q. 427 (1973). Two more recent articles have studied the U.S. Supreme Court using a similar information-gathering approach, and they touch on a few of the topics discussed in this book: A Miller and J. Barron, The Supreme Court, the Adversary System, and the Flow of Information to the Justices: A Preliminary Inquiry, 61 Va. L. Rev. 1187 (1975); and C. Lamb, Judicial Policy-Making and Information Flow to the Supreme Court, 29 Vand. L. Rev. 45 (1976). Elements of such an approach can also be found in C. Swisher, The Supreme Court and "the Moment of Truth," 54 Am. Pol. Sci. Rev. 879 (1960); J. Howard, Adjudication Considered as a Process of Conflict Resolution: A Variation on Separation of Powers, 18 J. Pub. L. 339 (1969); and W. Chambliss and R. Seidman, *Law, Order, and Power* Ch. 7 (1971).

This book does not contain the customary preliminary discussion of the prior literature on the subject and of how the book builds on that literature. I find those discussions generally tedious, uninformative, and biased, often seemingly devoted to setting up straw men. More important, this book is substantially different from other studies of appellate courts (except of course the Miller-Barron and Lamb studies) in its approach. In specific subject areas it overlaps a very large range and number of prior studies, but none, except K. Llewellyn, *The Common Law Tradition, Deciding Appeals* (1960), is relevant to more than a small portion of the book. As for the social science literature on appellate courts, works classified as "role studies" or "traditional scholarship" are relevant to several specific topics discussed here; however, the large body of "judicial behavioralism" work is almost totally unrelated to this book.

2. I know of no exceptions to this general statement. No comprehensive study has been made of judicial secrecy, but the subject quite often crops up in the literature

on appellate courts. The secrecy applies only to the details of what is being done in each individual case toward reaching a decision; it does not apply to descriptions of the decision-making procedures used. Judges often write about the latter (see Bibliography A) and there is an accelerating trend toward publishing details of the procedure. See *ABA Standards Relating to Appellate Courts* No. 3.30; and J. Hopkins, Book Review, 77 Colum. L. Rev. 332 (1977).

3. The great majority of the judges interviewed and a number of clerks were asked about the reasons for judicial secrecy. The reasons they gave were very similar to those given in the literature on the subject. In one study Iowa Supreme Court justices were asked "What function do you feel is played by the veil of secrecy concerning judicial deliberations?" and they answered that secrecy encouraged "the free flow of information and frank discussions." J. Beatty, *An Institutional and Behavioral Analysis of the Iowa Supreme Court—1965-1969* 229, 230 (unpublished Ph.D. dissertation, University of Iowa, 1970). For similar statements by a judge, a law clerk, and a social scientist see: E. Wright, Observations of an Appellate Judge: The Use of Law Clerks, 26 Vand. L. Rev. 1179, 1189 (1973); J. Wilkinson, *Serving Justice* 41 (1974); J. Howard, Comment on Secrecy and the Supreme Court, 22 Buffalo L. Rev. 837 (1973). Justice Rehnquist, in a recent and lengthy defense of judicial secrecy, gives several reasons for it: (1) It permits candid discussions among the judges; (2) it forces the judges to prepare well for conference, since they cannot rely on staff; (3) it isolates the court from excessive influence of public pressure—for example, if tentative votes were known, interested people might lobby for vote changes; and (4) it helps preserve the cordiality among the Justices. He gives more attention to the first reason (though he says the second is equally important), claiming that open conferences may lead to little communication there, hedging of views, or presentations aimed at the public rather than colleagues. In addition to the four reasons just listed, he has also suggested that openness would make the judges' job uncomfortable and would deter competent lawyers from becoming judges. See W. Rehnquist, Sunshine in the Third Branch, 16 Washburn L.J. 559, 564-570 (1977). A journalist studying the Supreme Court has also given a somewhat similar list of reasons for secrecy, D. Grey, *The Supreme Court and the News Media*, 15, 16 (1968).

In all, the literature discussing judicial secrecy seems to give more attention to dangers of public pressure should the decision process be open than is evidenced in the interview results. Other examples of this are: F. Frankfurter, Mr. Justice Roberts, 104 U. Pa. L. Rev. 311, 313 (1955); R. Kluger, *Simple Justice* 586 (1976). Probably, however, this rationale is more important at the Supreme Court level, where most issues are of greater importance than those decided by the judges interviewed.

A caveat about the interviews should be mentioned. Here and subsequently in the book where I have asked judges about their reasons for what they do, it is obvious that they may not list all their reasons or indicate which of those mentioned are the most important; hence the frequency with which any particular reason is mentioned is an inexact indication of its importance. However, if one reason is mentioned a good deal more than another, it is probably the more important.

4. C. Newland, Personal Assistants to the Supreme Court Justices: The Law Clerks, 40 Ore. L. Rev. 299, 310 (1961).

5. Llewellyn, *supra* note 1, at 324; see S. Ulmer, Leadership in the Michigan Supreme Court, in *Judicial Decision-Making* 13, 14 (G. Schubert ed. 1963). The only

hint of such a reason given by a judge that I know of is by Justice Rehnquist, as discussed in note 3.

6. For judges' and clerks' concerns about secrecy see the references cited in notes 3 and 7. Also, F. Hamley, Condensation of Remarks to Ninth Circuit Law Clerks Schools, 63 F.R.D. 478, 479 (1974); W. Erickson, Why an Oath for Law Clerks? 14 Judges' J. 20 (1975); R. Aldisert, Duties of Law Clerks, 26 Vand. L. Rev. 1251, 1256 (1973); J. Goodwyn, The Supreme Court at Work, 21 Ala. Lawyer 5, 8 (1960); T. Clark, The Supreme Court Conference, 37 Texas L. Rev. 273, 274, 275 (1959); L. Powell, Myths and Misconceptions About the Supreme Court, 61 A.B.A.J. 1344 (1975); D. Sweeney, Law Clerkships—Three Inside Views: III. In United States Court of Appeals, 33 Ala. Lawyer 171, 172, 175 (1972); and Louisiana Code of Judicial Conduct, No. 3A(4). The ABA Code of Judicial Conduct, No. 3A(6) says that judges and their employees should not comment publicly about pending cases.

On the other hand, the curtain of secrecy is not absolutely opaque and free of resistance, and there are signs of a slight opening up. First, as is true for just about every topic in this book, the judges are not all of the same view concerning secrecy. Two focal court judges actually placed supposedly confidential memorandums in their published opinions, and a Massachusetts justice said he believed that in some kinds of cases it might be helpful to have counsel sit in the conference room and speak out when they think a judge is wrong. Second, at present there is considerable thought among judges and scholars that memorandums written by staff attorneys should be made public, especially as a response to criticism that some busy judges have come to rely too much on staff work. Among the numerous suggestions along this line see P. Carrington, Report on Group Discussions, in *Appellate Justice 1975, Volume V: Supplement, Proceedings, and Conclusions* 62, 66, 67 (1975), and R. Thompson, One Judge and No Judge Appellate Decisions, 50 Calif. St. B.J. 476, 516, 517 (1975). Third, another crack in the curtain is that some judges have willed that their papers be made open to scholars, leading to quite a few interesting historical studies of the U.S. Supreme Court and one lower court, for example, W. Murphy, *Elements of Judicial Strategy* (1964), J. Howard, *Mr. Justice Murphy, A Political Biography* (1968), and M. Schick, *Learned Hand's Court* (1970). The latter is probably the best political science study of the operations of an appellate court below the Supreme Court level. There are, however, indications that papers of federal judges, at least, will be less available in the future. For problems in this type of study see S. Ulmer, Biocolage and Assorted Thoughts on Working in the Papers of Supreme Court Justices, 35 J. Pol. 286 (1973). Fourth, at least one court has allowed into conferences consultants hired to study its internal procedures; see National Center for State Courts, *Report on the Appellate Process in Alabama* 166 (1973). Fifth, some courts, probably no more than a few, bring secretaries or court officers into the conference room to take notes and run errands, but they must not repeat what they hear. This practice, however seems to be declining. Sixth, in the past few years the judges have been bringing law clerks or staff attorneys into conference to discuss their work. The bulk of this practice is limited to administrative conferences —those dealing with rule making and supervision of the courts, rather than appeals. But at least three courts discuss appeals with law clerks or staff attorneys in some conferences. These are the Washington Court of Appeals, the Minnesota Supreme Court, and the D.C. Circuit Court of Appeals. See National Center for State Courts,

Washington Appellate Courts Project 118 (1975); D. Meador, *Appellate Courts, Staff and Process in the Crisis of Volume* 177, 227 (1964); and United States Court of Appeals for the D.C. Circuit, Job Announcement for Court Law Clerks, October 5, 1976. Seventh, at least two courts tape-record judges' conferences. The New York Court of Appeals has long done this, D. Karlen, *Appellate Courts in the United States and England* 38 (1963), and the Virginia Supreme Court has recently begun to do it, T. Morris, *The Virginia Supreme Court, An Institutional and Political Analysis* 76 (1975). The New York court transcribes the recordings; thus at least the typists have access to them, but outsiders cannot see them. The Virginia law clerks have access to the tape recordings. It has been suggested that appellate courts tape record, and then make public transcripts of, the judges' conferences, largely to help historians and appellate counsel understand how decisions are made. M. Schnitzer, Court Conferences and the Doctrine of Exclusivity of the Record, 30 Rutgers L. Rev. 482 (1977). Eighth and lastly, although in my interviews the judges and clerks generally steered clear of pending cases and details of the judges' decision-making activities, several judges (mostly from the same court) described at length their views about pending issues and a few recounted incidents that had occurred in conference.

Although this is a sizable list of inroads on judicial secrecy, they add up to little information from the scholar's viewpoint, except, of course, access to judges' papers.

7. Concern about such leaks can be seen in M. Schick, *Learned Hand's Court*, 88, 89 (1970); L. Brown, The Handling of Supreme Court Cases—Processing, Practice, and Procedure, 22 Ark. L. Rev. 679, 688; 689 (1969); and P. Fish, Secrecy and the Supreme Court: Judicial Indiscretion and Reconstruction Politics, 8 Wm. & Mary L. Rev. 225, 234-236 (1967).

8. Llewellyn, *supra* note 1 at 324; A. Miller and S. Sastri, Secrecy and the Supreme Court: On the Need for Piercing the Red Velour Curtain, 22 Buffalo L. Rev. 799 (1973); T. D'Alemberte, Let the Sunshine in: The Case for an Open Judicial System, 58 Judicature 61, 64, 65 (1974).

9. F. Morrison, The Swiss Federal Court: Judicial Decision Making and Recruitment, in *Frontiers of Judicial Research* 133 (J. Grossman and J. Tanenhaus ed. 1969); D. Karlen, *Appellate Courts in the United States and England* 80-116 (1963); Miller and Sastri, *supra* note 8, at 810-814; R. Young, Comments on "Secrecy and the Supreme Court," 22 Buffalo L. Rev. 863 (1973).

10. B. Cardozo, *The Nature of the Judicial Process* 9 (1921).

11. W. Schaefer, Precedent and Policy, 34 U. Chi. L. Rev. 3, 22, 23 (1966). For examples of other judges saying they cannot, or have great difficulty in, describing their decision process see J. Hopkins, Fictions and the Judicial Process: A Preliminary Theory of Decision, 33 Brooklyn L. Rev. 1, 3, 11 (1966); E. Prettyman, Some Observations Concerning Appellate Advocacy, 39 Va. L. Rev. 285; F. Frankfurter, The Process of Judging in Constitutional Cases, in *An Autobiography of the Supreme Court* 267, 268 (A. Westin ed. 1953). The latter complained about the meager amount of judges' writings explaining how they make decisions. Perhaps the judges' increasing use of judicial seminars to discuss decision-making methods has helped here. See A. Tate, Bob Leflar's Impact on the Judicial Process. 25 Ark. L. Rev. 105, 106-108 (1971).

12. Cardozo, *supra* note 10, at 11, 12, 167-178.

13. For example, various political scientists have asked well over a hundred appel-

late judges how important their idea of "justice" is in deciding cases, and nearly all said it is important, often very important. See Beatty, *supra* note 3, at 268-270; G. Mason, *Judges and Their Publics: Role Perceptions and Role Expectations* 264, 265 (unpublished Ph.D. dissertation, University of Kansas, 1967); F. Rich, *Role Perceptions and Precedent Orientation as Variables Influencing Appellate Judicial Decision-Making* 100 (unpublished Ph.D. dissertation, University of Georgia, 1967); J. Howard, *Role Perceptions on the U.S. Courts of Appeals for the 2d, 5th, and D.C. Circuits*, 37, 38 (Research Report No. 2, Federal Judicial Center, 1973); C. Sheldon, Contrasting Judicial Roles: Trial vs. Appellate, 11 Judges' J. 72 (1972); J. Masuda, *The Politics of a State Intermediate Appellate Process: The California Court of Appeal* 71, 80 (unpublished Ph.D. dissertation, University of Iowa, 1976).

Recently an appellate judge has expounded on the vagueness of "justice," giving the three meanings I have listed in the text. J. Day, Why Judges Must Make Law, 26 Case W. Res. L. Rev. 563, 565 (1976).

14. Quite a few judges have written about the importance of this type of thing in judicial decision making, using terms such as "intuition" and "feeling." Often these articles also quickly mention the main point here—that they cannot easily describe their decision process. See Wright, *supra* note 3, at 1180; Hopkins, *supra* note 11, at 2, 11, 12; J. Hutcheson, The Glorious Uncertainty of Our Lady of the Law, 23 J. Am. Jud. Soc'y 73, 74 (1939); R. Traynor, Badlands in an Appellate Judge's Realm of Reason, 7 Utah L. Rev. 157, 160 (1960); W. Douglas, The Meaning of Due Process, 10 Colum. J. L. and Soc. Prob. 1, 10 (1973); K. Keating, Today's Values—Yesterday's Constitution, 24 N.Y.Co.B. Bull. 106, 108 (1966); B. Cardozo, *The Growth of the Law* 89 93 (1924); E. Lampron, Observations on Appellate Advocacy, 14 N.H.B.J. 105, 106 (1973). See also the discussions in R. Leflar, *Appellate Judicial Opinions* 101-103 (1974); R. Aldisert, *The Judicial Process: Readings, Materials and Cases* 374-389 (1976); R. Pound, The Theory of Judicial Decision, 36 Harv. L. Rev. 940, 951 (1923); and M. Pollack, The Civil Appeal in *Counsel on Appeal* 29, 48, 49 (A. Charpentier ed. 1968). For expressions that these feelings play a small part in judicial decision making see: J. Weintraub, Writing, Consideration and Adoption of Opinions, 83 N.J.L.J. 477, 479 (1960), and H. Friendly, Reactions of a Lawyer—Newly Become Judge, 71 Yale L.J. 218, 229, 230 (1961).

15. A. Fite, Law Clerkships—Three Inside Views: I. In Alabama Supreme Court, 33 Ala. Lawyer 156, 158, 159 (1972).

16. For example, a political scientist asked appellate judges: "How would you describe the way a judge should go about reaching a decision in a case?" (a common type of question asked by political scientists) and then categorized them mainly in terms of whether they answered by describing the decision-making stages (oral argument, etc.) or by describing what elements went into their decisions (applying the law, etc.). See H. Glick, *Supreme Courts in State Politics* 72-77 (1971).

17. Llewellyn, *supra* note 1, at 43. See also pages 104, 105, 196, 197, 264-267, 392.

18. On this point see note 30 of Chapter 10, especially the Clark and Trubek article.

CHAPTER 2

1. The descriptions of appellate court internal operations in this chapter are based on information from the interviews, from court rules and other publications at the

six courts, and from the writings on appellate court internal operations listed in Bibliography A.

2. What is said here about the criteria is based on a few comments in the interviews and on the following writings about state court practices: K. Taft, How to Get into the Supreme Court, 47 Ohio B. 847 (1953); P. Herbert, Obtaining Certification in the Supreme Court of Ohio: Cases of Public or Great General Interest, 18 W. Res. L. Rev. 32 (1966); M. Cuomo, The New York Court of Appeals: A Practical Perspective, 34 St. John's L. Rev. 197, 202, 203 (1960); R. Traynor, Some Open Questions on the Work of State Appellate Courts, 24 U. Chi. L. Rev. 211, 214 (1957); D. Wright, Criteria for Selecting Cases for Review, in *Proceedings, Twenty-Third Annual Meeting of the Conference of Chief Justices* 2 (1971); G. Lilly, *The Appellate Process and Staff Research Attorneys in the Supreme Court of Virginia* 24 (National Center for State Courts 1974); F. Thompson, Practice in the Supreme Court, in W. Dodd and P. Edmunds, *Appellate Jurisdiction and Practice in the Courts of Illinois* 23, 26 (1929); R. Calvert, The Mechanics of Judgment Making in the Supreme Court of Texas, 21 Baylor L. Rev. 439, 445-447 (1969); D. Johnedis, Massachusetts' Two-Court Appellate System in Operation, 60 Mass. L.Q. 77 (1975); Note, To Hear or Not to Hear: A Question for the California Supreme Court, 3 Stan. L. Rev. 243 (1951); L. Baum, Decisions to Grant and Deny Hearings in the California Supreme Court: Patterns in Court and Individual Behavior, 16 Santa Clara L. Rev. 713 (1976); National Center for State Courts, *Washington Appellate Courts Project* 68-71 (1975); B. Witkin, Appellate Court Opinions, A Syllabus for Panel Discussion, 63 F.R.D. 515, 531, 532 (1974).

The U.S. Supreme Court probably emphasizes the importance of issues more than state courts, as many Justices have said. That, though, does not mean that the Justices' views about the correctness of the lower court decision are not important. Justice Stevens recently remarked that his colleagues' reaction to the lower court's result has "a significant impact" on their votes on certiorari petitions. J. Stevens, Address to the Illinois State Bar Association's Centennial Dinner, 65 Ill. B. J. 508, 512 (1977). Likewise, a political science study found that the Justices voting for certiorari also tend to vote to reverse. S. Ulmer, The Decision to Grant Certiorari as an Indicator to Decisions "On the Merits," 4 Polity 429 (1972).

3. G. Edwards, Exorcising the Devil of Appellate Court Delay, 58 A.B.A.J. 149 (1972).

4. W. Shafroth, Survey of the United States Courts of Appeals, 42 F.R.D. 247, 284 (1967).

5. Federal Judicial Center, A Summary of the Third Circuit Time Study (Washington, 1974). I asked most of the clerks interviewed how long their judges work, but they were only able to guess because so much work was done outside the office.

6. Elements other than the lawmaking aspects of a case may enter the decision to publish or not, for example, the general public interest in the case. Published criteria for when opinions should be published, however, strongly emphasize the lawmaking element. See, for example, Advisory Council on Appellate Justice, *Standards for Publication of Judicial Opinions* (1973), and *ABA Standards Relating to Appellate Courts* No. 3.37.

7. "The adversary process is better designed to serve the dispute-deciding function of the courts than to serve their lawmaking function, but law grows through the

adversary process nevertheless'' (R. Leflar, Sources of Judge-Made Law, 24 Okla. L. Rev. 319, 336 (1971)).

CHAPTER 3

1. On the advantages of the adversary system see especially, Note, Judicial Determination in Nonadversary Proceedings, 72 Harv. L. Rev. 723 (1959). This excellent note covers much of the same ground as this chapter.

2. F. Hamley, Appellate Advocacy, 12 Ark. L. Rev. 129, 131 (1958).

3. Justice Stevens (then a circuit judge) has said: ''We have great confidence in the adversary system as a means of bringing out the truth in difficult cases as well as in easy cases.'' Testimony of John Paul Stevens to the Commission on Revision of the Federal Court Appellate System, June 10, 1974, p. 513. On the whole, though, comments by judges on the adversary system in appellate courts (as opposed to trial courts) are extremely rare.

4. See, for example, M. Frankel, The Search for Truth: An Umpireal View, 123 U. Pa. L. Rev. 1031 (1975) and the articles that follow it. See also M. Neef and S. Nagel, The Adversary Nature of the American Legal System from a Historical Perspective, 20 N.Y.L.F. 123 (1974). These articles give different meanings to the term ''umpire.''

5. I. Kaufman, The Court Needs a Friend in Court, 60 A.B.A.J. 175 (1974).

6. R. Traynor, Badlands in an Appellate Judge's Realm of Reason, 7 Utah L. Rev. 157, 159 (1960).

7. In all, I found over fifty discussions about the quality of appellate advocacy by judges—in law review articles, books, congressional testimony, judicial conferences, and (secondhand) through others who have talked to judges. This is too many to cite. Among the last listed sources the major ones are: P. Carrington, Report on Group Discussions, in *Appellate Justice 1975, Vol. V, Supplement, Proceedings, and Conclusions* 62 (1975); M. Osthus and R. Shapiro, *Congestion and Delay in State Appellate Courts* 83, 90 (American Judicature Society, 1974); K. Llewellyn, *The Common Law Tradition, Deciding Appeals* 30 (1960); M. Schick, *Learned Hand's Court* 91 (1970); National Center for State Courts, *The Appellate Process in Alabama* 42, 97, 145 (1973); J. Harley, *Establishing Criteria for Effective Oral Argument Before a Court of Appeals* 129-176 (unpublished Ph.D. dissertation, Case Western Reserve University, 1976); *Final Report of the Advisory Committee to the Judicial Council on Qualifications to Practice Before the United States Courts in the Second Circuit on Proposed Rules for Improvement of Performance of the Present Members of the Bar* (1977); A. Partridge and G. Bermant, *The Quality of Advocacy in the Federal Courts* (Federal Judicial Center, 1978).

The Partridge and Bermant monograph is by far the most elaborate study of judges' views on appellate advocacy. Federal circuit judges were asked whether they believed ''there is, overall, a serious problem of inadequate appellate advocacy by lawyers with cases in your court?'' About two thirds said no, and one third yes (*Id.* at 22, 178). However, when judges were asked to rate actual performances in the oral arguments and briefs, only 6 percent of the ratings were ''inadequate,'' 16 percent were ''adequate but no better,'' and 78 percent ''good,'' ''very good,'' or ''first rate'' (see *Id.* at 191). Similar results were presented in the *Final Report* cited above. Second

Circuit judges rated over a thousand attorneys appearing before them; 6 percent were deemed "to a substantial extent, not satisfactory," and 94 percent "overall, satisfactory." Thus, judges' judgments seem much less harsh when evaluating individuals appearing before them than when evaluating the overall state of appellate advocacy.

The Partridge and Bermant monograph (*supra* at 191) clearly sets forth the great variation in quality of appellate advocacy. The percentages for different ratings were as follows: first rate (18%), very good (29%), good (31%), adequate but no better (16%), inadequate (6%). These are combined ratings for briefs and arguments. The percentages would probably be higher at the extremes if briefs or arguments alone were rated.

8. J. Lumbard, Appellate Advocacy 9, 11, 12 (unpublished paper, Institute of Judicial Administration, 1962). See also J. Lumbard, The Responsibility of the Bar for the Performance of the Courts, 34 N.Y.St.B.J. 169 (1962).

9. Llewellyn, *supra* note 7, at 196; Lumbard, *supra* (both); J. Frank, *The Marble Palace* 93, 94 (1958).

10. D. Lay, Modern Administrative Proposals for Federal Habeas Corpus: The Rights of Prisoners Preserved, 21 De Paul L. Rev. 701, 734 (1972).

11. W. Pope, Suggestions for Lessening the Burden of Frivolous Applications, 33 F.R.D. 409 (1962).

12. The impressions about the types of attorneys who do better jobs are, of course approximations, since attorneys vary greatly. The impressions are, though, in accord with those of over two dozen judges and clerks who have commented in writing on the quality of various types of attorneys. The most commonly expressed distinction is between appointed counsel in criminal cases and attorneys from the public appellate defenders; the latter are routinely said to be better. In one study Illinois intermediate appellate court judges were asked whether the introduction of appellate defenders had improved the legal process, and twelve of the thirteen judges answering said they had. See G. Yuhas, Statewide Public Defender Organizations: An Appealing Alternative, 29 Stan. L. Rev. 157, 169 (1976).

The Partridge and Bermant study (*supra* note 7) attempted to discern which categories of lawyers are better appellate advocates than others. When the circuit judges were asked to rate the quality advocacy in appeals heard, very little difference was found among broad characteristics of lawyers and their backgrounds (*id.* at 187-208). However, when asked what types of lawyers in general present serious problems of inadequate advocacy, the judges clearly indicated that some types present fewer problems than most (e.g., public defenders and private lawyers for corporations) and that some present more problems than most (e.g., state or local government lawyers and prosecutors and private lawyers in criminal cases). See *id.* at 193.

13. The two committees are: (1) The Committee of the Judicial Conference of the United States to Consider Standards for Admission to Practice in the Federal Courts, and (2) the Committee on Appellate Advocacy of the Appellate Judges' Conference, Judicial Administration Division, American Bar Association. The former is considering standards for the federal district courts as well as the circuit courts; it has a special subcommittee to deal with circuit court standards. The Second Circuit Court of Appeals has a local rule, which went into effect at the beginning of 1976, requiring that new attorneys who appear before it have had a fair amount of

appellate experience (e.g., have argued three appeals). Since 1976 the Committee on Appellate Advocacy has been conducting training programs for law students and practicing lawyers, beginning with a pilot project in Arizona, designed to upgrade appellate advocacy.

Also, a new approach is being tried at several courts, especially in New York and California. Judges or staff attorneys meet with counsel early in the appeal, trying, among other things, to persuade them to concentrate on and narrow the key issues. There is some evidence of a little success in accomplishing this. This procedure, however, is aimed more at reducing the case load than upgrading advocacy; most of the effort is directed at getting cases settled so that the court does not have to decide them.

14. This discussion is based on eighty books and articles published from 1950 through 1977. In all there are writings by eighty-two judges; a few wrote more than one piece, and two articles contain writings by several judges. The writings are listed in Bibliography B, along with a few cautionary remarks about the meanings to be given to the relative frequency of different comments. (In addition, I asked a number of judges to list the major mistakes made by the attorneys. But the interviews are a poor place to learn about this topic because complete answers take too much time. I will not mention the interview material in the following discussion, except in the one place where it differs substantially from the judges' writings.) The cutoff line of comments mentioned by at least fifteen judges was used because it lies at a natural break. Almost no comments were made by eleven to fourteen judges.

15. In contrast, the judges who talked about advocacy in the interviews complained about incomplete legal arguments more often than about incomplete statements of fact. I do not know the reason for this difference.

16. A. Tate, The Appellate Advocate and the Appellate Court, 13 La. B.J. 107, 111 (1965).

17. M. Conford, The Appellate Division, New York and New Jersey: Varying Problems in Organization and Advocacy, 26 Record 301, 303 (1971).

18. J. Harlan, What Part Does the Oral Argument Play in the Conduct of an Appeal? 41 Cornell L.Q. 6, 8 (1955).

19. W. Carswell, The Briefing and Argument of an Appeal, 16 Brooklyn L. Rev. 147, 153 (1950).

20. E. Prettyman, Some Observations Concerning Appellate Advocacy, 39 Va. L. Rev. 285, 297 (1953).

21. Tate, *supra* note 16 at 111.

22. A. Denecke et al., Notes on Appellate Brief Writing, 51 Ore. L. Rev. 351, 360 (1972).

23. C. Fahy, Book Review, 3 J. Legal Ed. 471, 473 (1951).

24. H. Medina, The Decisional Process, 20 N.Y.Co.B. Bull. 94, 98, 99 (1962), Some Reflections on the Judicial Function at the Appellate Level, 1961 Wash. U.L.Q. 148, 154, 155, and Some Reflections on the Judicial Function: A Personal Viewpoint, 38 A.B.A.J. 107, 108 (1952). C. Magruder, The Trials and Tribulations of an Inter-mediate Appellate Court, 44 Cornell L.Q. 1, 5 (1958); R. Gustafson, Some Observations About California Courts of Appeal, 19 U.C.L.A.L. Rev. 167, 182 (1971). See also T. Thacher, The Presentation of an Appeal, 18 N.Y.St.B. Bull. 219, 220 (1946); Llewellyn, *supra* note 7, at 31; J. Wetter, *The Styles of Appellate Judicial Opinions, passim,* esp. 52, 53 (1960); Committee on Federal Courts, *Appeals to the Second*

Circuit 35 (1975); *Practitioners' Handbook for Appeals to the United States Court of Appeals for the Sixth Circuit* 39 (1977).

In one political science study, over 80 percent of the appellate judges on six courts that returned questionnaires considered a "highly competent advocate" an "important" factor influencing their decisions. See C. Sheldon, Contrasting Judicial Roles: Trial vs. Appellate, 11 Judges' J. 72 (1972). Another political science study found that Kansas Supreme Court justices believed the quality of advocacy might affect the outcome. See G. Mason, *Judges and Their Publics: Role Perceptions and Role Expectations* 305, 306 (unpublished Ph.D. dissertation, University of Kansas, 1967).

Another study found that public defenders obtained reversals twice as often as appointed counsel in criminal appeals in Indiana. As was mentioned previously, the public defenders are usually considered better than appointed counsel. See R. Brown et al., Appellate Representation of Indigents in Indiana, 50 Ind. L.J. 154, 186 (1974).

A number of the law clerks interviewed were asked about the effects of imbalance of counsel, and their views were similar to the judges'. As might be expected, they usually added that their research at least partly compensated for poor advocacy.

On the other hand, Justice Tate believes the quality of advocacy has very little effect: A Tate, Sua Sponte Consideration on Appeal, 9 Trial Judges' J. 68 (1970), and The Judge as a Person, 19 La. L. Rev. 438, 440 (1959). See also M. Schick, *Learned Hand's Court* 92, 93 (1970), and J. Thorton, Expertise in Judicial Arguing, 37 Ala. Lawyer 54 (1976).

Most of these writings, in both groups, say that counsel's effect is largely limited to close cases, where the winning side is not immediately evident. Thus the effect of counsel may depend mainly on the number of such cases the court decides.

25. H. Medina, Some Reflections on the Judicial Function: A Personal Viewpoint, 38 A.B.A.J. 107, 108 (1952).

26. The data for the ratings and backgrounds of the attorneys here and in the following sentences came from the interviews, from the briefs, and primarily from Martindale Hubbell. Not all of the 112 appeals presented to the court that year are included. As will be seen later, there is considerable doubt about who wins some cases; I had no idea who won 3 (and made an educated guess in a dozen or so more). In 14 cases one or both sides did not argue; these were not included. (Arguing attorneys were used rather than brief writers because when two or more lawyers worked on a case, the top lawyer tended to do the arguing and because if one or both sides did not argue, it suggested that something out of the ordinary had happened, e.g., the lawyer might think his case too weak to bother arguing, or the case might be moot.) Lastly, there was no information about one or both attorneys in a few cases, the number varying with the background characteristic. In all, 80 to 90 cases were used.

27. I used their ratings of "a," "b," and "c." The effect of the imbalance is the same whether unranked attorneys were considered below "c" or not used at all.

28. The top schools are Chicago, Columbia, Harvard, the University of Michigan, Stanford, and Yale. These six ranked far higher than any other law schools in a poll of law school deans. P. Blau and R. Margulies, The Reputation of American Professional Schools, 6 Change Magazine 42 (Winter 1974-75). The vast majority of others went to the state's local law schools.

29. S. Nagel and F. Gagliano, Attorney Characteristics and Courtroom Results, 44 Neb. L. Rev. 599 (1965).

30. I rated each brief and argument on a five-point scale. Averaging the briefs and arguments (if any) produced the following figures:

Difference Between Attorneys	Number of Cases	Better Won	Better Lost
0 or ½	40		
1 through 2	50	34	16
2½ through 4	14	13	1
Total	104	47	17

This does not include three cases in which it was impossible to tell who won (see note 26) and five cases that contained virtually the same issues as other cases. If there was more than one brief or argument on a side (including amicus and including cases with the same issues), the better one was used. The results were very similar using the briefs or arguments alone, and there was little difference between cases reversed or affirmed.

Much can be said against these findings. I am a lawyer without appellate experience; my only qualification for doing this is that I studied a great many briefs and arguments even before starting on these cases. I had no firm criteria upon which to base the ratings. They were just my impression gained from many factors, for example, the thoroughness of research, organization, whether the reasoning made sense to me, and the handling of questions in the arguments. I studied the briefs and arguments after reading the opinions in a case; thus I probably rated a lawyer better if he covered what the court was concerned about—which may or may not indicate good advocacy. In the arguments the losers may have received tougher questioning from the judges, leading me to rate them too low. Lastly, the winner may have had a much better case, making his presentation look better, though it was often said that the court only handled difficult cases because it has discretionary jurisdiction.

However, the differences in the attorneys' products seemed very obvious to me at the time I studied the cases. And the results here came as a complete surprise; until I actually totaled up the figures, I has supposed that no relationship would result.

There were many comments in the interviews about the work of specific lawyers, and I compared these with my ratings. The attorneys normally commented on how good a job their opponent had done, and several clerks, judges, and attorneys commented on the quality of presentations they had witnessed. In all, there were comments on sixty different presentations in which an attorney was said to have done a "good job" or a "bad job" or the like. Rating a good job as 1 to 2½ and a bad job as 3½ to 5, my scoring matched the commentators 78 percent of the time, and in most of the mismatches I had given the attorney a rating of 3. Also, in ten of the eleven situations in which more than one peson commented on the same attorney, there was agreement. Furthermore, most of the attorneys I interviewed commented on how good they thought various of their own briefs and arguments were. Of the twenty times they rated an argument or brief good, I ranked it 1 or 2 eighteen times, and of the four times they rated one bad, I ranked it 4 or 5 twice. Three of the four mismatches were given a 3 rating by me. In all, there seems to be a good consensus on how to rate the attorneys' appellate work. (My ratings could have been affected by these comments; to the best of my memory, however, I rarely had them in mind when studying the briefs and arguments.)

31. I looked at whether an attorney won more often if the length of his brief, the number of authorities cited for issues decided by the court, the length of case facts in his brief, and the length of social facts in the brief were greater, 50 percent greater, 100 percent greater, and 200 percent greater, than his opponent's. The effects were almost uniform over the different degrees of imbalance. Attorneys presenting more legal authority and more case facts won less than 5 percent more often than opponents; in effect, then, there was no difference. Attorneys presenting more social facts won almost 20 percent more often, a finding that is discussed further in Chapter 12, note 8. The variation in the amount of information in the opposing briefs was very large. In about half the cases one side presented at least twice as much legal authority as his opponent. The same proportions hold true for case facts (of course, the appellant generally presented the greater number of case facts). In about two-thirds of the cases one side mentioned at least twice as many social facts as the other.

32. See K. Davis, The Liberalized Law of Standing, 37 U. Chi. L. Rev. 450, 468 (1970); L. Albert, Standing to Challenge Administrative Action: An Inadequate Surrogate for Claim for Relief, 83 Yale L.J. 425, 440, 441 (1974); and Note, Taxpayers' Suits: A Survey and Summary, 69 Yale L.J. 895 (1960).

33. For a list of comments about the uncertainty and complexity of this area of law, along with a good concise bibliography, see Albert, *supra,* at 425, n. 1.

34. Baker v. Carr, 369 U.S. 186, 204 (1962).

35. Poe v. Ullman, 367 U.S. 497, 503 (1961).

36. See, for example, Davis, *supra* note 32, at 469, 470; K. Davis, Standing 1976, 72 Nw. L. Rev. 69, 81 (1977); K. Scott, Standing in the Supreme Court—A Functional Analysis, 86 Harv. L. Rev. 645, 669-690 (1973); Comment, The Impact of Policy on Federal Standing, 45 Fordham L. Rev. 515, 518, 519 (1976); Comment, Standing to Sue in Federal Courts: The Elimination of Preliminary Threshhold Standing Inquiries, 51 Tul. L. Rev. 120, 141-145 (1976); M. Tushnet, The New Law of Standing: A Plea for Abandonment, 62 Cornell L. Rev. 663 (1977). Other writers, however, have given considerable importance to the need for adverseness as a reason for the standing rules. See F. Scharpf, Judicial Review and the Political Question: A Functional Analysis, 75 Yale L.J. 517, 529-534 (1966); and H. Monaghan, Constitutional Adjudication: The Who and When, 82 Yale L.J. 1363, 1371, 1372 (1973). The Supreme Court itself, it should be added, quite often suggests reasons for standing other than the need for adverseness; but adverseness seems to be the reason given most often.

37. For example, Schlesinger v. Reservists to Stop the War, 418 U.S. 208, 217-222 (1974); Arlington Heights v. Metro. Housing Corp., 429 U.S. 252, 261 (1977); Hunt v. Washington Apple Advertising Comm'n, 432 U.S. 333, 341-345 (1977).

38. Schlesinger v. Reservists, *supra* at 221. The court then contrasted appellate court information gathering to that of legislatures; the latter can initiate inquiries, define issues, and make a record in a hearing. The quality of advocacy, however, is specifically mentioned as a reason for jus tertii standing restrictions in Singleton v. Wulff, 428 U.S. 106, 114, 118 (1976).

39. On the practice here in the Supreme Court see *Hart and Weschsler, The Federal Courts and the Federal System* 104, 105 (2d ed. 1973). The courts, of course, need not agree with the prosecutor that there was error below.

40. See S. Diamond, Federal Jurisdiction to Decide Moot Cases, 94 U. Pa. L. Rev. 125, 128-130 (1946).

41. For example, in U.S. v. Johnson, 319 U.S. 302 (1943) it appears that the collusion might not have been brought to the Court's attention if the U.S. government had not become an intervener and raised the point. And the Court apparently has decided some friendly suits in the past, *Wright, Law of Federal Courts* 36 (1970). It has been suggested that the U.S. Supreme Court use staff members to investigate the background of appeals before it to determine whether a true controversy exists and to ensure that cases are adequately briefed. C. Vose, *Constitutional Change: Amendment Politics and Supreme Court Litigation Since 1900,* 370 (1972).

42. In view of the later discussion on mootness, many other states probably do the same. For one example see Collier v. Lindley, 203 Cal. 641 (1928).

43. This is a simplified definition; one writer has said that attempts to define mootness are fruitless. Note, Mootness on Appeal in the Supreme Court, 83 Harv. L. Rev. 1672, 1673, 1674 (1970).

44. DeFunis v. Odegaard, 416 U.S. 312 (1974).

45. On the discretion accorded under the mootness (and standing) rules see: Note, The Mootness Doctrine in the Supreme Court, 88 Harv. L. Rev. 373, 375 n. 12, 377 (1974); D. Kates and W. Barker, Mootness in Judicial Proceedings: Toward a Coherent Theory, 62 Calif. L. Rev. 1385, *passim,* esp. 1428 (1974); D. Donaldson, A Search for Principles of Mootness in the Federal Courts. Part One—The Continuing Impact Doctrines, 54 Texas L. Rev. 1289, 1291 (1976). These three articles also contain good discussions of the first exception to the mootness rule. For a description of the second exception see Note, Cases Moot on Appeal: A Limit on the Judicial Power, 103 U. Pa. L. Rev. 772, 787-793 (1955).

46. Courts ordinarily learn about mootness when the parties petition to abandon the appeal because of mootness. Also, judges sometimes question attorneys at oral arguments about possible mootness, and facts outside the record are permissible here. When the U.S. Supreme Court suspects that a case may be moot, it sometimes sends it back to the lower court to consider the question, for example, Spomer v. Littleton, 414 U.S. 514 (1974). In a recent case the justices, especially Justice Burger, were openly annoyed when the attorneys did not tell them that new state legislation might have rendered the case moot. See Fusari v. Steinberg, 419 U.S. 379, 387, 390, 391 (1975). For a discussion of a case decided by the Supreme Court when the justices did not know it was apparently moot, see J. Howard, *Mr. Justice Murphy, a Political Biography* 447 (1968). About how the Supreme Court learns of mootness, see especially Robertson and Kirkham, *Jurisdiction of the Supreme Court of the United States,* sec. 275 (2d. ed. R. Wolfson and P. Kurland, 1951).

47. The best and most recent writings on mootness claim that case load management is the prime reason for the rules (and, secondarily, considerations of judicial restraint) and that the attorneys' motives to present thorough arguments are of lesser or no importance. Note (1974), *supra* note 45, at 374-379, 395, and Kates and Barker, *supra* note 45, *passim.* However a number of student notes had earlier given attorney motivation as the foundation for mootness rules, though usually adding case load management as a secondary reason. See Note, Constitutional Law—Exceptions to the Prohibition Against Considering Moot Questions, 17 De Paul L. Rev. 590, 591 (1968); Comment, Mootness and Ripeness: The Postman Always Rings Twice, 65

Colum. L. Rev. 867, 873 (1965); Note (1970), *supra* note 43, *passim*; and Note (1955), *supra* note 45, at 773-775, 778. The U.S. Supreme Court has emphasized the adverseness aspect in Sibron v. New York, 392, U.S. 40, 57 (1968).

48. The discussion in this section is based on the dozen writings on advisory opinions in the past thirty years. See especially C. Carberry, The State Advisory Opinion in Perspective, 44 Fordham L. Rev. 81 (1975), and G. Stevens, Advisory Opinions— Present Status and an Evaluation, 34 Wash. L. Rev. 1 (1959). Although the justices on three of the six courts in this study—the Massachusetts court, the Rhode Island court, and the focal court—issue advisory opinions, I did not regularly ask about this function in the interviews, which was a mistake. Several judges on these courts, however, did comment on their and their colleagues' views of it. The Massachusetts justice quoted in the text is Justice Braucher speaking to a conference of U.S. circuit judges, Federal Judicial Center Cassette J-128 (1975). The only writings by judges about advisory opinions I am aware of are by other Massachusetts justices. See P. Reardon, The Internal Operations of Appellate Courts, in *Proceedings, Eighteenth Annual Meeting of the Conference of Chief Justices* 13, 16, 17 (1966); E. Hennessey, The State of the Judiciary, 62 Mass. L.Q. 3, 14 (1977). Justice Reardon liked the function. Chief Justice Hennessey said that they disrupt the court's work and that the need to decide abstract questions "not as applied in the context of their practical application" is a major difficulty.

Recently the term "advisory opinion" has been applied to state supreme court decisions in cases certified by federal courts for rulings on questions of state law involved in federal court cases. The state court proceedings, however, involve adversary counsel and a real controversy.

49. Good summaries of the arguments on this point can be found in Note (1974), *supra* note 45, at 375 n. 13, and Kates and Barker, *supra* note 45, at 1409, 1410.

50. For a musing on this point see J. Weinstein, Rendering Advisory Opinions— Do We, Should We? 54 Judicature 140 (1970).

51. Fed. R. Civ. P. 23(a) (4) gives as one criteria for class actions that "the representative parties will fairly and adequately protect the interests of the class." Courts have frequently included in this the requirement that the class be represented by a competent counsel. See M. Kane, Standing, Mootness, and Federal Rule 23—Balancing Perspectives, 26 Buffalo L. Rev. 83, 112, 113 (1977). This article also discusses the use of this requirement in mootness and standing suits. A notable Supreme Court application is Sosna v. Iowa, 419 U.S. 393, 403 (1975).

Although the actual quality of adversary presentation apparently is not used as a factor in deciding whether to reach the merits (except in class actions), the existence of adversary counsel has been cited at least once as a reason for granting a request for an advisory opinion, In Re Opinion to the Governor, Fla. 239 So.2d 1, 8, 9 (1970).

CHAPTER 4

1. The discussion in this paragraph comes from comparing the characteristics of the lawyers who appeared before the court in the 112 appeals (information obtained as described in note 26, Chapter 3, and for a few attorneys information was not obtained about all categories) with the figures in American Bar Foundation, *The 1971 Lawyer Statistical Report* (1971).

The characteristics of the attorneys appearing before the focal court are similar to those of attorneys appearing before the Second, Third, and Sixth Circuit Courts of Appeals at about the same time. See T. Drury et al., *Attorney Attitudes Toward Limitation of Oral Argument and Written Opinion in Three U.S. Courts of Appeals*, 5-14 (Federal Judicial Center, 1974). The attorneys differed somewhat from circuit to circuit, but in general the similarity holds, especially with compared with the Second Circuit, for the portion of government attorneys and private practitioners, the portion of sole practitioners, the size of the law firm for law firm lawyers, and the length of time the lawyers had been practicing. On the other hand, one study found that appellate lawyers are very similar to lawyers in general, including age and proportion living in metropolitian areas. See G. Rathjen, Lawyers and the Appeals Process: A Profile, 34 Fed. B.J. 21, 24-26 (1975). But in general that study looked at different variables than those discussed here.

2. Half the attorneys were asked if they changed their briefs much from those presented to the intermediate court, and most said there was little change, except, some added, the legal authority was updated. Also, a few clerks and court employees mentioned that the briefs at the final stage differed little from those presented to the lower court and those accompanying the application for leave to appeal at the focal court.

3. Information about attorneys handling the various stages comes from the appendixes of cases argued before the focal court over a year. The appendixes gave no indication of who handled the appeal to the intermediate court in a good number of cases, but the trial attorney was virtually always named.

4. There is evidence that time problems hindered some attorneys. Several complained that the court had allowed too little time to prepare the briefs, usually adding that their work suffered for it. Two private practitioners said they had to limit the amount of work on the appeals because their clients were only willing to pay a small fee. Two more said they disliked writing briefs and spent relatively little time on them, adding that if their client had more money, they would have transferred the appeal to another lawyer. Except for these four, incidentally, there was no hint that the amount of money the client could pay had limited the amount of work on the briefs. A good number of lawyers, however, complained about the high cost of appealing.

5. See especially F. Wiener, *Briefing and Arguing Federal Appeals* Chapter XI (1961) and *Appellate Justice: 1975, Volume III: Criminal Justice on Appeal* 97-106 (P. Carrington et al. ed. 1975).

6. From 76 to 79 percent of the attorneys appearing before the Second, Fifth, and Sixth Circuit Courts during one year's time handled only one case during that year (Drury, *supra* note 2, at 4). But the great majority of attorneys had appeared in the circuit courts earlier (see *id.* at 10, 11). On the other hand, Judge Godbold of the Fifth Circuit has said that more than half the lawyers appearing there are appearing for the first time. See J. Godbold, Twenty Pages and Twenty Minutes—Effective Advocacy on Appeal, 30 Sw. L.J. 801 (1976). The situation at the Second Circuit was even more extreme several years earlier; only 97 of 625 counsel appearing there during a year in the early 1960s appeared more than once. J. Lumbard, *Appellate Advocacy* (unpublished paper, Institute of Judicial Administration, 1962). Only 20 percent of the lawyers appearing before the Kansas Supreme Court in the 1965 term appeared more than once (and only 1 percent had appeared more than three times).

G. Mason, *Judges and Their Publics: Role Perceptions and Role Expectations* 43 (unpublished Ph.D. dissertation, University of Kansas, 1967). During a forty-one month period, from 1965 to 1969, 74 percent of the almost 800 law firms appearing before the Iowa Supreme Court appeared only once. J. Beatty, *An Institutional and Behavioral Analysis of the Iowa Supreme Court* 109-113 (unpublished Ph.D. dissertation, University of Iowa, 1970).

7. The Solicitor General's Office, within the U.S. Justice Department, handles the vast majority of U.S. government litigation in the U.S. Supreme Court. See Wiener, *supra* note 5, at 383, 384; Note, Government Litigation in the Supreme Court: The Roles of the Solicitor General, 78 Yale L. J. 1442 (1969). And federal agencies and U.S. attorneys' offices tend to have separate appellate offices (Wiener, *supra*, at 384, 385). But there is no real appellate bar of private attorneys in the Supreme Court or, surely, the circuit courts. See J. Frank, *The Marble Palace* 94 (1958); J. Casper, *Lawyers Before the Warren Court* 88 (1972). Two lawyers I interviewed had been in appellate sections of government agencies before their present jobs and thus knew a good deal about appellate work. There are probably many lawyers throughout the country in this category.

There is considerable information about appellate specialization in the defense of indigent defendants on appeal. In most states, the trial attorney is usually appointed as appellate counsel. In some ten states including the focal court state and generally the northern industrial states, the courts usually appoint a new counsel. In a few other states either trial counsel or new counsel are often appointed. Ordinarily, when new counsel is appointed, he is from the appellate public defenders or from the appellate division of state or local public defender programs; that is, the attorneys specialize in appellate work. See W. Kramer, *Outline of Basic Appellate court Structure in the United States, passim* (1975); National Legal Aid and Defender Association, National Study Commission on Defense Services, *Draft Report and Guidelines for the Defense of Eligible Persons*, 587, 588 (1976); G. Yuhas, Statewide Public Defender Organizations: An Appealing Alternative, 29 Stan. L. Rev. 157 (1976); R. Brown et al., Appellate Representation of Indigents in Indiana, 50 Ind. L. Rev. 154 (1974); D. Meador, *Appellate Courts, Staff and Process in the Crisis of Volume*, 154 (1974).

Practices vary greatly among the U.S. circuit courts, but most appear to favor retaining trial counsel in indigent appeals. R. Hermann, Frivolous Criminal Appeals, 47 N.Y.U.L. Rev. 701, 709 (1972). The debate about whether to appoint trial counsel or new counsel for indigent defendants has one major element not often applicable to civil appeals: Trial counsel is not likely to argue on appeal that the defendant was not given adequate representation at the trial.

8. Wiener, *supra* note 5, at 359.

9. Much of this was fireside equities (equities between the immediate parties), which are discussed in Chapter 10. Some of these arguments listed in the text could have been legitimately made, however, had there been facts in the record to support them. Most of the attorneys in the interviews commented on their views of their clients, and the great majority commented on their views of the opposing party.

10. But a study of lawyers before the U.S. Supreme Court found that some lawyers, apparently representing criminal defendants, "spoke of their clients with distaste if not antipathy." Casper, *supra* note 7, at 92.

11. Though the attorneys normally talked about how well they knew the other

side (usually in response to questions), only half mentioned how well they got along. A couple said they got along with opposing counsel in appellate work better than in trial work.

12. This view is in accord with lawyers' ethics, ABA Code of Professional Responsibility, EC 2-26 to EC 2-32, though prosecutors and government lawyers should be more selective, EC 7-13 and 7-14 and DR 7-103 (A).

13. This may be a common practice among government attorneys. See Wiener, *supra* note 5, at 104; Note, *supra* note 7, at 1467-1475; ABA Code of Professional Responsibility EC 7-14.

14. Wiener, *supra* note 5, at 359, 360, is elegant on this topic. Among other things he says that agreeing with one's case "is often self-induced, frequently by an involved process of rationalization." Social scientists might call this an example of the operation of cognitive dissonance. But that is stretching things because much of the effect may be simply due to the lawyers' focusing on the favorable aspects of their cases in order to prepare them.

15. Most of the attorneys interviewed talked about when they would appeal a case. A similar conclusion was reached in a study based on questionnaire returns from over a hundred lawyers who had handled circuit court cases. The lawyers were asked what factors lead them to appeal to the circuit court from a loss in the district court and to the Supreme Court from a loss in the circuit court. The factor mentioned much more often than others was the chance of success upon appeal. Most of the other factors were things that indicate that the attorney thought the lower court ruling was wrong. The clients' wishes and the expense of the appeal were considered only minor factors. See G. Rathjen, *supra* note 2 at 32, 33. Similarily, a study of decisions made by the U.S. Department of Justice about whether to appeal supports the findings here that the main factor by far is the lawyers' opinions about the chances of success. See P. Carrington, United States Appeals in Civil Cases: A Field and Statistical Study, 11 Houston L. Rev. 1101 (1974). See also a more recent study of the Department of Justice appellate policy: D. Horowitz, *The Jurocracy*, 46-71 (1977).

On the other hand, there are two reasons often mentioned why attorneys might not agree with their appeal. One is that criminal defense lawyers often bring what they believe to be meritless appeals. See, for example, Hermann, *supra* note 7, *passim.* Indigent defendants are allowed to appeal and are provided counsel irrespective of the strength of their case, and their counsel often believe their claim has little or no merit (Anders briefs are not often used because it is easier to file a regular brief). The focal court has discretionary jurisdiction, so that this situation is not likely to arise there. I do not know why the situation did not show up more in Rathjen's data (his study was done while the circuit courts still published opinions in all but a few cases; thus many of his attorneys probably handle meritless appeals). See Rathjen, *supra* note 2.

Second, appealing to gain a bargaining position is often thought by judges to be important. See W. Doyle, The Battle of the Backlog in the Supreme Court, 33 Rocky Mt. L. Rev. 489, 490 (1961); H. Goodrich, A Case on Appeal—A Judge's View, in *A Case on Appeal* 4 (4th ed. 1967). Appeal is made, it is thought, in the hopes of persuading the other side to settle for something more to the appellant's liking than the lower court gave. This procedure may be more common at courts other than the focal court, because the law of the state effectively prevents insurance companies from doing it. But, again, there was very little sign of it in Rathjen's data either (however, a good number of appeals to the circuit courts are settled before decision, suggesting that appeals are often made by attorneys searching for settlements). This type of appeal, it should be added, does not mean that the attorney necessarily believes his case has little merit.

Of course, all this does not mean that attorneys always appeal when they believe their side is correct. They may not because of the expense (see B. Willcox et al., Justice Lost—By What Appellate Papers Cost, 33 N.Y.U.L. Rev. 934 (1958)), because the case is not important enough to the client, or because the case is not thought to be a good vehicle for establishing a particular rule.

16. Most of the material in this section was gathered by asking the attorneys specifically about the various ways they might gain by winning; but they also volunteered comments. I asked half the attorneys what they had riding on the case, and all but two said nothing. But usually they also asked what I meant by the question, and I then asked about the specific topics. The great majority of the attorneys talked about one or more of the topics.

17. Rathjen (*supra* note 2, at 30-33) made a similar finding with respect to lawyers appearing before circuit courts. Only 5 percent said that the "significance of the issue" was the most important factor in deciding to appeal, and no other similar motives were listed by the author. Also, the attorney's "perception of the importance of the issue to society as a whole" was, overall, considered a minor factor in deciding whether to appeal to the Supreme Court. And only a quarter of the attorneys considered themselves "group advocates" or "civil libertarians" (as opposed to "advocates"), who are essentially lawyers who appeal largely to establish a legal principle.

On the other hand, studies of lawyers before the Supreme Court have found a greater interest in establishing a legal principle, especially in civil liberties cases. Casper (*supra* note 7, *passim*, esp. 96) found that 70 percent of his sample of attorneys in civil liberties cases were group advocates or civil libertarians. See also N. Hakman, Lobbying the Supreme Court—An Appraisal of "Political Science Folklore," 35 Fordham L. Rev. 15 (1966), and N. Hakman, The Supreme Court's Political Environment: The Processing of Noncommercial Litigation, in *Frontiers of Judicial Research* 199 (J. Grossman and J. Tanenhous ed. 1969).

18. This point is often made by lawyers. For example, see the references in note 20.

19. The problem of not knowing what aspects of a case will interest the various judges seems common even among experienced counsel. See M. Pollack, The Civil Appeal, in *Counsel on Appeal* 29, 49-53 (A. Charpentier ed. 1968); M. Lasky, A Return to the Observatory Below the Bench, 19 Sw. L.J. 679, 692 (1965). Both suggest that the court tell attorneys what points it wants covered in oral arguments or in supplemental briefs. The California Supreme Court announces the issues that it considers the major issues in each appeal when it decides to take a case under its discretionary jurisdiction, and this announcement is published in legal newspapers. As far as I know, this happens in no other state.

20. Lawyers often recommend that this be done if possible. See especially S. Gates, Hot Bench or Cold Bench, in Charpentier, *supra* note 19, at 107, 111, and K. Llewellyn, *The Common Law Tradition, Deciding Appeals* 34, 42, 43, 251, 391 (1960). For some reason, judges writing about appellate advocacy rarely suggest that counsel do this. The major exception is by a former appellate attorney. T. Marshall, The Federal Appeal, in Charpentier, *supra* note 19, at 139, 143.

21. Attorneys' lack of knowledge of internal procedures has long been a source of concern to judges and to the bar. Many judges have written articles explaining the workings of their courts (see Bibliography A, where many of the writings listed have been authored by judges). Many appellate courts have now written, or are preparing, descriptions of their internal procedures, under the impetus of suggestions that they do so by: Commission on Revision of the Federal Court Appellate System, *Structure and Internal Procedures: Recommendations for Change* 44-46 (1975) and ABA *Standards Relating to Appellate Courts* No. 3.30 (1977).

22. A Partridge and G. Bermant, *The Quality of Advocacy in the Federal Courts* 187-208 (Federal Judicial Center, 1978). On the other hand, substantial relationships were found with respect to trial advocacy in the U.S. district courts. The judges, for example, rated lawyers from large offices, middle-aged lawyers, lawyers with trial court experience, and lawyers from top law schools better than average. The reason for this difference between trial and appellate advocacy is not clear.

23. See Chapter 3 at notes 27-30. The categories I used are listed there. They differ from those in the federal court study. Those not discussed here seemed unrelated to the quality of advocacy.

24. This finding cannot be compared to the Partridge and Bermant finding that "office size" is not related to the quality of advocacy (as rated by the judges). "Office" includes both government offices and law firms, and a substantial number of lawyers were government lawyers (Partridge and Bermant, *supra* note 22 at 190, 191, 198-200).

CHAPTER 5

1. The main basis for the descriptions in this chapter is the bibliography of writings on appellate decision-making procedures found in Bibliography A. Another basis for the six courts studied here is interviews with judges and others at the courts as well as the court rules. Since it would be too unwieldy to cite authority for each point, notes are used only for statements not derived from these sources and for points of major importance that can be found in only a few sources.

2. A Charpentier, *Law Libraries Currently Receiving Appellate Records* (Ass'n B. City of N.Y. 1961).

3. The more thorough discussions of these reasons are A. Vanderbilt, Improving the Administration of Justice—Two Decades of Development, 26 U. Cin. L. Rev. 155, 266, 267 (1957); J. Hopkins, The Winds of Change: New Styles in the Appellate Process, 3 Hofstra L. Rev. 649, 655, 656 (1975); F. Wiener, *Effective Appellate Advocacy,* 12-20 (1950).

4. Federal Judicial Center, *A Summary of the Third Circuit Time Study* 4 (1974).

5. This statement is based on the slips of paper on the tape boxes that noted who had taken the tapes from storage. Also the man in charge of the tapes told me they were "rarely" used by judges. Judges on other courts, however, have suggested that their tapes are used more often. See F. Kenison, Electronic Recording of Oral Arguments in the States, in *Proceedings of the Thirteenth Annual Meeting of the Conference of Chief Justices* 117 (1961); C. Donworth, The Value of Tape Recording Oral Arguments in Appellate Courts, 7 Trial Judges' J. 11 (Oct. 1968); Federal Judicial Center Cassette Recordings Nos. J-52 and J-53, Preparation for Decision-Making (1973). When the tapes are used, it is because the judge missed the arguments, be-

cause the case is important or technical, or because the attorney made a very important statement (especially admitting a point or waiving an issue).

6. Less than half the judges interviewed were asked or otherwise talked about this. All but one of the half dozen judges who have given an opinion about the relative importance in the legal literature were of this opinion. See especially, U.S. Court of Appeals for the Third Circuit, In the Matter of Oral Argument, 1 Prac. Law. 12, 17, 18 (Jan. 1955). Also a political scientist asked thirteen Fifth Circuit judges how influential the briefs and arguments are in reaching decisions. Ten ranked the briefs as "most influential" and more influential than the arguments, while three ranked both the briefs and arguments one knotch lower, as "very influential." Incidently, ten said the arguments are "very influential" and three of "some influence." F. Rich, *Role Perceptions and Precedent Orientation as Variables Influencing Appellate Judicial Decision-Making* 100 (unpublished Ph.D. dissertation, University of Georgia, 1967). Another political scientist found perhaps that judges on four state supreme courts more often viewed arguments as important as the briefs, though the results are not clearly presented. See J. Wold, *Internal Procedures, Role Perceptions and Judicial Behavior: A Study of Four State Courts of Last Resort* 55, 56, 87-90, 118, 124, 144, 145 (unpublished Ph.D. dissertation, The Johns Hopkins University, 1972).

7. Most of the judges interviewed talked about the importance of oral arguments, but the statements in the text about this subject are based mainly on over 200 statements by appellate judges in law review articles, testimony, judicial conferences, and in response to questionnaires. For the latter see Rich, *supra*; Wold, *supra*; M. Bright, The Changing Nature of the Federal Appeals Process in the 1970's, 65 F.R.D. 496, 505 (1975); Institute of Judicial Administration, *Appellate Courts. Internal Operating Procedures. Preliminary Report*, 50-86 (1957). All told, about 80 percent of these 200 judges said that the oral arguments are very important. In addition, a study of circuit judges, 40 of whom answered, asked whether arguments are "essential," "moderately valuable," or "dispensable" for several categories of appeals. Although there is a large gap between "essential" and "moderately valuable," the results of the study are consistent with the 80 percent figure. The importance of arguments, though, varied greatly between different types of cases, for example, 8 percent of the judges said arguments are dispensable in appeals involving the constitutionality of state statutes or actions, while half said they are in collateral attacks on state or federal convictions. See J. Goldman, *Attitudes of United States Judges Toward Limitation of Oral Argument and Opinion-Writing in the United States Court of Appeals*, 8-12 (Federal Judicial Center, 1975).

For a collection of statements by U.S. Supreme Court Justices about the importance of oral arguments, see S. Wasby et al., The Functions of Oral Argument in the U.S. Supreme Court, 62 Q.J. Speech 410, 411 (1976).

8. An illustration of this difference between judges and clerks is found in the National Center for State Courts, *The Appellate Process in Alabama* 99 (1973). The authors wrote that the arguments in the Alabama Supreme Court tended to be dull and that the lawyers mainly just covered things already in the briefs. Then a footnote states that some of the justices disagreed with this statement "and believe that argument in their Court is vigorous and productive." The footnote continues by saying that the statement in the text represents the view of the law clerks and the author's observations. Then at page 154, the report says that the Alabama clerks "tend to

view oral argument as a waste of time.'' One Alabama justice, it should be added, wrote earlier that the arguments were often useless. See P. Merrill, Appellate Practice, 25 Ala. Lawyer 33, 39, 40 (1964). A good example of law clerks' attitudes toward arguments is found in T. Ragatz and J. Shea, Supreme Court Law Clerks, 35 Wisc. B. Bull. 33, 35 (Aug. 1962).

9. About standards as to when arguments are held see R. Leflar, *Internal Operating Procedures of Appellate Courts* 33-35 (1976). Published standards for screening out the argument stage, however, are inexact, and the general criteria seems to be that judges will ask for arguments if they think they will be worth their time, taking into consideration such things as the caliber of counsel and the amount of travel the judges must do to hold arguments.

10. The discussion on the frequency of oral arguments is taken largely (but along with the other materials in Bibliography A), from the Institute of Judicial Administration, *supra* note 7, at 50-86; S. McCronkie, Decision-Making in State Supreme Courts, 59 Judicature 337, 340, 341 (1976); Administrative Office of the United States Courts, *1977 Annual Report of the Director* 71. The latter, however, is difficult to interpret.

11. This discussion is based on comments by over a hundred judges in the types of sources listed in note 7. A substantial amount of the information is in Institute of Judicial Administration, *supra* note 7, at 50-86, and Goldman, *supra* note 7, at 16. I did not ask about this topic in the interviews, but a dozen judges volunteered comments. As with other topics in this section, there was little difference between what the judges said in the interviews and what was said in these other sources. Of course, the fact that a judge mentioned one purpose but not others does not mean that the others are unimportant to him, especially since the discussions were nearly always very short (the most frequent purpose was mentioned by only half the judges), but the relative frequency of the purposes gives some indication of the weight the judges give them. This caveat applies also to several following notes.

12. Statement of William E. Doyle to the Commission on Revision of the Federal Court Appellate System, April 16, 1975, p. 826.

13. Judges mention several other functions of oral arguments, though much less often than these two. Arguments give counsel a chance to mention things they failed to put in their briefs, and they may help judges get a better understanding of certain aspects of the case than they can from the briefs—they can get a better "feel" for the case, or they can more easily grasp the justice or policy implications involved. Judges occasionally say that they benefit from the personal contact with counsel: They learn more from listening than reading; the arguments are a pleasant relief from the long hours of reading and research; or human contact gets some points across better than the "cold" briefs can. Lastly, arguments give counsel the assurance that he has had his day in court—has had the opportunity to present his views to all the judges deciding the case. This public relations function is especially important when attorneys suspect that not all judges read the briefs or that the court's staff plays a major role in the decision process.

14. I asked most of the judges interviewed about the purpose of their questions (including six of the seven sitting on the focal court at the time I studied the arguments), and I have found discussion on this topic in almost thirty judges' writings, mostly articles on appellate advocacy in which the judges tell the attorneys that ques-

tions should be welcome. The most thorough discussion of the purpose of questions is by Justice Tate. See A. Tate, The Appellate Advocate and the Appellate Court, 13 La. B.J. 107, 111 (1965), and On Questions from the Bench, 7 La. B.J. 128 (1959). See also, I. Goldberg, Preparation for Hearing Oral Argument, 63 F.R.D. 499, 503, 506 (1974); Wasby et al., *supra* note 7, at 413-420.

15. T. Drury et al. *Attorney Attitudes Toward Limitation of Oral Argument and Written Opinion in Three U.S. Courts of Appeals, passim* (Federal Judicial Center, 1974). The three courts are the Second, Fifth, and Sixth Circuits.

16. *Supra*, at 37-42.

17. None of the attorneys I interviewed mentioned the clients' wish for a day in court (perhaps the attorneys in the circuit court study considered themselves the "litigants"), and the circuit court study did not ask about the chance to present non-legal arguments (the attorneys were asked about the importance of specific functions and benefits of the arguments that were listed by the authors). Several attorneys interviewed (and a few judges, but not asked in the circuit court study) gave as another purpose the chance to tell the court about things missed or not available when writing the briefs.

18. *Supra*, at 38. However, attorneys practicing before courts that ask few questions would probably agree less with this view.

19. Institute of Judicial Administration, *supra* note 7, at 145-155.

20. See Chapter 9, about legal authority, 12, about social facts, and 13, about empirical data.

21. Comment, The Amicus Curiae, 55 Nw. U.L. Rev. 469, 477-482 (1960). Amicus briefs were submitted in only eighty-four cases—not much over four a year—though they were much more common in the 1950s than earlier. The Virginia Supreme Court received amicus briefs in less than 2 percent of its appeals from 1961 to 1966. See T. Morris, *The Virginia Supreme Court, An Institutional and Political Analysis* 93 (1975).

In another study a sample of 646 U.S. Supreme Court cases decided over forty-five years prior to 1970 showed that amicus briefs were filled in 13 percent of the cases (though over a quarter of the cases decided in the 1960s). In 15 percent of the opinions that cited "nonlegal evidence" (which is, essentially, anything cited except cases, statutes, regulations, and constitutions), at least some of the nonlegal evidence was cited in an amicus brief; but only 4 percent of these opinions (there were some 400 such opinions in the sample) cited nonlegal evidence found in the amicus briefs but not in the parties' briefs. Only a small minority of the nonlegal evidence cited by the Court was references to empirical data. See J. Johnson, *The Dimensions of Non-legal Evidence in the American Judicial Process: The Supreme Court's Use of Extra-Legal Materials in the Twentieth Century* 211-215 (Unpublished Ph.D. dissertation, University of Minnesota, 1974).

In a study of briefs and opinions in over 200 U.S. Supreme Court cases decided from 1954 to 1974, it was found that over 40 percent of the citations to social science works in the briefs were in the amicus briefs, as opposed to the parties' briefs, and that the Court was as likely to cite the works mentioned in amicus briefs as those in the parties' briefs. See V. Rosenblum et al., *Report on the Uses of Social Science in Judicial Decision Making* 68 (unpublished manuscript, Northwestern University Law School, 1977).

22. Less than half the judges and clerks were asked about the helpfulness of amicus briefs. From what has been written on the subject it appears that judges elsewhere are of very differing views about the importance of amicus briefs, but probably think less of them on the whole than the judges interviewed. In Maryland they are not considered influential and are seldom filed; in New York they are considered "moderately influential"; in Virginia two justices considered them "very important" factors in their decision making, and four "moderately important"; and in Delaware they had only a "slight effect." See Wold, *supra* note 6, at 55, 90, 118, 144, 145. A political scientist studying the Kansas Supreme Court said "there was a tendency among the judges to rate the briefs submitted by the litigants as less helpful than those submitted as amicus curiae." See G. Mason, *Judges and Their Publics: Role Perceptions and Role Expectations* 300 (unpublished Ph.D. dissertation, University of Kansas, 1967). None of thirteen Fifth Circuit judges said amicus briefs are either "most influential" or of "no influence." In between, two said they are "very influential," five, "of some influence," and six, of "slight influence." See Rich, *supra* note 6, at 100.

Judges' writings hardly ever refer to amicus briefs, which in itself suggests they are of limited importance. Judge Jerome Frank called them "often helpful," Aero Spark Plug Co. v. B. G. Corporation, 130 F. 2d 290, 299 (1942). Justice Denecke said the Oregon Supreme Court gets many amicus briefs, but "they seldom have more expertise on the particular issue than other competent practicing attorneys." See A. Denecke, The Judiciary Needs Your Help, Teachers, 22 J. Legal Ed. 197, 202 (1969). However, Justice Denecke, as well as several other appellate judges, have asked for more help through amicus briefs from law professors or from the government. See K. O'Connell, Streamlining Appellate Procedures, 56 Judicature 234, 236, 237 (1973); R. Traynor, Badlands in an Appellate Judge's Realm of Reason, 7 Utah L. Rev. 157, 170 (1960). I. Kaufman, Judicial Reform in the Next Century, 32 Record 9, 16, 17 (1977). These judges suggested that the court might pay the professors for their efforts. This has never been done, as far as I know. Judge Kaufman suggests that courts might employ experts on a full-time basis or establish research organizations for that purpose.

The *ABA Standards Relating to Appellate Courts* No. 3.33 (and the following commentary) rather strongly encourage the use of amicus briefs to help appellate courts in their lawmaking function.

23. P. Kurland, Jurisdiction of the United States Supreme Court: Time for Change? 59 Cornell L. Rev. 616, 632 (1974). In one extreme example of the importance of amicus briefs in the Supreme Court, however, the appellee attorney dropped out, and the court used an amicus as the adversary supporting the appellee. See Mathews v. Weber, 423 U.S. 261, 265 n. 2 (1976). Some students of the use of amicus briefs in the Supreme Court have suggested that the briefs can be valuable. See Note, Government Litigation in the Supreme Court: The Roles of the Solicitor General, 78 Yale L.J. 1442, 1475-1477 (1969); S. Krislov, The Amicus Curiae Brief: From Friendship to Advocacy, 72 Yale L.J. 694 (1963).

24. F. Harper and E. Etherington, Lobbyists Before the Court, 101 U. Pa. L. Rev. 1172 (1953).

25. Appellate courts are attempting more and more to consider cases with similar issues at the same time. Courts without discretionary jurisdiction often have issue

files, in which every case is entered under each issue it raises as soon as the appeal is brought to the court. This enables the courts to place cases with similar issues before the same judges at the same time. Courts with discretionary jurisdiction can grant leave (or certiorari) to several cases with similar issues. This not only enables the courts to obtain arguments from more than two adversaries, but the several appeals present a broader picture of the factual possibilities with which to formulate law.

The discussion here is only about cases before the court at roughly the same time. Judges or their staff can also read briefs of cases decided sometime earlier containing issues similar to an appeal being decided. Justice Schaefer says that "hardly a term of court goes by but that" the court does that (but largely to see how strong the precedent is). W. Schaefer, Precedent and Policy, 34 U. Chi. L. Rev. 3, 11 (1966). I talked with a number of law clerks (and but one judge) about this practice, and most said they looked at old briefs a few times a year, but again largely to elucidate what the precedent was—for example, whether a specific argument had been raised in the earlier case—and not to gain information from the attorneys' arguments to apply to the present appeal. On the other hand, three clerks from three different courts said they had sent for briefs of pending or recently decided cases in other courts, using the briefs to get information about the issues under consideration. Only one clerk said he did this at all often: "I deal a lot on briefs in other courts where there is a pending issue like ours. I write to other courts for briefs and records in the case. You know, if I can't get them for freebies, I'll borrow them and send them back."

Attorneys can also use the briefs of prior cases when preparing appeals. The librarian in the state law library (located very close to the focal court) said that attorneys often look at the old briefs. However, I asked a number of attorneys if they did this, and they typically answered that they never or rarely used the briefs. None made frequent use of them. On the other hand, some attorneys often use old briefs written by their firm or office; the public defenders have a "brief bank" that is routinely used.

26. This information comes from the court clerks at the six courts, several judges and clerks interviewed, and the focal court records. These courts are probably typical, though there is little published on the subject. The *ABA Standards Relating to Appellate Courts* No. 3.33(a) (and commentary) states, "Appellate courts do not always demand of the adversary system the assistance it is capable of providing," and then encourages the use of supplemental briefs, especially when counsel's main briefs are inadequate. Judge Leventhal, talking about appeals involving technical material, said that the court could call for supplemental materials. "Theoretically there are ways for a judge to amplify his knowledge [using counsel]. But the fact is that most of the time you don't. You just do the best you can, you struggle along." See H. Leventhal, Cues and Compasses for Administrative Lawyers, 20 Ad. L. Rev. 237, 241 (1968). Judge Leventhal later advocated the use of supplemental briefs—H. Leventhal, Environmental Decisionmaking and the Role of the Courts, 122 U. Pa. L. Rev. 509, 545 (1974)—as has a Fifth Circuit judge, Goldberg, *supra* note 14, at 505. Apparently, California appellate courts often ask for rebriefing. See R. Traynor, Some Open Questions on the Work of State Appellate Courts, 24 U. Chi. L. Rev. 211, 216, 219 (1957); R. Peters, Five Years of the Conference System, 19 Calif. St. B.J. 399, 402 (1944). Elsewhere, probably the main use of supplemental briefs is when a court wants to decide an issue not raised, a topic discussed in Chapter 8.

27. A 1957 survey of appellate courts found that rearguments are rare in all courts answering the survey. Institute of Judicial Administration, *Appellate Courts. Internal Operating Procedures. 1959 Summary and Supplement* 12.

28. See *ABA Code of Judicial Conduct*, No. 3(A) (4) and *ABA Code of Professional Responsibility*, DR 7-110(B).

29. Only several judges and clerks interviewed, but all the court clerks, talked about the topics in this paragraph. They had generally experienced or knew of incidents in which clients, lawyers, or other interested parties had tried to contact people at the court about the cases under consideration. The court clerks, of course, got the bulk of it. All said it was improper to discuss pending appeals, though a few would give a broad guess as to when an appeal would be decided, and two law clerks told me of incidents in which they had briefly talked with attorneys on one side concerning the merits of their case before the court, once even giving the attorney advice. At one time the U.S. Supreme Court justices were very annoyed by people involved in their cases sending them letters. See Krislov, *supra* note 23, at 710, 711.

30. I asked several clerks and judges about this (but none from the First Circuit). A judge and a clerk at the focal court told me about different examples of the practice, but no others I talked to about the subject knew of it; so it seems it went on rather secretly.

The New Jersey and Wisconsin Supreme Courts and the Fifth Circuit Court of Appeals have had such conferences with lawyers (and at the two state courts with technical experts) after the arguments. J. Francis, Joseph Weintraub—A Judge for All Seasons, 59 Cornell L. Rev. 186, 191 (1974); G. Currie, Appellate Courts Use of Facts Outside the Record by Resort to Judicial Notice and Independent Investigation, 1960 Wisc. L. Rev. 39, 47; Testimony of G. Bell before the Commission on Revision of the Federal Court Apellate System, April 15, 1975, p. 686. And Judge Leventhal of the D.C. Circuit has suggested this procedure, especially for technical cases. See Leventhal, *supra* note 26, at 546; H. Leventhal, Appellate Procedures: Design, Patchwork and Managed Flexibility, 23 U.C.L.A.L. Rev. 432, 446, 447 (1976).

31. I asked the court clerks, several judges, and a number of law clerks about this practice. All said it was not done often. The judges and court clerks generally volunteered that the attorney must send a copy to the opponent. The practice seems to be the same at all six courts, though the Sixth Circuit judges are more likely to frown on it. Two distinguished texts on appellate advocacy disapprove of the practice. See F. Wiener, *Briefing and Arguing Federal Appeals*, 266, 267 (1961); E. Re, *Brief Writing and Oral Argument* 207 (4th ed. 1974). But a Texas justice has encouraged its use, J. Greenhill, Presentation of a Case to the Supreme Court of Texas, 38 Texas L. Rev. 538, 548 (1960). No other judges writing about appellate advocacy mentioned the practice (in the writings in Bibliography B), suggesting it is not often used.

32. Institute of Judicial Administration, *supra* note 27, at 22. This appears to be the situation on the six courts studied here, judging from comments by a dozen clerks and judges. And there are many other scattered references in the legal literature suggesting that IJA findings still apply, for example, National Center for State Courts, *Wisconsin Appellate Practice and Procedure Study* 50 (1975). However, it appears that rehearing petitions were slightly less common earlier in the century. See W. Cook, The Rehearing Evil, 14 Iowa L. Rev. 36, 51, 52 (1928).

Judges, also, often express annoyance at frivolous petitions, and the Second Circuit has passed a local rule (Rule 40) providing for a fine up to $250 for petitions "wholly without merit, vexatious, and for delay."

33. Wiener, *supra* note 31, at 365. See Institute of Judicial Administration, *supra* note 27, at 24.

34. H. Goodrich, A Case on Appeal—A Judge's View, in *A Case on Appeal* 31 (4th ed. 1967). The standards, if any, as to when rehearing will be granted are very vague. D. Louisell and R. Degnan, Rehearing in American Appellate Courts, 44 Calif. L. Rev. 627, *passim* (1956). The bulk of the successful petitions for rehearings before the focal court were the result of a turnover in judges. This is probably true of many other courts. See Louisell and Degnan, *supra*, at 637, 638, and G. Rossman, Appellate Practice and Advocacy, 16 F.R.D. 403, 418, 419 (1955). Similarly, petitions for rehearings in circuit courts routinely ask for en banc consideration of a panel's decision, trying to persuade those outside the panel that the case is important and that the panel is wrong.

35. See American Bar Association, *Methods of Reaching and Preparing Appellate Court Decisions* 34 (1942), and R. Pound, *Appellate Procedure in Civil Cases* 214 (1941). This function of rehearing—essentially a check on the opinion writer—was more common in the past.

36. Leventhal, *supra* note 6, at 546.

37. R. Jackson, Advocacy Before the United States Supreme Court, 37 Cornell L.Q. 1, 6 (1951).

38. These two possibilities have been suggested by two appellate judges, R. Thompson, One Judge and No Judge Appellate Decisions, 50 Calif. St. B.J. 476, 516, 517 (1975); and Leventhal, *supra* note 26, at 546.

39. Justice Weintraub of New Jersey has asked if it might not be proper to use rule-making procedures when deciding appeals, especially inviting comments from the public on proposed decisions. See J. Weintraub, Judicial Legislation, 81 N.J.L.J. 545, 549 (1958). Administrative agencies, it should be noted, have been shifting from adjudicative-type decision making to rule making when creating laws, probably because of information-gathering considerations. See B. Boyer, Alternatives to Administrative Trial-Type Hearings for Resolving Complex Scientific, Economic, and Social Issues, 71 Mich. L. Rev. 111 (1972).

CHAPTER 6

1. The information about law clerks in this section is based on the interviews with judges and clerks and on the rather large literature about clerks. The major writings are listed in Bibliography C, though there are numerous shorter references to clerks' duties elsewhere. Specific points will not be noted unless they are important points and are derived from only a few sources or from authorities not listed in Bibliography C. I interviewed thirty-one clerks; nineteen worked for eleven different focal court justices; four worked for four Sixth Circuit judges; and two each worked for different judges in Rhode Island, Massachusetts, Ohio, and the First Circuit. (In two interviews, at the focal court and the Sixth Circuit, two of a judge's clerks were interviewed together. These are counted as only one interview each.)

2. All circuit courts and all state supreme courts, except the Wyoming Supreme

Court, use law clerks, though a few rare judges do not have them even though authorized. See Council of State Governments, *State Court Systems* 40-41 (Rev. 1976). Three older judges interviewed in this study did not have clerks, and they are not included in the following discussions. All three had clerks years ago but then decided they did not need them.

3. Information about the clerks' broad duties—for example, about whether they draft opinions—was obtained for the great majority of the judges interviewed who had clerks and for four judges not interviewed (two were dead and two refused to be interviewed) from their clerks. For three-eighths of the judges the information came from judges only; for an equal number it came from clerks only; and for a quarter, from both. In three of the ten cases where both a judge and his clerk talked about the clerks' duties, the clerks implied that they did much more drafting than the judges implied (though two of these judges were interviewed before the clerks interviewed were hired). Here I took the clerks' views, suspecting that the judges were less than forthright—virtually the only time I suspected this in the interviews. This, of course, casts some doubt on what the other judges said; thus the text may understate the extent of clerk drafting.

Information about the details of the clerks' duties was obtained largely from the clerks; therefore, it is based mainly on the practices in the focal court. But these practices seem typical, based on the other interviews and on the literature about clerks' jobs.

4. J. Frank, *The Marble Palace* 116 (1958).

5. See especially, P. Carrington, Report on Group Discussions, in *Appellate Justice 1975, Vol. 5, Supplement, Proceedings, and Conclusions* 62, 65 (1975).

6. Federal Judicial Center Cassette J-135, The Role and Functions of the Court of Appeals (1975). See also G. Edwards, Exorcising the Devil of Appellate Court Delay, 58 A.B.A.J. 149, 153 (1972). Leflar is also against opinion writing by law clerks (or staff attorneys). See R. Leflar, *Internal Operating Procedures of Appellate Courts* 93, 94 (1976).

7. In a recent study (Council of State Governments, *supra* note 2) twenty-five state supreme courts reported that one of the clerks' duties was drafting opinions; but it is uncertain what portion of the clerks on each court wrote drafts. The remaining twenty-five courts either reported that the clerks' duties varied with individual judges (or did whatever work the judge directed) or did not indicate that the clerks wrote drafts but indicated other specific duties (the questionnaire listed several possible duties a clerk may perform, and the person filling out the questionnaire, probably the chief justice, did not check "preliminary drafts"). Of the twelve that reported that duties varied with the judge, two had answered the Council of State Government questionnaire two years earlier by stating that one duty of the clerks was to draft opinions. Four had answered an earlier questionnaire (institute of Judicial Administration, *Appellate Courts, Internal Operating Procedures, Preliminary Report*, appendix 28-33 (1957), and all said that clerks sometimes wrote drafts. For one of these four there is independent confirmation that the clerks do write opinion drafts: The preargument memos written by the California Supreme Court clerks are in effect draft opinions. See P. Johnson, Foreword: The Accidental Decision and How It Happens, 65 Calif. L. Rev. 231, 250 (1977). Of the thirteen courts that mentioned some specific duties, but not writing drafts, there is independent information about

several. In the 1957 study, three courts in this category reported that the clerks did not write drafts and one reported that they did. There are publications mentioning the topic for three of the thirteen, all reporting that clerks sometimes wrote drafts. See National Center for State Courts, *Wisconsin Appellate Practice and Procedure Study* 22 (1975); J. Beatty, *An Institutional and Behavioral Analysis of the Iowa Supreme Court* 38-45 (unpublished Ph.D. dissertation, University of Iowa, 1970); R. Braucher, Choosing Law Clerks in Massachusetts, 26 Vand. L. Rev. 1197, 1200 (1973); and, of course, interviews in Massachusetts. On the other hand, the New Mexico Supreme Court was marked, in the Council of State Governments report, as using clerks to write drafts, but an earlier article by a justice there said the clerks do not write drafts, M. Nobel, The Law Clerk, 7 Trial Judges' J. 4 (Oct. 1968). On the other hand, a law clerk at that court has complained publicly that his judge delegated too much, including opinion drafting. See The New York Times, March 2, 1975. In sum, extrapolating from these sources, it appears that some judges on the great majority of state supreme courts use clerks' draft opinions.

From the interviews and from scattered references in the literature, it seems that federal circuit judges use clerks' drafts more often than state judges, probably because of the huge case loads and because they tend to have better clerks.

A cloud, it should be added, always hangs over published reports of the amount of delegation to clerks. Judges seem to be leary about admitting that much of their opinions are ghostwritten. Also, an interesting point discovered in the interviews, judges (and less often, clerks) often have little idea of how clerks are used in other offices at their court. Thus when a judge speaks for his court as a whole on this matter, as is the case in most of the preceding sources, he may not really know what he is speaking about.

8. Perhaps one would think the clerks' praise of their bosses should be taken with a grain of salt. But the respect shown appeared genuine; in general, the clerks seemed very frank in the interviews, and most were interviewed after they had left the court. Moreover, these comments were all volunteered—the clerks were not asked what they thought of their judges but almost always brought the subject up on their own. Four clerks showed disrespect in rather strong terms; two others did not praise their judges and, I suspected, were holding back criticism.

9. Most of the judges were asked if they liked their clerks to argue with them, and all said yes, except for a couple who said that they liked clerks to speak frankly, but not really "argue." A few judges said there were some exceptions: Two said that they did not like clerks to argue if they did not know what they were talking about, and two more said clerks should argue only about legal matters, and not social philosophy or the like.

10. I. Goldberg, Preparation for Hearing Oral Argument, 63 F.R.D. 499, 503 (1974). This statement was made in a seminar of circuit judges, and it seemed to represent the consensus of the judges there. Federal Judicial Center Cassettes J-52 and J-53, Preparing for Decision-Making (1973). See also, H. Medina, The Decisional Process, 20 N.Y.Co.B. Bull. 94, 96 (1962); R. Aldisert, Duties of Law Clerks, 26 Vand. L. Rev. 1251, 1255-1257 (1973). On the other hand, some judges seem wary of clerks who continually agitate for moral or political reform. See Braucher, *supra* note 7, at 1199.

11. At all six courts studied, and at a few others referred to in the literature on

clerks, the clerks are, on the whole, more liberal than the judges. For example, a study of the Iowa Supreme Court concluded that the clerks are a good deal more liberal, apparently more so than at the courts here. See Beatty, *supra* note 7, at 210-214. Terms like "liberal" and "conservative" are, of course, virtually undefinable, and some clerks and judges refused to use them.

12. Clerks writing about their jobs routinely emphasize that their judges make the final decision. See the writings listed in Bibliography C, and C. Wright, The Overloaded Fifth Circuit: A Crisis in Judicial Administration, 42 Texas L. Rev. 949, 961 (1964). In the Iowa Supreme Court study referred to in the preceding note both the clerks and judges considered the clerks' influence slight. Of course, the fact that the judges do not delegate the actual deciding does not mean the clerks are without influence, for judges to varying degrees accept the clerks' draft opinions and research findings without double-checking everything, and I suppose in some instances without understanding everything.

13. This was said during a seminar for circuit judges, Federal Judicial Center Cassette J-53, Preparation of Opinions (1973). Similar comments are routinely made by those writing about the value of clerks. For examples not in Bibliography C, see K. Llewellyn *The Common Law Tradition, Deciding Appeals* 322 (1960); Report of *the Study Group on the Caseload of the Supreme Court* 44 (1972) and Testimony of W. Gewin Before the Commission on Revision of the Federal Court Appellate System, August 23, 1973, at page 411. Judge Gewin said, "I like to expose myself to fresh, young law clerks. . . . They bring new thoughts to us and new techniques, new methods of doing things. It's a refreshing thing to get fine, young lawyers to come in who are in the top 10 percent of their classes and who are well trained. It makes me think that I am not casting myself into a mold." On the other hand, a lawyer and student of appellate courts has labeled this view "more romantic than realistic." See B. Witkin, Appellate Court Opinions—A Syllabus for Panel Discussion at the Appellate Judges' Conference, 63 F.R.D. 515, 547 (1947).

14. Thus the present Justice Rehnquist said, soon after he clerked on the Court, that the clerks may slant their memorandums on certiorari petitions and misinform the justices. See W. Rehnquist, Who Writes Decisions of the Supreme Court? *U.S. News & World Report*, Dec. 13, 1957, p. 74, 75.

15. See especially D. Meador, *Appellate Courts, Staff and Process in the Crisis of Volume* (1974); T. Lesinski and N. Stockmeyer, Prehearing Research and Screening in the Michigan Court of Appeals: One Court's Method of Increasing Judicial Productivity, 26 Vand. L. Rev. 1211 (1973); S. Flanders and J. Goldman, *Screening Practices and the Use of Para-Judicial Personnel in the U.S. Court of Appeals: A Study in the Fourth Circuit* (Federal Judicial Center 1974); J. Cameron, The Central Staff: A New Solution to an Old Problem, 23 U.C.L.A.L. Rev. 465 (1976).

16. This practice is described in M. Wall, What the Courts Are Doing to Improve Judicial Opinions, 32 J. Am. Jud. Soc'y 148, 149, 150 (1949). However, she claims the checkers' role is largely limited to matters of grammar and writing style. Meador has suggested that drafts be sent to staff attorneys for comments, which seems like a good idea. See D. Meador, Appellate Case Management and Decisional Process, 61 Va. L. Rev. 255, 288 (1975).

17. The court clerks were asked about this; only the focal court clerk had done it, and he only two or three times in the past two decades.

18. Also one judge said he just never thought of doing it; another said he would not be able to get much help; and two more said they were concerned about confidentiality. Of course, some judges gave more than one reason, and others probably would agree with some of the reasons they did not mention.

A few judges, in explaining why they did not get advice from law professors or did not get it more often, said they had little respect for the professors because professors have little practical experience. An Oregon justice has written that some judges —a "large enough number so they cannot be ignored"—felt the same way, though he himself did not. See A. Denecke, The Judiciary Needs Your Help, Teachers, 22 J. Legal Ed. 197, 199 (1969). Some scholars have said that law professors are much more interested in the logical manipulation of rules than practical implications: R. Pound, The Theory of Judicial Decision, 36 Harv. L. Rev. 940, 953, 958 (1923); J. Deutsch, Neutrality, Legitimacy, and the Supreme Court: Some Intersections Between Law and Political Science, 20 Stan. L. Rev. 169, 240 (1968); M. Weber, *On Law in Economy and Society* 276-278 (M. Rheinstein ed. 1954); Llewellyn, *supra* note 13, at 348, 355. See also J. Frank, *Courts on Trial* 225-246 (1949).

One further point that ought to be mentioned is that appellate judges never, as far as I know, discuss the substance of a pending case with the judge who tried the case below. See Medina, *supra* note 10, at 103. However, in one case at the focal court the trial judge sent the court a letter trying to explain his decision further.

19. The original draft circulated by the ABA for comments did not contain the last section in what is now Canon 3A(4), in effect prohibiting advice from experts except through amicus briefs. See A.B.A. Spec Comm. on Standards of Judicial Conduct, *Canons of Judicial Ethics, Tentative Draft* (1971). The provision was inserted because those drafting the Code learned of many communications between judges and professors or judges on other courts, because they felt that these communications might be helpful, and because the amicus curiae route might be too time consuming and cumbersome in some instances; but they still wanted to limit "possible inroads on the adversary system" or, more strongly, would not "allow the adversary process to be subverted." See E. Thode, *Reporter's Notes to the Code of Judicial Conduct* 53, 54 (1973); E. Thode, The New Code of Judicial Conduct, 12 Judges' J. 34 (1973). One commentator said that "Many law teachers believe that it is not uncommon for a judge, particularly an appellate judge, to discuss with a law teacher a troublesome point of law that he must pass upon." J. Sutton, A Comparison of the Code of Professional Responsibility with the Code of Judicial Conduct, 1972 Utah L. Rev. 355, 363. A similar statement was made in D. Weckstein, Introductory Observations on the Code of Judicial Conduct, 9 San Diego L. Rev. 785, 787 (1972). This article said the original version of 3A (4) drew the most fire from law school professors and quoted Andrew L. Kaufman of Harvard Law School to the effect that such advice was valuable and there is not much difference between it and library research on the law.

The publications discussed previously mention a good many problems in interpreting Canon 3A(4). Probably the most important, however, is that the canon states that a judge may obtain the advice of an expert "on the law"—does this exclude obtaining advice on facts? Those involved with drafting the provision seemed to have had in mind advice from law professors, and not experts in other fields; but the latter are often asked for advice. The New Jersey court, which gets advice on scientific and technical matters (see note 22) changed 3A(4) to allow advice on "the law applicable to or the subject matter of" cases being decided. At any rate, however, social facts can probably be considered part of "the law," since they are used in establishing the law; but advice about the facts of the case seems prohibited. (In this regard, a suggestion that circuit judges borrow the technical advisers employed by the Court of Customs and Patent Appeals for help in interpreting technical data in the records of cases such as patent cases seems disallowed under 3A(4), whether notice is given to counsel or not. See note 17 of Chapter 11.)

20. One of the circuit judges interviewed said he would get outside advice if it were not for 3A(4), and Judge Oakes of the Second Circuit is of the same view: J. Oakes, Law Reviews and Judging, 50 N.Y.U.L. Rev. 2, 4 (1975). Also, either from the interviews, talking with law professors, or from the legal literature, I know of six state supreme courts on which judges got outside advice before adopting the code or part of it (including the three courts studied here), and in four the notice requirement in 3A(4) was not adopted. The other two are the New Jersey and Oregon courts, which are discussed in note 22. The New Jersey court added to 3A(4) a requirement that the parties be notified before the advice is sought and be allowed to participate, which appears to have been their practice beforehand. At the Oregon Supreme Court there was dislike of the practice by at least one judge.

It should be noted that a recent and major use of outside advice is possible even under the 3A(4) notice requirements. In a pilot project started in 1977 many Federal judges have received legal research aid (for example, in questions of legislative history) from the Library of Congress staff. See, 10 Third Branch 4, 6 (Jan. 1978). Presumedly the research results are transmitted in writing and are sent to counsel. See also note 22 of Chapter 5.

21. As of the end of 1977, the code was adopted at least in part by the Judicial Conference of the United States (which controls the circuit courts in such matters) and forty-five states—all except Hawaii, Illinois, Kentucky, Montana, and Wisconsin. (Rhode Island and Maryland adopted only a few parts of the code, though.)

The Judicial Conference and twenty-seven states adopted the ABA version of 3A(4). Three other states made slight changes: Idaho to say the judges cannot solicit advice from people outside the court without notice to the parties and opportunity to respond, Vermont to allow for advice only about out-of-state law, and New Jersey to allow for advice on nonlaw matters and to give counsel a chance to participate. Kansas, Texas, and Washington prohibited outside advice altogether.

Twelve states apparently changed 3A(4) to allow outside advice without notice to the parties. Alabama, Arizona, Michigan, and North Carolina allow it either overtly or by obvious implication. In Nevada judges need not give notice if the advice is only about "case citations or other abstract legal references." Massachusetts, New Hampshire, Rhode Island and Virginia provide that a judge should "not permit private interviews, arguments or communications designed to influence his judicial action, where the interests to be affected thereby are not represented before him, except in cases where provision is made by law for *ex parte* application." This language is taken from Canon 17 of the Canons of Judicial Ethics, which was adopted by the ABA in 1924 and which the Code of Judicial Conduct replaced. Canon 17 apparently was interpreted to allow advice from outside experts. Louisiana, Maine, and Pennsylvania have language similar to that of Canon 17.

In all but four of the forty-five states the supreme court adopted the code. In the four it was adopted by various bodies made up of some or all of: trial and appellate judges and lawyers. The four adopted the ABA version. The Judicial Conference of the United States consists of the chief judges of all the circuit courts, and thus would likely reflect the overall views of circuit judges (though obviously not some on the Second Circuit).

22. A New Jersey justice has said the court has talked to technical experts, but with the lawyers present. See J. Francis, Joseph Weintraub—A Judge for All Seasons, 59 Cornell L. Rev. 186, 191 (1974). Also, a political scientist was told by justices there that they had consulted psychiatrists for one case, and had received statistics about automobiles for another; though there is no indication about whether counsel were present. See H. Glick, *Supreme Courts in State Politics* 84 (1971). The Wisconsin Supreme Court has long obtained advice from state agencies, at least on social facts. See G. Currie, Appellate Courts Use of Facts Outside of the Record by Resort to Judicial Notice and Independent Investigation, 1960 Wisc. L. Rev. 39, *passim.* Wisconsin has not adopted the new Code of Judicial Conduct.

There are a number of references elsewhere in the legal literature about this subject. The Michigan Supreme Court justices once obtained a law professor's help in interpreting a will: H. Butzel, Justice Butzel Reminisces, 34 Mich. St. B.J. 25, 28 (Dec. 1955). At least three of the six Second Circuit judges in the 1940s sought advice from law professors. See M. Schick, *Learned Hand's Court* 124-130 (1970).

An Oregon justice has written about a case in which "The seven justices of the Oregon Supreme Court corresponded with Professor Green and Dean Prosser, as well as with other professors." This was an important tort case decided in 1963. See A. Goodwin, Chief Justice O'Connell: A Colleague Looks Back, 56 Oregon L. Rev. 183, 188, 189 (1977). However, Justice Denecke of that court says, "ex parte conversations or correspondence with experts, law teachers or otherwise, is unfair and can be misleading. The facts given may be incomplete or inaccurate, the problem can be incorrectly stated or other matters can be incorrectly stated." See Denecke, *supra* note 18, at 203. On the other hand, Justice O'Connell of the same court has written that he has on many occasions puzzled over problems in areas of law where he had little knowledge, and that "a telephone call to one of my teacher friends working in the particular field" would help him. He did not say he actually made such calls, but he suggested that advice on questions of law, not specifically related to the facts of the appeal, are proper. K. O'Connell, Continuing Legal Education for the Judiciary, 16 J. Legal Ed. 405, 412, 413 (1964). Thus, there has apparently been quite a debate on the Oregon Supreme Court about this topic.

Karl Llewellyn, *supra* note 13, at 323-332, strongly advocates this practice, mainly for nonlaw advice, and discusses at length its drawbacks and benefits. As was noted in note 20, the Federal courts now use legal research aid from the Library of Congress. U.S. Supreme Court Justices are rumored to get advice from law professors and government agencies, as is discussed in C. Lamb, Judicial Policy-Making and Information Flow to the Supreme Court, 29 Vand. L. Rev. 45, 98, 116, (1976). There is stronger evidence that Justice Murphy and possibly others received outside advice. See J. Howard, *Mr. Justice Murphy, A Political Biography*, 242, 473 (1968).

CHAPTER 7

1. Again, the source for the discussion in this chapter is the interviews at the six courts and the authorities listed in Bibliography A on decision-making procedures in appellate courts. The authorities will not be cited here unless an important point is substantiated by only a few authorities or by authorities not in Bibliography A.

2. Only several judges and less than half the law clerks were asked about whether judges await vehicles. Most said it happens, generally adding that it is not often. There was a strong tendency to believe that other judges do it more than one's self (or one's judge). Judges more often decide that they want to study an area and await a case to do that, but without definitely deciding what the outcome will be. Justice Brandeis is often said to have decided issues and awaited vehicles; see, for example, his law clerk's account in H. Friendly, Reactions of a Lawyer—Newly Become Judge, 71 Yale L.J. 218, 233 (1961). Judge Medina said he encountered this among other judges: H. Medina, Some Reflections on the Judicial Function at the Appellate Level, 1961 Wash. U.L.Q. 148, 151. See also, B. Witkin, Appellate Court Opinions, A Syllabus for Panel Discussion, 63 F.R.D. 515, 564, 565 (1974).

3. Llewellyn claims that all but a few judges learn to delay final judgment to the end. See his *The Common Law Tradition, Deciding Appeals* 46, 47, 104, 105 (1960). There are numerous comments in judges' writings that judges should keep an open mind during the various stages of the procedures, for example, G. Broadfoot, How I Go About Making Up My Mind, 31 Wisc. B. Bull. 30 (Aug. 1958). In what seems to be a counterexample an Arizona justice recently wrote that usually "the central staff is more important in preparing the information that will be considered by the court in reaching a decision, while the law clerk is more important in justifying that decision after it is made." See J. Cameron, The Central Staff: A New Solution to an Old Problem, 23 U.C.L.A.L. Rev. 465, 469 (1976).

4. Petitions for rehearing after the decision is announced, on the other hand, are probably greeted with anything but an open mind. I did not ask about this in the interviews, however. An often quoted remark is that they are received "with the upmost prejudice."

5. Alabama, Oklahoma, Tennessee, and Texas have intermediate courts or courts of last resort that decide only criminal appeals. There are a few specialized courts in the federal system, the Court of Military Appeals, the Court of Customs and Patent Appeals, the Temporary Emergency Court of Appeals, and the Court of Claims. At the trial level and among administrative tribunals, of course, there is a good deal more specialization.

Judges and lawyers, in general, frown upon the creation of specialized courts. There is an enormous amount of writing on this subject. See especially, P. Carrington, Crowded Dockets and the Courts of Appeals, 82 Harv. L. Rev. 542, 604-612 (1969); Commision on Revision of the Federal Court Appellate System, *Structure and Internal Procedures: Recommendations for Change* 28-30 (1975); *ABA Standards Relating to Court Organization* No. 1.13(b)(i). For an empirical research study, see L. Baum, Judicial Specialization, Litigant Influence, and Substantive Policy: The Court of Customs and Patent Appeals, 11 L. & Society Rev. 823 (1977); However, there is some sentiment now to place tax and patent appeals in specialized courts, mainly prompted by Judge Friendly's suggestion in H. Friendly, *Federal Jurisdiction: A*

General View 156-171 (1973). These are technical areas in which uniform law is important for the business community. For the same reasons there have been proposals that special courts decide admiralty appeals, labor appeals, appeals in environmental cases, or appeals from regulatory agencies in general. The major objections to specialized appellate courts are that the quality of judges might be low because the court is likely to have less prestige than the circuit courts and because special-interest groups may dominate the selection of judges. Also, the judges may become isolated from the mainstream of judicial thought, getting bogged down in the esoteric aspects of the speciality, and they may become bored by the lack of variation. Attorneys often believe that specialized judges are less open-minded than generalists.

6. A number of judges talked about specialization, at least one from each court. All said there was no specialization on their courts. "Specialization," however, seems to mean to some judges that the vast bulk of cases of a certain type go to specific judges, rather than a lesser tendency to give cases to judges with expertise in the area. There is no specialization, they say, if each judge gets at least a few of every type of major case.

Judges elsewhere also routinely say that they would not like to be considered specialists. See especially Friendly, *supra* note 2, at 219-225, and J. Wold, *Internal Procedures, Role Perceptions, and Judicial Behavior: A Study of Four State Courts of Last Resort* 60-64, 92-97, 118-123, 146-150 (unpublished Ph.D. dissertation, Johns Hopkins University, 1972).

7. For good discussions about the relative merits of the two assignment methods see B. Witkin, *supra* note 2, at 543-545; National Center for State Courts, *The Appellate Process in Alabama* 127-131 (1973); G. Smith, The Appellate Decisional Conference, 28 Ark. L. Rev. 425, 431-433 (1975); R. Leflar, *Internal Operating Procedures of Appellate Courts* 39, 40 (1976); E. Slotnick, Who Speaks for the Court? The View from the States, 26 Emory L.J. 107, 111, 112, 133-138 (1977).

8. H. Medina, The Decisional Process, 20 N.Y.Co.B. Bull. 94, 98 (1962).

9. A study of opinion assigning patterns in state courts also found some deviation from strict rotation, but resulting mainly from assigned judges being in the minority: Slotnick, *supra* note 7, at 112-114, 137.

10. The most thorough study of state court practices is Slotnick's questionnaire survey of state supreme court chief justices. Seventeen chief justices said they assigned cases (out of forty-five answering the questionnaire, though it appears that some of the seventeen assigned cases on a rotation basis). They were asked the importance of a long list of possible factors entering into their assignment decisions. The most important were getting all the court's work done and equalizing the opinion work load. But expertise was considered a very important factor by six chief justices and somewhat important by seven. (Also of considerable importance were maintaining harmony on the court, the importance of the case, and the need to hold a majority together.) See Slotnick *supra* note 7, at 129. Similar views concerning the New Jersey, Maryland, and Delaware courts can be found in J. Weintraub, Writing, Consideration, and Adoption of Opinions, 83 N.J.L.J. 477, 478 (1960), and Wold, *supra* note 6, at 60-64, 146-150.

As for the federal circuit courts, one study has found a quite uneven pattern of assignments, especially in labor and tax cases, but rarely does a judge get assigned no cases in a major area of the law. See B. Atkins, Opinion Assignments on the United States Court of Appeals: The Question of Issue Specialization, 27 W. Pol. Q. 409

(1974). This is generally supported by other descriptions of the assignment process, though balancing the work load is considered the most important criteria. (Atkins found some imbalance in the number of opinions written, but the number of opinions need not reflect the actual amount of work involved. Also there was some tendency for the chief judges to give themselves more cases then they gave colleagues.) On opinion assignments in circuit courts, see: Committee on Federal Courts, The Association of the Bar of the City of New York, *Appeals to the Second Circuit* 45, 46 (1975); Cincinnati Chapter of the Federal Bar Association, *Practitioners' Handbook for Appeals to the United States Court of Appeals for the Sixth Circuit* 47 (1973); M. Schick, *Learned Hand's Court* 100, 101, 217 (1970); Medina, *supra* note 8, at 98, 101, 102; J. Parker, Improving Appellate Methods, 25 N.Y.U.L. Rev. 1, 12 (1950).

11. This is the practice on at least the D.C., Second, Fifth, and Ninth Circuits. Remarks of George Fisher, Proceedings of the Thirty-seventh Annual Judicial Conference of the District of Columbia Circuit, 73 F.R.D. 141, 155-159 (1977); Committee on Federal Courts, *supra* note 10, at 25, 48; United States Court of Appeals for the Fifth Circuit, *Internal Operating Procedures Manual*, 19-22 (1976); Statements by E. Wright and R. Chambers before the Commission on Revision of the Federal Court Appellate System, First Phase, August 28, 1973, pages 729, 730, 764, 765. The assignment of judges to panels and then the assignment of cases to the panels tend to be a very complicated business on the circuit courts; considerable effort is made to isolate the judges from the actual assignment of cases to specific panels, to make sure that each judge sits an equal number of times with each other judge, and to make sure time-consuming cases are spread evenly among the panels.

Several important scholars have advocated that large intermediate courts operate with broadly specialized parts, mainly to ensure consistency in a court's rulings. A court would be divided into about a half-dozen sections, each having sole jurisdiction in one or several areas of law, and the judges would rotate between divisions every few years. See P. Carrington, D. Meador, and M. Rosenberg, *Justice on Appeal* 174-184, 204-206 (1976). However, the Commission on Revision of the Federal Court Appellate System (*supra* note 5, at 60) rejected this idea for the circuit courts, largely because it felt that the person assigning cases to panels would have considerable discretion and, therefore, power to affect results by chosing panels with known leanings. The Arizona intermediate court has had a panel that specialized in workman's compensation cases, but specialized panels are extremely rare even in state courts. *ABA Standards Relating to Appellate Courts* No. 3.54 calls for assignment of cases to panels by strict rotation.

12. W. Schaefer, The Advocate as a Lawmaker: The Advocate in the Reviewing Courts, 1956 U. Ill. L.F. 203, 204.

13. The great majority of judges and clerks were asked about this. The judges so routinely said they put their reasons in their opinions that in several interviews I asked if they favored short opinions and, when they said yes, I asked if that led them to leave out reasons for the decisions. All but one said it did not.

14. A good many judges have written that opinions should be short. See especially the comments in Witkin, *supra* note 2, at 567-575. As is discussed in Chapter 10, one type of facts of the case, called "supporting case facts," is rarely mentioned (probably because mentioning them would make opinions extremely long); and the use of case facts in lawmaking is often not evident from the opinions.

15. R. Leflar, Some Observations Concerning Judicial Opinions, 61 Colum. L.

Rev. 810, 817 (1961). Leflar later wrote that judges should recognize that judge-made law changes with the times, and then "above all, the opinions of the court would be honest; the true reasons, in contrast to technical or clever formalistic ones, would be given for its decisions." See Leflar, *supra* note 7, at 131. Just how often the Supreme Court actually does cite social facts, as Leflar said it does, is uncertain. Davis states:

> How much the Supreme Court goes beyond the record for legislative facts to guide the making of law and policy cannot be accurately ascertained from the opinions because the practice undoubtedly exceeds specific formal acknowledgments of the practice. But the acknowledgments are numerous enough to show that the practice is a commonplace one. *K. Davis, Administrative Law Treatise* sec. 15.03 (1958).

16. Half the clerks were also asked about this, and they tended to believe that the social facts were mentioned in the opinions more often than the judges believed, though the difference was not great.

17. Only a few judges and clerks discussed this point. They generally said some research in this area was not mentioned in the opinions, though it very often is. A Kansas justice has said that he believes social science materials are important in deciding cases, but the court usually limits its citations from these sources. See G. Mason, *Judges and Their Publics: Role Perceptions and Role Expectations* 283 (unpublished Ph.D. dissertation, University of Kansas, 1967).

18. For general statements that opinions often do not reflect the reasons for decisions, see Leflar, *supra* note 15, at 816-819; W. Schaefer, Precedent and Policy, 34 U. Chi. L. Rev. 3, 5, 10, 11, 16 (1966); J. Frank, *Courts on Trial* 258 (1949); C. Horowitz, Judging Judgments, 7 Gonzaga L. Rev. 1, 3 (1971); J. Oakes, Law Reviews and Judging, 50 N.Y.U.L. Rev. 2 (1975); R. Aldisert, *The Judicial Process, Readings, Materials and Cases* 464 (1976); C. Breitel, Book Review, 61 Colum. L. Rev. 931, 939 (1961); see also the statement by Justice Cameron in note 3. The only writings by judges I have found expressing the opposite view are: S. Fuld, The Voices of Dissent, 62 Colum. L. Rev. 923, 929 (1962); and B. Shientag, The Personality of the Judge, in *Handbook for Judges* 67, 71 (American Judicature Society, 1961).

Judge Breitel, like the earlier cited ex-justice Leflar, claims that judges often do not mention social fact or policy arguments underlying decisions, but that they should do so: C. Breitel, The Lawmakers, 65 Colum. L. Rev. 749, 774, 775 (1965) and The Courts and Lawmaking, in *Legal Institutions Today and Tomorrow* 1, 39 (M. Paulsen ed. 1959).

Besides Breitel and Leflar, several other judges have said that policy considerations are sometimes left out of opinions: J. Craven, Pean to Pragmatism, 50 N.C.L. Rev. 977, 981, 983 (1972); J. Hopkins, Fictions and the Judicial Process: A Preliminary Theory of Decision, 33 Brooklyn L. Rev. 1, 6, 7 (1966); R. Neely, A Glimpse into Judges' Chambers, 7 Juris Doctor 33, *passim* (Dec. 1977); A. Tate, "Policy" in Judicial Decisions, 20 La. L. Rev. 62, 65, 67, 70, 71 (1969). Two other judges strongly imply, without specifically stating, that they often leave these factors unstated: G. Smith, A Primer of Opinion Writing for Law Clerks, 26 Vand. L. Rev. 1203, 1207 (1973); Parker, *supra* note 10, at 12, 13. It should be noted, also, that when a judge cites a prior case or an accepted rule, he may also have in mind the policy arguments behind the precedent or rule and feel he need not mention them.

There is, in addition, a great deal of comment by law professors to the effect that reasons often are not in the decisions, especially professors in the "realist" school earlier this century.

19. But the judges cited in note 18 freely admit in writing that opinions need not reflect a judges' reasons, though several seemed to talk in terms of other judges and said that reasons should be in the opinions.

20. Federal Judicial Center Cassette No. J-122, Nature of Judge-Made Law (1975). In a later conference Judge (now Justice) Stevens criticized the Supreme Court for not candidly giving its reasons for deciding a case, and Judge Aldisert of the Third Circuit announced "the Aldisert thesis: that a judge who would be intellectually honest should equate the reasons set forth *publicly* in his opinion with his motivation for reaching the decision. The "why" a decision was made should be *publicly expressed in the essay*," not because of ethics, but to indicate to the bar how future cases will be decided: Federal Judicial Center Cassette N. J-130, October 1973 Term (1975), and Cassette N. J-131, Appellate Judicial Opinions (1975).

Other judges saying that opinions have become more candid are Hopkins, *supra* note 18, at 6, and Breitel (1959) *supra* note 18, at 39. But note that there are more recent articles saying that opinions still do not reflect the judges' reasons.

21. Reasons for or against stating one's reasons were seldom given in the interviews. This discussion is based mainly on the sources mentioned in notes 18 and 20. Llewellyn, *supra* note 3, at 42, 43, discusses the problems attorneys have when reasons for decisions remain hidden, and Davis suggests that there be a rule requiring that courts state influential social facts they use when not free from doubt so that the parties can answer them, although the "mainstream of practice" is for the courts to state these facts anyway. See K. Davis, Judicial Notice, 1969 L. and Soc. Order 513, 526.

22. The great majority of judges were asked this, and the Massachusetts and Ohio justices were more likely to say they cared about impressing themselves only. Most of the judges when answering this question mentioned audiences they wrote to, clearly distinguishing this from trying to impress. As far as I know, virtually nothing has been written about who judges try to impress; much has been written about their audience, however, for example, Leflar, *supra* note 15, at 811-814; Weintraub, *supra* note 10, at 478; F. Hale, The Court's Perception of the Press, 57 Judicature 183, 187 (1973).

23. Less than half the judges were asked about the effect of public opinion on their votes; several, all from the focal and Ohio courts, said it might affect votes in some cases, and the rest said it did not affect votes. Judges on these two courts are elected, and they usually added that that was the reason public opinion had an effect. The Rhode Island justices can be recalled by the state legislature, but I asked three if they worried about legislative reaction and all said no. Political scientists have asked more than seventy appellate judges whether "public opinion" or "public demands" affect their decisions, and the great majority said it has little or no effect. There does not seem to be any difference between elected and appointed judges here, however. See Mason, *supra* note 17, at 293, 294; J. Howard, *Role Perceptions on the U.S. Courts of Appeals for the 2d, 5th, and D.C. Circuits* 38 (Federal Judicial Center,

1973); J. Beatty, *An Institutional and Behavioral Analysis of the Iowa Supreme Court—1965-1969* 275-277 (unpublished Ph.D. dissertation, University of Iowa, 1970); C. Sheldon, Contrasting Judicial Roles: Trial Vs. Appellate, 11 Judges' J. 72 (1972). Also, according to judicial ethics, a judge should not be swayed by "public clamor," *ABA Code of Judicial Conduct* No. 3A(1).

Based on what some judges said in the interviews and in numerous writings, they are very thick-skinned about press criticism of their decisions, viewing it as ill-founded and unknowledgeable, except as it affects the respect given courts. See especially Hale, *supra* note 22. Many courts, nevertheless, have recently employed public relations officers, mainly to condense and explain opinions for the press.

24. This idea is probably universal among judges. They often make speeches about it, and it cropped up many times in the interviews. I found that if you ask a judge what he thinks of his robes, he will say that they are good because they help preserve the image of the courts and the legal system. Also, public opinion is a prime impetus behind judicial restraint, as will be discussed later, and is, of course, behind the numerous things judicial ethics require so that judges will appear impartial.

Another important aspect of public opinion in appellate courts is taking into account customs and attitudes of people in the same manner as other social facts when making law. Judges place great value in keeping the laws up with the times, as is said in Chapter 10, and this necessarily involves keeping track of changes in public opinion. Some broad legal rules have elements of public opinion built into them, such that it is often part of fashioning specific rules—for example, the prohibition against cruel and unusual punishment and the moral aspects in immigration laws.

25. Only a dozen judges talked about the effect of public opinion on the language of opinions; most said it did have an effect in a few rare cases, mainly again at elected courts.

26. Only several judges discussed this topic, and most said they never do it. One study found that this was the practice on at least some state intermediate courts. See M. Wall, What the Courts Are Doing to Improve Judicial Opinions, 32 J. Am. Jud. Soc'y 148, 151 (1949).

27. A number of judges and clerks talked about whether judges tried for majority or unanimous opinions. The focal court justices are less interested in these than judges on the other five courts, and dissenting and concurring opinions are much more frequent there.

28. Oakes, *supra* note 18, at 2. Whether dissenting or concurring opinions reflect the authors' reasons more than majority opinions is a difficult question. Cardozo has written, "Comparatively speaking, at least, the dissenter is irresponsible. The spokesman of the court is cautious, timid, fearful of the vivid word, the heightened phrase. . . . Not so, however, the dissenter. He has laid aside the role of the hierophant, which he will be only too glad to resume when the chances of war make him the spokesman of the majority." B. Cardozo, *Selected Writings of Benjamin Nathan Cardozo* 353 (1947). One judge interviewed volunteered that he writes his thoughts more freely in dissents. However, I know of no more statements by judges suggesting that dissentioning opinions express a judge's reasons more fully or accurately than majority opinions. Probably the opposite is the case; minority opinions often address only areas of disagreement with the majority, instead of fully explaining the authors' views.

29. At least two state supreme courts tape-record judges' conferences (see note 6

of Chapter 1); so that the judges there have a rather complete account of colleagues' views if the conference discussions are comprehensive. Elsewhere, judges may take notes, more or less thoroughly, of colleagues' views.

30. Institute of Judicial Administration, *Appellate Courts, Internal Operating Procedures. 1959 Summary and Supplement* 14. The Arkansas court has since stopped doing this. See G. Smith, A Primer of Opinion Writing, for Four New Judges, 21 Ark. L. Rev. 197, 202 (1967).

31. I received information on the topics in this and the previous paragraph about the great majority of judges interviewed, either from the judges or their clerks. There is discussion on the topic in the legal literature about a dozen circuit courts and state supreme courts, mainly judges' writings. They all substantiate the thrust here that courts differ greatly in the amount of minor changes and that major changes are not often made. (The U.S. Supreme Court Justices, though, often make major changes). Two research studies have discussed the topic. One found that changes are very frequently requested in the Maryland and Virginia courts of last resort, and less often in the New York and Delaware courts. However, at all four suggestions for major changes are unusual. See Wold, *supra* note 6, at 66, 67, 97, 98, 103, 127, 151. The second study, made almost thirty years ago, appears to have found the same pattern, though the results are not clearly presented. See Wall, *supra* note 26, at 149.

32. Most of the judges and clerks talked about each topic in this paragraph. The emphasis on getting along well is probably typical of all courts. Judges' writings, for example, often mention that relations with colleagues are friendly. Two political scientists, studying eight state courts of last resort, found that emphasis. See Wold, *supra* note 6, at 171, 236, 237, 242, 243, 246-248; H. Glick, *Supreme Courts in State Politics* 58-63 (1971). One of the courts Glick studied, the Pennsylvania Supreme Court, was well known at that time for the rancor among some of its members. Also, there used to be considerable animosity at the Second Circuit. Schick, *supra* note 10, at Chapter 7 especially.

33. Judges definitely do not feel that one should "go along to get along." See Glick, *supra* note 32, at 65; Beatty, *supra* note 23, at 224, 225.

34. Schaefer, *supra* note 18, at 10. Most judges, though, say that criticism is less hindered than Justice Schaefer suggests. In Texas, for example, it is given "unrestrained by fear of giving offense to the author." See R. Calvert, The Mechanics of Judgment Making in the Supreme Court of Texas, 21 Baylor L. Rev. 439, 449 (1969). The judges' stress on judicial secrecy, discussed in Chapter 1, of course facilitates frankness among the judges.

35. The California Supreme Court certainly has such a rule. See L. Burke, Chairman's Column, 15 Oyez Oyez 1 (July 1972).

36. The justices often say the strong language in the opinions does not reflect ill will. See, for example, C. Whittaker, The Role of the Supreme Court, 17 Ark. L. Rev. 292, 300 (1963); L. Powell, Myths and Misconceptions About the Supreme Court, 61 A.B.A.J. 1344 (1975).

37. Almost half the judges were asked about this.

38. This is the gist of what several judges and clerks said about influence among the judges. It is a difficult subject because of judicial secrecy and because of the considerations discussed in the last chapter with respect to the clerks' influence. One thing seems certain, however: there is no logrolling on the courts.

39. Llewellyn, *supra* note 3, at 131, 132, and see also pp. 52-59 and 124-135. He

also gives convincing evidence that a cited case virtually always supports the point for which it is cited, *supra* at 101-106, 258, 260. Justice Breitel criticizes Llewellyn for relying too much on the opinions to discover the reasons for deciding. See C. Breitel, Book Review, 61 Colum. L. Rev. 931, 939 (1961). And Llewellyn does rely largely on opinions as a source of information about how judges decide (though he often reads between the lines of opinions, also). Thus, like myself, he is subject to a common bias: One who relies on a source of data is tempted to overstate its accuracy. It is difficult to know whether one is being objective in a situation like that.

40. Because law clerks draft many opinions, perhaps parts of some reflect the clerks' views rather than the judges'. But, as was seen in Chapter 6, the judges ordinarily either discuss the issues at length with the clerks before or during the drafting, or greatly edit the drafts afterward. The opinions, then, are unlikely to contain major departures from the judges' thinking on this account; although a few judges may leave details to the clerks' discretion, for instance, the particular cases cited in support of a contention.

CHAPTER 8

1. "A decision is not authority as to any questions of law which were not raised or presented to the court, and were not considered and decided by it, even though they were logically present in the case and might have been argued, and even though such questions, if considered by the court, would have caused a different judgment to be given." See Black, *Law of Judicial Precedent* 37 (1912), as quoted in E. Re, *Brief Writing and Oral Argument* 91 (4th ed. 1974).

2. Note, Raising New Issues on Appeal, 64 Harv. L. Rev. 652, 653 (1951).

3. The word "issue" is the more commonly used, but "question" is the formal term—the list of issues at the beginning of a brief is called the "statement of questions" in the focal court. "Error" (in the court below) is sometimes used also. When these three terms are used, one can be quite sure they refer to what I mean by "issue" here. Many other words can refer to an issue, but are also used to refer to a legal argument within an issue, for example: ground, contention, theory, argument, point, problem, claim, and aspect. "Assignments of error" under appellate rules common earlier this century, but largely abandoned now, are much more restrictive than "issues."

4. Examples of this distinction will be given later in the chapter. As a practical matter, I seldom used these definitions except when determining whether the court used issues not raised. In the interviews I just asked about issues, and only one judge and one clerk asked what the term meant, and there was no sign that people had differing notions of its meaning. When studying the focal court cases, I just used the judges' and attorneys' designation of issues if I could. Generally, there was broad agreement on what the issues were. When there was not, I used the court's definition. In the few times that was unsatisfactory, I had to make a rough determination based on the definitions in the text.

A problem similar to the present one of defining and differentiating between issues results from Sanders v. United States, 373 U.S. 1 (1963), in which the Supreme Court held that the federal courts need not entertain an application for habeas corpus or other postconviction relief if the prisoner had argued "the same grounds presented" in an earlier application. A "ground" is apparently similar to what I mean by issue, though the court's definition of the term is vague. At page 16, it is defined as "a sufficient legal basis for granting the relief sought by the applicant," for example, a contention that a confession was involuntary. The same "ground" can include separate contentions based on different facts and different legal arguments. The court said a claim of involuntary confession alleging psychological coersion is not a different ground from one alleging physical coersion. The problem here, as with my definition of issues, is that there is little with which to judge how different the facts and legal arguments must be for there to be separate grounds. However, as a practical matter, the lower federal courts have evidenced little trouble in determining whether separate grounds are involved. See R. Williamson, Federal Habeas Corpus: Limitations on Successive Applications from the Same Prisoner, 15 Wm. & Mary L. Rev. 265, 274 (1973). This provides some evidence that distinguishing between issues is not very often difficult.

5. This reluctance certainly exists at other courts as well. See A. Vestal, Sua Sponte Consideration in Appellate Review, 27 Fordham L. Rev. 477, *passim* (1958-1959); 5 *Am. Jur. 2d* Appeal and Error, secs. 654, 655 (1962).

6. Only about half the judges were asked about the reasons for their reluctance to decide issues not raised. The three reasons mentioned in the text (unfairness to counsel, lack of information, and reluctance to decide issues not raised below) were given with equal frequency. Also, a few judges said that they did not have enough time to decide these issues or did not want to do the extra work required. (Deciding an issue not raised, however, may save time and work if doing so would obviate the need to decide more difficult issues in the case.) Several judges, in addition, said that one reason for not deciding many issues not raised is simply that the attorneys did not often miss the major issues. The reasons given in the legal literature are very similar to those given by the judges interviewed. See Vestal, *supra* note 5, at 483-495, 508-510; D. Rendleman, The Scope of Review in Criminal Appeals and the Iowa Judgment on the Record Statute, 22 Drake L. Rev. 477, 479 (1973); Note, Appellate-Court Sua Sponte Activity: Remaking Disputes and the Rule of Non-Intervention, 40 So. Calif. L. Rev. 352, 360-364 (1967).

7. Lawyers would certainly like the chance to speak to these issues, as is evidenced by the discussion at the end of this section. See also the comments in B. Witkin, Appellate Court Opinions—A Syllabus for Panel Discussion, 63 F.R.D. 515, 565 (1974). However, Judge Medina and Justice Tate claim that it is not often worthwhile to ask for rebriefing, since the attorneys are not likely to add much and they have a chance to make objections in rehearing petitions. See H. Medina, Some Reflections on the Judicial Function at the Appellate Level, 1961 Wash. U.L.Q. 148, 152; A. Tate, Sua Sponte Consideration on Appeal, 9 Trial Judges' J. 68 (1970). Justice Tate also, like the Ohio judge in the text, says rebriefing would delay the appellate process. Other judges, though, feel that the attorneys should always be given a chance to file supplementary briefs, for example, M. Conford, Management of Oral Argument by an Appellate Court, 14 Judges' J. 14, 15 (1975).

8. Only several judges talked about the reasons for not deciding issues not raised below. Another reason given is that trial counsel should not be tempted to ignore issues below in order to leave himself a second chance on appeal, but this hardly applies if the issue is not raised in the briefs. Most of these reasons are also the rea-

sons commonly given in the legal literature. See Vestal *supra* note 5, at 490-492; Re, *supra* note 1, at 71-78; Rendleman, *supra* note 6, at 483-486; Note (1951), *supra* note 2, *passim*; Note (1967), *supra* note 6, at 355, 356.

9. In only three cases did the opinions (two majority and one dissenting) say that the issue had not been raised; but in three others this could be guessed from a close reading of the opinions.

The total of nineteen issues does not include cases in which the court spotted an issue in the application for leave process and summarily reversed the case or sent it back to a lower court for consideration of the issue. This happened quite often, especially when the issue related to a recent ruling of the court. Also, this does not include issues not raised discussed in dissenting or concurring opinions, which happened in four more cases. Four of the nineteen issues not raised had been argued and decided in the lower courts but not briefed in the final appeal.

10. A court decides an issue not raised when the issue involves case facts or legal arguments unrelated and dissimilar to those in the issues presented by counsel. This is not a precise definition, but as a practical matter there was seldom any doubt that the issue was new. All nineteen of the issues not raised involved legal arguments that differed from those presented in the briefs, but about half the time the facts involved were similar to those emphasized by counsel with respect to other issues. Only one of these nineteen involved any real problem about classifying it as a new issue; the plaintiff in an automobile accident case argued that the defense did not lay a proper foundation for the introduction of an automobile part into evidence because the part was not shown to be similar to the one used in the car involved in the accident. The court, besides agreeing with the plaintiff, added that the expertise of the witness demonstrating the part had not been established.

It may be helpful to give an example of a case in which the court was fairly close to deciding an issue not raised, but the legal arguments used were similar enough to those in plaintiff's issue to call it the same issue. Plaintiff argued that a law requiring him to connect with the town's sewer system, even though his septic tank was adequate, was an unconstitutional taking of property without compensation. He also argued that a provision in the state's constitution requiring that the body of the act fall within the scope of its title was violated because the title said the statute would apply to counties with a population of over 75,000 people, while the applicable section of the statute was limited to counties over 300,000. The court ruled for the plaintiff on the grounds that the title of the act referred only to requiring properties that emanated sewage to connect with the sewage system, and it was not shown that the plaintiff's property did so.

11. This habit of deciding new issues not really needed to decide the case is probably unusual. Several judges on other courts said they only decide dispositive issues not raised, and Vestal (*supra* note 5, at 505) says that courts will probably only consider issues not raised that are of real importance in the case.

12. Mass. Ann. Laws ch. 278 sec. 33E. At least a half-dozen other states have had search-the-record statutes for criminal cases. See Rendleman, *supra* note 6, at 481. But during the past few years the laws have been repealed in half these states.

13. See the authorities in note 5, which, however, base their discussion on the courts' opinions. Judges often mention quickly that they will not consider issues not raised in the appellant's brief—for example, see Justice Hammond's remarks in A.

Scanlan, Effective Appellate Advocacy in the Court of Appeals of Maryland, 29 Md. L. Rev. 126, 132 (1969). On the other hand, Judge Medina (*supra* note 7, at 152) said that the Second Circuit sometimes decided issues not raised, and he has known one or two judges who were always on the alert for them. And two judges, from Idaho and Louisiana, have urged that these issues be decided to provide justice in the individual case: R. Bakes, Appellate Procedure— An Evolutionary Backwater, 10 Idaho L. Rev. 117 (1974); Tate, *supra* note 7. See also G. Currie, Questions to the Court, 31 Wisc. B. Bull. 34, 37 (Aug. 1958).

In an experimental use of staff attorneys at four state courts, the staff found, but did not actively search for, issues not raised. The Nebraska Supreme Court refused to consider them, unless they were jurisdictional issues. The Supreme Court of Virginia, the Appellate Court of Illinois, First District, and the Superior Court of New Jersey, Appellate Division, apparently considered issues found by the staff. See D. Meador, *Appellate Courts, Staff and Process in the Crisis of Volume* 45, 46 (1974). Staff attorneys in the U.S. Court of Military Appeals and the Michigan Court of Appeals are instructed to raise new issues. *Id.* at 219, 220, 223, 224; T. Lesinski and N. Stockmeyer, Prehearing Research and Screening in the Michigan Court of Appeals: One Court's Method for Increasing Judicial Productivity, 26 Vand. L. Rev. 1211, 1217 (1973).

Two judges on the Court of Appeals of Ohio, Eighth Appellate District (Cleveland) mentioned in tape-recorded interviews that they often decide issues not raised; one said "at least thirty-five percent of the time we resolve cases on issues not raised by appealing counsel," and the other said the court finds issues not raised in 10 percent of the cases. See J. Harley, *Establishing Criteria for Effective Oral Argument Before a Court of Appeals* 130, 131, 139 (unpublished Ph.D. dissertation, Case Western Reserve University, 1976).

There is some thought now that appellate courts should actively search for issues in criminal cases and decide them even though not raised in order to lessen the chances of further attack on the conviction, for example, National Advisory Commission on Criminal Justice Standards and Goals, *Courts* 119-124 (1973). See also P. Carrington, D. Meador, and M. Rosenberg, *Justice on Appeal*, 85, 109-113 (1976).

Apparently it was quite common for courts to decide issues not raised in the middle of the past century, and the practice lessened considerably by the end of the century. See R. Pound, *Appellate Procedure in Civil Cases* 185, 186 (1941). The practice was probably more common in equity appeals. See L. Orfield, Appellate Procedure in Equity Cases: A Guide for Appeals at Law, 90 U. Pa. L. Rev. 563, 576-579 (1942).

The U.S. Supreme Court sometimes decides cases on issues not raised. The most famous examples are Erie v. Tompkins, 304 U.S. 64 (1938) and Mapp v. Ohio, 367 U.S. 643 (1961). The Justices have done this quite a bit recently; for example, there were at least four cases in 1974: O'Shea v. Littleton, 414 U.S. 488 (1974); Vachon v. New Hampshire, 414 U.S. 478 (1974); Mayor v. Educational Equality League, 415 U.S. 605, 642 (1974) (Justice White dissenting); Fuller v. Oregon, 417 U.S. 40 (1974).

Some scholars frown on the practice of deciding on issues not raised, for example, K. Llewellyn, *The Common Law Tradition, Deciding Appeals* 29, 325 (1960); National Center for State Courts, *The Appellate Process in Alabama* 143-148 (1973); G. Christie, Objectivity in the Law, 78 Yale L.J. 1311, 1329-1333 (1969). However, see *James, Civil Procedure* sec. 1.2 (1965).

14. In a recent study the Second Circuit judges were asked to answer questions about several hundred cases, including whether any essential issues were omitted from the briefs. Almost 85 percent answered no, suggesting that in roughly 15 percent of the cases the judges noticed essential issues not raised. See J. Goldman, *An Evaluation of the Civil Appeals Management Plan: An Experiment in Judicial Administration* 68 (Federal Judicial Center, 1977). There is no indication in the study about how many of these issues were decided by the court.

15. Vestal, *supra* note 5, at 499-502. Mootness, standing, and appealability are often subsumed under the label of jurisdiction for this purpose. (None of the nineteen issues not raised that the focal court decided, however, was of this type.) Courts, also, will probably look for and decide issues not raised when defendant's appellate counsel in a criminal case asks to withdraw from the case, claiming that there are no issues worth appealing, under Anders v. California, 386 U.S. 738 (1967). I suspect that there are some kinds of issues that courts so routinely raise on their own that it has never come to light in the opinions, for example, whether an error is harmless and whether an objection has been made below.

16. Vestal, *supra* note 5, at 503-506; "Illusive" is Vestal's description of the fundamental error concept. The U.S. Supreme Court Rule 40(1) (d)(2) says bluntly that the Court "at its option, may notice a plain error not presented." Justice Bakes said, "these rules are noted mostly for the indiscriminate manner of their application." See Bakes, *supra* note 13, at 121.

17. This statement is based on comments by most of the judges and clerks interviewed. Even the U.S. Supreme Court has this problem. J. Wilkinson, *Serving Justice* 30 (1974).

A few courts, notably the Second Circuit, now often require counsel to meet with staff attorneys before oral arguments, partly to try to settle the case and partly to get lawyers to simplify the issues. See the Committee on Federal Courts, The Association of the Bar of the City of New York, *Appeals to the Second Circuit* 15 (1975). Former Supreme Court Justice Clark has said of this procedure:

> Now, this coordinating clerk also talks to them about points; what points are you raising? It is amazing the number of points these people raise. They raise eight and ten points in a case. Well, you know as well as I do that there are not that many points in a case, and there surely are not that many points that are of a reversible nature that would require reversal. They could narrow them down. Hearings before the Commission on Revision of the Federal Court Appellate System, Second Phase, 247 (1974).

18. The court's opinions did not mention 38 percent of the issues raised in the briefs. Half of these were not needed for the decision because the case was decided on other issues, and half were needed for the decision but apparently were not discussed because they were considered frivolous (a few were moot). This first category of issues is not included when deriving the figure of one-fourth to one-third because there is no indication of how many were considered insubstantial, though many of them certainly were. The determination of whether the court covered an issue in the opinion only quickly is, of course, very subjective; thus only a rough estimate is possible.

CHAPTER 9

1. This is the gist of what a number of judges said in the interviews (and many others have said elsewhere) about statutes and the willingness to depart from precedent. Judges also vary greatly in their willingness to consider statutes ambiguous and precedents distinguishable such that they need not be applied in the case.

There is an especially large body of literature showing the importance of precedent in appellate decision making. Political scientists have asked judges on ten state courts of last resort and four federal circuit courts how important precedent is in deciding cases. Virtually all said it is important; the vast majority say it is very important. See J. Wold, *Internal Procedures, Role Perceptions and Judicial Behavior: A Study of Four State Courts of Last Resort* 200, 201 (unpublished PhD. dissertation, The Johns Hopkins University, 1972); H. Glick, *Supreme Courts in State Politics* 76 (1971); J. Beatty, *An Institutional and Behavioral Analysis of the Iowa Supreme Court* 264, 265 (unpublished Ph.D. dissertation, University of Iowa, 1970); G. Mason, *Judges and Their Publics: Role Perceptions and Role Expectations* 270 (unpublished Ph.D. dissertation, University of Kansas, 1967); J. Howard, *Role Perceptions on the U.S. Courts of Appeals for the 2d, 5th, and D.C. Circuits* 37, 38 (Federal Judicial Center Research Report No. 2, 1973); F. Rich, *Role Perception and Precedent Orientation as Variables Influencing Appellate Judicial Decision-Making: An Analysis of the Fifth Circuit Court of Appeals* 100 (unpublished Ph.D. dissertation, University of Georgia, 1967).

As to judges' writings, probably the strongest indication of the importance of precedent is that even those who argue for more leeway in overruling precedent accord precedent great importance, for example, B. Cardozo, *The Nature of Judicial Process* 20 (1921); W. Schaefer, Precedent and Policy, 34 U. Chi. L. Rev. 3, 4, 5 (1966); J. Hutcheson, The Glorious Uncertainty of Our Lady of the Law, 23 J. Am. Jud. Soc'y. 73, 76 (1939); R. Traynor, Interweavers in the Reformation of Law, 42 Cal. St. B.J. 817, 819 (1967).

2. In the interviews most clerks talked about the judges' first deciding how they would like the issues decided and then studying the legal authority to see whether that outcome could be supported. They generally said it happened frequently, often calling it "result oriented." I only talked to several judges about this, but most said it was sometimes done. However, I do not know how the clerks and judges could tell on most issues which of the two approaches was taken because information about legal authorities arrives at the court along with the other information the judges receive about the case and because the judges often already know a good deal about the law in the area before hearing the appeal; thus one would have to separate out the influence of the legal authorities from that of other elements involved in the issues, a difficult task—especially for the clerks, when talking about someone else's thinking process.

Judges do not often write about this topic. Justice Tate has said that, when there is no legal authority directly on point, he sometimes, though rarely, decides on a result and then looks for supporting authorities. See A. Tate, "Policy" in Judicial Decisions, 20 La. L. Rev. 62, 68, 72 (1959). Also see his Book Review, 39 Tulane L. Rev. 163, 174 (1964). Judge Craven strongly implies that there is much result orientation, especially in important cases. See J. Craven, Paean to Pragmatism, 50 N.C.L. Rev.

977, 980, 981 (1972). Judge Magruder wrote that when the U.S. Supreme Court had
not decided a point, the First Circuit sometimes decided by guessing how the Supreme
Court would go and sometimes by making what the court thought to be the best
decisions. He said there was no particular reason for doing one or the other, and any
reason he gave would seem a mere rationalization. See C. Magruder, The Trials and
Tribulations of an Intermediate Appellate Court, 44 Cornell L.Q. 1, 5 (1958). New
Hampshire Justice Lampron has advised appellate lawyers that one purpose of oral
argument is "to arouse the emotions of the members of the court so that they will be
moved to act on behalf of your client," but the litigant will lose if "you convince
them on the emotional level that your client had a raw deal, but fail to convince them
on the intellectual level that there is anything they can properly do about it." See E.
Lampron, Observations on Appellate Advocacy, 14 N.H.B.J. 105, 106 (1972). Along
the same line, see B. Shientag, The Appellate Division, First Department, Its Jurisdiction, How It Functions in Conference, Briefs and Oral Arguments Presented to
It, 5 Record 377, 415, 416 (1950), and T. Chadick, An Effective Appellate Brief, 26
Texas B.J. 923, 972 (1963). But on the whole this type of advice is unusual in the
judges' writings on appellate advocacy. On the other side, Judge Medina said that
before he sat on the bench he believed that as a judge he would "look to see what I
wanted to do and then . . . find a way to do it." But that is not what happened:
"When you have the responsibility it looks a little bit different. I get up there and I
am trying to find out what the law is, not what I want it to be," unless there is no
authority in the area. See H. Medina, The Decisional Process in the United States
Court of Appeals, Second Circuit, Part III, 149 N.Y.L.J. 4 (Feb. 20, 1963).

For factors that may lead a judge to reach a decision independent of the authorities
see the discussion of "justice" and deciding by emotions in Chapter 1, and the discussion of fireside equities and social facts in Chapter 10.

3. "The labor of judges would be increased almost to the breaking point if every
past decision could be reopened in every case." See B. Cardozo, *supra* note 1, at 149.
See also J. Frank, *Courts on Trial* 254, 255, 272-274 (1949).

4. In the interviews, most of the judges talked about reasons for following precedent; the great majority said it was to preserve predictability. Also, several gave as a
reason the need to respect the wisdom of the past judges, which might imply the
second reason for the importance of legal authority above—the impossibility of restudying the legal rules in every case. The need to preserve predictability is often cited
elsewhere by judges and others as the basis for following precedent. "The most
frequent, and perhaps the most substantial, argument made against a court's departure from precedent is that a sudden shift in the law will frustrate past transactions
made in reliance on existing law" (Schaefer, *supra* note 1, at 15). However, perhaps
people really do not rely much on precedent. See Judge Frank in Aero Spark Plug
Co. v. B. G. Corporation, 130 F. 2d 290, at 298 (1942), and S. Macaulay, Elegant
Models, Empirical Pictures, and the Complexities of Contract, 11 L. & Soc'y Rev.
507 (1977). And the problem of reliance can be greatly mitigated by prospective overruling. See Schaefer, *supra*, at 15-17. Cardozo (*supra* note 1, at 34, 112) gives an additional reason for following precedent: to make the courts appear impartial. For
long lists of reasons for following precedent, adding a few not discussed here, see J.
Merryman, The Authority of Authority, 6 Stan. L. Rev. 613, 621 (1954); C. Lobin-
gier, Precedent in Past and Present Legal Systems, 44 Mich. L. Rev. 955, 990 (1946).

5. A number of judges talked about this saying; they were evenly split between those who flatly disagreed with the notion and those who believed it to be true for at least some areas of the law.

6. The majority of attorneys interviewed talked about this point. There was little difference between private practitioners and government attorneys.

7. On the many ways precedent can be used, see K. Llewellyn, *The Common Law Tradition, Deciding Appeals* 62-120 (1960), and Frank, *supra* note 3, at 275-280.

8. However, texts and articles used solely as a source of empirical data are not considered "legal authorities" for the purpose of this chapter.

9. Parallel authority actually does exist on some issues, though it is difficult to tell whether the court missed or purposely ignored the prior authority. A decision may or may not be taken as overruling a prior inconsistent unmentioned ruling by the court. A few judges, clerks, and attorneys mentioned examples of parallel authority by the focal court, but I did not ask about this topic in the interviews. On problems of parallel authority in other courts, see Llewellyn, *supra* note 7, at 85, 134, 256-260, 450-461; H. Friendly, Reactions of a Lawyer—Newly Become Judge, 71 Yale L.J. 218, 225 (1961); R. Traynor, Badlands in an Appellate Judge's Realm of Reason, 7 Utah L. Rev. 157, 159, 160 (1960). Justice Traynor said:

> How can [a judge] be sure that between counsel's efforts and his own all pertinent materials have been rounded up? Suppose there lies undiscovered some pertinent statute still at large? Many a judge is haunted by the muddle that ensues when a court overlooks such a statute even when it is in plain sight.

A similar problem exists on courts that sit in panels; without proper research one panel may decide an issue differently from the way another panel did earlier. See, for example, J. Gardner, Ninth Circuit's Unpublished Opinions: Denial of Equal Justice? 61 A.B.A.J. 1224 (1975).

10. Many courts, however, limit the search for the law of local governments, such as municipal ordinances. American courts used to limit the search for the law of other states to that presented by the parties, but probably no court continues this practice.

11. This flat statement leaves many details to be explained. In all there were almost 2,000 authorities cited in the opinions and over 7,000 in the briefs, though of course there was much duplication between majority and minority opinions and between appellant and appellee briefs. There were 179 opinions in the 112 cases, 104 majority opinions, 30 concurring and plurality opinions, and 45 dissenting opinions. A few opinions, however, did not cite any authorities. Authorities mean all those types listed at the beginning of the chapter. Sometimes it was difficult to tell whether two citations should be classified as the same or different authorities, and the following rules were used: The same case in different courts was counted as separate authority; different sections of a constitution were considered separate authority; and different sections of the same statute or text were considered separate authority unless they were only two sections apart. All authority mentioned in the briefs was counted, except the lower court decisions, even if in footnotes or quotations. The text of the briefs was used in counting the authorities, since the indexes were often incomplete. In the opinions all authority was counted, including those in quotations and foot-

notes, except the following: the lower court opinion in the case and authority in quotes from the lower court opinion, literary pieces, empirical data sources, authorities in the footnotes added by the court reporter, authorities in agreed statements of facts copied in the opinions, and authorities that were obviously completely extraneous to the decision (such as the court rule under which amicus briefs were submitted). These exceptions were made because these are not "legal," because there is no question about where the authorities came from or because they were too unimportant to the decision; but except for the lower court opinions and empirical data sources, these exceptions were very rare. On the other hand, an authority cited in the briefs was counted as being used if used by the court in one of these categories.

12. In a few cases it was difficult to align the issues as defined by the court with those defined by the attorneys, and thus the designation of the issues not decided may be inaccurate. The opinions cited twenty-five authorities that were not available in time for the attorneys to present them to the court. In four cases the new authorities disposed of an issue, making the attorneys' presentations—and 4 percent of the total amount of authorities they cited—superfluous. But deleting these only raised the proportion of authorities used by 1 percent.

As can be seen in the table in note 15, counsel cite a far larger portion of court decisions not binding on the focal court (numbers 4 and 5) than the court's opinions do. And the opinions tend to give a higher proportion of the court's precedent and of statutory and similar material (numbers 2 and 3) than counsel do. These differences probably reflect both the judges' propensity to cite these different kinds of authority and the attorneys' ability to judge what kinds of authorities the judges will find persuasive.

13. This pertains only to issues decided by the court. A fourth of the authorities given by counsel in these issues were emphasized. An authority was considered emphasized if: (1) the attorney said he relied on the authority or otherwise treated it as very important, (2) he quoted from it at all, if in the oral arguments, or for five lines or over, if in the briefs, or (3) he gave a long detailed account of its provisions. Authority contra to his position and lower court decisions in the case were not included. (I also kept track of case authority—but not other types—mentioned and emphasized by the attorneys in the oral arguments, for all the issues presented. The court used about 25 and 30 percent respectively.)

14. There is some indication that this low figure is caused partly by some judges' wish to keep down the number of citations in their opinions, citing only the most important and leaving out the rest, even though some of the others may have been considered relevant. The justices' opinion-writing styles differed greatly in that some cited as few authorities as possible and others cited almost anything connected to the decision they could find. Three justices averaged from eighteen to twenty-six citations of legal authority in majority opinions, while the remaining four averaged from six to nine. The first group, on the average, cited a quarter of the authorities cited by counsel for the issues decided by the court, while the latter four cited, on the average, a sixth. (The two groups did not differ in their tendency to cite authorities not raised by counsel.)

Also, there was a substantial tendency to cite authority from the briefs of the attorney who won the particular issue; therefore, it seems that some authority cited by the attorneys went unused because it did not support the court's holding. (In most majority opinions more authority of the attorney who won the issues was cited than authority of his opponent, and in the other majority opinions the authority cited was usually mentioned equally by both sides. Seldom was more authority of the issues' loser than of the winner used. All in all, for both authorities cited and authorities emphasized in the majority opinions, authorities cited in the losing briefs for the various issues amounted to only 70 percent of those brought up by the attorneys who won the issues.)

15. This includes both majority and minority opinions, as does the following discussion unless stated otherwise. The figures for minority opinions are very close to those for majority opinions all through this section.

The fact that an authority cited in an opinion was also cited in a brief does not imply that the briefs lead the opinion writer to use the authority. The real importance of an authority or its place in the chain of reasoning used by the judge may have been missed by the attorney. Also, I do not mean to imply that half the opinions came from the briefs. The use of the attorneys' reasoning is not one of the topics covered here, but in my experience the opinions seldom were similar to either party's briefs in their organization or method of reasoning or language. A few attorneys I interviewed felt very flattered when the court did follow their reasoning closely or quoted from their briefs.

The figures also differ greatly for different types of authority. The following table covers all legal authority in all opinions in the 112 cases and all authority cited by the parties in the issues decided by the court:

	Percent of All Authority in the Opinions	Percent of All Authority Given by Counsel	Percent Used in Opinions Given by Counsel	Percent Given by Counsel Used in the Opinions
1. U.S. Supreme Court opinions	12	12	66	24
2. Statutes, constitutional provisions, court and agency rules	24	15	58	39
3. Precedents of the focal court	37	31	40	19
4. Decisions of courts in other jurisdictions	14	24	52	16
5. Decisions of lower tribunals or agencies in the state	4	10	46	8
6. Texts, restatements, C.J.S., Am. Jur., and other reference books	7	7	27	11
7. Law review articles	1	1	20	7

The authorities are listed in order of lessening authoritativeness, though there is probably no difference between numbers 4 and 5 and numbers 6 and 7 in this regard. The more authoritative the authority, the more the authorities used by the court tend to be presented by counsel and the more the authorities presented by counsel tend to be used by the court. This mainly reflects the fact that there is a greater match between the opinions and the briefs for authorities emphasized.

16. These two categories are an attempt to pick out the authorities the justices considered major factors in their opinions' reasoning. By quoted, I mean any authority from which more than a few words were quoted, unless the quote was in a footnote or within another quote. It included overruled and distinguished cases. Whether an authority was relied upon was more subjective. Often the court said it was relying upon an authority, but many other times I had to use my judgment. If the court said "See . . . " or "cf. . . ." or "see also . . ." there was a strong presumption against the authority being in this category. If one authority was discussed and relied upon, other authorities simply cited as supporting this position were not considered relied upon. In all, about 60 percent of the authority labeled as emphasized was considered relied upon and three-quarters was quoted.

17. I tried asking a number of judges how often the attorneys missed important authorities, but the answers were on the whole not helpful, probably because the judges really did not know the answer. At times they dodged the questions, and if they gave an answer, it was usually very imprecise, for example, "sometimes." And even when they gave answers, they often differed greatly from their colleagues. A First Circuit judge said, "More than half the cases we cite in an opinion that we take seriously—worry about whether we're doing a good enough job on tough questions —more than half the cases we don't find in the briefs." At the Sixth Circuit one judge said a "very small percentage" of cases cited in the opinions are not in the briefs, and another said, "We decide cases on cases that aren't ever cited in the briefs . . . I suppose 25 percent of the time." Two Massachusetts justices said important authorities are often missed by counsel, and a third said this was not common. One Ohio justice said they were found in 60 percent of the cases and another said in 15 percent. Two Rhode Island justices agreed that counsel hardly ever missed important authorities.

Several studies have compared authorities cited in the opinions with those in the briefs. One is C. Newland, Legal Periodicals and the United States Supreme Court, 3 Midwest J. Pol. Sci. 58, 62 (1959). The author found that a little less than 20 percent of the law reviews cited by the justices who used them the most between 1924 and 1956 were in the briefs. (Twenty percent—five out of twenty-five—of the law review articles cited in the focal court opinions were in the briefs.)

A second study is rather confusing. The author studied "non-legal evidence" used by the Supreme Court in a sample of over 600 cases decided between 1925 and 1969. "Non-legal evidence" is authorities not having the force of law—that is, authorities other than cases, statutes, constitutions, and regulations issued by government bodies. It includes empirical data sources, but consists mainly of congressional documents and law reviews. In almost 300 cases at least 1 opinion cited this nonlegal evidence (almost 400 opinions in all), and for 70 percent of the opinions at least 1 such authority cited was mentioned in the briefs. The author, however, does not say what percentage of this type of authority was in the briefs. But he broke the category down into 8 subcategories, and for each he calculated what percentage of the opinions citing each subcategory were in appeals in which the briefs cited at least 1 of the subcategories used in the opinion. That is, for example, for 64 of the 165 (or 39 percent)of the opinions using law reviews, the briefs mentioned at least 1 of the law reviews used. The percentages for the other subcategories (which are defined more thoroughly in the original study) are: legal treatises, 47 percent, quasi-legal documents, 42 percent, congressional documents, 81 percent, other government documents, 40 percent, nonlegal texts, 40 percent, nonlegal journals or newspapers, 34 percent, unpublished documents, 46 percent. These percentages are probably higher than the percentages of authorities used that are in the briefs, but they do indicate that the focal court is similar to the U.S. Supreme Court in this regard. See J. Johnson, *The Dimensions of Non-Legal Evidence in the American Judicial Process: The Supreme Court's Use of Extra-Legal Materials in the Twentieth Century*, 184-187, 208, 209, 216-218 (unpublished Ph.D. dissertation, University of Minnesota, 1974).

Chief Justice Vanderbilt of the New Jersey Supreme Court asked his staff to study a year's worth of cases and discovered: "In 111 opinions in the Supreme Court out of 135—or 82 percent of all our cases—there were 397 New Jersey cases cited by the court—or 3.5 per opinion—that did not appear in the briefs." Somewhat lower figures were found for the New Jersey intermediate court. A. Vanderbilt, Our New Judicial Establishment: The Record of the First Year, 4 Rutgers L. Rev. 353, 361 (1950).

Chapter 13, at note 21, discusses studies comparing empirical data sources mentioned in opinions with those cited in the briefs.

18. These thirty cases are the appeals reported in 500-503 Federal Second for which briefs were available in the library. Because briefs for both sides were rarely available in criminal cases, I only studied civil cases. And briefs were missing for almost half the civil cases, though not for any specific, obvious categories of appeals. Because the opinions were published, the cases were among the more substantial ones decided by the court, and thus comparable to the opinions of the focal court, which has discretionary jurisdiction. However, nine of the thirty cases had per curium opinions, and often seemed quite routine. Authorities in the per curiums were generally in the briefs, and in the signed opinions (including three dissents) 50 percent of the authorities and 62 percent of the emphasized authorities were in the briefs. This is very close to the focal court figures, as are the medium values.

19. A national study of state appellate judges asked what percentage of their time they spend "doing legal research." A third each said they spend 11-20 percent and 21-30 percent of their time on legal research, 11 percent spend 10 percent or less, and 23 percent over 30 percent of their time. This is considerably less time than they said they spend writing opinions, and considerably more than hearing oral arguments. In this regard there is little difference between intermediate court and supreme court judges. See M. Osthus and R. Shapiro, *Congestion and Delay in State Appellate Courts* 76 (1974). Probably all appellate judges have a copy of the jurisdiction's reports and statutes in their offices. The courts themselves tend to have rather small law libraries, but the judges and clerks have access to larger libraries nearby, used by the bar in general.

20. Questionnaires were submitted to judges in four appellate courts asking how often independent research was done for the memorandums prepared by their law clerks. The great majority of the judges answered that the memorandums "usually" involved independent research (the highest category in the question), several said the

memorandums "sometimes" involved independent research, and none said the memorandums involved "little or no" independent research. See G. Lilly, *The Appellate Process and Staff Research Attorneys in the Supreme Court of Virginia* 185; J. Lake, *The Appellate Process and Staff Research Attorneys in the Supreme Court of Nebraska* 189; J. Lucas, *The Appellate Process and Staff Research Attorneys in the Illinois Appellate Court* 134; and T. Farer and C. Jacob, *The Appellate Process and Staff Research Attorneys in the Appellate Division of the New Jersey Superior Court* 108. (All four are Reports of the Appellate Justice Project of the National Center for State Courts, 1974.) A question in a questionnaire sent to appellate judges in 1966, "on whether independent research should be the normal procedure, [was answered] overwhelmingly in the affirmative." See B. Witkin, Appellate Court Opinions, A Syllabus for Panel Discussion, 63 F.R.D. 515, 558 (1974). A political scientist asked justices in New York, Maryland, and Delaware how important was the influence of the aid of their clerks and their own independent research. In New York and Maryland the clerks' aid was seen as quite important, presumably because they did most of the research. In Delaware there was only one clerk for the three justices, and the clerk's aid was seen as only moderately important. All the justices considered their own research important. In fact, on the whole the justices rated the importance of the clerks' aid and their own research at least as great as the importance of the briefs. See Wold, *supra* note 1, at 55, 64, 89, 90, 144, 150. See also M. Cuomo, The New York Court of Appeals: A Practical Perspective, 34 St. John's L. Rev. 197, 211 (1960); T. Lesinski and N. Stockmeyer, Prehearing Research and Screening in the Michigan Court of Appeals: One Court's Method for Increasing Judicial Productivity, 26 Vand. L. Rev. 1211, 1217 (1973); R. Aldisert, Duties of Law Clerks, 26 Vand. L. Rev. 1251, 1253 (1973); A. England and M. McMahn, Quality Discounts in Appellate Justice, 60 Judicature 442, 446 (1977).

21. I only talked to several judges and less than half the clerks about this topic. All said essentially the same thing. Information about other courts is scanty. An early study of appellate courts in the country found that on the "great majority of courts" the nonassigned judges did not make a practice of doing independent research. See the American Bar Association, *Methods of Reaching and Preparing Appellate Court Decisions* 28 (1942). That is also the case on the Alabama Supreme Court, National Center for State Courts, *The Appellate Process in Alabama* 167, 168 (1973).

22. Ethical Considerations are not mandatory, but this rule is repeated in Disciplinary rule 7-106(B). These references are to the American Bar Association's version of the Code of Professional Responsibility, but the rules have been widely adopted. The most thorough discussion of this ethical rule is in J. Weinstein, Judicial Notice and the Duty to Disclose Adverse Information, 51 Iowa L. Rev. 807, 808-814 (1966). Judge Weinstein (then a professor) expressed firm belief in the rule, believing it workable because self-interest should prompt attorneys to bring up the adverse authority.

23. Less than half the judges and clerks were asked about this, at least two from each court. Several said they had no idea how often it happened. Only a couple said the attorneys regularly do it.

The U.S. Supreme Court was recently very annoyed when counsel did not inform it of an important amendment to the state statute being attacked. See Fusari v. Steinberg, 419 U.S. 379, 387 (1975). Justice Burger, concurring, said "This Court must rely on counsel to present issues fully and fairly, and counsel have a continuing duty to inform the court of any development which may conceivably affect the outcome." *Id.*, at 391.

24. For an example of this view, see R. Carson, Conduct of the Appeal—A Lawyer's View, in *A Case on Appeal* 34, 62 (H. Goodrich ed. 4th ed. 1967). One justice has written that an attorney following this rule "established himself as a man whose expressed conclusions as to the state of the law are based on knowledge and preparation and can be received by the court with confidence in their accuracy." See D. Webber, Appellate Advocacy with Main Flavor, 18 Maine L. Rev. 59, 64 (1966). See also Weinstein, *supra* note 22, at 810, 811.

25. An opposing precedent should be brought out if it is "one which the court should clearly consider in deciding the case." See ABA Comm. on Professional Ethics, Opinion No. 280, 35 A.B.A.J. 876 (1949).

CHAPTER 10

1. R. Jackson, Advocacy Before the United States Supreme Court, 37 Cornell L.Q. 1, 6 (1951). Justice Miller was surprised at how readily the justices "came to an agreement upon questions of law, and how often they disagreed in regard to questions of fact." Quoted in J. Frank, Facts Are Guesses, in *A Man's Reach* 180, 208 (B. Kristein ed. 1965). Likewise, a circuit judge has written that "judges much more often disagree on the facts or the proper inferences to be drawn from the facts than on the law." See J. Craven, The Impact of Social Science Evidence on the Judge: A Personal Comment, 39 Law & Contemp. Prob. 150, 151 (1975).

2. The concepts of case facts and social facts are similar to Kenneth Culp Davis's adjudicative and legislative facts. See his *Administrative Law Treatise* sec. 15.03 (1958). He defines adjudicative facts as "facts concerning the immediate parties— who did what, where, when, how and with what motive or intent" and facts "to which the law is applied in the process of adjudication. They are the facts that normally go to the jury in a jury case. They relate to the parties, their activities, their properties, their businesses." His definition of legislative facts is: "facts which help the tribunal determine the content of law and of policy and help the tribunal to exercise its judgment or discretion in determining what course of action to take. Legislative facts are ordinarily general and do not concern the immediate parties." (In sec. 7.02, however, he says legislative facts "do not usually concern the immediate parties but are general facts" used in lawmaking.)

Davis's terminology is not used here for a number of reasons. "Facts of the case," abbreviated to "case facts" here for the sake of literary style, is the common and fairly unambiguous term used to describe adjudicative facts. And there is much confusion in the legal literature about what "legislative facts" are. The term is used sometimes to refer to ideals, case facts used in developing the law, supporting case facts, or legislative history materials, and some use it to refer to scientific and social science data only. Also, although it is an important concept, many are not familiar with the term. I rarely used it in interview questions (and then generally unsuccessfully), and only one person used that term in all the briefs, arguments, and opinions in the focal court I studied, or volunteered it in the interviews. Also, virtually none of the numerous writings by judges in this area uses this terminology. (However, after virtually all the interviewing was done, Davis's terminology was enacted in Fed. R. Evidence 201.) Lastly, the term used here, "social fact," is quite often used instead of "legislative facts" in the law review literature.

Davis distinguishes between legislative facts and adjudicative facts because courts and administrative agencies gather (or should gather, according to Davis) the two in different ways. They can search for legislative facts themselves, whereas they are expected to use only adjudicative facts in the record or those properly subject to judicial notice, and adjudicative facts should be found in trial-type hearings and legislative facts mainly in rule-making proceedings.

The concepts of supporting case facts and case facts used as social facts have been mentioned by a few writers, as is discussed in note 12 of Chapter 11 and note 12 of this chapter.

3. An example of facts not falling within any of the four categories is historical facts used in trying to determine legislative intent or the intent of the framers of the Constitution. Legislative hearings, debates, and reports and proceedings of constitutional conventions were placed under the category of legal authority in this study. There was little of this at the focal court, as I presume is typical of state courts. Besides legislative history, historical facts about the state of affairs at the time legislation or a constitution became law are sometimes used to determine legislative intent. There was none of this at the focal court during the year studied, though the U.S. Supreme Court uses it quite regularly. See C. Miller, *The Supreme Court and the Uses of History, passim* (1969).

4. The case facts in the table that follows are those that were not obviously case facts used as social facts. As will be seen later, the judges may have often used the case facts at least partly as social facts without this use being obvious. The case fact category includes hypothetical questions about what would have happened if someone had acted differently in the case, but not questions about what the law would be in fact situations not before the court.

Although exact percentages are given in the table, it should be emphasized that the findings are not that precise because of uncertainties in categorizing facts, possible inaccuracies in measuring time in arguments and portions of pages in briefs and opinions, and possible clerical mistakes. I would estimate that each percentage given is probably correct within 5 percent of the percentage given.

The table is presented in terms of the average percent of time, questions, or pages devoted to case facts and social facts. This figure was used instead of the percent of the total of all time, and so on, or the median time, and so on, because it appears to be the most meaningful figure in view of the great variation in lengths of briefs and so on. These two other indicators are as follows:

	Briefs	*Oral Argument Time*	*Judges' Questions*	*Majority Opinions*
Case facts				
Percent over all cases	28	33	38	32
Median percent	33	30	35	35
Social Facts				
Percent over all cases	8	9	11	9
Median percent	3	4	4	0

The seven justices differed greatly in their attention given to case facts in the arguments, varying between a fourth and a half of their questions on that subject.

When questioning an attorney, a judge was more likely to ask a series of questions on a single topic than one isolated question; and half of these series contained one or more questions about case facts.

5. I kept track of the time spent on case facts and the percentage of questions on case facts in the arguments of about ten cases each in the First Circuit, Sixth Circuit, and Rhode Island Supreme Court. Roughly half of the time and half of the questions were on case facts. The judges prepare beforehand; hence the greater attention to facts than in the focal court is probably due to the types of issues these courts heard. In the arguments of seven appeals before the Massachusetts court, where the judges have discretionary jurisdiction but do not prepare for arguments, 40 percent of the argument time was spent in explaining the case facts, but only a quarter of the questions were in that category.

6. K. Llewellyn, *The Common Law Tradition, Deciding Appeals* 268-285 (1960). Using fireside equities is very similar to Max Weber's substantive irrational mode of legal thought, or khadi justice. Here the "decision is influenced by concrete factors of the particular case as evaluated upon an ethical, emotional, or political basis rather than by general norms." See M. Weber, *On Law in Economy and Society* 63 (M. Rheinstein ed. 1954).

7. The notion of justice in the particular case is also used in connection with whether a court having discretionary jurisdiction will grant leave to appeal to a case decided wrongly below but of little importance to the development of the law. A few justices mentioned that they are paying attention to the equities of the particular case when they grant leave in such a case and ignoring them when they do not.

8. I also talked with most of the clerks about how important fireside equities are in the judges' decision making. Like the judges, their opinions varied, but on the whole they considered these equities more important than the judges did.

In neither the interviews with the judges nor with the clerks did I learn much about how often fireside equities are important. All that can be said is that they are important in some cases.

Judges do not often mention this topic in their writings. In the writings on appellate advocacy discussed in Chapter 3 for example, a fifth said that attorneys should mention the justice or equities of their positions. But a great many of these seemed to be aimed only at presenting case facts to be used in developing the law. Only three clearly spoke about fireside equities (and an equal number cautioned attorneys against overemphasizing that their client is the more deserving party, probably cautioning against presenting fireside equities). The three are A. Denecke et al., Notes on Appellate Brief Writing, 51 Ore. L. Rev. 351, 352 (1972), T. Chadick, An Effective Appellate Brief, 26 Texas B.J. 923, 971, 972 (1963), and C. Breitel, Discussion, in *Counsel on Appeal* 97 (A. Charpentier ed. 1968). Justice Denecke told counsel, "Fireside equities may be suggested if one is not too obvious about it." Judge Breitel, then on the New York intermediate court, said:

I don't agree . . . that judges do not try to test the fact of innocence or guilt in a criminal case or, in a civil case, do not test the fact that the judgment rendered is right or wrong, despite the risk of sleeplessness and the risk of enhancing the burdens that they have. As a matter of fact, if anything there is a greater danger that judges, in their anxiety, will depart from the rules of the game, from what has been provided for them by the advocates, and decide, on some basis not supportable by the record or the law or even by reason, that a person is innocent or guilty or that a civil case is right or wrong as it has been decided. As I say that, I recognize that judges may vary, although my experience is that this practice is fairly common among them.

Lawyers' writings on appellate advocacy often advise lawyers to write the statement of facts so as to emphasize the justice of the client's situation, but this is probably aimed at case facts used as social facts more than fireside equities. See, for example, E. Re, *Brief Writing and Oral Argument* 8, 88, 167 (4th ed. 1974), and F. Wiener, *Briefing and Arguing Federal Appeals* 4, 45, 56-58 (1961). Karl Llewellyn (*supra* note 6, at 43, 44, 121, 268-285) does not believe they dictate the outcome very often by themselves. There are numerous comments by judges and others to the effect that equities of the particular case should not lead to a decision that contradicts the law, though without suggesting how often these equities are important. See especially ABA *Canons of Judicial Ethics* No. 20.

9. See the statement by Judge Breitel in note 8. From a study of criminal cases over a four-year period in the Second and D.C. Circuit Courts of Appeals, it was claimed (without a great deal of proof) that many rulings are based on the judges' feelings about the probable guilt of the defendant, rather than the rules used in the opinions to justify the decision. See J. Carney, The Constant Factor: Judicial Review of the Fact Finding Process in the Circuit Court of Appeals, 12 Duquesne L. Rev. 233 (1973). This tendency is probably most pronounced in harmless-error issues: The judge may feel that the error is harmless or not because he believes the defendant is guilty or not, rather than because the error might have affected the jury decision. See R. Traynor, *The Riddle of Harmless Error* 49, 50 (1970). The National Advisory Commission on Criminal Justice Standards and Goals, *Courts* 124 (1973), suggests that appellate courts be given more flexible review procedures because now "in a case where the court is convinced that the conviction works on injustice it is driven artificially to find some legal error on which a reversal can respectably be based, even if this necessitates a distortion of legal doctrine."

10. I questioned a number of judges about the meaning of objectivity (and impartiality, which is usually used interchangeably with objectivity), and judges often write about the subject. The most common meanings are those mentioned in the text, plus not having one's mind made up before hearing the attorneys and not being emotional, which two may be variants of the meanings in the text. Judges do not often use objectivity in the sense that they should not let their ideologies or feelings about what is right affect decisions, except in the sense that this may lead one to run afoul of one of the meanings just given. Objectivity does not mean refusing to overrule precedent, a definition political scientists sometimes use.

11. J. Lumbard, Appellate Advocacy, 4, 5 (unpublished paper, Institute of Judicial Administration, 1962). This statement was virtually copied in Committee on Federal Courts, The Association of the Bar of the City of New York, *Appeals to the Second Circuit* 37 (1975) and Cincinnati Chapter of the Federal Bar Association, *Practitioners' Handbook for Appeals to the United States Court of Appeals for the Sixth Circuit* 40 (1973). And a very similar thought is expressed by another circuit judge in H.

Goodrich, A Case on Appeal—A Judge's View, in *A Case on Appeal* 27, 28 (4th ed. 1967).

12. For example, R. Pound, The Theory of Judicial Decision, 36 Harv. L. Rev. 940 (1923); Llewellyn, *supra* note 6, at 122, 238, 268-274, 293 (1960); W. Schaefer, The Advocate as a Lawmaker: The Advocate in the Reviewing Courts, 1956 U. Ill. L. F. 203, 204, 205; J. Hopkins, Fictions and the Judicial Process: A Preliminary Theory of Decision, 33 Brooklyn L. Rev. 1, 4 (1966); R. Traynor, Some Not So Lost Causes of Action, 22 Sw. L.J. 551, *passim* (1968); R. Traynor, What Domesday Books for Emerging Law? 15 U.C.L.A.L. Rev. 1105, 1111 (1968); A. Tate, The Justice Function of the Judge, 1 Southern U. L. Rev. 250, *passim* (1975); J. Wright, No Matter How Small, 2 Human Rights 115, 118-120 (1972).

13. Davis, *supra* note 2, at sec. 21.02; Note, Judicial Determination in Nonadversary Proceedings, 72 Harv. L. Rev. 723, 727, 735 (1959); G. Vining, Direct Judicial Review and the Doctrine of Ripeness in Administrative Review, 69 Mich. L. Rev. 1445, 1529 (1971).

14. For more discussion on this point, see Chapter 12 at notes 19-23.

15. C. McGowan, Rule-Making and the Police, 70 Mich. L. Rev. 659, 660 (1972). Also, in Furman v. Georgia, 408 U.S. 238, 313 (1972), Justice White based his major point, that there is no meaningful basis to distinguish cases in which the death penalty is imposed from those in which it is not, on "a conclusion based on 10 years of almost daily exposure to the facts and circumstances of hundreds and hundreds of federal and state criminal cases involving crimes for which death is the authorized penalty."

However, the facts judges get are incomplete and perhaps often inaccurate. Llewellyn says:

> What with the screening through legal theory and through the rules of procedure and of evidence, what with the unavailability or unreliability of oral testimony, the facts of life show up even in the trial courtroom only as unrecognizable distortion, let alone then in an appellate judge's little selective essay built to put rouge and lipstick on his court's decision! Llewellyn, *supra* note 6, at 359.

16. "The history of the common law shows a constant pattern of questions once treated as fact growing into matters of law after the courts have gained knowledge and experience concerning them." See H. Korn, Law, Fact, and Science in the Courts, 66 Colum. L. Rev. 1080, 1105 (1966). See also N. Isaacs, The Law and the Facts, 22 Colum. L. Rev. 1, 3 (1922).

17. This is one argument made by those saying that the U.S. Supreme Court should often let problems "percolate" in the lower courts. Judge Lay, for example, has stressed "the value of having important national questions resolved slowly, allowing many lower courts to approach an issue anew, each considering what others have done and yet rethinking the justice and policy of the question as it is presented on the particular facts before each court." See Hearings on S. 2762 Before the Subcommittee on Improvements in Judicial Machinery of the Senate Committee on the Judiciary, 94th Cong., 2d sess., pt. 1, at 141 (1976).

The argument that an appellate court can learn of problems in life, especially through the numerous certiorari petitions in courts with discretionary jurisdiction, is forcefully made in W. Brennan, Justice Brennan Calls National Court of Appeals Proposal "Fundamentally Unnecessary and Ill Advised," 59 A.B.A.J. 835, 839 (1973).

18. A description of legal literature discussing this type of fact is in note 12, Chapter 11.

19. B. Cardozo, The Bench and the Bar, 34 N.Y.St.B.J. 444, 454 (1962) [a 1929 speech].

20. W. Schaefer, Appellate Advocacy, 23 Tenn. L. Rev. 471, 476 (1954).

21. W. Douglas, The Supreme Court and Its Case Load, 45 Cornell L.Q. 401, 413 (1960).

22. "Public policy" is used in a technical area of the law, contracts against public policy, and "policy" is used by judges and people generally to describe an organization's rules or its standard operating procedures. These uses, however, are unusual compared with those described in the text.

23. O. Holmes, *The Common Law* 31, 32 (M. Howe ed. 1963). The open use of social facts and the term "public policy" to describe that use had been common in Holmes's state of Massachusetts for some time. See L. Levy, *The Law of the Commonwealth and Chief Justice Shaw, passim* (1957). Holmes says of Justice Shaw: "Few have lived who were his equals in their understanding of the grounds of public policy to which all laws must ultimately be referred" (Holmes, *supra*, at 85). Holmes uses the words "public policy" or "policy" about twenty times in this book, most of the time referring to specific examples, nearly all of which involve social facts.

24. Throughout my research the distinction between ideals and social facts was thought to be that ideals, being goals, cannot be proved or disproved without the use of another ideal, whereas social facts, being facts, can theoretically be shown to be true or false. But on reflection this seems rather silly because it is probably impossible actually to prove many social facts and probably impossible even to gather evidence about some of them. Saying that something can be done "theoretically" is really an admission, at least as the term is used in sociology, that it probably cannot be done. What then distinguishes social facts from broad policy? The only criterion I can think of (and probably the only criterion ever available, in the end, for definitions) is a commonsense definiton based on the shared meanings of words—here, the difference between facts and goals.

This distinction between ideas and legal rules is sometimes fuzzy. In this study any statement expressing what seemed to be a legal rule, no matter how broad, was not classified as an ideal. If legal authority was cited for a proposition, the proposition was assumed to be a legal rule. Words like "fair," "just," and "unconscionable" strongly indicated statements of ideals. Any statement within a statute was not considered an ideal, including language about the broad purposes of the statute. Ideals include both the political science type of broad policy considerations and narrower goals dealing with a specific area of the law. On the difference between political scientists' and lawyers' use of "policy," see J. Blawie and M. Blawie, The Judicial Decision: A Second Look at Certain Assumptions of Behavioral Research, 18 Western Pol. Q. 579, 583-587 (1965).

25. In over 100 situations in which the terms "policy" and "public policy" were used by judges, clerks, and attorneys in law review articles, interviews, briefs, arguments, or opinions, and in which it was possible to tell from the context how the terms were used, they were used almost equally to refer to social facts and to ideals.

About a quarter of the time the judges and others used "policy" to refer to both, and many more surely would have if they had given more examples.

Incidently, social facts and ideals were rarely used together. One might think that arguments would be in the form of: "This is the ideal that should be furthered, and these facts indicate that ruling a certain way would further the ideal." In practice, either the social fact or ideal was virtually always left as an unstated step in the reasoning. In some issues, especially equal-protection issues, social facts were applied to legal propositions, and there was no implicit or explicit ideals. (Courts often apply social facts directly to legal propositions in several areas other than equal-protection issues, for example, due process, nuisance, conflict of laws, commerce clause, and admissibility of scientific tests.)

26. See Chapter 1 for a fuller discussion of why ideals are outside the scope of this study, and see Chapter 7 for more about leaving ideals out of opinions.

27. This is for the 112 cases studied. It includes both minority and majority opinions, as does the discussion in the rest of the chapter unless noted otherwise. Also, here and elsewhere the figures are about the same for the majority and minority opinions. By "tiny part" I mean less than 5 percent. The statements about ideals generally seemed to be part of a chain of reasoning supporting the holding, but rarely the sole reason. The focal court is probably typical in the small place given to ideals in opinions; perhaps it even makes more use of it than is normal. A study of opinions on three courts (the Second and D.C. Circuits and the New York Court of Appeals) found that the courts very rarely explicitly relied on "social policy"; but it is uncertain what was meant by that term. See R. Daynard, The Use of Social Policy in Judicial Decision-Making, 56 Cornell L. Rev. 919 (1971). A study of two years' opinions in the Arkansas Supreme Court apparently found very few statements of "morality" or "philosophical and religious ideas" in the opinions. See R. Trammell, The Unprovided Case in the Arkansas Supreme Court—A Jurisprudential Inquiry, 7 Ark. L. Rev. 77, 91-94 (1953). Also, F. Cohen, Field Theory and Judicial Logic, 59 Yale L.J. 238, 262 (1950), states that value judgments (which are clearly distinguished from factual statements) are almost never found in opinions.

28. Less than 10 percent of the statements about ideals in the opinions, briefs, and arguments were about the court's method of making decisions or its role in society. (The rest were about the substance of the cases.) Social facts are important here, as will be seen later, along with ideals. For example, a social fact justification often given for following precedent is that otherwise people would not be sure what the law is and thus their interactions would be hampered; however, behind this is the assumption that these interactions should be encouraged, an ideal.

29. The terms were used a few times to refer to the effect of a decision on related issues, to fireside equities, or to the type of decree to be entered in a case.

30. Davis's definition of legislative facts is discussed in note 2. Cardozo's method of tradition is the incorporation of customs, especially business practices, into the judge-made law; it rests completely on social facts (the existence of customs). His method of sociology includes the consideration of both social facts and ideals. See B. Cardozo, *The Nature of the Judicial Process*, 31-141 (1921). Frankly, I do not know what Llewellyn (*supra* note 6, *passim*) means by "situation sense"; he does not define it, and it is not always clear what he is getting at in the numerous examples he gives. I would guess that the term is meant to include social facts, plus case facts used as

social facts and, even, ideals. But, in all, the meaning is left to (and is easily supplied by) the reader's imagination. For two articles that have discussed Llewellyn's lack of definition of "situation sense" and other terms, see C. Clark and D. Trubek, The Creative Role of the Judge: Restraint and Freedom in the Common Law Tradition, 71 Yale L.J. 255, 260-264 (1961); A. Becht, A Study of "The Common Law Tradition: Deciding Appeals," 1962 Wash. U.L.Q. 5, 34-36.

31. A further indication that not all social facts are placed in the opinions is that the social fact topics of the judges' questions from the bench were rarely mentioned in the opinions at the focal court.

Some evidence suggests that judges vary in their tendency to include social facts in the opinions. There is a great difference between the seven justices in the amount of social facts used in the opinions; for example, from one-third to two-thirds of each justice's opinions contained some social facts. This varied closely with the length of opinions the various justices tended to write. They also differed greatly in the amount of questions from the bench about social facts, from 8 to 15 percent of their questions, but this was totally unrelated to the amount of social facts placed in the opinions. (Incidently, the judges' reputations for being liberal or conservative were related to neither the amount of attention given social facts in the opinions nor that given in the arguments.)

32. In the arguments I studied in the First Circuit, Sixth Circuit, and the Rhode Island and Massachusetts courts (see note 5), 9, 7, 3, and 1 percent of the questions were about social facts. Several judges and clerks in Ohio said that there was very little social fact discussion in the arguments there, but I did not watch any of the arguments. Only a half-dozen of the opinions in thirty Sixth Circuit cases studied (see note 18 of Chapter 9) contained social facts that seemed important to reaching the holding.

33. C. Breitel, The Courts and Lawmaking, in *Legal Institutions Today and Tomorrow* 1, 24, 25 (M. Paulsen ed. 1959). See also 2A *Sutherland, Statutory Construction* secs. 54.04, 54.07, 56.01, 56.05 (4th ed. C. Sands 1973).

34. The law clerks who were interviewed agreed with their judges about the importance the latter placed on social facts, substantiating both their judges' views and the variation between judges.

The quotations from judges writings are from: R. Fellows, Practice Before the Supreme Judicial Court of Maine, 43 Me. St. B. Ass'n 85, 89 (1954), E. Hallows, The Role of the Wisconsin Supreme Court in Our Democratic Society, 29 Milwaukee B. Ass'n Gavel 13, 14 (1968), and J. Breitenstein, The United States Court of Appeals for the Tenth Circuit, 52 Denver L.J. 9, 13 (1975). Many other appellate judges have written about the importance of social facts, by whatever name they are called, often in association with ideals. See the quotations from Justices Cardozo, Schaefer, Douglas, and Breitel above at notes 19, 20, 21, and 33. For some other, extensive statements see: J. Frank, *Courts on Trial* 342, 343 (1949); F. Coffin, Justice and Workability, 5 Suffolk L. Rev. 567 (1971); A. Tate, "Policy" in Judicial Decisions, 20 La. L. Rev. 62 (1959); J. Van Voorhis, Cardozo and the Judicial Process Today, 71 Yale L.J. 202 (1961); R. Aldisert, The Role of the Courts in Contemporary Society, 38 U. Pitt. L. Rev. 437, 444-456 (1977). No judge has written, as far as I know, that social facts are not important, though it is sometimes said that "policy" should be left to the legislature, probably referring to ideals only. But many judges have written about appellate decision making or, especially, appellate advocacy without mentioning this topic, suggesting perhaps that they consider it of limited importance. On this subject, see note 6 of Chapter 12.

Of course, law scholars have written about the importance of social facts, especially many of those considered to be within the vague areas of judicial realism or sociological jurisprudence. See especially Holmes, *supra* note 23; Llewellyn, *supra* note 6, and Pound, *supra* note 12.

Political scientists have asked appellate judges about the importance of common sense, public needs, public policy, and practical considerations in judicial decision making. These terms are never defined, but a substantial part of each probably consists of social facts. Judges on three circuit courts and two state supreme courts generally believed common sense to be very important—at the state courts, as important as precedent. See J. Howard, *Role Perceptions on the U.S. Courts of Appeals for the 2d, 5th, and D.C. Circuits* 37 (Federal Judicial Center, 1973); F. Rich, *Role Perceptions and Precedent Orientations as Variables Influencing Appellate Judicial Decision-Making: An Analysis of the Fifth Circuit Court of Appeals* 100 (unpublished Ph.D. dissertation, University of Georgia, 1967); G. Mason, *Judges and Their Publics: Role Perceptions and Role Expectations* 261 (unpublished Ph.D. dissertation, University of Kansas, 1967; J. Beatty, *An Institutional and Behavioral Analysis of the Iowa Supreme Court—1961-1969* 270, 271 (unpublished Ph.D. dissertation, University of Iowa, 1970). On the other hand, only a small minority believed that consideration of the public's needs was very important, and a substantial minority said it had little or no importance. See Howard, *supra*; Rich, *supra*; Mason, *supra*, at 287, 288, 311; Beatty, *supra*, at 277, 278. Likewise, in a questionnaire returned by twenty-six out of thirty-five judges on the top courts in Nevada, Utah, Vermont, Maine, and New Hampshire and an intermediate court in New York, about 40 percent said "needs of the community" are "important" or "highly important" factors influencing their decisions (and the rest presumedly considered it moderately or hardly important). See C. Sheldon, Contrasting Judicial Roles: Trial vs. Appellate, 11 Judges' J. 72 (1972). Howard asked thirty-four circuit judges how important the "needs of public policy" are when precedent is absent or ambiguous; the majority said it was very important, and most of the rest said it was moderately important (Howard, *supra*, at 38). Nine Iowa justices and five Kansas justices were asked the importance of "weighing competing practical considerations and forming a practical judgment in your decision." All said it was important—though fewer than half considered it very important—and about half said they considered practical implications in many cases (Mason, *supra*, at 267, 313; Beatty, *supra*, at 271). Mason asked if it is important for a judge to be an economic scholar, and three justices said it was and two said it was not (Mason, *supra*, at 90-92). In a study of four state courts of last resort, the justices were asked, "How about the influence of nonlegal factors in deciding cases? Of what importance are they? I mean things such as those contained in a Brandeis Brief, for example." The reference to the Brandeis brief here may have suggested to the justices that the question was referring to the social sciences (which will be discussed in Chapter 13) and not social facts in general. In any event, the New Jersey justices all believed it very important; the great majority of the Pennsylvania justices believed it very or moderately important; the Massachusetts justices varied between considering it of moderate to no importance; and one Louisiana justice considered it very important, but the rest said it had no importance. See H. Glick, *Supreme Courts in State Politics* 83-85 (1971).

Of all these courts studied by the political scientists, only the New Jersey, the Pennsylvania, and the Louisiana courts had discretionary jurisdiction at the time studied. The Beatty and Glick studies suggested a relation between the judges' conservativeness and their lack of interest in social facts. The Rich study suggested there was none, and the other studies did not explore the subject.

35. Most of the judges talked about this topic, usually in response to questions about how often there was ample authority to go either way. Even the focal court judges generally said there was not in most appeals. Judges elsewhere have stated that a large percentage of the appeals are cut-and-dry, especially on courts with little discretionary jurisdiction. Cardozo has said most cases could be decided only one way because the law and its application are plain and, later, that the decision in at least 90 percent of the cases is predetermined. See B. Cardozo, *supra* note 30, at 164, and *The Growth of the Law* 60 (1924). Agreeing with Cardozo is H. Friendly, Reactions of a Lawyer—Newly Become Judge, 71 Yale L.J. 218, 222, 223 (1961). Also, Judge Tate, *supra* note 34, at 62 said 90 percent or more of the cases involve "routine application of precedent and word-logic." Judge Clark of the Second Circuit estimated that 10 percent of the cases were "clear one-way cases" and only 10 percent were "highly original cases giving scope to the method of social values." See Clark and Trubek, *supra* note 30, at 256. Howard (*supra* note 34, at 36, 39) reported that most of the thirty-four circuit judges he interviewed believed that only about 10 percent of their cases offered an opportunity to innovate. On the other hand, Justice Schaefer of the Illinois Supreme Court, which has a good deal of discretionary jurisdiction, said almost every case embodies a competition for supremacy among multiple legal doctrines (Schaefer, *supra* note 20 at 475, 476).

This discussion only concerns the number of cases the judges believe determined by existing law; there is no objective means of finding out how many actually are in that category. Most of the law clerks spoke to this subject in the interviews, and on the average they believed decisions either way could be supported by ample authority in a much higher proportion of the cases than the judges believed. A good number of clerks made sweeping statements to the effect that one can find support for almost any position one wishes to take. Also, two important scholars of appellate courts have emphasized that even what may be considered the cut-and-dry cases often involve situations different from those found in precedent, and thus are important in lawmaking (Llewellyn, *supra* note 6, at 24, 25, 99, 108, 109, 237; R. Pound, *supra* note 12, at 941).

It should be noted that the amount of lawmaking, at least as determined by the number of opinions published as discussed in Chapter 2, is higher than the figures given here for the portion of appeals not determined by existing authority. The difference is probably accounted for by cases decided by what is considered the necessary extension of existing authority.

36. Judges on other courts have often mentioned change in times as a reason for overruling precedent, sometimes, as with the judges interviewed, in conjunction with other reasons. See especially: Cardozo, *supra* note 30, at 150-158; W. Schaefer, Precedent and Policy, 34 U. Chi. L. Rev. 3, 10-14 (1966); R. Traynor, Interweavers in the Reformation of Law, 42 Cal. St. B.J. 817, 821-823 (1967); J. Weintraub, Judicial

Legislation, 81 N.J.L.J. 545 (1958); R. Leflar, No Task for the Short Winded, 54 Judicature 366 (1971); Breitel, *supra* note 33, at 5, 6; T. Kavanagh, The Ethics of Urban Law and Practice: A Challenge for the Common Law, 19 De Paul L. Rev. 496 (1970). Justice Kenison's list of factors that may lead a court to overrule a precedent suggests, but does not explicitly include, changing social conditions. See F. Kenison, Some Preliminary Observations on the State Appellate Judge Today, 61 Colum. L. Rev. 792, 795 (1961).

A political scientist asked the justices on four state courts when they believed a justice should depart from precedent. Seventy-two percent said when conditions have changed, and many of the remainder said in order to avoid an unfair or unjust result. J. Wold, *Internal Procedures, Role Perceptions and Judicial Behavior: A Study of Four State Courts of Last Resort* 201-207 (unpublished Ph.D. dissertation, The Johns Hopkins University, 1972).

37. Williams v. City of Detroit, 111 N.W.2d 1, 23, 24 (1961). The author, Judge Edwards, is now on the Sixth Circuit.

38. All of these social fact assumptions can be questioned. As has been discussed in Chapter 4, the relationship between the thoroughness of counsel's presentation and what he might gain from winning is not clear; perhaps few rely on or even know the law when they act; perhaps the demeanor of witnesses serves to mislead trial court fact finders more than to indicate the trustworthiness of witnesses (see J. Hutcheson, *Judgment Intuitive* 27 (1938); perhaps new case facts could be presented at the appellate level, as is done in England; legislatures may give their enactments little study; and perhaps, as one judge interviewed said, people dislike an appellate court only when they disagree with the substantive result of its decisions.

As far as I know, only one of these points, the public reliance on precedent, has received much attention from appellate judges. For example, precedent is less powerful in areas where it is believed people are less likely to rely. Also, some judges have taken a skeptical look a the notion of reliance in general (Frank, *supra* note 34, at 268-271; Cardozo, *supra* note 35, at 122). A more important reason behind all of these might be the judges' time and work load problems, for each requires less work by the judges than the alternative decision-making method.

CHAPTER 11

1. The word "record" does not have a uniform definition, but this seems to be the most common one. Sometimes it refers to the appendix, sometimes to everything the attorneys submit to the appellate court, and sometimes just to the papers filed with the court below without including the transcript of testimony. The definition used here is essentially that in Rule 10a of the Federal Rules of Appellate Procedure: "The original papers and exhibits filed in the district court, the transcript of proceedings, if any, and a certified copy of the docket entries prepared by the clerk of the district court." The docket entries are the dates at which different actions were taken in the case. The exhibits, which may or may not be sent to the appellate court, are documents and various other things entered into evidence at the trial—for example, technical gadgets in patent cases or movies in pornography cases.

Under the old appellate practice, which may still be used in a few rare states, the court did not receive a verbatim transcript of the testimony. Instead, the parties prepared a bill of exceptions— a narrative description of the testimony—because there was no court reporter at the trial level to take the testimony down verbatim. With the advent of verbatim recordings, appellate courts slowly began receiving these instead of the bill of exceptions. See D. Louisell and M. Pirsig, The Significance of Verbatim Recording of Proceedings in American Adjudication, 38 Minn. L. Rev. 29, 39-41 (1953); R. Pound, *Appellate Procedure in Civil Cases* 152-158 (1941).

2. In some ten states the legislature has given appellate courts the authority to take in evidence largely at the judges' discretion, except when the fact finding below was by a jury. However, the courts have tended to construe these statutes narrowly and have used them extremely rarely. See R. Millar, New Allegations and Proof on Appeal in Anglo-American Civil Procedure, 47 Nw. L. Rev. 427, 435-441 (1952); D. Louisell and R. Degnan, Rehearing in American Appellate Courts, 44 Calif. L. Rev. 627, 629 (1956); F. Lapardo, Findings and New Evidence, in *California Civil Appellate Practice* 413, *passim* (California Continuing Education of the Bar, 1966). In the few situations in which appellate courts have truly original jurisdiction—for example, the U.S. Supreme Court in litigation between states—they often appoint masters to gather the case facts in a trial-type hearing.

The reason why appellate courts do not take evidence beyond this meager amount is not clear, but most likely the judges do not want to take the time and do not want to damage the morale of the lower courts by usurping what is commonly seen as a trial function.

It should be noted that new evidence is allowed and quite often taken in the U.S. Court of Military Appeals and in the English Court of Appeal Criminal Division. See E. Abamkewicz, Appellate Consideration of Matters Outside the Record of Trial, 32 Military L. Rev. 1 (1966); A. Samuels, Fresh Evidence in the Court of Appeal Criminal Division, 1975 Crim. L. Rev. 23.

3. For example, Rule 52 of the Federal Rules of Civil Procedure provides that findings of fact by a trial judge "shall not be set aside unless clearly erroneous, and due regard shall be given to the opportunity of the trial court to judge of the credibility of the witnesses."

4. I talked with half the judges about this, and the great majority said the reason was that the appellate judges cannot view the witnesses. A few, however, said the reason is simply that that is the way it is done. A couple said that if trial court fact findings were easily overturned, the number of appeals would greatly increase.

The legal literature contains innumerable statements by appellate judges that they will give the benefit of the doubt to findings of fact below because they cannot see the witnesses. "The principle that the trier of fact, whether judge or jury, is in a far better position to determine where the truth lies than the appellate court with only the cold record before it has been stated and restated so often that it has become a truism." S. Hofstedter, Appellate Theory and Practice, 15 N.Y.Co.B. Bull. 34 (1957). See especially J. Frank, *Courts on Trial* 23 (1949). Much less attention is given to time problems and to decreasing the number of appeals; for one scholar who emphasizes this see C. Wright, The Doubtful Omniscience of Appellate Courts, 41 Minn. L. Rev. 751, 779, 780 (1957).

However, there is an indication that the inability to view the witnesses' demeanors may not be such a decisive factor. If the findings of fact below were based solely on written materials—for example, on documentary evidence, written depositions, and affidavits—appellate judges can evaluate the evidence as well as the trial court. For this reason some federal circuit courts have lessened or removed the presumption of correctness applied to the findings below. But this is a minority position and is losing favor because of the case load problems, because the judges wish to maintain public confidence in the district court decisions, and, as one judge told me, because they wish to maintain the self-confidence of the district judges. See Wright, *supra*, at 764-771; *Wright & Miller, Federal Practice and Procedure* sec. 2587 (1971). State courts are also split on this issue: 5 *Am. Jur. 2d.* Appeal and Error sec. 823 (1962). On the other hand, appellate judges routinely interpret contracts, a very important kind of written evidence, without relying on findings below. In the old equity cases, where there was no oral testimony, appellate judges reviewed the facts all over again. After testimony was allowed in equity, however, appellate courts began using a "clearly erroneous" test or something similar. See C. Clark and F. Stone, Review of Findings of Fact, 4 U. Chi. L. Rev. 190, 207, 208 (1937); Pound, *supra* note 1, at 298-302.

There are experiments now in which trials are videotaped and shown to the jury; here, of course, the videotape can be also shown to the appellate court, which, thus, has no less information about case facts than the jury. How this might affect the scope of review is uncertain, but it seems unlikely that the judges will take the time to view the testimony.

5. See, for example, H. Leventhal, Environmental Decisionmaking and the Role of the Courts, 122 Pa. L. Rev. 509 (1974).

6. The tests used to determine whether error is harmless differ greatly from court to court, and even from decision to decision in the same court. See R. Traynor, *The Riddle of Harmless Error* (1970); S. Saltzburg, The Harm of Harmless Error, 59 Va. L. Rev. 988 (1973).

7. Questions of this type probably come up often in appellate courts. For example, a criminal defense lawyer has said, "One key issue which is very often the subject of clarification at oral argument is the ground for defense counsel's objection at trial and whether the objection was sufficient to preserve the issue for appeal" (Statement of Phyllis Bamberger to the Commission on Revision of the Federal Court Appellate System, October 1, 1973, p. 1121).

8. While studying the six courts I saw only three examples of garbled or missing records; in each case all consideration of the merits stopped while the court determined what to do about the record. Appellate court rules often provide rather elaborate procedures to supply a record when the transcript cannot be obtained (e.g., when the reporter dies and no one else can read his notes) or to correct what counsel feel to be mistakes in the transcript.

9. There are a few examples of investigation of case facts at the Second Circuit. Judge Clark once obtained the advice of a music professor about whether one songwriter had plagiarized another's songs. See M. Schick, *Learned Hand's Court* 126-129 (1970). Judge Frank twice made his own surveys in trademark infringement cases, seeking evidence about whether consumers confused similar trademarks. See Triangle Publications v. Rohrlich, 167 F.2d 969, 976 (1948), and LaTouraine Coffee Co. v. Lorraine Coffee Co. 157 F.2d 115, 120 (1946).

Under the new ABA Code of Judicial Conduct No. 3C(1) (a) a judge should disqualify himself if he has "personal knowledge of disputed evidentiary facts concerning the proceedings." A law clerk told me he had investigated the facts of one case—

"kind of dug around a little bit. I know a few people. Talked to a few people," and found out "exactly what the hell was going on." But he did so without his judge's knowledge. Compare this with what another clerk said: When he began as a clerk, his judge ordered him not to go into the trial courtrooms, "because there's always a chance," his judge said, "that the case that's being heard will eventually come to us for review, and we might be assigned it, and if that happens you might take something into consideration as you're going over that case that wasn't in the record.' "

The judges can also get some information by viewing the audience in oral arguments. Sometimes the judges spot a litigant. One judge mentioned in an interview that he saw that a criminal defendant's wife was pregnant. In two focal court cases the courtroom and lobby were jammed with supporters of litigants. I have no real evidence about whether the presence of a client or his supporters makes any difference in the outcome of the case, but I cannot imagine that it does.

Judges are much more likely to investigate supporting case facts. They use dictionaries to understand technical terms, and they sometimes even search for empirical studies.

10. That case facts are supposed to come from the record see, for example, 4A *C.J.S.* Appeal and Error sec. 680 (1957). There are quite a few exceptions, however. Several appellate courts have the authority to take new evidence, as was discussed in note 2. Probably all appellate judges feel they can use any source to determine if a case is contrived or moot or the court lacks jurisdiction. There are, however, a number of situations in which appellate judges have used facts outside the record, and outside the judicial notice restrictions, while appearing to believe they are justified in doing so. The U.S. Supreme Court often mentions facts outside the record that were given by counsel in oral arguments. See Cox v. Louisiana 379 U.S. 559, 592 (1965) (Justice White dissenting); Brown v. Louisiana, 383 U.S. 131, 137 (1966) (Justice Fortas concurring); Washington Game Dept. v. Puyallup Tribe 414 U.S. 44, 48 (1973); O'Shea v. Littleton, 414 U.S. 488, 495 (1974); Spomer v. Littleton 414 U.S. 514, 522 (1974); Steffel v. Thompson, 415 U.S. 452, 456 (1974). But none of the facts here seems important to the holding. Thurgood Marshall, before he was on the Court, claimed that the Solicitor General can bring in facts outside the record if well documented, although private litigants probably cannot. See T. Marshall, The Federal Appeal, in *Counsel on Appeal* 139, 158 (A. Charpentier ed. 1968). A circuit judge interviewed said that sometimes when events take place at trial outside the presence of the court reporter, the judges ask counsel what happened then and will accept facts agreed to by both sides. Likewise, Judge Leventhal of the D.C. Circuit said that the court sometimes uses substantive facts not in the record if agreed to in the arguments by the attorneys. H. Leventhal, *supra* note 5, at 550. Admissions by an attorney against his interest and affidavits brought to the court upon appeal are allowed by some courts (4A *C.J.S.* Appeal and Error sec. 1210, 1211 (1957)). Another circuit judge interviewed said that facts outside the record are often allowed in injunction cases when there is not enough time to develop a trial court record.

11. As to when judicial notice may be taken of case facts see Federal Rules of Evidence 201(b) and 29 *Am. Jur. 2d.* Evidence secs. 14-122 (1967). In practice the judicial notice rules are much more complicated than is suggested in the text. For a good discussion about the general uncertainty in the area see: E. Roberts, Preliminary Notes Toward a Study of Judicial Notice, 52 Cornell L.Q. 210 (1967).

12. *McCormick on Evidence* sec. 328, 334 (E. Cleary ed. 1972); F. Guidice and C.

Kraft, The Presently Expanding Concept of Judicial Notice, 13 Vill. L. Rev. 528, 533, 559, 560 (1968); *Weinstein-Korn-Miller, New York Civil Practice* sec. 4511.01; Advisory Committee's Notes on the Proposed Rules of Evidence for the United States Courts, 56 F.R.D. 183, 203, 204 (1973); K. Davis, Judicial Notice, 1969 L. and Soc. Order 513, 520. See also, K. Davis, A System of Judicial Notice Based on Fairness and Convenience, in *Perspectives of Law* 69, 73, 74 (R. Pound ed. 1964). These writers have different labels for the concepts, which are all similar to, but not exactly the same as, supporting case facts; McCormick and Guidice and Kraft call them "general facts," which appear to be supporting facts used to determine an ultimate fact. Here judicial notice is often relaxed. McCormick later (in sec. 334) also refers to "subliminal-like data" used in the same manner. The judicial notice restrictions do not apply to them. Weinstein calls it "hypotheses and generalized knowledge," definitely referring to this same use, and this is considered outside the judicial notice restrictions. Davis claims that "peripheral facts" are noticed more liberally than "critical facts" but does not really say what they are (1969 article). In the earlier article he talked about facts needed to understand words and the significance of ideas expressed, but within the context of judicial notice. The advisory committee referred to "non-evidence facts" to which the judicial notice restrictions do not apply. These included definitions of words and facts used "to appraise or assess the adjudicative facts."

For numerous examples of supporting case facts outside the record and of the uncertainty in the area, see *K. Davis, Administrative Law Treatise* sec. 15.03 (1958), and the 1970 supplement.

13. McCormick, *supra*, at sec. 334; Advisory Committee, *supra*; Davis (1964), *supra*, at 73, 74. Davis added that judges instinctively tend to bring to the attention of the parties questionable facts along this line; he cites no evidence for this, and I doubt that it is true.

14. McCormick, *supra*, at sec. 13.

15. Weinstein-Korn-Miller, *supra* note 12.

16. Testimony of H. Markey and D. Dunner, *Hearings Before the Commission on Revision of the Federal Court Appellate System, Second Phase*, 670, 674-677, 842, 843 (1975).

17. The major suggestions are in H. Leventhal, *supra* note 5, at 550-554, and Commission on Revision of the Federal Court Appellate System, *Structure and Internal Procedures: Recommendations for Change, Preliminary Draft* 82-84 (1975). The latter suggested that the technical advisers employed by the Court of Customs and Patent Appeals be loaned to the circuit courts when needed. This recommendation was left out of the commission's final report, probably because of the objections voiced in its hearings. Circuit judges were about two to one against the proposal during the hearings; those against the proposal thought the advice should not be given outside of counsel's presence, though the objection was not so much that this supporting case fact information should be in the record as that advice from outside experts must be made available to the parties, a topic discussed in Chapter 6. See *Hearings Before the Commission on Revision of the Federal Court Appellate System, Second Phase*, 679, 827, 877, 942, 985, 994, 995, 1004, 1116, 1302, 1382 (1975). Judge Robb of the D.C. Circuit said that in a patent case a law clerk who had studied chemistry helped him understand the terms in the record (at page 995).

A major controversy in this area surrounds U.S. District Judge Wyzanski's use of an economist as a law clerk when deciding a major antitrust case; the clerk wrote a long report analyzing the evidence, and the report was not shown to counsel, as many believe it should have been. See especially, C. Kaysen, An Economist as the Judge's Law Clerk in Sherman Act Cases, 12 ABA Antitrust Section Rep. 43 (1958).

Counsel often supply technical supporting case facts at the appellate stage. See especially Judge Leventhal's directions to attorneys to present this information in H. Leventhal, Cues and Compasses for Administrative Lawyers, 20 Ad. L. Rev. 237, 241 (1968). The New Jersey Supreme Court has, in a few rare cases involving technical facts, sat down with counsel and with the parties' experts who testified at trial, getting information needed to understand the record. J. Francis, Joseph Weintraub— A Judge for All Seasons, 59 Cornell L. Rev. 186, 191 (1974).

18. For an interesting example of appellate judges' use of discretion here, see: P. Luckenbill, Judicial Notice—Disputability and Appellate Practice Regarding Judicial Notice of Stopping Distances, 38 Mo. L. Rev. 678 (1973).

19. Fewer than half the judges talked about this. Almost all said the record comes alive.

20. Most of the judges interviewed talked about this subject; the vast majority said they read between the lines. Judges surely also read into the record their knowledge based on experience to evaluate the evidence, but I did not ask about this. Two judges volunteered examples, though. One used his knowledge of power boats to judge whether insurance should be paid, deciding that the boat was probably purposely set afire; and another used his knowledge of power brakes in automobiles to judge the testimony about an auto accident.

21. K. Llewellyn, *The Common Law Tradition, Deciding Appeals* 28 (1960). For a judge's vivid description of reading between the lines and the importance of prior experiences in this process, see E. Wright, Observations of an Appellate Judge: The Use of Law Clerks, 26 Vand. L. Rev. 1179, 1180, 1182 (1973).

22. The Rhode Island case is State v. Fortes, 330 A.2d 404 (R.I. 1975). The court here asked counsel to supply these figures after the appeal arrived, while counsel in the focal court case supplied them on his own motion. The Rhode Island court did not discuss the judicial notice restrictions; the focal court claimed that the figures fell within a technical exception to the restrictions that permits use of information in court records.

23. The number of case facts outside the record was determined by counting the number of statements containing such a fact. If a statement contained more than one specific fact, it was only counted once. These statements were generally isolated, so that there was no trouble counting them. When they were not isolated—when there was a lengthy discussion of facts not in the record—each sentence was counted as a separate fact not in the record. For the judges, I simply counted the number of questions containing facts not in the record. If the same fact was mentioned by an attorney or judge more than once in a brief or argument, it was only counted once. But the same fact was counted more than once in the few cases where an attorney mentioned it both in his brief and in the argument and where more than one judge asked about it. Also, when a judge asked about such a fact and the attorney gave the fact in his answer, it was counted for both the judge and the attorney.

I considered a fact to be outside the record only if there was very little doubt about it being such. This determination was made in a number of ways: (1) I went back to the trial court and read the record in the two cases that appeared to have the most facts outside the record, and I read the appendixes in eight other cases in which there was little question but that the appendix contained all the case facts on the point, usually because there was a judgment on the pleadings. This accounted for about 20 percent of the attorneys' statements and judges' questions about facts not in the record at the focal court. (I did not read the appendixes in other cases because there is no assurance that they contained all the facts.) (2) The attorneys often admitted that statements were outside the record, accounting for about 30 percent of the facts. This includes attempts by attorneys in six cases to introduce affidavits at the appellate level, which is not a proper way to introduce case facts into the record at the focal court. (3) About 40 percent of the facts outside the record were about the state of somebody's mind—the motives or knowledge of the attorneys, parties, trial judge, or jury. If this concerned what happened at the trial level, there was virtually no .chance it was in the record. Most were in this category. Statements about motives and knowledge at other times were often obviously not the sort of thing that would have been introduced as evidence at trial, especially when it was not relevant to any of the issues at the trial. (4) Eight percent of the questions and statements about facts outside the .record concerned events taking place after the last lower court proceedings and, thus, could not be in the record. (5) Fifteen percent were hypothetical facts —what would have happened if a hypothetical event took place somewhere in the history of the dispute or what would be done in the present case after the court ruled. These facts could not have been in the record because they did not exist. (This category of facts is discussed in Chapter 10 as a possible lawmaking use of case facts.) (6) There was considerable overlap in the preceding categories, and they did not account for 5 percent of the facts outside the record. These were classified as such because of many varying indications that they were almost certainly not in the record.

Because this method was used to determine whether the facts were outside the record, it cannot be said that the judges had no way of knowing that they were asking about facts outside the record in the great majority of the instances. Also, I have surely understated the amount of facts outside the record, but I have no idea by how much.

There was one category of statements outside the record so clearly trivial and irrelevant that I did not include it in these figures on facts outside the record. In many arguments the attorneys mentioned something about their work—what they had to prepare for the appeal (e.g., what cases they had read or which issues they deemed important when writing the briefs) or about their work in general (e.g., how long they had practiced).

Supporting case facts were not included in these figures for the amount of facts not in the record. But including them would not change the figures much, since supporting case facts were mentioned so infrequently.

24. This is based on only a few arguments in four of the other five courts studied here (see note 5 of Chapter 10). The Massachusetts justices asked virtually no questions about facts outside the record, but they did not ask many fact questions anyway. At the two circuit courts and the Rhode Island court questions about facts outside the record were roughly as frequent as at the focal court. (I did not listen to the

arguments in Ohio, but one justice there told me there were many questions about facts outside the record.) I noticed fewer comments about facts outside the record volunteered by the attorneys; but this is probably because I did not tape-record these arguments, as I did in the focal court, and I missed much of what the attorneys said while concentrating on the judges' questions.

The legal literature contains very little on this topic; so I cannot say whether these courts are typical. Note 10 mentions some examples of courts' use of facts outside the record, but these account for only a small portion of the facts outside the record in the arguments I observed. There is some indirect suggestion that one of the most common facts outside the record in the focal court is not unique—asking attorneys about what motive they had for actions taken at trial. Justice Clark said that one problem with having a new counsel on appeal is that:

> He does not get all the nuances that are in the trial. Many things come up that are not in the record, that the reporter does not get; perhaps something that the defendant told his counsel to do, and things like that, particularly with reference to strategy. That counsel would know the trial strategy is very important, very important. He might decide to waive some right the defendant might have rather than bring out some testimony that would be against him. Statement of Justice Tom C. Clark to the Commission on Revision of the Federal Court Appellate System, May 20, 1974, p. 246.

And a California attorney writing about appellate advocacy advised attorneys who are new counsel on appeal to ask the trial attorney why he did what he did at trial because the judges are likely to ask about his motives. See N. Sokolow, "Just a Minute Counsel—I Have a Question," 46 L.A.B. Bull. 251, 255, 256 (1971).

25. A few opinions did contain facts outside the record, but, except for one dissenting opinion, these were clearly not a basis for the decisions.

26. Asking about judges' questions outside the record was difficult; quite a few judges, for example, seemed upset at the question or appeared to dodge it by simply saying that they tried to stay in the record. Only several judges really gave any information on this topic. At most courts the judges differed among themselves about the amount of questions outside the record, though at least one from each court except the Massachusetts court said there were questions outside the record, but only at the focal court and the Ohio court did a judge say they were frequent.

27. This information comes from interviews with court clerks. One study found that "it is rare for a partial transcript to be ordered" in the circuit courts, even though many cases need only a partial transcript or no transcript at all. See W. Whittaker, Differentiated Case Management in United States Courts of Appeals, 63 F.R.D. 457, 459 (1974). See also J. Godbold, Twenty Pages and Twenty Minutes—Effective Advocacy on Appeal, 30 Sw. L.J. 801, 806 (1976). In Kentucky, for another example, "It is a rare occasion indeed that counsel complies" with a rule requiring that only matters essential to the appeal be in the appellate record, and the whole record is sent up in nearly every case. B. Martin, Kentucky's New Court of Appeals, 42 Ky. Bench & Bar 8, 12 (April, 1977).

Some appellate procedural rules also provide for an agreed statement of facts instead of the record, but counsel very rarely do this.

28. The six courts studied here, and probably the great majority of other circuits and state supreme courts, use the appendix system (though not necessarily the term "appendix"). Many of these courts, though, do not use the appendixes in certain types of cases, especially criminal cases. The appendix system was first used in the 1940s in the federal courts and then spread to the state courts. The earlier system, by and large, was the settled record system, under which the appellant court did not receive a transcript of the testimony but a narrative condensed account of what was said at trial, agreed to by the attorneys and the trial judge. In some courts now, but probably no more than a few, such a narrative condensation serves as an appendix. A few courts—for instance, the Seventh and Ninth Circuits—have dropped the appendixes and receive only the record. For general discussions of the methods of presenting the transcripts used in appellate courts see: B. Willcox et al., Justice Lost— By What Appellate Papers Cost, 33 N.Y.U.L. Rev. 934 (1958), and Note, Form of Appellate Records in Iowa, 48 Iowa L. Rev. 77 (1962).

29. The court clerks and a number of judges—mostly at the focal court and the Sixth Circuit—were asked about the appendixes. The Massachusetts court had just begun using appendixes, so there was little comment on them there. The court clerks usually complained about the appendixes, and at least one judge from the other five courts did also.

The legal literature is full of complaints about the appendix system (as well as other systems), mainly for the reasons in the text. An Eighth Circuit judge said he made a careful study of the appendixes his court received and decided that so much unneeded material was included that the attorneys could save half the cost of printing if they did an adequate job. H. Johnsen, Practice in United States Court of Appeals Discussed, 21 Hennepin Lawyer 134, 136 (1953). For a small sample of other writings on the problems with the appendix system, see T. Kavanagh, Remarks, in *Proceedings, Sixteenth Annual Meeting of the Conference of Chief Justices* 77 (1964); J. Weintraub, Remarks, in *supra* at 87; H. Goodrich, A Case on Appeal—A Judge's View, in *A Case on Appeal* 9 (4th ed. 1967); Notes on the Draft of Proposed Rule 30, Uniform R. Fed. App. P., 41 F.R.D. 311, 321, 322 (1966); Improvement on "Appendix Method" Suggested, 33 J. Am. Jud. Soc'y 57 (1949).

30. E. Tuttle, Book Review, 33 Miss. L.J. 147 (1961).

31. The discussion here is based on comments by all but a few of the clerks and judges interviewed, though quite a few were not very specific about just how much of the transcript was read. The court clerks were asked how often the records were sent to the assigned judges and to the nonassigned judges. From the information published about how often the record is read, it seems that courts elsewhere, like these six courts, differ greatly in their practices, though overall the six courts probably give a bit more attention to the record than is normal. Judges often write that they study the record thoroughly, but this statement is too general to be helpful. One study asked, "What judges read the record (or transcript) in a case?" A substantial minority of the courts said all the judges did, and nearly every remaining court said the assigned judge did. However, there is no indication of how much of the record was read, how often it was read, and what was meant by the word "record." Institute of Judicial Administration, *Appellate Courts. Internal Operating Procedures. 1959 Summary and Supplement* 6. In the Fifth Circuit at least some of the clerks read the record. N. Johnson, What DO Law Clerks Do? 22 Texas B.J. 229, 234 (1959); D.

Sweeney, Law Clerkships—Three Inside Views: III. In United States Court of Appeals, 33 Ala. Lawyer 171, 174, 178 (1972). Louisiana's 1921 Constitution, Art. 7, Sec. 6, required that two judges read the record in every case. This provision was left out of the 1974 Constitution. See also Institute of Judicial Administration, *A Study of the Louisiana Court System* 185 (1972). On the Arkansas Supreme Court the judge assigned the case normally reads the transcript, but not the others. L. Brown, The Handling of Supreme Court Cases—Processing, Practice and Procedure, 22 Ark. L. Rev. 679, 690 (1969). Likewise, the whole record was read, in the recent past at least, in the California Supreme Court, Second Circuit, Eighth Circuit and maybe the Oregon Supreme Court. Only in the Second Circuit were the nonassigned judges likely to read it. R. Traynor, Some Open Questions on the Work of State Appellate Courts, 24 U. Chi. L. Rev. 211, 216 (1957); H. Medina, The Decisional Process, 20 N.Y.Co.B. Bull. 94, 100 (1962); Marshall, *supra* note 10, at 158; F. Gibson, Some Observations on Our United States Court of Appeals, 35 U.M.K.C.L. Rev. 261, 268 (1967); Denecke et al., Notes on Appellate Brief Writing, 51 Ore. L. Rev. 351, 358 (1972). Three judges on the Ohio Court of Appeals, Eighth District, mentioned that they regularly read the record, but a fourth said he did so only if the briefs presented conflicting facts. J. Harley, *Establishing Criteria for Effective Oral Argument Before a Court of Appeals* 130, 132, 139, 140, 143, 171, 172 (unpublished Ph.D. dissertation, Case Western Reserve University, 1976). And some Wisconsin Supreme Court justices read the record completely and others only partly: H. Wilkie, Supreme Court Practice, 36 Wisc. B. Bull. 27 (Dec. 1963); T. Fairchild, Setting the Stage, the Synopsis, and Issues Stated, 31 Wisc. B. Bull. 14, 39 (Aug. 1958). On the other hand, judges in New Jersey, Maine, Connecticut, and the Ninth and Tenth Circuits do not often look at the transcript: Weintraub, *supra* note 29; D. Webber, Appellate Advocacy with Maine Flavor, 18 Maine L. Rev. 59 (1966); R. Baldwin, Suggestions for Appeals to the Supreme Court, 34 Conn. B.J. 1, 7, 8 (1960); F. Hamley, Condensation of Remarks to Ninth Circuit Law Clerks School, 63 F.R.D. 478, 481 (1974); W. Doyle, Testimony Before the Commission on Revision of the Federal Court Appellate System, April 16, 1975, p. 832. See also S. Hufstedler, California Appellate Reform— A Second Look, 4 Pacific L.J. 725, 731 (1973).

There is probably a trend, because of the case load pressures, toward less study of the record in the judges' offices. In the more routine appeals in courts without discretionary jurisdiction the staff attorneys, instead of judges or law clerks, now probably do the bulk of the reading of the transcript. A proposal that has received increasing attention and that will probably be implemented soon is to actually do away with the record, or at least the transcript of testimony, in as many civil appeals as possible. See E. Jacobson and M. Schroeder, Arizona's Experiment with Appellate Reform, 63 A.B.A.J. 1226 (1977); CBA Judiciary Section's Proposed Expedited Appeal Process, 6 Col. Lawyer 1132 (1977).

32. See note 12 of Chapter 8. Note also the Louisiana constitutional provision mentioned in the preceding note.

CHAPTER 12

1. B. Cardozo, *The Growth of the Law* 85, 86, 98 (1924).
2. See Table 2 in Chapter 10 at note 4.
3. In three cases the opinions mentioned social facts to a much greater extent

than in the remaining cases. Excluding these, the figure of one-half becomes one-third. Social facts in minority opinions were slightly less likely to have been mentioned by counsel than those in majority opinions, except that in the three cases the social facts in minority opinions were much more likely to have been. All seven judges were about equal in their propensity to use social facts not mentioned by counsel.

Social facts were counted in the same manner as facts outside the record. See Chapter 11, note 23. That is, each factual statement was counted as a separate fact, and when there was a lengthy discussion of social facts, each sentence was considered a different fact. In the Brandeis briefs, I took the average number of social facts per page over a number of pages, and figured the total number of facts by counting the pages discussing them. The social facts in the records or appendixes, as opposed to the briefs, were not counted, but this made little difference, since in the cases in which social fact testimony was taken below, almost all the social facts used in the opinions were in the briefs. If the same fact was used in more than one opinion or more than one brief or argument in a case, it was counted separately for each. There was, however, virtually no overlapping except in two equal-protection cases. Except in the Brandeis briefs, I tried to eliminate repeated assertions of the same fact by an attorney. But statements by attorneys in the briefs and the arguments were counted separately. It was sometimes difficult to tell whether two factual statements involved the same or different facts. The general rule I followed here was that if there was any doubt, they were considered the same.

4. It has been suggested that courts inform attorneys when they plan to rely on a social fact not mentioned in the briefs or arguments and give them a chance to argue the point—both for the sake of fairness and to make sure the court is not mistaken. See K. Davis, Judicial Notice, 1969 L. and Soc. Order 513, 526, 527; F. Guidice and C. Kraft, The Presently Expanding Concept of Judicial Notice, 13 Vill. L. Rev. 528, 553, 561 (1968); T. Kungsgaard, Judicial Notice and the California Evidence Code, 18 Hastings L.J. 117, 136-140 (1966). There is no evidence that this is done, except in a few rare cases involving empirical data. An extreme suggestion is that attorneys be supplied social facts and other information by means of transcripts of judges' conferences. M. Schnitzer, Court Conferences and the Doctrine of Exclusivity of the Record, 30 Rutgers L. Rev. 482, 490 (1977).

5. J. Weinstein, Judicial Notice and the Duty to Disclose Adverse Information, 51 Iowa L. Rev. 807, 823 (1966).

6. A. Vanderbilt, *Forensic Persuasion* 24 (1950). See also the statement by Justice Schaefer cited in Chapter 10, note 20. The judges' writings on appellate advocacy are discussed in Chapter 3. The figure of one out of seven is imprecise because of the terminology problems discussed in Chapter 10. It includes a few judges who said counsel should argue "policy" but does not include requests that the attorneys argue the "equity" or "justice" of the client's cause. If the latter were included, the number of judges calling for social fact arguments would increase by one-third.

There are a few statements by judges elsewhere, not in writings on appellate advocacy, about the inadequacy of counsel's presentation of social facts: C. McGowan, Rule-Making and the Police, 70 Mich. L. Rev. 659, 678 (1972); G. Currie, Appellate Courts Use of Facts Outside the Record by Resort to Judicial Notice and Independent Investigation, 1960 Wisc. L. Rev. 39, 53. See also, R. Neely, A Glimpse into Judges' Chambers, 7 Juris Doctor 33, 37 (Dec. 1977). Judge Breitel wrote that, because judges in the past refused to admit in their opinions that they were "influenced by

the social and economic facts of life, or what they were believed to be," counsel did
not know of their importance and, thus, ignored them; however, he said it is now
pretty well accepted that these facts are important. C. Breitel, The Courts and Lawmaking, in *Legal Institutions Today and Tomorrow* 1, 39 (M. Paulsen ed. 1959).
Justice Frankfurter complained that the lawyers before the Court were poor advocates mainly because they were not sufficiently "cultivated"—not widely enough
read in general subjects—by which he probably meant that the lawyers did not present
the social facts well. F. Frankfurter, *Of Law and Life and Other Things That Matter*
163, 164 (P. Kurland ed. 1965). Others have commented on incomplete presentation
of social facts to the Supreme Court, for example, H. Friendly, *Benchmarks* 307
(1967), K. Karst, Legislative Facts in Constitutional Litigation, 1960 Supreme Ct.
Rev. 75, 83, 91-100. A book about lawyers arguing civil rights and civil liberties cases
before the U.S. Supreme Court claims, but with little substantiation, that the great
majority of attorneys representing defendants in criminal cases—apparently mostly
appointed counsel—were "typically not concerned with (and may not even be aware
of) the broader implications of the litigation in which they became involved" because
they concentrated on freeing their clients. J. Casper, *Lawyers Before the Warren
Court* 90-110, quote at 96 (1972).

7. Most of the judges and clerks were asked about this topic, though a few said
they could not, or otherwise did not, answer the question.

8. As is mentioned in Chapter 3, at note 31, there was a moderate relationship
between the amount of social fact information presented by counsel and his chances
of winning. Counsel presenting the most social facts won some 55 percent of the
time. However, after deleting cases in which very little attention was given social
facts in the briefs (less than a quarter-page in each brief), the attorney presenting
more social facts won almost 60 percent of the time (in 79 cases). This relationship is
not large, but it is consistent over varying degrees of imbalance in the presentation of
social facts. Perhaps, however, better counsel tend both to win more often (because
of the overall quality of his presentation) and to present more social facts. There was
no relationship between whether an attorney won and whether the opinion mentioned
social facts in his brief.

9. This is only social fact argument volunteered, and not that given in response
to my questions about the subject. Half of the attorneys mentioned in the interviews
social fact argument that they did not give the court. I do not know why they did
not. Overall, though, social fact arguments mentioned in the interviews generally
were also given the court.

10. Scholars have noticed for some time that judges use social facts without complying with the judicial notice restrictions. See especially, O. Holmes, *The Common
Law* 120 (M. Howe ed. 1963); K. Davis, An Approach to Problems of Evidence in
the Administrative Process, 55 Harv. L. Rev. 364, 402-407 (1942); *K. Davis, Administrative Law Treaties* sec. 15.03 (1958); *McCormick on Evidence* sec. 331 (E. Cleary
ed. 1972). The new Federal Rules of Evidence Rule 201(a) states that the judicial
notice restrictions apply only to adjudicative facts (case facts). This clearly means
that judges may use social facts not in the record. *Weinstein's Evidence* sec. 200(03)
(1975). As will be seen in the next chapter, there is some feeling that empirical data
used to support social facts should be in the record.

11. Karst, *supra* note 6, at 109. I only ran across three examples of stipulated social facts in my research of the courts, all of which the courts refused to accept; in two of the cases the court found the facts to be substantially different from what was stipulated. See Mobile Oil Corp. v. Attorney General, 361 Mass. 401, 416, 420 (1972).

12. Note, Social and Economic Facts, Appraisal of Suggested Techniques for Presenting Them to the Courts, 61 Harv. L. Rev. 692, 700 (1948).

13. Although the judges were not asked specifically about the effect of their backgrounds on their philosophical views, a number volunteered that this effect was important. They usually added that one should make an effort to recognize certain of these effects—those considered biases—and try to counteract them.

14. The references to past experiences were in many contexts, and there was little uniformity in the questions asked judges here. Several were asked how important their experiences are in decision making and how these are important, but the subject was usually volunteered or arose out of more specific questions, such as the importance of trial court experience, whether colleagues with greater experience in an area are helpful, and how one evaluates social fact arguments.

15. Holmes, *supra* note 10, at 5; R. Pound, The Theory of Judicial Decision, 36 Harv. L. Rev. 940, 950 (1923); B. Cardozo, *The Nature of the Judicial Process* 113 (1921); K. Llewellyn, *The Common Law Tradition, Deciding Appeals* 263 (1960). Each is talking about social facts, but also probably about ideals and perhaps case facts used as social facts. See also, C. Clark, The Limits of Judicial Objectivity, 12 Am. U.L. Rev. 1, 10-12 (1963).

16. Most of the clerks interviewed talked about each of the two topics in this paragraph.

Testimonials written by clerks about their judges often emphasize the importance of the latters' practical experiences, for example: Chief Justice Vinson and His Law Clerks, 49 Nw. U. L. Rev. 26, 34 (1954); J. Pickering, E. Gressman, and T. Tolan, Mr. Justice Murphy—A Note of Appreciation, 48 Mich. L. Rev. 742 (1950).

17. V. Brudney and R. Wolfson, Mr. Justice Rutledge—Law Clerks' Reflections, 25 Ind. L. Rev. 455, 560 (1950). However, there was little evidence of this as a major source of social facts for the judges in the courts studied here.

18. The ABA Code of Judicial Conduct, Canon 5, prevents a judge from practicing law, severely restricts his business activities, and even prohibits some charitable work. Canon 7 prohibits any active or public political activities, except when running for judgeships or on matters of court administration. Canon 4, on the other hand, encourages judges to engage in activities and organizations concerned with court administration. Even before the Code of Judicial Conduct was adopted, appellate judges stayed pretty well within these bounds, based on comments by most clerks and a few judges interviewed. Political scientists studying ten state courts and the U.S. Fifth Circuit found the same thing. The bulk of these studies are cited in note 34 of Chapter 10: Beatty at 230-255, Mason at 200-232, Rich at 90, and Glick at 123-130. See also, J. Wold, *Internal Procedures, Role Perceptions and Judicial Behavior: A Study of Four State Courts of Last Resort* 257-271 (unpublished Ph.D. dissertation, The Johns Hopkins University, 1972). A study of a years' work habits on a circuit court found that the judges spent 8 percent of their time on "pro bono activities." Federal Judicial Center, *A Summary of the Third Circuit Time Study* 3 (1974).

Judicial conferences where appellate judges exchange ideas are one kind of outside activity allowed and are increasingly important. See especially F. Kenison, The Continuing Contribution of Robert A. Leflar to the Judicial Education of Appellate Judges, 25 Ark. L. Rev. 95 (1971).

In L. Friedman, Epitaph for Judicial Isolationism, 6 Trial Judges' J. 1 (Oct. 1967), a California intermediate appellate court judge strongly urged more involvement in general community affairs. He said judges traditionally have withdrawn from civic, charitable, and other activities,

> often placing the law in intellectual isolation from the organic processes of social action and interaction of which the law is only a part. They recognized of course that legal techniques had to be supplemented by considerable knowledge of human behavior. As source of this knowledge, they relied almost entirely upon personal experience and a set of intuitions called "common sense."

But, on the whole, this reasoning has lost out to the view that judges must not be involved in outside activities that would give any hint of impartiality in their case deciding.

19. A. Smith and A. Blumberg, The Problem of Objectivity in Judicial Decision-Making, 46 Social Forces 96, 101 (1967); J. Beatty, *An Institutional and Behavioral Analysis of the Iowa Supreme Court—1965-1969* 190 (unpublished Ph.D. dissertation, University of Iowa, 1970). The former mentions a sociological study of thirty judges:

> Two-thirds of the respondents identified their isolation as the least favorable aspect of being an appellate judge. "I am segregated from the political, social, and economic arenas of life in which our destinies are shaped." was a comment that tended to summarize other similar comments. Two judges simply responded with one word, "loneliness." Another judge deplored his "lack of personal contact with the litigants, witnesses and others who play a part in each case."

Two other studies have asked appellate judges how their role differed from that of trial judges, and a common answer was that appellate judges are more secluded. J. Wold, *Internal Procedures, Role Perceptions and Judicial Behavior: A Study of Four State Courts of Last Resort* 184-187 (unpublished Ph.D. dissertation, The Johns Hopkins University, 1972); J. Howard, *Role Perceptions on the U.S. Courts of Appeals for the 2D, 5TH, and D.C. Circuits* 18 (Federal Judicial Center, 1973).

I did not ask the judges interviewed about whether they felt cloistered, though several did volunteer comments to that effect.

In the past century appellate judges routinely sat as trial judges also, picking up experience that way, but this is rare now. Every once in a while a federal circuit judge will sit in a district court, and trial judges may sit in circuit courts and many state appellate courts. Only in two or three states do appellate judges also try cases. See D. Carmody, Trial of Cases by Appellate Judges, 5 Trial Judges' J. 1 (Oct. 1966); Institute of Judicial Administration, *The Supreme Judicial Court and the Superior Court of the State of Maine* 1, 3 (1971).

20. F. Hiscock, The Court of Appeals of New York: Some Features of Its Organization and Work, 14 Cornell L.Q. 131, 134 (1929).

21. C. Breitel, The Lawmakers, 65 Colum. L. Rev. 749, 770 (1965).

22. Quoted in W. Gibson, Literary Minds and Judicial Style, 36 N.Y. U.L. Rev. 915, 924 (1961).

23. On this point see especially McGowan, *supra* note 6, at 678, 679. The U.S. Supreme Court, on the other hand, can delay entering an area until sufficient fact patterns have developed in lower court litigation.

24. In arguing against cutting back the jurisdiction of federal courts, a circuit judge and a district judge wrote:

> Many of [the judges'] contacts with the everyday affairs of life and with people in all walks of life would be lost. Their feel of the pulse of America would cease. A judge, if he is to render a high order of judicial service, must keep in touch with the practical day-to-day affairs of life. He must know and understand people, their emotions and prejudices, their hopes and aspirations, their virtues and their shortcomings, their strength and their frailties. He must understand human nature. He must be practical.

See O. Phillips and A. Christenson, The Historical and Legal Background of the Diversity Jurisdiction, 46 A.B.A.J. 959, 965 (1960).

25. On the importance of advice from colleagues who are experts in a particular area see Llewellyn, *supra* note 15, at 334; R. Traynor, Some Open Questions on the Work of State Appellate Courts, 24 U. Chi. L. Rev. 211, 217 (1957). Both Llewellyn and Traynor were apparently talking about social fact considerations. Political scientists, however, have found that advice from expert colleagues is considered to be of only limited value. One political scientist asked circuit judges how important the "views of the court's most expert member" were as a factor they were likely to follow when deciding cases where the precedent is unclear. About half said it was moderately important, several said it was very important, and several said it was not important (Howard, *supra* note 19, at 38). Another political scientist, studying the Iowa Supreme Court, asked judges how important the views of other judges with special competence in the area were in reaching decisions. Only three of nine judges said these views were important. Most other judges said there were no areas of special competence (Beatty, *supra* note 19, at 289). There is, of course, no indication in these two studies of how the advice of judges with expertise in an area may be helpful—whether it is advice about social facts or not.

26. See, for example, J. Breitenstein, The United States Court of Appeals for the Tenth Circuit, 52 Denver L.J. 9, 16 (1975).

27. Of course, a judge's background may lead to factors other than social fact information that affect decision making—for example, philosophies, biases, and work habits. These complicate the picture even further. Many political science studies have attempted to find correlations between judges' decisions (e.g., the propensity to decide for criminal defendants, labor unions, or plaintiffs in tort cases) and various background characteristics (e.g., political party, trial judge experience, and religion), and they tend to find very little correlation. For a thorough study of this type, see S. Goldman, Voting Behavior on the United States Courts of Appeals Revisited, 69 Am. Pol. Sci. Rev. 491 (1975). One study, however, using inapposite statistical techniques, as the author admits, obtained some high correlations. S. Nagel, Multiple

Correlation of Judicial Backgrounds and Decisions, 2 Fla. St. U.L. Rev. 258 (1974). These two articles contain references to the bulk of the studies in this area.

28. Karst, *supra* note 6, at 107, 108, claims that these facts are treated somewhat as *stare decisis*, though less so than propositions of law. This is supported by the focal court's habit of quoting social facts from its own decisions or U.S. Supreme Court decisions, that is, the two courts whose decisions are the most binding on the court.

Sometimes the line is very fine between citing or stating a social fact and citing or stating a legal rule. See H. Korn, Law, Fact, and Science in the Courts, 66 Colum. L. Rev. 1080, 1107 (1966); Davis, *supra* note 10, at sec. 15.04. However, in practice very rarely in this study did I have any problem distinguishing law statements from social fact statements.

That a judge cites a social fact in a prior opinion does not mean, of course, that he necessarily discovered the fact there originally. He may have known of the social fact and cited the statement in the prior opinion as an authoritative means of presenting it.

29. Many writings have emphasized this problem, for example: A. Miller and J. Barron, The Supreme Court, the Adversary System, and the Flow of Information to the Justices: A Preliminary Inquiry, 61 Va. L. Rev. 1187 (1975); J. Weintraub, Judicial Legislation, 81 N.J.L.J. 545, 549 (1958). M. Cohen, *American Thought* 164 (1954); R. Seidman, The Judicial Process Reconsidered in the Light of Role-Theory, 32 Modern L. Rev. 516, 525-527 (1969); Llewellyn, *supra* note 15, *passim*, esp. 323-335; C. Horowitz, Judging Judgments, 7 Gonzaga L. Rev. 1, 10-13 (1971); M. Rosenberg, Anything Legislatures Can Do, Courts Can Do Better? 62 A.B.A.J. 587 (1976). D. Horowitz, *The Courts and Social Policy* (1977); W. Friedmann, Legal Philosophy and Judicial Law Making, 61 Colum. L. Rev. 821, 842-845 (1961); Karst, *supra* note 6; R. Pound, *The Spirit of the Common Law* 213-216 (1921).

CHAPTER 13

1. R. Traynor, Some Open Questions on the Work of State Appellate Courts, 24 U. Chi. L. Rev. 211, 219 (1957).

2. For a description of the possible uses of empirical data for supporting case facts see I. Robbins, The Admissibility of Social Science Evidence in Person-Oriented Legal Adjudication, 50 Ind. L.J. 493 (1975). Although not one of the topics emphasized here, it seems that many judges use empirical data not in the record for supporting case facts, though not for regular case facts.

3. These statements are based on the interviews with the judges and clerks, studying the focal court appeals, and listening to some oral arguments at other courts. In the interviews, I asked how often they considered "scientific or statistical or social science studies or findings" when deciding cases. As one would expect, the answers were seldom specific figures, rather "sometimes," "rarely," or the like; so definite figures about how often empirical data was used in the courts, except the focal court, were not obtained. Also, it was sometimes difficult to tell whether the judges, especially, were talking about empirical data as social facts or case facts. Usually I added some reference to social facts—e.g., the use of empirical data when determining "policy or practical implications"—but this was not always possible due to difficulties in establishing some word to refer to social facts, as has been discussed in Chapter 10. Some answers, then, were mainly about case facts, and I had to study the context

—especially examples—to see whether the judge or clerk had social facts in mind. Even if the question was phrased in terms of social facts, the judges sometimes referred to case fact empirical data in the answers.

Another problem with questioning on this subject was that the question might not be taken to apply to professional journals, newspaper articles, and a great many other means of obtaining social facts from experts that the judges may not consider "scientific or statistical or social science" materials. Also, they may read about these materials secondhand in law review articles. (Until recently, hardly any law review articles contained this type of material, and it is still quite seldom cited. See J. Gazell, An Overdue Revolution Deferred: Researching the Law, 1972 Utah L. Rev. 22.) However, a few judges did mention these sources when asked about scientific, etc., materials, and I know of no case in which these sources were used but the judge did not mention it in the interviews.

4. In all, about a fifth of the social facts mentioned in the opinions were supported by empirical data. The use of empirical data was, of course, highly skewed, with great use being made in four opinions in three cases. One judge wrote three of these four opinions, but all the others, except one judge who wrote far fewer opinions than his colleagues, used empirical data. The source of the empirical data in the four opinions using much of it differed little from that of the data in the nine other opinions, on the average. Also, except for one judge, the judges using empirical data were about equally prone to use data not presented by counsel.

5. See Chapter 7, at note 17.

6. In D. Ziskind, The Use of Economic Data in Labor Cases, 6 U. Chi. L. Rev. 607 (1939), the author and a colleague read the briefs in Supreme Court labor cases and found that, by my count, the court did not mention empirical data presented by the attorneys in about one-third of the cases in which attorneys presented data to support social facts. For a further explanation of this article see note 17.

7. As Justice Van Voorhis of New York wrote in 1961: "Only recently in modern times have judges had the temerity to cite sociologists, economists, historians and other writers having knowledge essential to the intelligent decision of the law applicable to the case at the bar." J. Van Voorhis, Cardozo and the Judicial Process Today, 71 Yale L.J. 202, 205 (1961). Justice Traynor, in an article outlining the possible uses of empirical data, said "Here and there forward-looking courts have been alert to the implications for law of law-related learning. They are still an all too small vanguard, however." R. Traynor, What Domesday Books for Emerging Law? 15 U.C.L.A.L. Rev. 1105, 1109 (1968). In the past ten years, this vanguard has probably grown larger, but how much so is uncertain.

Empirical data have been emphasized in U.S. Supreme Court briefs and opinions at least since the turn of the century. For surveys of the Court's use of empirical evidence, see Ziskind, *supra* note 6; J. Kohn, Social Psychological Data, Legislative Fact, and Constitutional Law, 29 Geo. Wash. L. Rev. 136 (1960); K. Karst, Legislative Facts in Constitutional Litigation, 1960 Supreme Court Rev. 75; P. Rosen, *The Supreme Court and Social Science* (1972); A. Davis, *The United States Supreme Court and the Uses of Social Science Data* (1973).

A recent study of Supreme Court opinions in every five years from 1954 through 1974 found that the opinions cited social science sources in 10 percent of the some 600 cases studied. There is a slight tendency toward more use in later years. The use of empirical data by the Court is probably considerably greater, because the authors only studied social science sources. V. Rosenblum et al., *Report on the Uses of Social Science in Judicial Decision Making* 7-16 (unpublished manuscript, Northwestern University Law School, 1977). In the authors' opinion, however, not many of the social science sources were greatly relied upon by the justices in the opinions' reasoning (*id.*, at 21). Two other studies of Supreme Court opinions have found somewhat less use of empirical data. The first, studying one year's cases, concluded that there was a "paucity of these citations"—26 in 218 opinions, though the author did not say how many opinions cited them. He also concluded that these authorities were not fundamental to any opinions. N. Bernstein, The Supreme Court and Secondary Source Material; 1965 Term, 57 Geo. L.J. 55, 69-77 (1968). The second study was of 85 criminal cases decided in 1958-1962, and it found that the court used empirical data in seven cases, citing at least 30 authorities. J. Scurlock, Scholarship and the Courts, 32 U. Mo. Kan. City L. Rev. 228, 242-252 (1964).

Studies of state appellate courts have found great variations among courts but, on the whole, little use of empirical data references. Seven state supreme court justices reported in the 1920s that they did not believe in using, or at most rarely used, statistical and other sociological data. Queries Concerning Methods of Work in Supreme Courts, 8 J. Am. Jud. Soc'y. 165, 169 (1925), and 10 J. Am. Jud. Soc'y. 57, 58 (1926). But well before that time some state courts (along with the U.S. Supreme Court) used empirical data in economic due process cases. See note 8.

Scurlock (*supra*, at 228-241) studied about 100 criminal cases in the Missouri, California, and New York courts of last resort in the late 1950s and early 1960s. The Missouri court cited no empirical references, and the California and New York courts each cited about ten references in three or four cases. Scurlock also (*id.*, at 252-258) studied 189 criminal cases nationwide dealing with subjects that seemed to him to call for empirical data—for example, insanity defenses and the admissibility of scientific tests. Even here only about 10 percent of the cases cited authority for social facts. (The figures from Scurlock's article are based on citations supporting social facts; in the state courts most of these citations were to law review articles rather than nonlegal publications. There was no way to tell from the article whether a particular law review article cited incorporated empirical data to support the social facts or merely contained a law professor's opinion; so the figures may be too high. The focal court, incidentally, seldom cited law reviews to support social facts, and it may be unusual in this. Judge Oakes of the Second Circuit has said that the empirical data used by appellate courts come "in great measure" from law review articles. J. Oakes, Law Reviews and Judging, 50 N.Y.U.L. Rev. 2, 5 (1975).) Studies of citation practices of the California Supreme Court have found that in 1950 and 1960 the court cited only one or two nonlegal sources for empirical data each year, and then in 1970 about fifteen such cites appeared. One judge cited the bulk of these fifteen, however, and they probably were in no more than a half-dozen cases. J. Merryman, The Authority of Authority, 6 Stan. L. Rev. 613, 671, 672 (1954); J. Merryman, Toward a Theory of Citations: An Empirical Study of the Citation Practice of the California Supreme Court in 1950, 1960, and 1970, 50 So. Calif. L. Rev. 381, 409, 410 (1977). A similar study of the Ohio Supreme Court for the years 1951 through 1955 showed no such citations: R. Archibald, Stare Decisis and the Ohio Supreme Court, 9 Western Reserve L. Rev. 23, 26-28 (1957).

Political scientists have asked appellate judges in several courts about the importance of social science in decision making. See Glick's study in footnote 34 of Chapter 10, suggesting that the justices' attitude toward using social science varied greatly among the New Jersey, Pennsylvania, Massachusetts, and Louisiana courts of last resort (listed in order of decreasing importance given the material). Studies of the Iowa and Kansas Supreme Courts found that about half the justices considered literature in the social sciences important or very important; the justices' views varying greatly on each court, though overall the two courts were about the same. However, the justices said that social science literature was not used in very many cases. Also, from the answers quoted it seems that some of the judges were referring to case facts rather than social facts. G. Mason, *Judges and Their Publics: Role Perceptions and Role Expectations* 283, 284 (unpublished Ph.D. dissertation, University of Kansas, 1968); J. Beatty, *An Institutional and Behavioral Analysis of the Iowa Supreme Court* 282 (unpublished Ph.D. dissertation, University of Iowa, 1970). Seven of the eight justices on a New York intermediate appellate court said the findings of social scientists had a value in their decision making, but again the judges may have been thinking of case facts. M. Palley, *The Appellate Division of the New York State Supreme Court, First Department: A Study in Role Behavior* 87, 88 (unpublished Ph.D. dissertation, New York University, 1966). When asked about the importance of "non-legal" sources in reaching decisions, California intermediate court judges gave greatly differing answers, though less than half considered this information of much importance. J. Masuda, *The Politics of a State Intermediate Appellate Process: The California Court of Appeal* 80 (unpublished Ph.D. dissertation, University of Iowa, 1976).

Another indication of the general lack of interest in empirical data by appellate judges is that only one of the judges' writings on appellate advocacy (which have been discussed in Chapter 3) asked attorneys to supply this type of information. This is G. Rossman, Appellate Practice and Advocacy, 16 F.R.D. 403, 409 (1955). On the other hand, at least twenty appellate judges—but still a small number—have written elsewhere in law review articles that empirical data should be used more often, for example, T. Kavanagh, The Ethics of Urban Law and Practice: A Challenge for the Common Law, 19 De Paul L. Rev. 496, 500 (1970). Recently, however, a circuit judge has written that empirical data are of very limited importance: W. Doyle, Can Social Science Data Be Used in Judicial Decisionmaking? 6 J. L.&Ed. 13 (1977).

Innumerable lawyers and social scientists—I know of over five dozen—have written to urge the courts to use empirical data for social facts, giving arguments similar to this: "The formulation of law and policy . . . obviously gains strength to the extent that information replaces guesswork or ignorance or hunch or intuition or general impressions." K. Davis, *Administrative Law Treatise* sec. 15.03 (1958). The most detailed, but perhaps overly enthusiastic, argument for the use of empirical data is Rosen, *supra*. But nearly all of these writers also warn that the data—especially social science data—may be untrustworthy. Two recent articles have argued against the use of empirical data in most instances because of its frequent untrustworthiness. They are S. Miller and J. Kavanagh, Empirical Evidence, J.L. & Ed. 159 (1975), and R. Dworkin, Social Sciences and Constitutional Rights—The Consequences of Uncertainty, 6 J.L. & Ed. 3 (1977). See also E. Cahn, Jurisprudence, 30 N.Y.U.L. Rev. 150, 159-166 (1956).

8. See especially Kohn, *supra* note 7, at 137-162, and J. Wisdom, Random Remarks on the Role of Social Sciences in the Judicial Decision-Making Process in School Desegregation Cases, 39 Law & Contem. Prob. 135 (1975). Similar to this category is the old substantive due process cases. As opposed to equal-protection cases, the party initiating the use of empirical data generally was arguing in favor of the statute. In both the state and federal courts parties presented considerable data and judges often used it in their decisions, starting apparently with People v. Lochner 177 N.Y. 145 (1904) and Lochner v. New York, 198 U.S. 45 (1905).

The Rosenblum study (*supra* note 7, at 49, 50) found that the Supreme Court used social science materials in equal-protection cases far more than in cases with any other types of issues, and that there were only small variations in use in these other types of issues.

9. This and the following sentences are based on *McCormick on Evidence* secs. 203-211 (E. Cleary ed. 1972). Often, however, empirical data are not used in these cases because the court relies on other courts' findings. See the discussion of the Scurlock article in note 7.

10. For example, voice-print evidence was ruled admissible in Commonwealth v. Lykus, 327 N.E.2d 671 (Mass. 1975), and inadmissible in United States v. Addison, 498 F.2d 741 (D.C. 1974), and People v. Kelley, 17 Cal.3d 24 (1976). The three courts received much the same information on the topic.

11. What follows is an alphabetical listing of the more comprehensive writings about how judges obtain empirical data. They are mainly legal, as opposed to social science, articles. Many more writings quickly discuss the subject or cover only one aspect in detail; the latter group are cited elsewhere in this chapter.

Annotation—Consideration of Extrinsic Evidence on Questions of Constitutionality or Unconstitutionality of Statute, 82 L.Ed. 1244 (1938).

H. Baade, Social Science Evidence and the Federal Constitutional Court of West Germany, 23 J. Pol. 421 (1961).

J. Beuscher, The Use of Experts by the Courts, 54 Harv. L. Rev. 1105 (1941).

H. Bikle, Judicial Determination of Questions of Fact Affecting the Constitutional Validity of Legislative Action, 38 Harv. L. Rev. 6 (1924).

G. Currie, Appellate Courts Use of Facts Outside of the Record by Resort to Judicial Notice and Independent Investigation, 1960 Wisc. L. Rev. 39.

W. Denman, Trials of Fact in Constitutional Cases, 21 A.B.A.J. 805 (1935).

F. Frankfurter and J. Landis, *The Business of the Supreme Court* 312-318 (1928).

P. Freund, *On Understanding the Supreme Court* 86-91 (1949).

R. Fuchs and W. Freedman, The Wagner Act—Decisions and Factual Techniques in Public Law Cases, 22 Wash. U.L.Q. 510, 526-529 (1937).

S. Glueck, The Social Sciences and the Scientific Method in the Administration of Justice, 167 Annals 106, 112-117 (1933).

O. Grey, Judicial Legislation: Judicial Constructs and Social Facts, 31 U. Toronto Faculty of L. Rev. 75, 84-91 (1973).

H. Hart and J. McNaughton, Evidence and Inference in the Law, 87 Deadalus 40, 54-57 (Fall 1958).

P. Hogg, Proof of Facts in Constitutional Cases, 26 U. Toronto L.J. 386 (1976).

D. Horowitz, *The Courts and Social Policy* 279-283 (1977).

S. Kadish, Methodology and Criteria in Due Process Adjudication—A Survey and Criticism, 66 Yale L.J. 319, 358-362 (1957).

K. Karst, Legislative Facts in Constitutional Litigation, 1960 Supreme Court Rev. 75, 99-109.

J. Kohn, Social Psychological Data, Legislative Fact, and Constitutional Law, 29 Geo. Wash. L. Rev. 136, 163, 164 (1960).

B. Laub, The Courts and Social Reform—A Proposal to Meet New Challenges, 13 St. Louis U.L.J. 56 (1968).

A. Miller and J. Barron, The Supreme Court, the Adversary System, and the Flow of Information to the Justices: A Preliminary Inquiry, 61 Va. L. Rev. 1187 (1975).

C. Morris, Law and Fact, 55 Harv. L. Rev. 1303, 1319-1325 (1942).

C. Newland, Innovation in Judicial Technique: The Brandeis Opinion, 42 Sw. Social Sci. Q. 22 (1961).

Note, The Consideration of Facts in "Due Process" Cases, 30 Colum. L. Rev. 360, 370-372 (1930).

Note, The Presentation of Facts Underlying the Constitutionality of Statutes, 49 Harv. L. Rev. 631 (1936).

Note, The Presumption of Constitutionality Reconsidered, 36 Colum. L. Rev. 283 (1936).

Note, Social and Economic Facts, Appraisal of Suggested Techniques for Presenting Them to the Courts, 61 Harv. L. Rev. 692 (1948).

M. Rosenberg, Anything Legislatures Can Do, Courts Can Do Better? 62 A.B.A.J. 587 (1976).

F. Scharpf, Judicial Review and the Political Question: A Functional Analysis, 75 Yale L.J. 517, 524-529 (1966).

R. Traynor, What Domesday Books for Emerging Law? 15 U.C.L.A.L. Rev. 1105, 1111-1113 (1968).

Weinstein's Evidence, secs. 200(03), 200(04) (1975).

J. Weintraub, Judicial Legislation, 81 N.J.L.J. 545, 549 (1958).

E. Wilson, Consideration of Facts in Constitutional Cases, 17 So. Calif. L. Rev. 335, 338-344 (1944).

12. In several cases the court cited empirical data similar to that in the briefs, but not mentioned in the briefs.

The Rosenblum study (*supra* note 7, at 10, 63) of the Supreme Court's use of social science materials also studied the briefs. Reworking their data to take into account the method of sampling the briefs, a little over 20 percent of the briefs contained social science materials, almost the same proportion as at the focal court. However, the number of briefs before the Supreme Court containing empirical data is probably substantially higher than the number with social science materials alone. Also, extrapolating from Rosenblum's findings, it appears that the Supreme Court cited social science materials found in the briefs in only about 20 percent of the cases in which the briefs contained those materials.

13. Most of the attorneys gave reasons why they did not or very seldom used this material; all volunteered the information. A reason not mentioned by any attorneys, though surely important, is that many of the attorneys had handled very few cases reaching, or expected to reach, the appellate level and, thus, had little occasion to

use social facts, which are mainly applicable to appellate court decision making.

14. Law schools have traditionally paid little or no attention to the use of empirical data as social facts, though in recent years some schools, especially the major schools, have shown more interest in this area; also, there is some evidence of a trend among law students away from humanities majors in college to social science majors. See B. Boyer and R. Cramton, American Legal education: An Agenda for Research and Reform, 59 Cornell L. Rev. 221, 222-228, 239 (1974); Jurimetrics in Education, 16 Jurimetrics J. 74 (1975). The *Directory of Law Teachers* (Association of American Law Schools, 1975 Supplement) lists a little over 600 professors teaching in the areas of Law and Computers, Psychiatry, Science, Medicine, and Society (one-third are in each of the last two categories). Only 20 percent of them had taught these courses for more than five years, and half of these were law and medicine teachers. Throughout most of this century a few law professors have been doing empirical social science research; recently, especially with the help of federal research funds, this area has become quite fashionable, see L. Walker, Foreword, 52 N.C.L. Rev. 969 (1974).

15. For lengthy, but speculative, accounts of why lawyers do not use social science more often, see P. Lochner, Some Limits on the Application of Social Science Research in the Legal Process, 1973 L. & Social Order 815; S. Fahr and R. Ojemann, The Use of Social and Behavioral Science Knowledge in Law, 48 Iowa L. Rev. 59 (1962); and S. Fahr, Why Lawyers Are Dissatisfied with the Social Sciences, 1 Washburn L.J. 161 (1961). Lochner, especially, lists many reasons (at 824-835): Lawyers normally do not use social science research in their daily business (though they often have contact with social science practitioners—see Fahr's article, at 161), and thus do not know when it may be applicable or how to find and evaluate it; lawyers tend to stick to their habitual modes of research because of inertia; the costs in time and money often do not justify looking for social science research; and lawyers often have little respect for the social sciences. The last two were not mentioned in the interviews; the first of these, however, is probably important. The second is relevant only insofar as it affects the attorneys' views of the court's attitude toward social science.

These reasons probably apply as well to the physical sciences; most obviously do so, and even lack of respect may be involved: A study of lawyers interested in natural resources issues suggested "a serious credibility gap based on perceived lack of veracity and objectivity on the part of scientists and engineers." J. Curlin, Law, Science, and Public Policy, in *Scientists in the Legal System* 35, 43 (W. Thomas ed. 1974).

16. Kadish, *supra* note 11, at 361. For a similar view see I. Kaufman, Judicial Reform in the Next Century, 32 Record 9, 31 (1977).

17. Ziskind, *supra* note 6, *passim*. This old but competent study of the use of economic data (actually, social science data in general) by the U.S. Supreme Court in all types of labor cases, including appeals attacking legislation regulating working conditions under the due process clause, found that for those cases in which one party used the data and the other did not use it or used it only incidentally, victory went to the former sixteen times and to the latter three times. (In three of the sixteen the data appeared from the accounts given in the article to be used largely for case facts.) Ziskind said this may have been a coincidence but strongly suggests a causal relationship (*id.*, at 650). One of the most persistent areas of imbalance was in cases involv-

ing the National Labor Relations Board, whose own economic research division gave it far better resources to gather and present empirical data than its opponents (*id.*, at 621-631). On the inadequate presentation of empirical data in the U.S. Supreme Court, see also Karst, *supra* note 11, *passim.* In the present study there was no tendency for the side presenting the most empirical data to win when there was an imbalance. This may not be typical, however. A law professor has written:

> It is also regrettable that most attempts to introduce "voiceprint" evidence have been made in criminal cases by the prosecution, which has the resources at its disposal to bring in experts who are willing to testify in favor of admission. Generally defendants do not have the financial resources to introduce experts to rebut the prosecution's experts. The court, therefore, often is presented only one side of the evidence. W. Jones, Evidence vel non: The *Non* Sense of Voiceprint Identification, 62 Ky. L.J. 301, 302 (1974).

See also, W. Berns, Buck v. Bell, Due Process of the Law? 6 Western Pol. Q. 762, 765, 766 (1953).

18. The great majority of writings in note 11 suggest that it is all right for judges to investigate empirical data sources. See also notes 21, 25, and 28.

19. Except for the focal court, this statement is based on the almost total lack of examples of this practice and in the legal literature. The Rhode Island Supreme Court once in a while does ask for rebriefing in empirical data questions, and the U.S. Supreme Court earlier in the century remanded several cases to gather more empirical data testimony, as listed in Fuchs and Freedman, *supra* note 11, at 527. But the Court is, in general, reluctant to remand for this purpose. See Karst, *supra* note 11, at 95-98. The New Jersey Supreme Court sent a case back twice to the trial court for empirical data evidence, State v. Cary, 264 A.2d 209 (1970).

20. A little research for empirical data was also done for supporting case facts, and it was difficult to tell in a few interviews whether the judges were talking about researching social facts or supporting case facts.

21. This is based on forty-five references in the opinions. The Rosenblum study (*supra* note 7, at 64) found almost the same proportion with respect to social science citations in the U.S. Supreme Court opinions. He also found that majority opinions were much more likely than minority opinions to use social science sources not in the briefs (*id.*, at 71), though at the focal court the minority opinions were more likely to do so. In a recent study of U.S. Supreme Court decisions (see note 17 of Chapter 9 for a description of this study) it was found that for roughly 40 percent of the opinions citing what seems to be empirical data sources (nonlegal texts, nonlegal journals or newspapers, other government documents, and unpublished documents) the briefs brought out at least one of the authorities of those cited in the opinions in a case. Because the opinions may have cited more than one such authority, the percentage of such authorities brought up by counsel is probably close to the figure of one-third found at the focal court for empirical data sources. On the other hand, only four of the ten sources of empirical data cited in majority opinions in the 1965 term were not in the briefs (Bernstein, *supra* note 7, at 71).

22. Amicus briefs presented to other courts probably offer similar help in supplying empirical data. See note 21 of Chapter 5. Also, Rosenblum (*supra* note 7, at 68)

found that 43 percent of the social science citations in the briefs used by the U.S. Supreme Court were in the amicus briefs (apparently about that proportion of all social science citations in the briefs were in the amicus briefs).

23. I only know of one opinion of the six courts studied in which it was acknowledged that social fact advice was obtained from outside experts. For examples of this see: Currie, *supra* note 11, at 43-47 (the Wisconsin Supreme Court), and United States v. Roth, 237 F2d 796, 814 (1956) (J. Frank, concurring, Second Circuit). See also Beuscher, *supra* note 11, at 1107, 1108.

24. Examples of this practice in other courts are in the preceding note. Also the New Jersey Supreme Court obtained expert outside advice at least once. See H. Glick, *Supreme Courts in State Politics* 84 (1971). And this topic is discussed by Chief Justice Weintraub, *supra* note 11, at 549. Llewellyn highly recommends this practice. See his *The Common Law Tradition, Deciding Appeals* 323-332 (1960). It is also rumored that the U.S. Supreme Court occasionally asks for help from outside experts on empirical data matters. See C. Lamb, Judicial Policy-Making and Information Flow to the Supreme Court, 29 Vand. L. Rev. 45, 98 (1976). In England in the eighteenth century Lord Mansfield often obtained advice from experts about the practices of merchants when he was fashioning the commercial law (Beuscher, *supra* note 11, at 1108-1111).

25. Those making this suggestion are: E. Corwin, Reports of the National Conference on the Science of Politics, Round Table VI. Public Law, 18 Am. Pol. Sci. Rev. 148, 153 (1924); Glueck, *supra* note 11, at 115-117; F. Beutel, Some Implications of Experimental Jurisprudence, 48 Harv. L. Rev. 169, 181 (1934) [see also, F. Beutel, *Experimental Jurisprudence* 64-66 (1957)]; R. Pound, *The Spirit of the Common Law 214* (1921); C. Vose, *Constitutional Change: Amendment Politics and Supreme Court Litigation Since 1900*, 368-370 (1972); Laub, *supra* note 11, at 65; Fuchs and Freeman, *supra* note 11, at 527; M. Rosenberg, Let's Everybody Litigate? 50 Texas L. Rev. 1349, 1355 (1972); Rosenberg, *supra* note 11, at 590; B. Cardozo, *The Growth of the Law* 117 (1924); J. Frank, *Courts on Trial* 291, 343 (1949); C. Auerbach, AALS/AAAS Joint Panel Discussion on the Law-Science Interface, 16 Jurimetrics J. 24, 34, 35 (1975); Kaufman, *supra* note 18, at 31, 32. See also P. Freund, *supra* note 11, at 91.

But see Judge Frank's later objections to a proposed "commission of inquiry" to be used to supply lawyers with social science data on the grounds that there is little of value in the social sciences: J. Frank, The Lawyer's Role in Modern Society: A Round Table Comment, 4 J. Pub. L. 8, 16-18 (1955). Likewise, Baade (*supra* note 11, at 428) objected to an agency to help appellate courts evaluate social science data, because it "will in all probability be unable to transcend the state of relative uncertainty inherent in the present state of the social sciences." It has also been said that such an agency would probably not be established because it would imply too strongly that the courts make law like the legislature. *Weinstein-Korn-Miller, New York Civil Practice* sec. 4511.01.

26. This suggestion was made in Beuscher, *supra* note 11, at 1123-1126; and Note (1948), *supra* note 11, at 700, 701; see also Miller and Barron, *supra* note 11, at 1240-1242.

The Federal Constitutional Court of West Germany often takes testimony and exhibits concerning social fact empirical data, and it has even had empirical studies made under its direction (Baade, *supra* note 11, at 448-461).

The Canadian Supreme Court in at least one case has solicited and received arguments directly from social scientists, who appeared in adversary roles. See P. Hogg, *supra* note 11, at 399-407.

Actual empirical research by appellate judges, as opposed to using research findings by experts, appears totally out of the question because judges do not have the time, staff, or expertise for the research. I know of only one example of empirical research for social facts conducted by an appellate judge: Justice Murphy's dissent in Wolf v. Colorado, 338 U.S. 25, at 44-46 (1949) said that he asked police commissioners in thirty-eight large cities what instructions were given police about rules of search and seizure. Much more instruction was found to be given in states where illegally obtained evidence was excluded. Judge Frank of the Second Circuit conducted some empirical research for case facts in two trademark cases (see Chapter 11, note 9).

As explained in note 17 of Chapter 11, suggestions have been made that appellate courts use experts to help interpret records involving a great deal of technical data. These suggestions seem aimed only at case facts and supporting case facts; thus a stronger case can be made that this advice, as opposed to empirical data about social facts, should be in the record. Judge Leventhal has suggested that the parties be taxed the costs of hiring these experts, but that may not be fair when the advice sought is about social facts, since the questions involved deal not so much with the resolution of the dispute, but with the creation of precedent—that is, it is a "public question," the term often used by the focal court, at least, when not taxing costs to one side or the other in appeals. So it probably must be left to the courts to pay the experts, and funds may be hard to come by. Several appellate judges have suggested that law professors be paid by the court for work done in preparing amicus briefs (see note 22 of Chapter 5), but apparently this has never been done and, anyway, may pertain only to legal research and not the gathering of empirical data.

27. "The problem," said Judge Craven of the Fourth Circuit, "is not whether to use the social sciences, or whether it is proper to do so, but how to persuade the courts of the truth of the ultimate facts asserted." See J. Craven, The Impact of Social Science Evidence on the Judge: A Personal Comment, 39 Law & Contemp. Prob. 150, 151 (1975). Many writings on the use of empirical data by the courts have emphasized this problem; see especially Karst, *supra* note 11, at 105-107, and Kaufman, *supra* note 16, at 29-32.

28. Of the authorities listed in note 11, only Bikle, Denman, Laub, and Freund believe that the empirical data should always be in the record. A later expression of this view is M. Lasky, A Return to the Observatory Below the Bench, 19 Sw. L.J. 679, 690, 691 (1965). These writers would, of course, permit the use of empirical data not in the record if it satisfies the judicial notice restrictions. One political scientist would allow judges to search for empirical data but not allow counsel to mention it for the first time in the briefs. Horowitz, *supra* note 11, at 282. This suggestion is based on the mistaken notion that briefing schedules are inflexible and do not provide counsel enough time to answer opponents' empirical data.

29. *McCormick on Evidence* sec. 17 (W. Cleary ed. 1972). For an excellent discussion of the problems involved in presenting empirical data at the trial level, see H. Korn, Law, Fact, and Science in the Courts, 66 Colum. L. Rev. 1080 (1966). Included here, also, would be the use of a referee or special master to take evidence on the empirical data, as is sometimes suggested. This amounts to the same thing as testimo-

ny in an ordinary trial because no presumption of correctness is given a trial judge's findings of social facts.

In a related subject, there is some thought that administrative agencies cannot adequately decide complicated cases involving empirical materials in trial-type proceedings (that is, cannot rely on the parties to provide the information) and that they should use rule-making proceedings so that they will have more control over what empirical materials are used in the decision. See especially B. Boyer, Alternatives to Administrative Trial-Type Hearings for Resolving Complex Scientific, Economic, and Social Issues, 71 Mich. L. Rev. 111 (1972).

30. Frank (1955), *supra* note 25, at 21.

31. H. Leventhal, Cues and Compasses for Administrative Lawyers, 20 Ad. L. Rev. 237, 246, 247 (1968).

32. The bulk of these objections were discussed in the authorities cited in note 11.

33. It is sometimes said that rules of evidence hamper the presentation of facts at the trial court. See Horowitz, *supra* note 11, at 280, 281, and R. Seidman, The Judicial Process Reconsidered in the Light of Role-Theory, 32 Modern L. Rev. 516, 526 (1969). But in fact the rules of evidence probably need not be adhered to. See Karst, *supra* note 11, at 103-105; Korn, *supra* note 29, at 1113, 1114; Fed. R. Evidence 201. Juries, of course, do not decide social fact questions.

34. For example, trial counsel in *DeFunis* tried to frame the issue in the case at trial so as to make empirical data irrelevant, whereas those data were probably necessary for an appellate court decision on the merits. See L. Pollak, *DeFunis* Non Est Disputandum, 75 Colum. L. Rev. 494, 503-506 (1975).

35. J. Wright, Court of Appeals Review of Federal Regulatory Agency Rule-making, 26 Ad. L. Rev. 199 (1974). A similar passage is in D. Bazelon, Coping With Technology Through the Legal Process. 62 Cornell L. Rev. 817, 818 (1977). Both judges went on to say that it was sometimes hard to understand the technical materials. This insufficient scientific training in school is probably typical. Judge Friendly said he "avoided science courses because of lack of real comprehension." J. Friendly, *Federal Jurisdiction: A General View* 158 (1973). He said this in reference to appeals in patent cases, which often give federal judges trouble because of the technical material involved. See H. Goodrich, In the Matter of Oral Argument, 1 Prac. Lawyer 12, 13 (Jan. 1955); P. Wepner, Appellate Review of Patentability, 56 J. Patent Office Soc'y 216, 229 (1974). Often, however, circuit judges seem confident that with sufficient study they can understand technical materials. Judge Robb said, "A lawyer who is worth his salt and sits on a circuit court of appeals, if he puts his mind to it and studies long and hard enough, can master it and get at least an understanding of the most technical problems." R. Robb questioning Judge William Doyle, in Hearings Before the Commission on Revision of the Federal Court Appellate System, 830 (1975). Judge Doyle agreed with Judge Robb here. And Judge Griffin Bell made a similar statement (p. 679 of the Hearings). See also note 38.

Appellate judges, except in the rare instances when they obtain advice informally from experts, do not have the opportunity that trial judges have to talk to and be educated by experts about concepts in the cases before them.

36. Most judges were asked about this. A few rare judges, most notably Brandeis and Frank, have done an enormous amount of social science reading in their spare time. Quite a few judges have said that they believe judges should read widely in the

social sciences; one, Justice O'Connell of Oregon, said that judges should be given sabbatical leave for this and other purposes. See K. O'Connell, Streamlining Appellate Procedures, 56 Judicature 234, 238, 239 (1973). Occasionally, a judge will run into large doses of empirical data research in extracurricular law reform activities. See, for example, P. Reardon, Fair Trial-Free Press, 52 Marq. L. Rev. 547, 550 (1969).

37. United States v. Addison, 498 F.2d 741, 744 (D.C.C. 1974).

38. R. Traynor, Reasoning in a Circle of Law, 56 Va. L. Rev. 739, 750 (1970). Except for the first sentence, the passage first appeared in a 1967 article, R. Traynor, Interweavers in the Reformation of Law, 42 Calif. St. B.J. 817, 826 (1967). His thoughts on the matter are more fully set out in Traynor, *supra* note 11. The passage follows the same statement quoted in note 1 about judges' independent research for empirical data. That had been published in 1957, and a lawyer criticized it, saying the data should go through the safeguards of the trial court adversary fact-finding procedures (Lasky, *supra* note 28, at 690, 691). It seems likely that Justice Traynor's statement quoted here was intended as an answer to this criticism.

Justice Traynor believed that courts should inform counsel of empirical data found by the court, and he believed counsel's comments would further help the court evaluate the data. Also, he would like law professors to act as middlemen between the courts and the experts; they would help clarify the empirical data and integrate it into the law.

39. Most of the judges expressed their attitudes toward empirical data, particularly the social sciences. Much of it was volunteered; though I did ask a number of judges what they thought of the social sciences. Most showed a dislike or distrust, usually citing past experiences as a reason.

40. D. Bazelon, Psychiatrists and the Adversary Process, 230 Scientific Am. 18 (June 1974); Frank (1955), *supra* note 25, at 16 and *passim*. See also J. Frank, *Courts on Trial* 209-221 (1949). These two judges, as did several judges interviewed with similar views, sometimes used social science material when deciding cases. For a less skeptical view of psychiatry by another circuit judge familiar with the field, see J. Biggs, *The Guilty Mind, Psychiatry and the Law of Homicide* (1955).

41. R. Pound, The Theory of Judicial Decision, 36 Harv. L. Rev. 940, 950, 951 (1923).

42. *Id.*, at 952.

43. R. Pound, Judicial Councils and Judicial Statistics, 28 A. B.A.J. 98, 99 (1942). He is talking about court and legislative rule making as well as deciding appeals.

44. *Id.*, at 103.

45. *Id.*, at 102-104.

46. Hobson v. Hanson, 327 F. Supp. 844, 859 (D.D.C. 1971).

47. Rosen, *supra* note 7, at 157.

48. Morris, *supra* note 11, at 1319.

49. When courts use empirical data for facts about social life, they are just asking for trouble. For example, the U.S. Supreme Court has quite often been criticized for citing empirical data of dubious applicability and accuracy. Much of this is for the Brown v. School Board decision. See, for example, H. Garfinkel, Social Science Evidence and the School Segregation Cases, 21 J. Politics 37, 51-58 (1959), and M. Berger, Desegregation, Law, and Social Science, 23 Commentary 471, 475, 476 (1957).

For examples of criticism of social science use in other types of cases see: H. Zeisel and S. Diamond, "Convincing Empirical Evidence" on the Six Member Jury, 41 U. Chi. L. Rev. 281 (1974); Bernstein, *supra* note 7, at 73-76; Horowitz, *supra* note 11, at 176-185; and J. Witt, The Bases of Judicial Decision-Making: The Need for a Reappraisal, 59 Marquette L. Rev. 550 (1976).

Reasons why empirical data from the social sciences are often not reliable are discussed in more detail in Appendix A of this book.

Dworkin argues that courts should not use social science conclusions about causation, but that they can use interpretative judgments: R. Dworkin, Social Sciences and Constitutional Rights—The Consequence of Uncertainty, 6 J.L. & Ed. 3 (1977). He says, and I agree, that social science is very weak when studying causation and that the statistical techniques often used there are beyond the competence of judges. On the other hand, I do not understand what he means by interpretative judgments and how they differ from causal judgments. I do feel, however, that descriptive studies are more credible than those involving social science theory, partly because the latter ordinarily involve more uncertain causal assumptions; but social scientists do tend to isolate themselves in academic life, and descriptions by those more experienced in the particular subject area are probably more valuable.

50. Grey, *supra* note 11, at 87.

51. Various writers have suggested that counsel be given advance notice of the use of social facts. See note 4 of Chapter 12.

52. This is suggested in Note (1948), *supra* note 11, at 598. A couple of judges elsewhere have suggested that courts issue proposed opinions for comments. See note 38 of Chapter 5 and Appendix B.

CHAPTER 14

1. The distinction between information in the record and information in the briefs or arguments is sometimes a bit arbitrary; for example, issues ordinarily must be in both, as is discussed in the text. Background knowledge and independent investigation interact in that background knowledge guides investigation.

The table is based on the focal court appeals, but the categories are broad enough so that it probably applies also to most other courts, judging from the interviews at the five other courts and from the legal literature, even though judges and courts differ greatly in these matters. One exception is empirical data, for which the variation may be far beyond the categories. The categories, of course, are based on those discussed in Appendix A. There was nothing in the 70-85 percent range.

For issues, legal authorities, social facts, and empirical data, the total amounts of information in the table are that mentioned in the opinions. As has been said in Chapter 7, the opinions are not always a complete indication of the information used, social facts more so than the others. And it should be repeated that the fact that counsel mentioned information used in the opinion does not always mean that counsel's presentation led to the use of that information, because its importance might not have been apparent from the briefs or arguments. Supporting case facts are rarely mentioned in opinions, so references to them in the table are an educated guess. Case facts outside the record also are not apparent from the opinions, but they are from the briefs and arguments, though the extent of their use in deciding cases is not clear.

2. K. Llewellyn, *The Common Law Tradition, Deciding Appeals* 62-120, 521-535 (1960).

3. See for example, H. Leventhal, Technology Assessment and the Role of the Courts, 16 Jurimetrics J. 186, 199 (1976).

4. At an increasing number of appellate courts—especially intermediate courts—staff attorneys prepare thoroughly researched preargument memorandums. However, this was not done in the courts studied here (any preargument memorandums written were based almost solely on the briefs) and in the courts discussed in note 5.

5. The types of comments by the judges and clerks are not uniform and are sometimes hard to classify. A number would not give a percentage figure in the interviews, answering "not often" or the like, but in terms that seem to fit the percentage range given in the text. Several estimates were about how often the court changes or how often any judge changes, which of course, are lower and higher respectively than estimates about a particular judge.

A great deal of what is published about this is intended to illustrate the importance of oral arguments (i.e., that the impression right afterward is only changed in, say, 10 percent of the cases suggests that the arguments have an important effect on the decision). The judges read the briefs before the arguments on some of these courts, and afterward if at all in the others. When read afterward, any change in the tentative vote could be largely due to the briefs; thus the frequency of changing votes is less relevant. These are all estimates of how often the tentative vote is the final vote, and with one exception, do not indicate how often judges fail to give tentative votes because they do not feel they know enough after the briefs and arguments. The major writing on this subject is F. Wiener, *Effective Appellate Advocacy* 43-45 (1950). He wrote to judges, generally chief judges, on the circuit courts and state supreme courts asking how often their impressions at the close of oral arguments coincided with their final votes. Thirty-three answered; eleven did not give a percentage, and the rest were: 60-65 percent (1), 75 percent (4), 80 percent (4), 80-90 percent (3), and 90 percent or more (10).

A study of four state supreme courts gave this information: On the Maryland Court of Appeals the vote in the postargument conference is almost always the final vote; one justice said the voting alignment stays the same in 95 percent of the cases. One Virginia Supreme Court justice said votes change infrequently after the postargument conference. On the Delaware Supreme Court, the tentative decision in the postargument conference is almost always the final decision. All three courts prepared for the arguments and held conferences right after the arguments. The New York Court of Appeals justices do not read the briefs before the arguments and the first conference is a few weeks after the arguments. Within these few weeks the justices read the briefs, and a memorandum on each case is circulated by the assigned justice, who also does some independent research. Several justices said the voting alignment made in this conference is usually "frozen." J. Wold, *Internal Procedures, Role Perceptions and Judicial Behavior: A Study of Four State Courts of Last Resort* 58, 92, 132, 146, and *passim* (unpublished Ph.D. dissertation, Johns Hopkins University, 1972).

Three judges elsewhere have written about this topic. On the New Hampshire Supreme Court, where briefs are read before the arguments: "Several appellate judges have estimated that the final vote follows the tentative vote in more than eighty-five per cent of the cases." F. Kenison, Some Aspects of Appellate Arguments, 1 N.H.B.J.

5, 6 (Jan. 1959). In the Second Circuit, which had just begun reading briefs before arguments, in 20 percent of the cases the judges have no firm impression of how the case should be decided at the close of oral arguments. In 75 percent of the cases the final decision is in accordance with the tentative vote, and in the remaining 5 percent the decision is reversed. See J. Lumbard, Appellate Advocacy 9 (unpublished paper, Institute of Judicial Administration, 1962). Wisconsin Chief Justice Currie said that his opinion of how a case should come out at the close of oral arguments turned out to be correct at least 80 percent of the time, but he read the briefs after the arguments. See G. Currie, Some Aspects of Appellate Practice Before the Wisconsin Supreme Court, 1955 Wis. L. Rev. 554, 562.

CHAPTER 15

1. J. Frank, *Courts on Trial, passim* (1949).

2. On this latter point see especially J. Wright, Court of Appeals Review of Federal Regulatory Agency Rulemaking, 26 Ad. L. Rev. 199 (1974). In addition, of course, courts often say they give great weight to agency fact finding in adjudication, as opposed to rule making, because of the agency's greater expertise.

3. F. Coffin, Justice and Workability, 5 Suffolk U.L. Rev. 567, 573 (1971).

4. This has been a very general discussion of judicial restraint and has disregarded many nuances—for example, different reasons for restraint tend to be more appropriate for different types of issues. Also, the three are not completely separate reasons; the last two, for example, are connected because unwise decisions based on poor information may lead to less public support for the courts.

The judges' views about the superior capabilities of the legislature and the executive to gather lawmaking information does not, of course, mean that these two branches are in fact efficient information gatherers; they obviously are not in some jurisdictions.

Thirty-seven of the judges who were interviewed talked about the reasons for judicial restraint. About half gave more than one reason, and some probably left reasons unmentioned. Since I was mainly concerned with the information-gathering reason here, I usually asked specifically whether it was a reason. Of the twenty-two judges asked, eight said it was a reason, six said it was secondary, and eight said it was not a reason. Eight of the remaining fifteen judges volunteered it as a reason.

Other reasons given for judicial restraint, though much less often than those in the text, are (1) that courts have trouble fashioning remedies and orders in some areas, for example, problems of prospective overruling and the inability to appropriate money (on this point see especially Justice Powell's comments in Procunier v. Martinez, 416 U.S. 396, 404, 405 (1974)), and (2) that judges do not have enough time for the concentrated study needed when legislating—a reason given only at courts having exceptionally high case loads.

Appellate judges elsewhere quite often talk about the reasons for judicial restraint. Of the almost twenty judges discussing this in books, articles, and conference discussions (except those judges who were interviewed), most gave information-gathering problems as a reason for restraint; less than half mentioned the need for public acceptance; and only a few emphasized the separation of powers in and of itself— that is, about the same portion as in the present study gave the first reason, slightly more gave the second reason, and considerably less gave the third reason. The problems of fashioning remedies was mentioned more often than in the interviews, but still by only a small minority. Only one judge's writing gives all three of the major reasons, C. Breitel, The Lawmakers, 65 Colum. L. Rev. 749, 770, 771 (1965). Extensive discussions of the information-gathering reasons are given in C. McGowan, Rule-Making and the Police, 70 Mich. L. Rev. 659, 672-679 (1972), and R. Traynor, Interweavers in the Reformation of Law, 42 Cal. St. B.J. 817, 818-820 (1967). The major theoretical espousal of this view is F. Scharpf, Judicial Review and the Political Question: A Functional Analysis, 75 Yale L.J. 517 (1966). Judge Hand is the most noted advocate of the need for public acceptance: L. Hand, Contribution of an Independent Judiciary, in *The Spirit of Liberty* 155 (I. Dillard ed. 3rd ed. 1960); L. Hand, *The Bill of Rights* 71, 72 (1958). For lengthy discussions of the third reason by an appellate judge and by a legal scholar, see A. Adams, Judicial Restraint, the Best Medicine, 60 Judicature 179, 180-182 (1976), and J. Deutsch, Neutrality, Legitimacy, and the Supreme Court: Some Intersections Between Law and Political Science, 20 Stan. L. Rev. 169, 249-261 (1968).

Judicial opinions contain a wealth of information about the judges' reasons for judicial restraint, but no systematic search was made here. Justice Frankfurter, a strong advocate of restraint, has cited just about all the reasons for restraint. See, for example, Dennis v. United States, 341 US 494, 525 (1951); Sherrer v. Sherrer 334 US 343, 365, 366 (1948).

5. Most of the judges interviewed talked about the importance and reasons for narrow decisions. For a lengthy discussion of the U.S. Supreme Court's habit of writing broadly, see A. Miller and J. Barron, The Supreme Court, the Adversary System, and the Flow of Information to the Justices: A Preliminary Inquiry, 61 Va. L. Rev. 1187 (1975).

6. A few judges also said that they write narrow opinions so that other judges will sign them. Many other reasons were given, though only by three or fewer judges each: Broad opinions are contra to judicial tradition, confuse the bar, are more easily misinterpreted, result in opinions that are too long, and take too much time.

Judges' articles and books, oddly enough in view of the importance of this subject and the many debates within the courts about it, very seldom mention the need for narrow decisions and the reasons for this need; but concurring and dissenting opinions quite often do. When reasons are given, they are overwhelmingly that broad decisions may entail unintended consequences. See J. Dethmers, Delay in State Appellate Courts of Last Resort, 328 The Annals 153, 158 (1960); R. Gustafson, Some Observations About California Courts of Appeal, 19 U.C.L.A.L. Rev. 167, 178 (1971); R. Traynor, The Well-Tempered Judicial Decision, 21 Ark. L. Rev. 287, 291 (1967). For examples of minority opinions that have emphasized this point, see Justice Harlan dissenting in Sanders v. United States, 373 U.S. 1, 32 (1963); and Judge Frank, in Aero Spark Plug Co. v. B. G. Corporation, 130 F2d 290, 295-299 (1942).

Justice Stern of Pennsylvania made an interesting comment some time ago: He said that opinion writing had become "timid and guarded," as opposed to that in the past century when judges "scorned equivocal statements and eschewed words creating impressions of uncertainty or indecision." Perhaps, he said, this is because society has become more complicated, or perhaps there is much more precedent to worry about. That is, the judges have more trouble finding all important social facts and legal authority. H. Stern, The Writing of Judicial Opinions, 18 Pa. B. Ass'n Q. 40, 42 (1946).

7. Less than half the judges were asked this. Cardozo said he put little faith in dicta because they may be wrong—B. Cardozo, *The Nature of the Judicial Process* 29, 30 (1921)—but there is nothing elsewhere, as far as I know, about this subject in judges' books and articles; again, however, it crops up in some opinions. John Marshall, in an often quoted passage, said the reason was, "The question actually before the Court is investigated with care, and considered in its full extent. Other principles which may serve to illustrate it, are considered in their relation to the case decided, but their possible bearing on all other cases is seldom completely investigated." Cohens v. Virginia, 6 Wheat. 264, 399, 400 (1821).

8. J. Weintraub, Writing, Consideration and Adoption of Opinions, 83 N.J.L.J. 477, 478 (1960). The judges interviewed were not asked about this topic. Another reason for not deciding alternative grounds is that this may lessen the strength of the holding in any one issue. See J. Hopkins, Notes on Style in Judicial Opinions, 8 Trial Judges' J. 49, 51 (1969).

9. O. Holmes, *The Common Law* 98-103 (M. Howe ed. 1963).

10. H. Korn, Law, Fact, and Science in the Courts, 66 Colum. L. Rev. 1080, 1106, 1107 (1966).

11. M. Rosenberg, Judicial Discretion of the Trial Court, Viewed from Above, 22 Syracuse L. Rev. 635, 662, 663 (1971).

12. H. Friendly, Reactions of a Lawyer—Newly Become Judge, 71 Yale L.J. 218, 219 (1961).

13. B. Cardozo, *supra* note 7, at 166. Cardozo remained haunted by this topic; see *The Paradoxes of Legal Science* 1, 80, 81 (1927); The Bench and the Bar, N.Y. St. B.J. 444, 448, 449 (1962). Judge Learned Hand, also, was bothered by the uncertainty: L. Hand, *The Spirit of Liberty* 303-309 (I. Dilliard ed. 3rd ed. 1960); F. Frankfurter, *Of Law and Life and Other Things That Matter* 158 (P. Kurland ed. 1965). Some other judges writing about the uncertainty fully accept it, like the judges who were interviewed, or even revel in it. See especially: C. Clark and D. Trubek, The Creative Role of the Judge: Restraint and Freedom in the Common Law Tradition, 71 Yale L.J. 225 (1961); J. Hutcheson, The Glorious Uncertainty of Our Lady of the Law, 23 J. Am. Jud. Soc'y 73 (1939); W. Douglas, The Dissent: A Safeguard of Democracy, 32 J. Am. Jud. Soc'y 104 (1948).

Judges often say that their job cannot be compared to the workings of a computer or a slot machine: See, for example, I Kaufman, Judicial Reform in the Next Century, 32 Record 9, 32, 33 (1977); R. Traynor, Badlands in an Appellate Judge's Realm of Reason, 7 Utah L. Rev. 157, 158 (1960); H. Medina, Some Reflections on the Judicial Function at the Appellate Level, 1961 Wash. U.L.Q. 148, 155; Coffin, *supra* note 3, at 572; R. Leflar, The Task of the Appellate Court, 33 Notre Dame L. Rev. 548, 567 (1958); A. Tate, The Judge as a Person, 19 La. L. Rev. 438 (1959); Douglas, *supra* at 105. No judge or lawyer is likely to admit that his job is as routine as these analogies imply if only because, as Max Weber said, it would lessen their feelings of self-importance and sense of power. See M. Weber, *On Law in Economy and Society* 309-315 (M. Rheinstein ed. 1954).

14. The great majority of the judges were asked to comment on this, though only about half gave reasons for the uncertainty and discussed whether they were disheartened by it.

15. Again, the great majority were asked about this. Nothing has been written on this subject that I know of.

16. Again, the great majority were asked this.

17. Several judges mentioned this in the interviews, though no questions were asked about it. Justice Cardozo wrote, "A brief experience on the bench was enough to reveal to me all sorts of cracks and crevices and loopholes in my own opinions when picked up a few months after delivery, and reread with due contrition." Cardozo, *supra* note 7, at 29, 30. But few if any other judges have written about this experience.

18. He had clerked on the U.S. Supreme Court. For a very similar statement by a Supreme Court clerk see J. Wilkinson, *Serving Justice* 75 (1974). The responsibilities and uncertainties, of course, are much greater on the U.S. Supreme Court than on the courts studied. Justice Whittaker called his position on the Eighth Circuit "a very quiet and comfortable position" (though it probably would not be considered such now), but the Supreme Court he "found truly to be, as the fans say, 'the hot corner.' Then came the solemn quest for light that can proceed from the broodings of a human soul." C. Whittaker, Some Reminiscences, 47 A.B.A.J. 1087, 1090 (1961). It is often rumored that Justice Whittaker left the Court because he agonized too much, and he did say just before he left that "pains of adequacy troubled" him then (*id.*, at 1089). Another Supreme Court justice has said that the decision "process can be a lonely, troubling experience for fallible human beings, conscious that their best may not be adequate to the challenge. . . . The process is not without the tensions, quite agonizing tensions at times." P. Stewart, A View from Inside the Court, 39 Cleveland B.J. 69, 88, 90 (1968).

But the problems of agonizing can also hinder judges on lower appellate courts. I did not ask about this specifically in the interviews, though one judge did mention that he had had problems on this score (he said he had been horrified of the job when first appointed, but his anxiety was relieved by an experienced judge who told him that a judge should not try to give the last word but simply to do the best he can), and two others talked about other judges with this problem. Judge Medina wrote that "Some judges just cannot make up their minds. They play with things; they fuss with it. Time goes by. Even the simplest things." See H. Medina, The Decisional Process, 20 N.Y. Co. B. Bull. 94, 99 (1962). See also Cardozo, *supra* note 13, at 80, 81; C. Merrill, The Business of Judging, 40 Calif. St. B.J. 811, 812 (1965); and the discussions of Karl Llewellyn and Julius Stone in notes 22 and 25.

19. E. Spaeth, Reflections on a Judicial Campaign, 60 Judicature 10, 17 (1976). The author, an intermediate court judge, argues that campaigning counteracts the tendency toward arrogance. Several other appellate judges have written about the existence of and problem of arrogant or egoistical judges: R. Thompson, Selection of Judges on the California Court of Appeal, 48 Calif. St. B.J. 381 (1973); R. Neely, A Glimpse into Judges' Chambers, 7 Juris Doctor 33, 35 (Dec. 1977); H. Medina, Some Reflections on the Judicial Function: A Personal Viewpoint, 38 A.B.A.J. 107, 108 (1952). Only a few judges talked about this subject in the interviews (I was afraid to broach the subject myself); all said big egos are a problem, like the two quoted in the text, but they differed about how many judges are afflicted with it.

20. The great majority of the clerks spoke to this subject. In the first interviews with the focal court clerks, they generally talked about judges' egos, so in the later interviews I asked about the subject. Several clerks made sweeping statements that

judges in general have big egos, and several more said that no judges on their court had big egos. But most picked a small minority of their courts (generally the focal court clerks mentioning the same judges.)

21. J. Hutcheson, *Judgment Intuitive* 43, 44 (1938). He later warned, it should be added, that the uncertainty of the law should "not be the uncertainty of whim or caprice or of mere lust for power" (Hutcheson, *supra* note 13, at 81). On deciding issues by hunch, feeling, and the like, see the discussion in Chapter 1 at note 14.

22. Clark and Trubek, *supra* note 13, at 270. The Cardozo quote is from *The Nature of the Judicial Process*, at 172. The phrase "one right rule" probably comes from—or at least brings into mind—Llewellyn's phrase "one single right answer." He said judges tend to believe there is only one right answer to an issue, rather than acknowledging that there are often several possible answers having some merit. This attitude, Llewellyn says, "tends, along with the pressure of work and human avoidance of sweat, to encourage taking the first seemingly workable road which offers, thus giving the more familiar edge up on the more wise," and it prevents judges from taking a hard look at their lawmaking. But, according to Llewellyn, the attitude does have some good effects: It makes decisions more predictable in all but the most challenging cases, and it helps in "the preservation of self-confidence and good conscience in the law-personnel." K. Llewellyn, *The Common Law Tradition, Deciding Appeals* 24, 25 (1960).

23. R. Traynor, *supra* note 4, at 826, 827.

24. F. Kenison, Some Preliminary Observations on the State Appellate Judge Today, 61 Colum. L. Rev. 792 (1961); C. Magruder, The Trials and Tribulations of an Intermediate Appellate Court, 44 Cornell L.Q. 1 (1958); W. Schaefer, Good Judges, Better Judges, Best Judges, 44 J. Am. Jud. Soc'y 22, 24 (1960); Merrill, *supra* note 18, *passim*. Also, during this same period Judge Tate emphasized the fallibility of appellate judges at some length: A. Tate, *supra* note 13. See also Frankfurter in Rochin v. California, 342 U.S. 165, 171 (1952); T. Clark, Internal Operations of the United States Supreme Court, 43 J. Am. Jud. Soc'y 45, 51 (1959).

25. Judge Frank argues that trial judges should be required to write opinions explaining (or rather justifying) their decisions because this can "act as a partial check on" the subjectivity involved in deciding fact questions (Frank, *supra* note 1, at 183-185). Julius Stone, writing about appellate decision making, although agreeing with Judge Frank that explaining reasons and the resulting self-examination would lead a judge to do a better job in the individual case, said this may be outweighed by the damage to the "overall psychic economy of the man who is a judge"—that is, by the "resulting increases in stress" caused by the judges' "full awareness of uncertainty, of choices open, of the relevance of uncharted seas of social facts and ethical judgment." J. Stone, *Social Dimensions of Law and Justice* 670-686 (2d ed. 1971) (quotes at pp. 683, 684).

26. Schaefer, *supra* note 24, at 24.

27. Llewellyn, *supra* note 22, at 293.

APPENDIX B

1. R. Peters, Five Years of the Conference System, 19 Calif. St. B.J. 399 (1944); J. Molinari, The Decisionmaking Conference of the California Court of Appeal, 57

Calif. L. Rev. 606 (1969); National Center for State Courts, *The California Courts of Appeal* 119-124 (1974); R. Thompson, One Judge and No Judge Appellate Decisions, 50 Calif. St. B.J. 476 (1975); A. Vanderbilt, Improving the Administration of Justice—Two Decades of Development, 26 U. Cin. L. Rev. 155, 266 (1957). At least a dozen courts hold short conferences right before arguments to decide what needs to be discussed there; and probably most courts use prehearing or bench memorandums, outlining the facts, issues, and arguments of counsel, but they are sometimes rather skimpy.

2. Thompson, *supra*, at 516-518.

3. Statement by Judge Winslow Christian at the National Conference, Appellate Justice: 1975.

4. H. Leventhal, Environmental Decisionmaking and the Role of the Courts, 122 Pa. L. Rev. 509, 546 (1974).

5. See, for example, P. Carrington, Report on Group Discussions, *Appellate Justice: 1975, Volume V, Supplement, Proceedings, and Conclusions* 62, 66, 67 (1975); P. Carrington et al. *Justice on Appeal* 52, 53 (1976).

6. Institute of Judicial Administration, *The Supreme Court of Iowa, A Study of Its Procedure and Administration* 68 (1971). The Report, however, did not recommend this practice.

7. American Bar Association, *Methods of Reaching and Preparing Appellate Court Decisions* 34 (1942).

8. Thompson, *supra* note 1, at 478, 480.

9. *Id.*, at 517, 518.

10. See R. Leflar, *Internal Operating Procedures of Appellate Courts* 41 (1976).

11. A similar suggestion was made in L. Orfield, *Criminal Appeals in America* 161 (1939).

12. National Advisory Commission on Criminal Justice Standards and Goals, *Courts*, 119-124 (1973).

13. For an example of a judge who would like to get more advice from law professors see, K. O'Connell, Continuing Legal Education for the Judiciary, 19 J. Legal Ed. 405, 412, 413 (1964). Llewellyn said that a partial hedge against faulty advice from outside experts would be to place materials gained from the outside advice "on the face of a *proposed* opinion, the court remaining open to reargument addressed to that material." K. Llewellyn, *Deciding Appeals, The Common Law Tradition* 325 (1960).

14. K. Davis, Judicial Notice, 1969 L. & Social Order 513, 526.

15. Llewellyn, *supra* note 13, at 324.

16. See J. Francis, Joseph Weintraub—A Judge for All Seasons, 59 Cornell L. Rev. 186, 191 (1974). This procedure is quite different from the prehearing settlement conference that several courts use to settle appeals and to narrow issues. The judge presiding in those conferences (when a judge presides) never hears the case for a decision on the merits.

17. This suggestion was made in D. Meador, Appellate Case Management and Decisional Process, 61 Va. L. Rev. 255, 288 (1975).

18. *ABA Standards Relating to Appellate Courts* 52. This was stated in reference to a suggestion that supplemental briefs be requested more often.

Index

ABOUT THE AUTHOR
Thomas B. Marvell is an attorney-sociologist with the National Center for State Courts and the author of *The Federal Home Loan Bank Board*.